Feminism and Hospitality

Feminism and Hospitality

Gender in the Host/Guest Relationship

Edited by
Maurice Hamington

LEXINGTON BOOKS
A division of
ROWMAN & LITTLEFIELD PUBLISHERS, INC.
Lanham • Boulder • New York • Toronto • Plymouth, UK

Published by Lexington Books
A division of Rowman & Littlefield Publishers, Inc.
A wholly owned subsidiary of The Rowman & Littlefield Publishing Group, Inc.
4501 Forbes Boulevard, Suite 200, Lanham, Maryland 20706
http://www.lexingtonbooks.com

Estover Road, Plymouth PL6 7PY, United Kingdom

Copyright © 2010 by Lexington Books

All rights reserved. No part of this book may be reproduced in any form or by any electronic or mechanical means, including information storage and retrieval systems, without written permission from the publisher, except by a reviewer who may quote passages in a review.

British Library Cataloguing in Publication Information Available

Library of Congress Cataloging-in-Publication Data
Hamington, Maurice.
  Feminism and hospitality : gender in the host/guest relationship / Maurice Hamington.
    p. cm.
  Includes bibliographical references and index.
  ISBN 978-0-7391-3627-0 (cloth : alk. paper)
  1. Hospitality. 2. Hospitality industry. 3. Feminism. I. Title.
  BJ2021.H36 2010
  177'.1082—dc22
                                                           2010022261

∞™ The paper used in this publication meets the minimum requirements of American National Standard for Information Sciences—Permanence of Paper for Printed Library Materials, ANSI/NISO Z39.48-1992.

Printed in the United States of America

*Dedicated to Dorothy C. Miller
whose intellect and caring inspired this volume.*

Contents

Acknowledgments ix
Introduction xi
Maurice Hamington

Part I: Theories of Feminism and Hospitality

1. Hospitableness: A Neglected Virtue 3
   Nancy E. Snow

2. *Su Casa es Mi Casa?*
   Hospitality, Feminist Care Ethics, and Reciprocity 19
   Maureen Sander-Staudt

3. Hospitality: Agency, Ethics, and Gender 39
   Helen Daley Schroepfer

Part II: Gender and Domestic Hospitality

4. Shame in Feminine Hospitality 55
   Daniel Haggerty

5. Domestic Hospitality: Self, Other, and Community 71
   Jo-Ann Pilardi

6. From Saint Martha To Hurricane Katrina:
   A Feminist Theopolitical Ethic Of Hospitality 91
   M. Christian Green

Part III: International Explorations of Feminism and Hospitality

7. Welcoming Courtyards: Hospitality, Spirituality, and Gender 109
   Fauzia Erfan Ahmed

8. Feminism, Hospitality, and Women in Exile 125
   Ileana F. Szymanski

9. Hospitality and European Muslims 163
   Meyda Yeğenoğlu

10. Caring Hospitality and Mexican "Illegal" Immigrants 187
    Maurice Hamington

Part IV: Gender, Hospitality, and Commerce

11   The Home/Work Interface In Family Hospitality Businesses:
     Gendered Dimensions and Constructions   207
     MariaLaura Di Domenico

12   Hospitality in the Doctor's Office   223
     Patricia Boling

13   Providing Hospitality
     In Mid-Nineteenth Century West Virginia Cities   237
     Barbara J. Howe

Part V: Feminism and Hospitality in Film and Literature

14   Reading Levinas in *The Apartment*   263
     Jacqueline M. Davies

15   Reading Feminist Hospitality In Plato's *Timaeus*:
     Possibilities For Education   281
     Stephanie Burdick-Shepherd

Selected Bibliography   299
Index   307
Contributor Biographies   311

Acknowledgments

Many people contributed to creating this volume. It began when Dorothy C. Miller suggested the idea to me in the Summer of 2006. I was originally dubious about the project given contemporary attitudes toward hospitality, but she convinced me how important an exploration of feminism and hospitality was in the modern context. Apparently, quite a few people agreed as the response from all over the world to our call for papers was astounding. Political Scientist Amy Eckert of Metropolitan State College of Denver and philosopher Laura Hengehold of Case Western University read early versions of the manuscript and provided much appreciated input to our contributors. The anonymous reviewers provided by Lexington Books also offered important insight. The staff at Lexington Books including Editor John Parry and later Editor Lenore Lautigar, Editorial Assistants Tawnya Zenierski, and Mirna Araklian were very helpful and patient through the publishing and production process—particularly with all my questions. I appreciate the careful copyediting done by Mackenzie Carignan. I would also like to thank the employees of the Tokyo Joe's restaurants in the greater Denver area for their hospitality as I spent so many hours there working on this project and drinking green tea. Finally, the greatest thanks must go to all the scholars who generously contributed of their time and energy in the belief that ideas matter and that enriching our understanding of feminism and hospitality can make a positive difference to a world desperately in need of openness and caring.

Introduction
Feminism and Hospitality

Maurice Hamington

The term hospitality brings a certain ambivalence to feminists at best. On the one hand, it connotes a positive experience. Occasions of hospitality are usually social ones imbued with good feelings. They are often opportunities for not only pleasant exchanges but informative ones as well—the kind that build and sustain relationships. On the other hand, like most social engagements, gender has played a major role in the experience of hospitality. Women have historically been responsible for the logistics and delivery of hospitality, although they do not always receive the status or credit of "host." Conversely, women often have been unwelcome guests in social circles marked by gender exclusivity. Given the legacy of the gendered division of labor and the limits placed on women, the exploration of intersections between feminism and hospitality ostensibly appears dubious. However, other social developments reveal another story. One of those developments is the evolution of feminist theory. Although hospitality has been the subject of philosophical consideration, albeit somewhat marginalized, from Ancient Greek times to the present, only in the contemporary moment are there robust feminist ethical theories of care, connection, social epistemology, etc., to engage hospitality. The work done in feminist theory can provide unique insight into the nature and potential of hospitality. Another social development of significance to this project is what can be described as a contemporary global crisis of care. At no time in the history of the world are people so mobile and able to obtain extensive information about distant others. Yet, war, cruelty, and intolerance have not abated. The world appears to be a fairly intolerant place. Perhaps, as the editors believe, this is the time to rediscover and revalue the notion of hospitality and feminism can provide the intellectual foundation for such a renaissance.

For those who have not given hospitality serious consideration, this introduction provides a measure of historical and theoretical background. First a brief and partial history of hospitality is offered. A complete accounting of the many cultural manifestations of hospitality would fill numerous volumes. This history is provided to reinforce the notion that hospitality has a rich genealogy with meaning that goes beyond contemporary understandings. The history is followed by a discussion of why this moment in the history of the evolution of feminist thought is particularly ripe for addressing hospitality. In particular, theoretical work in feminist ethics and epistemology are explored for their implications in looking at hospitality afresh. Finally, an overview of the articles in this anthology is provided, which places them in a thematic framework as well as in trajectories extending from the historical and theoretical discussions offered in this introduction.

Hospitality Past and Present

Hospitality is an idea fraught with tension for both the host and guest. Who should be invited in? Who can be trusted? How much should be shared? What is the significance of the invitation? What will be desired in return? The very foundation of the word, "hospitality," rooted in two clusters of meaning, reveals elements of this tension. According to Tracy McNulty, "the institution of hospitality implies the union of somewhat contradictory notions."[1] The Latin *hostis* indicates a reciprocal relationship marked by sharing and exchange. However, the etymology of hospitality also poses *postis* as a root which signifies both a notion of personal identity and power. The complexity of hospitality is found in the very basis for the term as the constituent elements of reciprocity, power, and identity vie for centrality in its various historical and cultural manifestations.

Ancient Greek and Roman societies prized hospitality and elevated it to eligious status. For the Greeks, *xenia* or "guest-friendship" is often understood as hospitality. Xenia was to be offered to any stranger, no matter their social class, and it consisted of tending to physical requirements and comfort prior to any inquiry into identity. The host protected the guest, met needs, and offered gifts. The obligations of xenia went both ways. The guest was to offer service to the host moreover offer gifts as well as extending hospitality to those strangers presenting themselves. The guest-friendships that arose from acts of hospitality were much valued and could even be passed on to descendants. Xenia occurred between individuals, communities and individuals, and among communities.[2] Evidence for the significance of hospitality in Greek culture can be found in the central role it plays in the *Homeric* poems and the *Odyssey*. Acts of hospitality were believed to garner favor with the gods including Zeus who was often referred to as Zeus Xenios because of his special regard and protection for travelers. Conversely, inhospitality was considered an affront to the gods. Hospitality was so highly prized in Greek culture that some extant inscriptions praise guest-friendships as superior to other forms of friendship.[3]

Ancient Roman society also conceived of hospitality as a virtue although it may have been practiced with more public definition than in Greek culture.[4] Roman hospitality entailed care and protection of strangers and even legal representation. The relationship was instantiated with mutual gifts. Like Zeus, Jupiter was believed to watch over host-guest relations and took offense when hospitality was not justly offered. Guest-friendships were symbolized by the sharing of a token, *tessera hospitalis*, made of earthenware with an image of Jupiter on it, which could be passed on to subsequent generations.[5] Roman historian, Livy, describes ceremonies of hospitality ostensibly to cull favor from the gods where, "In every street doors were left open and viands [tasty dishes] of all sorts displayed for the promiscuous use of anyone and everyone; friends and strangers alike were, we are told, invited in and hospitably entertained."[6] Of course, history does not always record the psychology behind social phenomenon. Ladislaus J. Bolchazy speculates that ancient societies were often xenophobic and the Greeks and Romans were no exceptions. Given the strong mistrust of unknown others, the Greeks and Romans developed strong codes of hospitality and even evaluated other civilizations by the depth of their hospitality. According to Bolchazy, this hospitality was motivated by utilitarian concerns regarding how to navigate a dangerous world.[7]

Roman notions of hospitality would have been circulating during the development of early Christian communities. However, a separate Judaic tradition of hospitality, *hakhnasat orchim* or "bringing in of strangers," can be found in the Torah and the Talmud.[8] There are several examples of Abraham exhibiting hospitality (for example, Gen 18:1-5 and Gen 24:28-32). The Talmud teaches that Abraham always kept all four sides of his tent open so guests could easily enter. According to Hebrew Scriptures, Sodom and Gommorah were destroyed because of their inhabitants' lack of hospitality (Gen 19:24-25). Job boasts of his hospitality (Jb 31:32). As a *mitzvah*, hospitality can be interpreted as having the force of law. Like the Greek and Roman traditions, hospitality places demands on the host and guest. Although hosts must provide for their guests, in turn the guest is obligated to be grateful and offer additional blessings after meals. Given the continuity of the two faiths, it is not surprising that hospitality is praised in numerous passages of the Christian scriptures (Rm 12:13, 1 Tm 3:2, Tt 1:18, Heb 13:2, 1 Pt 4:9). The early Christian communities depended upon hospitality prior to the death of Jesus, as he was an itinerant preacher, and after Jesus' death as small communities met in people's homes.[9] Gender may have played an important role in early Christian communities as evidence reveals that women were some of the early benefactors as hosts of community meetings. Karen Jo Torjeson describes, "During the first and second centuries, when Christian congregations met in homes, women were prominent as leaders."[10] As the Christian religion became institutionalized, it reinforced hospitality as a central value in a number of ways. For example, at the Council of Trent, church ministers were admonished to "accustom themselves, as far as their revenues will allow, to exercise with alacrity and kindness the office of hospitality, so frequently commended by the holy Fathers; being mindful that those who cherish hospitality receive Christ in the person of their guests."[11] Thomas W. Ogletree argues that hospitality for the stranger is the guiding metaphor for Christian ethics.[12] Accordingly, numerous figures and communities in the history of Christianity have taken the theme of hospitality as a motivating force.

Of course, Christianity has far from a monopoly on hospitality traditions. Religion scholar Ronald M. Green has argued that moral reasoning is part of the deep structure that permeates all religions.[13] Although without systematic verification, perhaps hospitality is also part of this moral deep structure. The anecdotal evidence for a pervasive hospitality element in all religions is compelling. For example, the Qur'an describes an ethical imperative of generosity: "Be kind to parents, and the near kinsman, and to orphans, and to the needy, and to the neighbor who is of kin, and to the neighbor who is a stranger, and to the companion at your side, and to the traveler, and to [slaves] that your right hands own. Surely God loves not the proud and boastful such as are miserly, and bid other men to be miserly, and themselves conceal the bounty that God has given them" (4:36-37). Hindus are entreated to treat the stranger, *atithi*, as a god. According to the *Mahabharata*, one of the great Sanskrit epics of ancient India, "Even an enemy must be offered appropriate hospitality if he comes to your home. A tree does not deny its shade even to the one who comes to cut it down" (12.374). The various schools of Buddhism honor hospitality in different ways but the generosity of the Buddha is the starting point.[14]

A philosopher often associated with hospitality is Immanuel Kant. In 1795, Kant wrote a bold plan for creating world peace through hospitality: "Perpetual Peace." In the essay, Kant offers three aspects ("definitive articles") to end global belligerence: Every government should take a republican form; a league of nations should be formed; and, world citizenship should be funded by universal hospitality. In Kant's attempt to universalize hospitality, the concept became a very thin notion of visitation as compared to the more personal and affective hospitality practiced by the Ancient Greeks and Romans. For Kant, hospitality "means the right of an alien not to be treated as an enemy upon his arrival in another's country."[15] Despite the limitations of Kant's idea of hospitality, his influence cannot be underestimated. For example, contemporary political theorist, Seyla Benhabib, although dissatisfied with Kant's theory of hospitality, still uses his work for a starting point for developing her own theories of hospitality and cosmopolitanism.

In North America, hospitality was a significant theme in a number of social movements. In the late nineteenth and early twentieth centuries, the Settlement Movement was an outgrowth of the Progressive Era that at one time had over 400 settlements in North America. Driven by women college graduates with few career options such as Jane Addams, social settlements located in depressed urban areas and offered the hospitality of a good neighbor.[16] Often engaging in what was considered acceptable women's work, referred to by some commentators as "social housekeeping," social settlements endeavored to provide services based on the needs of the community. This form of community organizing was often philosophically differentiated from charity work as the settlement workers helped their marginalized neighbors to flourish in society by navigating social institutions from government aid agencies to educational organizations. Another movement that emphasized hospitality with a strong religious flavor is the Catholic Worker movement. Founded by Dorothy Day and Peter Maurin, the Catholic Worker movement, which continues to operate today, has loosely affiliated hospitality houses in major cities throughout North America. Combining anarchism with Roman Catholicism, the Catholic Worker offers soup kitchens and similar programs for the poor in continuity with Christian traditions of service and charity. Note that both of these hospitality-oriented movements have women as their founders.[17]

In the twentieth century, philosophers Emmanuel Levinas and Jacques Derrida took up the cause of reinvigorating discussions of hospitality. Actually, Levinas used the term "hospitality" rarely, but his work addressed the self's primordial relationship with the Other. Levinas argued for a fundamental moral responsibility to the other grounded in the subject's constitution. For Levinas, "The relation with the Other, or Discourse, is a non-allergic relation, an ethical relation; but inasmuch as it is welcomed this discourse is a teaching."[18] Derrida locates a philosophy of hospital-

Introduction

ity in a radical interpretation of Levinas' *Totality and Infinity*. In the latter part of his long career, Derrida takes up hospitality, as "not simply some region of ethics" but as "ethicity itself, the whole and the principle of ethics."[19] In hospitality, Derrida finds a fundamental tension of morality—an impossibility or *aporia*—that humanity must struggle with. Hospitality calls us to give of ourselves. In its pure form, or unconditional hospitality, absolute giving is demanded but one can no longer be the host or the giver, if all is given away. For Derrida, this paradox can be the source of morality: "the *aporia* is not simply paralysis, but the *aporia* or the *nonway* is the condition of walking: if there was no *aporia* we wouldn't walk, we would not find our way; path-breaking implies *aporia*. This impossibility to find one's way is the condition of ethics."[20] Hospitality is impossible, but in the striving for the ideal, morality takes place. Gender is not absent from the theorizing of Levinas and Derrida. For example, Levinas, somewhat mired in gender essentialism develops a notion of feminine hospitality that is self-sacrificial in a manner reminiscent of ideas complicit with "the problem which has no name" that Betty Friedan uncovered at the onset of the contemporary women's movement.[21]

Several contemporary feminist theorists have undertaken gender analyses of hospitality and born witness to the asymmetrical power relations within. Tracy McNulty finds the history of hospitality replete with gender hierarchy. Not only is the status of host traditionally "almost invariably male" the notion of "'feminine hospitality' is almost an oxymoron."[22] McNulty explores how hospitality informs identity and finds that property becomes a signification of the host's personhood. However, women and children are historically included in the category of property and therefore become part what can be offered to the guest. Accordingly, "The host's offer of hospitality often depends upon his ability to dispose of the female dependents who make up his personal property, who he offers to the guest as though giving some part of 'himself.'"[23] McNulty thus extrapolates that acts of hospitality leave women bereft of individual identity. Similarly, Mireille Rosello observes that, "No discussion of hospitality can ignore the troubling elimination of the female figure from the primordial guest-host pair and how hard it is for women to be treated as guests."[24] Investigating cultural artifacts of novels and films, Rosello leverages gender difference to expose the fragility of hospitality conventions. McNulty and Roselle represent relatively new voices in the chorus of hospitality theory. Their works, emerging since the turn of the millennia, foreshadow the potential for a larger body of feminist literature on hospitality.

Of course, in contemporary popular discourse, hospitality has little resemblance to the guest-host considerations given by the Ancient Greeks, Romans, Kant, Day, Addams, Levinas, Derrida, McNulty or Rosello. Commonly, hospitality is a comprehensive term used to describe the service industry including hotels, restaurants, travel, tourism, nightclubs, and bars. In this respect, hospitality is a commodity available for purchase in the marketplace. It is also part of a skill set taught in colleges and universities. The intersection of commodification and rhetorical appropriation can be witnessed in the euphemism, "hospitality worker" which sometimes used for prostitution, particularly in sex tourism. In the Philippines, "hospitality worker" is a legal and somewhat regulated designation for a bar worker which avoids the illegal category of prostitute.[25]

Hospitality is an enduring notion that has changed with time and culture and whose emphasis has waxed and waned but cannot seem to escape implications for gender.

The Feminist Moment

Hospitality is fundamentally about relationship. The host encounters the stranger, the other, or guest. Perhaps more than any other discipline, and in part because of its interdisciplinary nature, feminism has developed a rich body of theories regarding relationships. The metaphysical underpinning of feminist theories of relationships can be found in the notion that humans are not wholly atomistic beings. So much of traditional theory is based on the idea that people are independent agents. Feminism does not deny individual agency, but has strongly emphasized the interdependent nature of humanity. Accordingly, people are socially constituted and exist in contextual webs of relationships that are not insignificant to questions of existence, knowledge, and ethics. This recognition of situatedness, perhaps more than anything else, has led feminists to theorize so much about relationships and their implications. Accordingly, the editors contend that the present is the feminist moment to offer insight on social and political understandings such as hospitality. This introduction could not exhaustively address all the robust theoretical work on relationality coming from feminists today. Instead, a few themes will be offered including care theory, standpoint theory, and intersectionality.

Feminists first identified care theory in the 1980s and it subsequently spawned numerous publications. Today, care ethics has developed sufficient momentum that many nonfeminist theorists are working with its ideas. Care is a relational approach to morality that refocuses ethical content away from adjudication to consider the process, context, and affects of behavior. For example, Virginia Held describes care as both "a practice and a value. As a practice it shows us how to respond to needs and why we should. It builds trust and mutual concern."[26] Accordingly, any action of moral significance takes place in a particular context that includes and affects many other beings. Care ethics favors concrete considerations over abstract ones. Understanding the real people and implications involved in any situation is crucial to care. The moral agent is not simply an ambiguous other but a flesh and blood human being to which we have a connection despite significant differences of culture, class, or gender. Empathy and compassion are valued over hypothetical applications of moral reasoning. Care represents a reframing of morality that does not negate principles or consequences but suffuses those approaches with a fundamental concern for relationships and particularity. In many ways, care ethics does a different kind of work than many other ethical approaches. It does not provide a rubric for determining moral action in the abstract, but it does offer guidance as a situation unfolds or becomes more concrete. For those steeped in purely abstract ethical thinking this can be very frustrating because care does not offer the same clarity at the abstract level that other forms of ethics do. As philosopher Susan Hekman describes, care ethics is part of a modern intellectual "sea change" that is moving away from absolutism and universalism toward particularism and concreteness. Care ethicists often find themselves reconsidering the place of emotions in morality. Feelings are an outgrowth of beings who imaginatively consider the position of particular other beings in relation to themselves. This is not to assume that one can "own" someone else's experiences, however despite vast differences there is always room for some degree of understanding. By extension, knowledge is viewed not as simply an amalgamation of facts and propositions but as potentially disruptive to the routines of our lives when we care. Understanding one another leads to sympathetic connections that have the potential to draw us to act on behalf of others. Care theory, then, addresses both the nature of ethics and the nature of knowledge. Care ethics has enormous potential as a lens of analysis for hospitality, and, in turn, care theory may be enriched through engagement with philosophies of hospitality.

Another robust aspect of contemporary feminist theory that is ripe for application to hospitality is intersectional analysis. As championed by Kimberle Crenshaw, "intersectionality" is the notion that oppressive social forces—racism, sexism, classism, homophobia—are not independent phenomena, but exist as interlocking systems of repression that when combined create unique circumstances not captured by the constitutive originating oppression. Drawing from the marginalization of African-American women, Crenshaw describes, "Many of the experiences Black women face are not subsumed within the traditional boundaries of race or gender discrimination as these boundaries are currently understood, and that the intersection of racism and sexism factors into Black women's lives in ways that cannot be captured wholly by looking at the race or gender dimensions of those experiences separately."[27] Patricia Hill Collins characterizes intersectional analysis as spearheaded by African-American feminists since the 1970s. Collins describes intersectionality as, "An analysis claiming that systems of race, economic class, gender, sexuality, ethnicity, nation, and age from mutually constructing features of social organizations."[28] The host/guest relationship can be a social and political site of intersectional inquiry. An ethic of hospitality that attempts to problematize the power and privilege of the host and the reciprocal relationship with the guest can provide a fresh approach to intersectionality.

Since the mid-1970s, feminist theorists have also given special attention to the notions of voice and standpoint. Although there are disagreements regarding the nature of objectivity, many theorists including Alison Jaggar, Sandra Harding, Nancy Hartsock, Hilary Rose, and Dorothy Smith have advanced the notion that knowledge is situated. In particular, feminist standpoint theorists valorize the perspectives and theories derived from oppressed positions in society such as from women's experience. Harding describes a feminist standpoint as something to be achieved rather than a passive perspective. All women have lived experience in a woman's body and therefore have a woman's perspective but a feminist standpoint requires an effort at stepping back to gain a holistic picture of power struggles. She describes standpoint projects as exploring "'beneath' and 'behind' the dominant sexist and androcentric ideologies that shaped everyone's lives to the relations between, on the one hand, the actualities of women's everyday lives and on the other hand, the conceptual practices of powerful social institutions."[29] Through the understanding of the perspectival aspect of knowledge claims, standpoint epistemology can create libratory knowledge that can be leveraged to subvert oppressive systems, thus giving standpoint theories an ethical dimension as well as an epistemological one. The premise that standpoints matter provides an opportunity to interrogate the host/guest relationship by examining the standpoint of each position. How is the knowledge of the guest situated vis-à-vis the host? A challenge for standpoint theory is how to give voice to multiple positions without falling back on hierarchies that favor certain standpoints over others.

Explicated above are just a few areas of emphasis in recent works of feminist theory that engage relational understanding pertinent to hospitality. Other relational work coming out of feminist theorizing includes a broad range of topics including friendship, social epistemology, lesbian ethics, and moral repair. Given the prodigious contributions of feminist theorists to relational understanding, engagement with the notion of hospitality is appropriate and warranted, thus providing the theoretical impetus behind the present project, *Feminism and Hospitality: Gender in the Host/Guest Relationship.*

A Social/Political Imperative

There is another motivation for this project beyond an appropriate theoretical moment in the maturity of feminism. Bluntly stated, the world sorely needs to rediscover the values of hospitality, albeit one without oppressive power connotations. One report indicates that 5.4 million deaths have occurred because of war between 1955 and 2002.[30] The Stockholm International Peace Research Institute indicates that in 2008 there were 14 armed conflicts active around the world, and, whether at peace or war, the global community spent over $1.3 trillion on arms.[31] According to the UNHCR, over 300,000 individuals worldwide seek asylum every year.[32] Immigration is a high-profile political issue in both Europe and North America that has vilified illegal and legal immigrants on numerous occasions. Indeed, the world appears to be an inhospitable place.

Of course, statistics and political rhetoric do not tell the entire story of hospitality. Interestingly, given the credo of the women's movement that the "personal is political," hospitality is a concept that is both private and personal as well as political and international. There are many examples of generous and humble hospitality that are reminiscent of Derrida's notion of unconditional hospitality and, of course; there are plenty of examples of hospitality that reinforce hierarchical structures of power. Combining ideas about the potential for hospitality with experiences and cultural case studies, this project aspires to be analytical and critical as well as imaginative and hopeful.

The Organization of this Book

Feminism and Hospitality is divided into five thematic sections. Although all the chapters in this collection balance experience and theory, the first section, Theories of Feminism and Hospitality, emphasizes theoretical considerations including ideas such as virtue, reciprocity, agency and shame in the relationship of gender and hospitality. The chapters in the first section provide provocative themes and frameworks from which the specific applications or experiences found in subsequent chapters can be filtered. The impact of Jacques Derrida's work on contemporary theories of hospitality becomes evident in these chapters as almost all reference his work in an extensive manner.

In "Hospitableness: A Neglected Virtue," philosopher Nancy Snow engages an expansive definition of hospitality that she describes as "making others welcome." Furthermore, she investigates the potential for hospitableness to be a feminist virtue. In an intriguing response to traditional power dynamics ascribed to hospitality, Snow contrasts hospitableness construed as "making people feel welcome in one's *own* world with an alternative, namely making people feel welcome in a *shared* world." To accomplish this, Snow draws upon Buddhist philosophy because of its less individualistic metaphysic than traditional Western liberalism. She concludes by exploring how hospitality can be a feminist virtue in terms of its libratory elements in combating social oppression. Snow suggests "compassion has the potential to be a feminist virtue inasmuch as it is a form of solidarity with those who suffer, and can motivate us to act on their behalf. Hospitableness as an expression of unselfish compassion could have similar libratory value." Snow's careful examination of terms provides an excellent foundation for the rest of the collection.

In *"Su Casa es Mi Casa?* Hospitality, Feminist Care Ethics, and Reciprocity," Maureen Sander-Staudt agrees with Snow that care is a virtue but she also finds it to be a practice of feminist care ethics. Many care theorists such as Eva Feder Kittay contend that reciprocity is an essential element of a nonexploitative version of care ethics. There is a mutuality to reciprocal relations that does not demand the selflessness so often historically demanded of women in caring relationships. Sander-Staudt uses the reality of the absence of reciprocity in traditional relationships between host and guest to suggest that Derrida's ideal of unconditional hospitality is flawed because it fails to take into account context, and particularly women's experience, a hallmark of care ethics. Sander-Staudt concludes "hospitality functions best under conditions of discerning volunteerism on the part of hostess, and reciprocity on the part of guest that engages the central virtues of care—attention, response, respect, and competent completion." Sander-Staudt points to a theme found throughout the volume in suggesting that there are moral demands on the guest as well as the host.

Helen Schroepfer also explores Derrida's work on hospitality as well as the developmental psychology of Jean Piaget on self in "Hospitality: Agency, Ethics, and Gender." Schroepfer finds in an open and inclusive host-guest relation the potential for the development of self and personal agency necessary for human flourishing. Taking a more positive view of Derrida's unconditional hospitality than Sander-Staudt, Schroepfer reads Derrida as advocating the struggle against human limitation toward the unconditional: "We strain against the limits of these impossibles not theoretically, but performatively, through acts of hospitality and generosity." Schroepfer maps Piaget and subsequent literature in development theory onto Derrida's notion of hospitality to suggest that "Neo-Piagetian developmental theory describes a multi-faceted structure of hospitality closely akin to that articulated by Derrida, and this active and ongoing articulation of the relationship between self and other is crucial in human flourishing." Drawing on feminist theories of agency by Lorraine Code and others, Schroepfer reconfigures hospitality from a luxury of politeness to a necessity for rich human development of the notion of "self" and "other" with significant moral implications.

The second section, Gender and Domestic Hospitality, explores hospitality associated with the home. This is an area that is particularly challenging for feminists as women have often had roles that limited them to domestic preparations and management of hospitality. Is there any redeeming potential to domestic hospitality or is it merely a vessel of patriarchy?

Daniel Haggerty confronts the social forces of shame and pride that are used to discipline a particular form of "feminine" domestic hospitality generated by contemporary capitalism. In "Shame in Feminine Hospitality," Haggerty finds certain women's bodies as the site for a patriarchal struggle for which participation in hospitality is part of the contention: "shame often surfaces as hostility and heightened self-consciousness in the hostess/guest relationship." Like Sander-Staudt, Haggerty criticizes Derrida for neglecting the context of women in constructing unconditional hospitality, but Haggerty's analysis takes a corporeal turn. Haggerty claims that Derrida "ignores the embodied consciousness of the woman who invites and offers hospitality to the guest, to the foreigner, to the stranger." Although admittedly not applicable to all women, Haggerty uses psychoanalytic theory and Foucauldian analysis to come to a more negative conclusion than Schroepfer about the impact of patriarchal hospitality on self. Haggerty claims, "Shame in feminine hospitality destabilizes the hostess's *self*-identity." Applying analysis by Sandra Bartkey, Haggerty views this disciplined form of femininity as alienating because women's bodies become associated with their homes as the place of hospitality. He ends hopeful, however, by finding the home also a site of women's resistance.

Jo-Ann Pilardi's "Domestic Hospitality: Self, Other, and Community" strikes an intriguing counter note to Haggerty's criticism of domestic hospitality. Although they both agree on the negative influence of patriarchal disenfranchisement of women through narrow enforced performances of hospitality, Pilardi finds in domestic hospitality an empowering potential. Distinguishing domestic from public hospitality, Pilardi suggests that recent political theory has emphasized public hospitality and perhaps it is time for further feminist exploration of domestic hospitality. In particular, domestic hospitality is an important vehicle for community formation, and, given a feminist metaphysics of connection, self formation: "I welcome the Other to my home, a metaphysical and nonproprietary dimension of my existence, i.e., an aspect of my being, not a form of property. My home is the location from which I achieve my being." For Pilardi, domestic hospitality is an untapped resource for feminists to connect with a rich sense of women's culture.

In "From Martha to Katrina, From Fear to Openness: Prospects For A Feminist Ethic Of Hospitality," M. Christian Green begins with a discussion of Martha of Bethany who in a story recounted in the Gospel of Luke chooses to stay and listen to Jesus teach rather than help her sister, Mary, with household tasks of preparation. As Green explores, this story makes a fascinating metaphor for the role of women in domestic hospitality. Green engages the work of feminist biblical scholar, Elisabeth Schüssler Fiorenza and feminist theologian Letty Russell to find in hospitality both a Christian value and radical dynamic that challenges Christian churches to evolve and change regarding contemporary social demands. Green then turns to a case study of those displaced by Hurricane Katrina because it "raised concerns of race, class, gender and justice that feminists in particular cannot and should not ignore." Green concludes by drawing some principles for a feminist ethic of hospitality from the feminist readings of Martha's story and the lessons of Hurricane Katrina.

The third section of *Feminism and Hospitality*, International Explorations of Feminism and Hospitality, addresses what Pilardi refers to as public hospitality. Cultural and historical traditions of hospitality are innumerable and their implications for gender vary. This section offers just a few, but intriguing, explorations.

Fauzia Ahmed engages in an ethnographic study of Bangladeshi hospitality in "Welcoming Courtyards: Hospitality, Spirituality and Gender." Ahmed recounts the social progress that Bangladesh has made since gaining its independence in 1971. She contends that women have played a significant role in this advancement, but to date, the role of Bangladesh's tradition of hospitality, which Ahmed describes as "extravagant, spontaneous, and, at times, overwhelming" has not been explored. To this end, Ahmed provides essential background to the reader by describing the ancient Hindu philosophical tradition of hospitality and themes of hospitality in contemporary syncretic Islam as well as the sociocultural context of Bangladesh. Ahmed's report from a ten year ethnographic study includes observations and vignettes of hospitality analyzed through a feminist lens. Contrasting with Haggerty's analysis of domestic hospitality, Ahmed concludes that Bangladeshi hospitality not only "continues to sustain the women's movement" as "a feminist tool and strategy" but is also "a bulwark against rightwing Islam."

Those in exile, who have been displaced from their homes, provide a special and challenging case for the concept of international hospitality. Drawing upon numerous global examples, Ileana Szymanski claims in "Feminism, Hospitality, and Women in Exile," that women experience exile differently than men. Although the experiences vary by circumstance, women must contend not only with physical and cultural displacement, but also with the new standards of patriarchy in their place of exile. Szymanski offers a feminist strategy for mitigating the high level of disconnection experienced with exile by challenging the traditional metaphor of host and guest mapped onto the nation state: "the exile is more than a guest, and the new country is more than a host." Szymanski challenges the directionality of hospitality by suggesting that everyone should engage in giving hospitality to one another in order to foster greater community and imaginatively placing themselves in the position of exile. Although she admits this is a difficult task, Szymanski desires mutuality in hospitality reminiscent of Sander-Staudt's aspiration for reciprocity in host-guest relations.

During the 1990s, French national policy regarding the separation of church and state confronted values of openness and hospitality when the Muslim headscarf controversy arose in the public schools. A national commission determined in 2003 that "ostentatious" displays of religiosity were inappropriate and in the following year a ban of Muslim headscarves in schools was enacted. In "Hospitality and European Muslims," Meyda Yeğenoğlu interrogates the analysis of feminist theorists Julie Kristeva and Seyla Benhabib on Muslim immigrant women wearing headscarves in Europe, and finds their conclusions wanting. Yeğenoğlu claims Kristeva and Benhabib's treatment of the issue "symptomatic of a certain gesture of hospitality which ends up endorsing the means of reaffirming the European subject as a sovereign and self identical entity, a subject whose 'at home-ness' of identity is managed not to be disturbed or destabilized in its relation with Otherness." Yeğenoğlu addresses the fundamental question of how far does hospitality extend? She views the European headscarf issue as symptomatic of a dangerous trend but indicative of the shadow, which accompanies hospitality: "It is this transformation in the European attitude that explains how hospitality becomes imbued with hostility."

Migration is often metaphorically understood, even if not experienced, in terms of host-guest relations. In "Caring Hospitality and Mexican 'Illegal' Immigrants," Maurice Hamington challenges the popular notion that illegal immigration to the United States from Mexico is patently negative. Attempting to bridge domestic and public hospitality, Hamington describes caring hospitality as an essential interpersonal corollary to social policy regarding immigrant guests. The chapter begins with background information on Mexican immigration, particularly regarding women and follows with an argument that national hospitality is a feminist issue. Hamington then distinguishes "caring hospitality," drawn from feminist care ethics, from "hospitality of privilege," of which the latter serves to reinforce power differentials between people and between nations through a guise of hospitableness. Caring hospitality is described not only as an ethical position, but also as a means of personal and national identity development that is particularly important in a cosmopolitan world. Accordingly, whether arbitrarily designated as "illegal" or not, Hamington contends, "Mexican immigration to the U.S. is not a problem. People living lives of limited sustenance and where they cannot flourish are a problem."

Today, hospitality is most popularly associated as a commercial relationship for service. In section four, Gender, Hospitality, and Commerce, three particular instances of hospitality in business contexts are examined.

Although technology has recently served to obfuscate the distinction between home and work, those engaged in home-based businesses have a long-

Introduction xxiii

standing tradition of negotiating home and work life. In "The Home/Work Interface in Family Hospitality Businesses: Gendered Dimensions and Constructions," MariaLaura Di Domenico, addresses issues of hospitality within home-based businesses, such as bed and breakfasts, employing a dramaturgical analysis that views social relations as unfolding dramas. Di Domenico interviewed home-business owners in two Scottish cities and integrates narratives from the interviews in her analysis. Although the integration of public endeavors into the private sphere affected the roles of men and women in the home, Di Domenico also found that guests desired, and thus reinforced through monetary exchange, replication of traditional gender roles. Di Domenico describes, "The exchange of money in hospitality provision and consumption has a significant effect in altering the expectations surrounding the host-guest relationship." In this respect, commercial exchange plays a conservative role in the gender performances of hospitality by guest and host and reverses the usual power invested in the host. Di Domenico recounts that guests purchase idealized gendered hospitality and hosts endeavor to accommodate guests to attract their business.

Contemporary bureaucratic health care delivery does not evoke visions of robust hospitality but, of course, "hospital" etymologically shares the root and medicine ostensibly shares the spirit of hospitality through the care of the sick. Patricia Boling addresses the specific experience of long-term care of cancer patients in "Hospitality in the Doctor's Office." Motivated in part by her own diagnoses with breast cancer, Boling conducted interviews with cancer survivors who had received long-term treatment and engaged in focus group discussions with nurses, receptionists, schedulers, and technicians. Boling describes unidirectional and gendered expectations surrounding hospitality: "Both care providers and patients have internalized an understanding of care, generosity, sympathy, etc., as feminized, in the sense that women are thought to be better at expressing this than men, and in the sense that these virtues are expected of women more than men." Boling finds hospitality to be feminized and thus devalued in health care. Accordingly, those who are least paid have higher expectations of hospitableness than do more highly paid specialists. This relationship also correlates, albeit imperfectly, with the predominance of women among the least paid in the health industry.

In "Providing Hospitality In Mid-Nineteenth-Century West Virginia Cities," Barbara Howe offers a historical examination of women in the hospitality industry. This history is connected to present conditions: "understanding the hospitality industry in the nineteenth-century West Virginia cities helps us to understand the industry today." Drawing from historical records and artifacts, Howe explores the restaurant industry and reconstructs the world of nineteenth century prostitution in West Virginia. Howe contrasts the era's prostitution with contemporary forms, but the consistent theme is women's hospitality as a form of physical exploitation. As Howe describes, prostitution also created another class of women's work for madams, who managed the houses of ill repute. For Howe, it is not clear that much has changed for those in the less lucrative fields of the hospitality industry.

Although political philosophy has dominated contemporary discussions of hospitality, it is also a theme explored in the arts. The final section of chapters is Feminism and Hospitality in Film and Literature.

In *Totality and Infinity,* Emmanuel Levinas describes his relational ethic as the "I" who is accountable to the "Other." For Levinas, the Feminine is a complex notion of Otherness that is necessary for a relational morality but rooted in the female gender. Feminists disagree over the implications of Levinas's feminine other. In "Reading Levinas in *The Apartment,*" Jacqueline Davies addresses the controversy head on. Davis applies a Levinasian analysis on the 1960 classic film and six-time Academy Award winner, *The Apartment,* directed by Billy Wilder and starring Jack Lemmon and Shirley McLaine. Davies describes the film "subtly thematizes gender from its opening to its ending in ways that could be overlooked, unless you are attentive to the nuances of architecture, art direction and music which otherwise simply slip into the background." Furthermore, Davies finds in the protagonists, C. C. Baxter (Lemmon) and Fran Kubelik (McLaine), a Levinasian relationship. At the end of the movie, Baxter and Kubelik arrive home. Davies describes, "We do not know where they are headed next, but we know that they have come to the condition of exile that Levinas understood as the basis for hospitality."

Plato's *Timaeus* is a Socratic dialogue written by Plato that is usually understood as a treatise on the nature of the physical world. In "Reading Feminist Hospitality In Plato's *Timaeus*: Possibilities For Education," Stephanie Burdick-Shepherd claims that *Timaeus* "offers us images of hospitality that challenge our modern, everyday, and ordinary use of the concept." To support this claim, Burdick-Shepherd draws upon three episodes in *Timaeus*. The first scene focuses on Socrates as guest. The second is a discussion of *khōra*: a space between Socratic forms that Derrida appropriated in deconstruction to describe either/or logic. The third is the hospitality of the Socratic notion of the creator. Burdick-Shepherd's provocative interpretation of *Timaeus* supports a feminist understanding of hospitality: "In this reading, feminist hospitality enacts reception and invitation by enabling the feminine to be not merely a passive receiver but an active and challenging *reception.*"

The range of experiences, events, and theories addressed in this collection is a testament to the potency of hospitality, both existentially and metaphorically. Feminism continues to contend that gender matters and gender certainly matters in the history of the relationship between guest and host. We hope this collection contributes to a robust conversation regarding hospitality and how feminist work on relationality can help repair our world.

Notes

1. Tracy McNulty, *The Hostess: Hospitality, Femininity, and the Expropriation of Identity* (Minneapolis: University of Minnesota Press, 2007), xi.

Introduction

2. Stephanie Lynn Budin, *The Ancient Greeks: New Perspectives* (Santa Barbara: ABC-CLIO, 2004), 136.
3. Oscar E. Nybakken, "The Moral Basis of *Hospitium Privatum*" *The Classical Journal* 41:6 (Mar. 1946): 248-53.
4. Leonhard Schmitz, "Hospitium," in *A Dictionary of Greek and Roman Antiquities*, ed. William Smith (London: John Murray, 1875), 620-21.
5. James Yates, "Tessera," in *A Dictionary of Greek and Roman Antiquities*, ed. William Smith (London: John Murray, 1875), 1112-13.
6. Livy, *The Early History of Rome*, trans. Aubrey de Selincourt (London: Penguin Books, 1960), 5.13, 384.
7. Ladislaus J. Bolchazy, *Hospitality In Antiquity: Livy's Concept Of Its Humanizing Force* (Chicago: Ares Publishers, Inc., 1995), 2.
8. Ariel Scheib, "Hospitality," *Jewish Virtual Library* 2009, http://www.jewishvirtuallibrary.org/jsource/Judaism/hospitality.html (accessed November 25, 2009).
9. John L. McKenzie, *Dictionary of the Bible* (New York: Macmillan, 1965), 374.
10. Karen Jo Torjeson, *When Women Were Priests: Women's Leadership in the Early Church and the Scandal of their Subordination in the Rise of Christianity* (San Francisco: HarperCollins, 1993), 5.
11. Herbert Thurston, "Hospitality," in *The Catholic Encyclopedia* Vol. 7. (New York: Robert Appleton Company, 1910) http://www.newadvent.org/cathen/07475c.htm (accessed November 25, 2009).
12. Thomas W. Ogletree, *Hospitality to the Stranger: Dimensions of Moral Understanding* (Louisville: Westminster John Knox Press, 2003), 1.
13. Ronald M. Green, *Religion and Moral Reason: A New Method for Comparative Study* (New York: Oxford University Press, 1988), 3-32.
14. John B. Switzer, "Hospitality," in *Encyclopedia of Love in World Religions*, ed. Yudit Kornberg Greenberg (ABC-CLIO, 2007), 314.
15. Immanuel Kant, "To Perpetual Peace: A Philosophical Sketch" in *Perpetual Peace and Other Essays*, trans. Ted Humphrey (Indianapolis: Hackett Publishing Company, 1983), 118.
16. Judith M. Green, "Building A Cosmopolitan World Community Through Mutual Hospitality," in *Pragmatism And The Problem Of Race*, eds. Bill E. Lawson and Donald F. Koch (Bloomington: University of Indiana Press, 2004), 203-24.
17. For a comparison of the philosophies of Jane Addams and Dorothy Day, see Maurice Hamington, "Two Leaders, Two Utopias: Jane Addams and Dorothy Day," *National Women's Studies Association Journal*, 19 no. 2 (Summer 2007): 159-86.
18. Emmanuel Levinas, *Totality And Infinity: An Essay On Exteriority* (Pittsburgh: Duquesne University Press, 2002), 51.
19. Jacques Derrida, *Adieu to Emmanuel Levinas*, trans by Pascale-Anne Brault and Michael Naas (Stanford: Stanford University Press, 1999), 50.
20. Jacques Derrida, "Hospitality, Justice And Responsibility: A Dialogue with Jacques Derrida" in *Questioning Ethics: Contemporary Debates in Philosophy*, eds. in Richard Kearney and Mark Dooley (New York: Routledge, 1999), 73.
21. McNulty, *The Hostess*, xxv.
22. McNulty, *The Hostess*, xxvii.
23. McNulty, *The Hostess*, xxxvii.
24. Mireille Rosello, *Postcolonial Hospitality: The Immigrant as Guest* (Stanford, CA: Stanford University Press, 2001), 119.

25. Julia O'Connell Davidson, *Prostitution, Power, and Freedom* (Cambridge: Polity Press, 1998), 26-27.

26. Virginia Held, *The Ethics of Care: Personal, Political, and Global* (New York: Oxford University Press, 2006), 42.

27. Kimberle Crenshaw, "Mapping the Margins: Intersectionality, Identity Politics, and Violence Against Women of Color" *Stanford Law Review* 43, no. 6 (July 1991): 1241-1299.

28. Patricia Hill Collins, *Fighting Words: Black Women and the Search for Justice* (Minneapolis: University of Minnesota Press, 1998), 278.

29. Sandra G. Harding, *The Feminist Standpoint Theory Reader* (New York: Routledge, 2004), 6.

30. Ziad Obermeyer, Christopher J.L. Murray, Emmanuela Gakidou, "Fifty Years of Violent War Deaths from Vietnam to Bosnia: Analysis of Data from the World Health Survey Programme." *British Medical Journal* 336 (June 28, 2008): 1482-86.

31. Stockholm International Peace Research Institute (SIPRI), "SIPRI Yearbook 2008: Armaments, Disarmament and International Security." Sweden: Elanders. http://yearbook2008.sipri.org/files/SIPRIYB08summary.pdf (accessed November 25, 2009).

32. The Office of the United Nations High Commission for Refugees (UNHCR), "Asylum Levels And Trends In Industrialized Countries 2008," http://www.unhcr.org/statistics/STATISTICS/49c796572.pdf (accessed November 25, 2009).

Part I: Theories of Feminism and Hospitality

Chapter 1

Hospitableness: A Neglected Virtue

Nancy E. Snow

Reflections on the meaning of hospitality lead quickly to the concept of hospitableness. *Merriam-Webster's Online Dictionary*, for example, defines "hospitality" as hospitable treatment, reception, or disposition, and defines "hospitable" as "given to generous and cordial reception of guests; promising or suggesting generous and cordial welcome; and offering a pleasant or sustaining environment."[1] Ordinarily, we think of hospitality or hospitableness as making others welcome in one's place, such as in one's home or one's country.[2] My aim in this essay is to expand upon the core notion of hospitableness as "making others welcome" to argue that hospitableness should be considered a virtue, including a feminist virtue. Hospitableness as a virtue, I believe, has deeper and more extensive meanings than that which we usually ascribe to common usages of "hospitableness" or "hospitality."

In section two of the essay, I make preliminary comments about the conditions for hospitableness in its core or dictionary sense. In section three, I address the question of why hospitableness, understood simply in terms of its dictionary meaning, should be considered a virtue. There I suggest that, as a virtue, hospitableness is an expression of benevolence. In section four, I sketch two broader interpretations of the virtue of hospitableness and the worldviews they inhabit. I contrast hospitableness construed as making people feel welcome in one's *own* world with an alternative, namely, making people feel welcome in a *shared* world. These construals, I contend, assume very different perspectives on one's relation to one's life and world. Underlying the first construal of hospitableness, I argue, is a proprietary or controlling perspective on one's life and world which is congenial to liberal individualistic conceptions of the person and of social relations. The first construal is narrower than the second, which holds that hospitableness is welcoming others into lives and worlds that are shared. That we share our lives and worlds with others is a perspective taken by Buddhism. The Buddhist worldview is very different from that of individualism, and has features that animate the second conception.

By the end of section four, then, we will have seen three versions of the virtue of hospitableness: (1) in its core or dictionary meaning, in which it is the cordial welcoming of guests and, I maintain, an expression of the better-known virtue of benevolence; (2) in a broader interpretation in which it is making others welcome in one's own life and world, and is at home within the worldview of liberal individualism; and (3) in a more expansive alternative to (2), in which it is making others welcome in a shared life and world, and is at home in Buddhism.

In sections five and six, I inquire about the prospects for versions (2) and (3) from a feminist perspective. Hospitableness has often been viewed as the special province of women. Can the construals of the virtue articulated here be considered gender-neutral? What are the limits of the virtue, according to each construal? Is hospitableness on either construal an excessively demanding virtue? Does hospitableness conceived of in either of these ways unfairly burden women or further sexist oppression, and if so, how? How is hospitality on each construal limited by factors such as the needs for personal privacy, integrity, and autonomy? Can either construal of hospitableness be considered a feminist virtue, that is, a virtue that aids in struggles against oppression?[3]

Conditions for Hospitableness

Before turning to the question of why hospitableness in its core meaning should be considered a virtue, let me make a brief comment on the conditions for hospitableness. As mentioned, the core meaning of "hospitable" is "given to generous and cordial reception of guests; promising or suggesting generous and cordial welcome; and offering a pleasant or sustaining environment." Hospitable attitudes and behavior can, but need not, occur in settings where one has a special or proprietary relationship to that which is shared with guests. It is common to think it appropriate that a host welcomes visitors into her or his home or country, or an innkeeper welcomes travelers to hired lodgings. These are places to which the host has a relationship that can be called proprietary in some sense, either strictly speaking, as when one owns one's home, or owns or manages an inn or hotel, or more loosely, as when a country's citizens have a sense of "ownership" or responsibility for their nation. But, clearly, one need not stand in such a relationship in order to perform the duties of host and display hospitality. Suppose that Jane is hosting a party, but is called away from her guests on urgent business. Jake, a good friend, is asked to stand in and "play host" for Jane. Or Lucy is giving a party, and Lance, Lucy's significant other, assumes hosting duties out of love and a desire to help Lucy make her event a success. So having a proprietary relationship with that which is shared with guests is not necessary for the occurrence of displays of what can be called hospitableness or hospitality.

But neither is having a proprietary relationship to that which is shared with guests by itself sufficient for hospitableness. Consider a homeowner who admits a houseguest, but grudgingly, or a host who invites people to dinner but is stingy with food or drink. These people, though owners of what they offer, are unwelcoming and consequently, lack hospitality. They fall short of the hospitality ideal, which includes appropriate intent.

The foregoing considerations suggest that having a welcoming or cordial attitude toward others is both necessary and sufficient for hospitableness toward guests. Yet this is not quite correct, for consider how odd it would be if, barring some kind of emergency, a guest at a party simply assumed the role of welcoming host on her own without being asked to do so. Adding this factor to our previous discussion suggests that the necessary and sufficient conditions for displaying hospitableness toward guests are: (1) legitimately occupying the role of host, which can but need not entail a proprietary relationship with that which is shared with others; and (2) having a welcoming or cordial attitude toward those others. One legitimately occupies the role of host if one owns or manages that which is shared with others, or has been asked to perform the duties of hosting. So, according to the account thus far, one displays hospitality if and only if one legitimately occupies the role of host, and has a welcoming or cordial attitude toward guests.

This is still incomplete, however, for one can satisfy these conditions, yet fail to use practical reason in having a welcoming or cordial attitude toward guests, and, because of this lack, botch one's attempts at hospitality.[4] In other words, one's attempts at hospitableness can misfire because they're ill conceived or poorly executed. Let us amend the account to accommodate this point. The necessary and sufficient conditions for displaying hospitableness toward guests are: (1) legitimately occupying the role of host, which can but need not entail a proprietary relationship with that which is shared with others; and (2) having a welcoming or cordial attitude toward those others, which is (3) informed by practical reason. Having a welcoming or cordial attitude toward guests which is informed by practical reason makes it more likely that one will actually be successful in one's attempts at hospitableness, that is, one will in fact make one's guests feel welcome and at ease.

One final point should be noted. Successful efforts at hospitableness depend upon the guest as well as upon the host. A host cannot be faulted if he or she has made reasonable efforts at hospitality that fail because her guest is unreasonably demanding, ungrateful, surly, and so on. The success of hospitality is in an important sense relational. It depends on the qualities of the host, as well as upon the qualities of the guest.[5] A host should be welcoming, cordial, and responsive to guests without being overbearing, but guests should, in turn, be reasonable, gracious, and grateful for the host's accommodation. Thus, there is a reciprocity involved in the host-guest relationship that contributes to successful hospitality.

Why Hospitableness is a Virtue

Why should hospitableness, in its core meaning expressed in the Merriam-Webster definition, be considered a virtue? Why, in particular, should we think that, as a virtue, hospitableness is a form or expression of benevolence? Let me state at the outset that I endorse the notion, familiar from Aristotle, that virtue is an enduring character state, as well as his requirements for virtuous actions: virtuous actions spring from appropriate, that is, virtuous motivations, and such actions generally hit their target because they are guided by practical reason. If we assume that hospitableness can be an enduring character state and that hospitable actions generally satisfy the requirements for virtuous action, then hospitableness can be considered a virtue for three overlapping reasons: (1) it is other-regarding; (2) it helps us to live well in the sense that it makes social living go better; and (3) it contributes to the flourishing of the hospitable person and those around her.

The fact that hospitableness is other-regarding is an obvious reason for considering it a virtue. By definition, hospitableness expresses positive attitudes and behavior toward others: generosity, cordiality, and pleasantness. Hospitableness is making another feel welcome or at home; it sustains them. As such, one might say that it is a form of kindness. In any event, the fact that hospitableness is an expression of positive other-regarding attitudes and behavior counts in its favor when considering whether it is a virtue.

In addition, hospitableness helps us to live well by helping our lives go better socially. Other things being equal, social events, both large and small, run more smoothly when guests are treated hospitably. Hospitableness is a way of showing good will to others. Especially when relations are tense, as when a diplomat from a foreign country is unsure of his reception at an official function, the hospitality of the host can make a difference in building trust and positive relationships. Hospitality makes our social lives go better, then, by displaying good will and building trust. Since good will and trust are forms of positive other-regard, this second reason for considering hospitableness a virtue, namely, that it helps our lives go better socially, builds upon and overlaps with the first reason for regarding it as a virtue—that hospitableness expresses positive other-regarding attitudes and behavior.

Finally, how does hospitableness enable its possessor and those around her to flourish? The fact that it aids us in social living certainly contributes to its ability to help us flourish. In addition to the factors mentioned in the preceding paragraph, hospitableness aids in social living by helping us to make and cultivate friends and by building community. But friends and community, according to Aristotle, are necessary for flourishing. So I would say that, since hospitableness helps us with social living in various ways, including the formation and facilitation of friendships and community, it contributes to the flourishing of both the hospitable person and the recipients of her hospitality.

For these three overlapping reasons, hospitableness is a virtue: it expresses positive other-regarding attitudes and behavior; it helps our lives go well socially; and it contributes to our flourishing. Might it be that hospitableness is merely a social virtue, that is, suitable only for occasions requiring sociability, such as receptions, parties, visits, etc.? Could we be dour and curmudgeonly in everyday life, and put on our hospitable "party face" only occasionally, as circumstances require?

I think this would be to give hospitableness short shrift. I believe that true hospitableness consists not merely in the occasional display of superficial welcoming attitudes and behavior that might be conjoined with underlying pessimistic attitudes toward others, but is, instead, an expression of a deeper attitude toward life which we commonly call "benevolence." Contrast the miserliness of Ebenezer Scrooge with the kindness and benevolence of Bob Cratchitt in Dickens' *A Christmas Carol*. Admittedly, as Dickens portrays them, both characters are clichéd. Yet, each portrayal contains a kernel of truth. Miserly people are not warm-hearted. Their lack of hospitality stems not only from greed, but, as in Scrooge's case, from a negative, misanthropic outlook. By contrast, Cratchitt's easy hospitality seems inseparable from his kind-heartedness. Genuine hospitableness, it seems to me, expresses benevolence—a love of one's fellow person, and a desire to put him or her at ease and make him or her feel welcome. In short, I want to suggest that hospitableness as a virtue is not a superficial veneer

of sociability that could mask underlying negative attitudes, but instead, expresses genuine benevolence—fellow-feeling rooted in a love of humankind.
Contrasting hospitableness with Scrooge's miserliness might create the impression that my construal of hospitableness is similar to Aristotle's virtue of liberality.[6] Liberality is, after all, a mean between prodigality and miserliness. But hospitableness and liberality, in my view, are not the same or even similar. Liberality as described by Aristotle is a virtue whose proper sphere is the realm of small to moderate spending. Liberality is a virtue that guides our attitudes and behavior in regard to wealth on a smaller scale than the virtue of magnificence. That is, what we aim for when we aim for liberality is appropriateness with respect to wealth. By contrast, what we aim for in hospitality is appropriateness in the treatment of guests and visitors. These are different spheres of life. Though they might overlap, as when one displays liberality in providing for guests or visitors, liberality need not have anything to do with hospitableness. One can be hospitable even if, like Bob Cratchitt, one lacks the means for appropriate displays of liberality. In other words, though one's table can be poor, one can welcome others to it with grace and kindness. In sum, what is necessary for hospitableness is having and displaying kind and gracious attitudes and behavior toward others. These attitudes and behavior are motivated by benevolence–fellow-feeling that stems from a love of humankind.

At this point, one might suspect that hospitableness just *is* benevolence—applied, as it were, to the host/guest relationship. One might support this view by analogy with liberality and generosity. Liberality, it might be claimed, is a specific form or version of generosity. It is simply generosity applied to cases of small to moderate spending. Whatever one might think of the relation between liberality and generosity, I am not sure that much of importance depends on whether we consider the virtue of hospitableness, conceived of in its core or dictionary sense, as an independent virtue in its own right, or as a special application of benevolence. However, I favor viewing hospitableness in its core sense as an expression of benevolence, since doing so seems to imbue it with a depth that the virtue would otherwise lack. So I am content to think of hospitableness as an application of the broader virtue of benevolence to the specific relationship of host and guest.

Two Construals of Hospitableness

The preceding section was devoted to explaining why hospitableness in its core or dictionary meaning is a virtue and why, as a virtue, it is an expression of benevolence. So far, we've been considering hospitableness narrowly construed as the virtue whose proper sphere is the treatment of guests and visitors. In this section, I want to suggest that hospitableness be thought of as a virtue with a broader scope—as applicable to all of life. Here I consider two interpretations of this broader conception of hospitableness. Hospitableness can be conceived of as the virtue of making others feel welcome in a *shared* world, or as the virtue of making others feel welcome in one's *own* world. There are important differences between these two construals. Each relies on a different view of self and the world. In this section, I explore each construal and the larger worldview in which it is embedded.

Let us consider first the idea that hospitableness is making others feel welcome in one's own world. This construal assumes a proprietary conception of oneself and one's world. One's world, so viewed, is a certain ambit or sphere within which one operates and over which one has, if not outright ownership, at least a sense of ownership or control. This is the outlook of "mine" and "thine," according to which I see my home, my possessions, my country, and so on, as belonging to me, and view myself as having legitimate authority with respect to them. Hospitableness consists of welcoming another into one's territory, and sharing one's possessions with the other. The essence of this version of hospitableness is expressed by saying, "This is mine, and I welcome you to partake of it." In being hospitable, I give the other permission to share my life and world. The other has no right to my hospitality, and thus I have no duty to offer it. Hospitality can be seen as a form of generosity or largesse. It is always possible for me to foreclose or withdraw hospitality without infringing on the other's rights. If so, the other is then seen as an unwelcome intruder, an outsider with no right of access to that which I own or control.

Such a view of hospitality is at home in the context of liberalism individualism. Liberalism sees society as being composed of atomistic individuals, each of whom is sovereign over themselves and their possessions. This kind of perspective has dominated western democratic societies since the rise of modern philosophy, and is philosophically familiar in the work of Hobbes, Locke, Kant, and Mill, as well as contemporary liberalism. Key to this view is that the individual is an autonomous agent with the capacity to rule herself and manage her possessions. She has rights to self-ownership and, provided certain conditions have been met, to ownership of objects. These rights carve out a sphere of influence which is protected from the interventions of others. Her hospitality reflects her choice to permit others limited entry into this sphere. The legitimacy of their entry into her world is contingent upon her choice to give them access; she decides what they have access to and in what manner.

This conception of hospitality is common in Western societies and is reflected in social mores and customs. Consider, for example, the conventions surrounding inviting people to one's home for a dinner party. Hospitality reflects the host's choice to invite others into a selected space of his choosing: the dining area, the living room, and so on. It would be odd, if not downright rude, for dinner guests to assume they have the "run of the house," and ramble through bedrooms. That is, it's generally assumed that the access of guests is limited to areas of the host's choosing. If dinner guests want to see a bedroom, courtesy requires that they ask the host's permission. Even a houseguest is limited in her access to the host's quarters. The expectation is that the houseguest will respect the host's privacy by not intruding into places where, other things being equal, she has no business, for example, by rummaging through desk drawers or medicine cabinets.

There is an alternative to the western individualistic conception of hospitality and hospitableness. The alternative regards hospitableness as making others welcome in a *shared* life and world. According to the view of hospitableness discussed in the preceding paragraphs, one sees one's life and world as one's own, as one's rightful possessions. Hospitality consists in the choice to share one's possessions with others. According to the alternative, one sees one's life and world not as one's possessions, but as shared; hospitality follows as a matter of course, not as a matter of choice. It is not that the choice to be hospitable is not possible. Instead, it is unnecessary: hospitality is making available to others what is already shared among us.

I believe that this second conception of hospitality is at home in the context of the Buddhist worldview.[7] Buddhists hold that there is no self; the impression that we have a self is an illusion. This follows, I believe, from the more general doctrine that all is impermanent—the world, our lives, our thoughts, knowledge, feelings, sensory perceptions, and so on. Suffering, according to Buddhists, results from our selfish attachments to that which is impermanent, including our attachment to a self which is, in reality, non-existent. Whatever one might think of the tenability of Buddhist metaphysical doctrines, it is clear that, for Buddhists, the illusions of self-ownership and attachment to one's life and world are the causes of deep human suffering. Another metaphysical doctrine of relevance here is the concept of *ten del*, or dependent origination. All is intertwined. We are all parts of each other, and are dependent on each other. Given the facts of interdependency and impermanence, the kind of self-ownership and ownership of possessions endorsed by individualism is, for Buddhists, unnatural, unethical, and the cause of human suffering. It is unnatural in the sense that it is contrary to the true nature of the universe, unethical in the sense that it presumes rights of ownership we do not have, and the cause of suffering in the sense that it fosters attachment to and desire for that which we will someday lose—our lives, our loved ones, our possessions—and never really possessed in the first place.

Why would self-ownership and the ownership of things be unethical? How does it presume rights we do not have? After all, we need to take responsibility for ourselves and our well-being and to own some things in order to live. Buddhists do not deny this. What they decry is selfish attachment—to ourselves, to others, and to our possessions. To regard myself, my spouse, my family, and my home as mine in a selfish, clinging way is to court suffering. We should be mindful of the fact that nothing is really ours in the sense that all is impermanent. Someday I and all whom I love will die. I will no longer own my home or possessions. In fact, all of these things could be unexpectedly taken from me through illness or misfortune. For Buddhists, these things were never really mine, and we avoid suffering by not clinging to them.

Things are not really mine not only because they are impermanent, but also because everything is interconnected through dependent origination. Buddhists believe that metaphysically and, *a fortiori*, socially, we are all connected. But if we are all interlinked, and if I refuse another access to goods or resources that I "own," I deny another access to that to which he has a legitimate claim. Just as my life is not my own, my house, my food, and so on, are not my own in the sense that I should not withhold them from another.

A further element from Buddhist moral psychology should be added to this picture. Buddhists view suffering and the desire for happiness as facts of the existence of sentient creatures. As sentient beings, we all suffer. We also desire happiness. Given the fact of suffering and of our interdependence with others, the appropriate ethical attitude, according to Buddhists, is compassion. This creates an apparent paradox in the Buddhist worldview: we should be detached because of our impermanence, yet compassionate because of our interconnections with others who suffer. As I read Buddhism, however, the paradox dissolves. Detachment should not be understood as disengagement from the needs or suffering of others, but, instead, as an antidote to the selfish attachments that keep us emotionally bound to the world of impermanence. I should, as a Buddhist, feel compassion for others as I help them to overcome selfish desires and achieve a detached outlook. This requires me to maintain a psychological balance between becoming too attached to the one for whom compassion is felt, and becoming so detached that I feel nothing for her. To put the point slightly differently, my aim should be to have *unselfish compassion* for the other—compassion directed to helping her achieve a healthily detached perspective on the suffering that ails her.[8]

Hospitableness in the sense of making others welcome in a shared world is, in my view, an outgrowth of compassion and a central virtue of Buddhism. Given the Buddhist worldview, hospitableness is not an ethical option, as it is on the individualistic conception. Instead, it is essential to a Buddhist way of being in the world, since it follows naturally from the broader Buddhist metaphysical worldview of interdependency and impermanence. It reflects a detached perspective toward self and possessions that makes possible the recognition that, since all is shared, we should graciously welcome others into what is already rightfully theirs. Having unselfish compassion for others and desiring to help them as they live their lives should dispose us to be hospitable by welcoming fellow-sufferers into lives and worlds that we share.

Before moving on to consider how well these conceptions of hospitableness fare according to feminist lights, let us consider two questions. First, is hospitableness, on either construal, an unlimited virtue?[9] Second, doesn't hospitableness presuppose property ownership, such that, without a robust conception of property ownership, hospitableness is unintelligible?[10]

Let us address the first question first. Both the core and the liberal construals of hospitableness are clearly limited by the host's rights. That is, the host can choose not to be hospitable, as he or she pleases. Moreover, hospitableness is also limited by the reciprocity of the host/guest relationship. If a guest is ungracious or abuses the host and her property, she may withdraw hospitality without failing in virtue. As I will argue in section six, the Buddhist conception of hospitableness is also limited, though not by the host's rights, and not necessarily by the failure of guests to reciprocate appropriately.

The second question raises an interesting conceptual issue about hospitableness. If hospitableness is, in essence, sharing with others what is ours or what we legitimately manage, doesn't it presuppose the institution of property ownership? This seems to create a difficulty for the Buddhist conception of hospitableness, according to which we do not own ourselves or our property in any robust sense. Yet hospitableness is meaningful in Buddhist contexts in which western conceptions of property ownership are absent, provided that these contexts display differential power relations.[11] To illustrate, suppose that I have power within a Buddhist context, for example, that I am a Buddhist monk of some renown. My hospitableness can be displayed in the extent to which I allow others access to myself—to my knowledge, my teaching, my lifestyle, and so on. I might withhold my knowledge, or dispense it in a surly, mean-spirited way, without genuine concern for the salvation of others. Alternatively, I show hospitableness to others when I welcome them to share the learning I have, or invite them to share my spiritual journey. Consequently, hospitableness does make sense in contexts in which robust conceptions of property ownership are absent, provided that people have something of value to share with others. This sharing can be done in more or less gracious, thoughtful, and welcoming ways—ways which reflect degrees of hospitableness.

The Construals from a Feminist Point of View: Hospitableness from the Liberal Individualistic Perspective

Thus far, I've articulated three meanings of the virtue of hospitableness. The first is a narrow conception that closely tracks the dictionary definition of "hospitableness." According to this conception, hospitableness is, in essence, the virtue of making guests feel welcome. I have also developed and discussed two broader interpretations of this core conception within the context of the worldviews that animate them. The narrower interpretation construes hospitableness as making others welcome in one's own life and world, and is situated within the worldview of liberal individualism. A more expansive notion of hospitableness conceives of it as the virtue of making others welcome in a shared life and world, and is at home in Buddhism. How do the second and third interpretations fare according to feminist lights?

This question is the topic of this and the next section. Before delving in, here is a preliminary comment on the question of gender-neutrality. It should be evident that each construal of hospitableness is gender-neutral. There is nothing essential to their meanings that renders these virtues specially suited to either men or women. Like so many other virtues, however, hospitality has been gendered in the sense that, socially and historically, it has *de facto* been viewed as more appropriately the province of women. More interesting than hospitality's conceptual gender-neutrality, I think, is the extent to which either conception could in fact be misused to oppress women. Addressing this question will take us into a discussion of how the alternative notions of hospitality measure up to feminist standards.

How does each interpretation fare on the issue of its possible misuse in oppressing women? It would seem on the face of it that hospitableness as the virtue of making others welcome in one's own life and world would be less susceptible to this form of misuse. This is because hospitableness so conceived can be given a liberal feminist analysis that adopts central features of the liberal individualistic worldview. Given the liberal individualistic worldview, the host is assumed to have proprietary rights over herself and her possessions, and is thus free to choose to reject or deny claims from others on her hospitality. On a liberal feminist reading, then, the host clearly has the right to deny or withdraw hospitality. Since liberal feminists advocate equal rights of men and women, women who are hosts have the right to resist sexist and oppressive assertions that women have a special obligation to be hospitable that men lack.

The less expansive conception of hospitableness thus provides clear grounds on which women can stand to combat the sexist misuse of the virtue. This is because this conception places definite limits on how demanding the virtue can be: it is the choice of the host whether and how to offer hospitality. In denying hospitality to another, the host is not violating the other's rights. Moreover, the host's choice to deny hospitality need not be an unreasonable assertion of her rights. Liberal individualism recognizes the values of personal privacy, autonomy, and integrity, and posits individual rights to protect these values. The privacy of one's home is especially relevant to questions concerning the legitimate scope of hospitality. In the United States, constitutional law recognizes the importance of one's home as a place of private withdrawal is protected against the intrusion of the government.[12] Similarly, the intrusion of unwanted guests into one's life and home clearly violates the privacy of the individual, undermines her autonomy, and can threaten her integrity. In denying others access to her private domain, the host is reasonably protecting her own privacy, autonomy, and integrity.

To recapitulate, the liberal individualistic underpinnings of hospitableness as the virtue of making others welcome in one's own life and world render this conception congenial to analysis from a liberal feminist point of view. Given the perspective of liberal feminism, we can make the following claims. First, women are equal to men in the sense that both women and men may choose whether and how to be hospitable. Second, in virtue of these equal rights, women can legitimately resist sexist urgings that they have a special obligation to be hospitable that men lack. Third, in limiting their hospitality, women and men may reasonably stand on their rights. Finally, the rights that limit the demands of hospitality are not value-neutral, but are premised on the individual's own legitimate claims to privacy, autonomy, and integrity. Consequently, the narrower construal of hospitality seems well situated to resist oppressive misuse.

Could the narrower version of hospitableness be considered a feminist virtue in the sense of having liberatory value in struggles against sexism? One possibility is to view it as an expression of benevolence or generosity that seeks to overcome oppression by urging us to overlook and move beyond it. It is unclear, to say the least, how merely overlooking oppression allows us to genuinely move beyond it. To genuinely move beyond oppression, we need to confront it and work together to expunge it. To the extent that being hospitable under oppressive conditions would cause us to miss or ignore the essential steps of confrontation with and catharsis of oppressive tendencies, it would not aid in liberatory struggles.

Might the narrower version of hospitality be coupled with recognition of injustice? We could certainly be hospitable to the victims of oppression while recognizing the oppressive structures that keep them down. Hospitality then could be considered a form of solidarity with the oppressed. Would it be permissible or desirable from a feminist perspective to extend hospitality to oppressors, while acknowledging their roles and the consequences of their actions? The question is a hard one. On one hand, one can see hospitality coupled with an acknowledgement of wrongs as a gesture of forgiveness. A hospitable gesture might be viewed as expressing the following attitude: "Yes, you have wronged people, but we are willing to overlook that and extend our friendship to you." If the host is a member of the oppressed class, this could be a gracious and appropriate gesture. If the host is not a member of the oppressed class, however, hospitality becomes inappropriate. Graciously overlooking a wrong done to someone else and welcoming a perpetrator into one's own life and world could be interpreted as an insult to the oppressed, as identification with the oppressor, and as inappropriately trusting the oppressor.

As is clear from the preceding discussion, the basic tack of liberal feminists is to adopt the ideals of political liberalism, but argue that they have not been applied equally to women and men. The antidote to patriarchal injustice, they think, is to extend liberal ideals. Some feminists think that liberal feminism does not go far enough in its critique of patriarchy. For radical, Marxist, and socialist feminists, liberalism is deficient not merely in its practical application, but is flawed in the deeper sense that liberal ideals are conceptually biased against women. These feminists argue that because of this, liberalism should be jettisoned in favor of other, more women-friendly political and ethical ideals. For them, the liberal individualistic underpinnings of hospitality as the virtue of making others welcome in one's own life render it gender-biased from the outset, and are sufficient to disqualify it as a virtue. Hospitality so construed could be a feminist virtue only if it could somehow be turned against these underpinnings and used as a tool for liberatory struggle. As I previously suggested, there are conditions under which this could happen. However, not all displays of hospitality satisfy these conditions.

How does the more expansive alternative fare by feminist lights? Hospitality in the more expansive sense is the virtue of making others welcome in a shared life and world. At first glance, this version of hospitality seems even less promising than the other option, since it places no obvious limits on hospitality. Furthermore, Buddhism has been accused of being patriarchal.[13] If these concerns are correct, then the more expansive version of hospitality would seem liable to sexist misuse, and of little value as a feminist virtue in combating oppression. I turn to these questions in the next section.

A Feminist Look at the More Expansive Construal

From a feminist perspective, the main difficulties with the more expansive interpretation of hospitableness as making others welcome in a shared life and world are that it seems especially liable to sexist misuse, and seems to have no liberatory potential in struggles against oppression. The Buddhist underpinnings sketched earlier apparently do nothing to ameliorate these difficulties, creating instead the impression that there are no limits on hospitableness in a Buddhist worldview. This impression stems, I believe, from the implications of the metaphysical doctrines of impermanence and interdependence, as well as from an especially strong interpretation of the ethical demands of unselfish compassion. In other words, if we are all impermanent and interdependent, and if the suffering of all sentient beings requires us to have unselfish compassion, how could hospitableness to others possibly be limited? We all seem to have unlimited duties of hospitality. Moreover, there seems to be nothing intrinsic to Buddhist doctrine that might curb societal tendencies to shunt the burdens of hospitableness onto women. So an initial feminist assessment of the prospects for the more expansive version of hospitableness is not promising.

However, the Buddha himself eschewed metaphysics, preferring to educate his followers by giving them practical advice on how to attain Enlightenment—the highest state of spiritual awakening in which we are freed from all selfish attachments and experience bliss. I propose to follow the Buddha's lead. That is, even if Buddhist metaphysics place no limits on the hospitableness we should show to others, there are definite practical limits grounded in the need of each of us to strive for Enlightenment. Since women are as entitled as men to seek Enlightenment, women are also as entitled as men to place practical limits on their hospitality, and may invoke their equal need for Enlightenment to argue against sexist burdens that might detract from their spiritual growth.

The basic line of argument is this. Enlightenment, in the Buddhist tradition, is attained through attention to the inner self—to our spiritual and emotional states and purity of mind. The transformation of our inner states can be achieved only through meditation. But meditation requires that we have certain conditions available to us, most importantly, ample opportunities to sit and meditate, whether alone or with the *sangha*—the community of fellow seekers. However we meditate, we require privacy in order to do it—the time, place, and freedom from duties to others to attend to our inner states. The need to meditate in the search for Enlightenment places clear limits on the hospitableness we are required to show to others. If we voluntarily show too much hospitality to others, we risk shortchanging our own spiritual growth by neglecting meditation. If others force us to neglect meditation in order to show hospitality, for example, if men force women to host others to the neglect of women's meditation, men are guilty of a grave injustice, for they have no right to jeopardize others' spiritual development. A Buddhist might argue that the men should entertain the guests, thereby showing unselfish compassion to the guests by offering them hospitality, and to the women by freeing them to meditate.

Couldn't a Buddhist counter that unselfish compassion requires unselfish and unlimited hospitality? In showing unselfish hospitality, we thereby seek Enlightenment in a way that differs from meditation, for we seek to alleviate the suffering of fellow creatures with whom we are, after all, connected. An appropriate Buddhist rejoinder is to point out that meditation is indispensable, and that in daily life one must seek a middle path that balances the needs for meditation and hospitality. In other words, one must not neglect one's own spiritual development for the sake of welcoming others. Instead, the compassion, and, *a forti-*

ori, the hospitality, that we show to others should be rooted in the strength and wisdom we gain through meditation. Meditation is thus the *sine qua non* of genuine compassion. Consequently, despite the need for balancing the two at the level of everyday action, there is a deeper sense in which meditation comes first, for meditation is the source of the compassionate understanding and motivation expressed in hospitality.

Not only should we make time to meditate, we should also be careful about the company we keep. To the woman who is under sexist pressure to offer hospitality at the expense of her spiritual development, the Buddha would say, "If you find no one to support you on the spiritual path, walk alone."[14] This saying comes from a discussion of immaturity. There are two types of immaturity, according to the Buddha. The first type of immature person is ignorant, but, unaware of her ignorance, sees herself as wise. The second type is immature, and, knowing this, has a little wisdom. The message of the Buddha is not to waste one's precious time on the first type of immature person who "cannot understand the dharma [the way, the path to Enlightenment] even if they spend their whole life with the wise."[15] Similarly, the Buddha advises, "Make friends with those who are good and true, not with those who are bad and false."[16] One can infer from these passages that it is a mistake to associate with those who would prevent us from progressing in the *dharma*, whether they are guests we welcome into our homes and lives, or significant others who unfairly saddle us with the burdens of hospitality. Clearly, the Buddha would regard it as mistaken to extend hospitality at the expense of our spiritual lives, or even to associate with those who would cause us to do so.

The aforementioned texts do not address hospitableness directly, but suggest an outlook on appropriate hospitality that is consistent with remarks from the Buddha that guide us in shaping our social lives in ways beneficial for spiritual growth. These quotes are taken from *The Dhammapada*, an early work that purports to convey the sayings of the Buddha. Much later Buddhist advice to women comes from a collection of Zen stories. One such story tells the tale of Ryonen, an early nineteenth century Buddhist nun who started out as a beautiful lady in waiting to the empress of Japan.[17] After the sudden death of the empress, Ryonen's world changed. She sought several Zen masters to take her as a disciple. All refused, saying she was too beautiful. Finally, a master accepted her after she burned her face with a hot iron. On one level, the story is appalling—what sexist prejudice! Ryonen should not have had to mutilate herself in order to follow the *dharma*. Yet, her action was clearly approved by the Zen master. She did what she had to do, given the sexist barriers she confronted, to follow the path of Enlightenment. Similarly, it seems, women should refuse the burdens of hospitality if they interfere with spiritual growth.

The upshot of the reasoning pursued here is that the more expansive conception of hospitableness can, like the narrower version, resist sexist misuse, and like, the narrower version, draws on its contextual underpinnings to do so. Could the more expansive version contribute to the struggle against oppression? Perhaps hospitableness as an expression of unselfish compassion could lead us to offer succor to others who are oppressed, thereby aiding them in the struggle against injustice. Surely compassion has the potential to be a feminist virtue inasmuch as it is a form of solidarity with those who suffer, and can motivate us to act on their behalf. Hospitableness as an expression of unselfish compassion could have similar liberatory value. Such compassion and hospitality, though, should be offered with an awareness of injustice; that is, we can be compassionate, and perhaps, also, hospitable, while recognizing and combating the existence of injustice. So, as with our analysis of the narrower version of hospitality, more expansive hospitality, too, should be coupled with an appropriate recognition of the kinds of injustices that create oppression and the need to combat them.

Conclusion

In this essay, I've explored several versions of hospitableness, and have argued that they should be considered virtues. The core meaning of hospitableness, I've contended, is the display of cordiality or a welcoming attitude toward guests by someone who legitimately occupies the role of host. There are good reasons to regard this initial version of hospitableness as a virtue that expresses, in appropriate situations, the more familiar virtue of benevolence. In addition, I've explored two interpretations of this core conception of hospitableness: hospitableness construed narrowly as making others welcome in one's own life and world; and construed more expansively as making others welcome in a shared life and world. The former is at home within the perspective of liberal individualism; the latter, in the context of Buddhism. How well do these construals fare as possible feminist virtues? Both interpretations of the virtue are resistant to sexist misuse; the more expansive version, perhaps, has a slight edge in terms of its potential for aiding in liberatory struggles. On both interpretations, however, hospitality can aid in liberation only if it is coupled with an awareness of the injustice suffered by the oppressed and perpetrated by oppressors. Forgetting the facts of injustice, a host risks insulting the oppressed by displays of hospitality to oppressors. Such is the complexity of virtue under conditions of oppression.[18]

Notes

1. See http://www.merriam-webster.com/dictionary/hospitality.
2. Throughout this essay, I use "hospitableness" and "hospitality" interchangeably.
3. For the idea that a feminist virtue aids in struggles against oppression, I draw on Lisa Tessman, *Burdened Virtues: Virtue Ethics for Liberatory Struggles* (New York: Oxford University Press, 2005), 7.
4. I am grateful to Franco Trivigno for this point.
5. Thanks to Michael Monahan for this point.
6. See Aristotle, *Nicomachean Ethics*, trans. Terence Irwin (Indianapolis, Indiana: Hackett Publishing Company, 1985), Book IV.

7. My explanations of the Buddhist worldview draw on His Holiness the Dalai Lama, *Ethics for the New Millenium* (New York: Riverhead Books, 1999), esp. chapter 3; and Eknath Easwaran, trans., *The Dhammapada* (Tomales, California: Nilgiri Press, 1985, 2007), 80-98.

8. Clarifying what is meant by a "healthily detached perspective" on suffering would take us too far afield of the topic of hospitableness. However, it should be noted that achieving a detached outlook, say on an illness from which one suffers, can help one to put the suffering in perspective, to not be overwhelmed by it, and to manage it better.

9. I am grateful to Arun Iyer for raising this question.

10. I owe this point to David MacPherson.

11. Thanks to Melissa Mosko for bringing this up.

12. See *Stanley v. Georgia*, 394 U.S. 557 (1969).

13. See, for example, Rita M. Gross, *Buddhism after Patriarchy: A Feminist History, Analysis, and Reconstruction of Buddhism* (Albany, New York: State University of New York Press, 1993).

14. Easwaran, trans., 123.

15. Easwaran, trans., 123.

16. Easwaran, trans., 126.

17. Paul Reps and Nyogen Senzaki, compilers, *Zen Flesh, Zen Bones: A Collection of Zen and Pre-Zen Writings* (Boston, Massachusetts: Tuttle Publishing, 1988), 65-66.

18. This paper was presented at the Marquette Ethics and Political Philosophy Workshop, March 19, 2009. I am grateful to the audience for helpful questions and comments. I am also grateful to Maurice Hamington for helpful comments on an earlier version of this essay, as well as for his kind invitation to submit my work for this volume.

Chapter 2

Su Casa es Mi Casa? Hospitality, Feminist Care Ethics, and Reciprocity

Maureen Sander-Staudt

> I was about to go back inside when I heard voices coming from the house. I recognized one as Wahid's.
> "—Nothing left for the children."
> "We're hungry but we're not savages! He's a guest! What was I supposed to do?"
> he said in a strained voice.
> "—to find something tomorrow." She sounded near to tears. "What do I feed —"
> I tiptoed away. I understood now why the boys hadn't shown any interest in the watch.
> They hadn't been staring at the watch at all. They'd been staring at my food . . . When I was certain no one was looking . . . I planted a fistful of crumpled money under a mattress.
> —Khaled Hosseini, *The Kite Runner*

In an increasingly mobile, cosmopolitan world, hospitality is emerging as a moral and religious virtue to the extent that some ethicists construe it as the core of ethics. In light of the troubling historical correlations between ideals of hospitality, feminine subservience, and the deprivation of women and children, I argue for reciprocity as a key standard for a feminist care ethical account of hospitality. Defined as a set of practices aimed at producing and maintaining good relations between "guests" and "host/hostesses," in the first section I establish hospitality as a practice of care operating on domestic, professional, and international levels. Building on the writings of Joan Tronto and Daniel Engster, hospitality qualifies as a caring practice when it serves to maintain the world and meet basic needs. An obligation of domestic hospitality in care ethics correlates to Nel Noddings "dread of the proximate stranger" whose needs must be met, but who may compromisingly impinge upon the one who cares. But to the extent that hospitality is provided to those who could meet their needs on their own, it also qualifies as a personal, professional, and diplomatic service, raising feminist questions about power inequalities, exploitation, and the disparate benefits of hospitality to men, women, and children. Following this line of thought, the second section reviews historical, literary, and practical examples of hospitality, revealing distinct patterns of gender and privilege that yield unequally reciprocal benefits of hospitality. These examples suggest that although practices of hospitality can promote congenial relations, they are less likely to do so when hospitality is coerced, or standards of reciprocity are weakly stipulated. The third section thus employs a feminist care ethic to take issue with the suggestion of Emmanual Levinas, Jacques Derrida, and others, that hospitality is a gender-neutral duty of unconditional openness to all humans, without regret or expectation. The stipulation of reciprocity established by Eva Feder Kittay is used to argue that hospitality functions best under conditions of discerning volunteerism on the part of hostess, and reciprocity on the part of guest that engages the central virtues of care—attention, response, respect, and competent completion.

Hospitality and Care Ethics

As a moral and religious virtue, hospitality is enjoying a revival. Noting the vital historical importance of hospitality as a welcoming and sheltering of guests in diverse cultures, authors like Judith Green locate its modern relevance in how it creates preconditions for initiating and sustaining a global making peace process.[1] Emily Cook describes hospitality as a Christian duty to provide even enemies with the necessities of survival and to make everyone feel at home.[2] Despite its wide exploration as an ethical and political ideal, hospitality as a normative concept has been largely unconsidered by care ethicists, a surprising gap given that hospitality permeates and includes many caring practices. Care ethics is a moral theory that posits a fundamental relational ontology to human existence, stemming from the developmental origins of relational natality, and from the inherent dependency of humans at various times of life, including infancy, childhood, illness, old age, and times of unexpected calamity. Care ethicists argue that human dependency grounds a moral obligation to provide care for others when they need it, and hospitality seems to be one of the ways in which we do so, especially for visitors and travelers. Hospitality prima facie seems to be a caring ideal because of how it can help to solidify and strengthen relations between guests and host/hostesses. However, a feminist care ethic is also committed to the practical realities of how gender intersects with moral ideals and practices like hospitality. Feminist care ethicists are concerned with promoting care in more just ways, assuring that women receive care and are not burdened disproportionately with expectations to care for others. Along the same lines, hospitality is of interest to feminist care ethics both because of how women, and sometimes their children, may be in need of hospitality, and also because of how women typically bear different relationships to the provision of hospitality than men, such as being more responsible for work like cooking, cleaning, and making others feel at home. Clarifying how and when hospitality classifies as a feminist caring practice informs how one might go about promoting it as a valuable mode of social exchange that can strengthen social relationships, without recreating oppression and exploitation that characterize traditional hospitable norms.

The work of Elizabeith Telfer is a good place to start examining the ways in which the offer of hospitality qualifies as caring practice, and how its various understandings may or may not be consistently incorporated into a feminist care ethic.[3] Telfer defines hospitality as a welcoming to guests that generally includes offerings of food, drink, lodging, and a sharing of one's own personal provisions. While hospitality sometimes involves entertaining, Telfer distinguishes the former as an offering designed to meet the needs of another, and the latter as the giving of pleasure, although she uses the terms synonymously. She further delineates hospitable offerings into three types depending upon to whom they are directed— to one's friends; to one's circle of acquaintances including formal relations of family, work, or common interest; and in the spirit of Good Samaritanism, to any person in need, including strangers. Telfer characterizes hospitality as an optional virtue in all cases. While she thinks we should avoid being inhospitable to our circle and to strangers in need, she sees hospitality to one's friends as being of the strongest obligation, not only because individuals have limited resources with which to respond to the great many needs of myriad strangers, but also because we have stronger relational bonds with our friends. She observes that the ready existence of restaurants and hotels makes hospitality to known and unknown travelers less of a duty for most individuals today, but that hospitality continues to be a virtue of those living in rural areas, and that modern humans have needs that are newly emerging from changing circumstances.

Telfer's analysis is of special interest to feminists not only because of her view that hospitality is an optional virtue, but also because she associates it with a requisite motive, and acknowledges its association with gender norms. As a virtue, Telfer characterizes hospitality as requiring an appropriate motive, a consistent display, and a genuine desire to give pleasure unadulterated by ulterior desires. Telfer posits that persons who are hospitable out of duty but secretly resent their guests are better characterized as dutiful than hospitable. She states that a person is not inhospitable if he resents guests who wantonly damage his property, but he is if he resents their very presence while feeling that he has a duty to entertain them, adding further that if guests cannot tell the difference perhaps entertaining them is still the right thing to do. Although she does not tie this discussion to gender roles as extensively as she could, an oversight I rectify in the next section, she rejects common views that women as vocational nurturers have stronger duties of hospitality than men, that they more than men value the personal and caring side of morality to which hospitality belongs, or that they essentially have special, innate talents for being hospitable.[4]

Telfer's analysis of hospitality bears certain affinities with feminist care ethics. The first commonality is that Telfer implies that hospitality is best understood as a practice. Although Telfer explores hospitality primarily as a virtue, her definition of hospitality describes it more fundamentally as a practice normatively guided by virtues, a practice of welcoming. In a similar manner, feminist care ethicists tend to favor understanding care as a practice because doing so a) resists the tendency to romanticize care as a sentiment or dispositional trait, b) reveals the breadth of such practices as intertwining with virtually all aspects of life, and c) emphasizes that at its normative core care is work that must be done, and that it matters who does it, as well as how and why.[5] The same reasoning applies in favor of understanding hospitality as a practice that generates certain culturally specific accounts of virtue. Moreover, the definitions of care offered by Joan Tronto and Daniel Engster suggest that hospitality as construed by Telfer at least sometimes qualifies as a caring practice, namely, when a hospitable offering serves to "maintain, continue, and repair our world so that we can live in it as well as possible," or "helps individuals meet their vital biological needs, develop or maintain their basic capabilities, and avoid or alleviate unnecessary or unwanted pain and suffering."[6] According to these accounts, hospitality not only often involves caring practices—e.g. the giving of food and shelter, but is itself a caring practice to the extent that it serves to meet the needs of others who are dependent and vulnerable to certain forms of neglect or hostility. This potential classification gets lost in Telfer's tendency to overly conflate hospitality with the entertainment of friends, which is unfortunate because of how this undercuts the continued social relevance of hospitality as an ideal that inspires care for those who are foreign and in need, and that as a practice delivers care to strangers, encouraging evolving recognition of the particular other in the generalized other.

In addition to opening the door for understanding hospitality as a caring practice, Telfer's account resonates with care ethics in other ways, albeit in an inconsistent fashion. She characterizes hospitality as a ideal that is contextually determined, and finds that ideal applications of hospitality can be guided only so far by general principles, because a hospitable person responds to the specific interests and needs of the guest in question. This reflects care ethics' commitment to a contextual epistemology, although Telfer does not share the ethics' same aversion to general principles and universal injunctions. Telfer's claim that we have a stronger duty to hospitably benefit and meet the needs of our friends than we do to provide for those more unknown to us, also resonates with Nel Noddings' view that the duty to care applies more stringently toward the proximate than distant other, although the two authors' motivations are dissimilar.[7] For Noddings this is because a care-giver has a better chance of successfully completing care that is under her direct scope of influence, whereas for Telfer it is based on a universal principle that everyone has special duties to friends. Finally, like more recent feminist accounts of care, Telfer is careful to note the correlations between domestic hospitality and women without naturalizing or endorsing these associations.

Yet, while Telfer offers a good platform from which to think about hospitality as a form of care that feminists could endorse, there are certain problems and non-affinities with her account. Most notable is how Telfer only briefly acknowledges hospitality as a political practice, a common trend especially when it comes to gender. In construing hospitality as private and domestic, Telfer ignores its political aspects, both the ways in which offerings of hospitality are imbued with power inequities, and how hospitality is a significant part of political practice on many levels. Broadening the scope reveals forms of hospitality that are not explicit and overly distinct in Telfer's three categories, including diplomatic relations, immigration policies, health care systems, travel, tourist and service industries, and international exchanges, to mention a few.[8] Telfer's characterization of hospitality as a duty owed mainly to one's friends leads to possible parochialism and gives permission for the privileged to turn away the neediest in the world. Moreover, she does not seem to share the relational ontology of care ethics, in that Telfer's account of hospitality suggests that individuals are autonomous units who freely choose to give and receive hospitality against a backdrop of other options, departing from the fundamental commitment of care ethics to the essential inter-relational dependency of humans, and obscuring constraints on choice including involuntary and coercive gender socialization, embodied need, and systematic financial insecurities. Telfer's metaphysical grounding distracts away from attending to grave needs, from the moral imperative to question why there is extreme need for hospitality in certain cases and why some are distant from it, and from the move to establish better domestic and international chains of hospitality that respond to human matters of life and death.[9]

Furthermore, those who feel that hospitality is a socially vital and increasingly neglected virtue could take issue with Telfer's claim that hospitality ought be viewed as morally optional, as does Raymond Boisvert when he declares simply that "ethics is hospitality."[10] Feminist care ethicists have cause to share Boisvert's more stringent view of hospitality as a morally obligatory practice, but for different reasons. Although care ethicists may look favorably on Telfer's claim that hospitality is an optional virtue, given how women have historically suffered under the weight of expected domestic service to others, they may not conclude as does Telfer that hospitality is a mere moral nicety in modern society. Noddings suggests that hospitality is more than an optional virtue for one who is caring, such that the proximate other is a source of dread because "the stranger has an enormous claim on me, because I do not know where he fits, what requests he has a formal right to make, or what personal needs he will pass on to me . . . I fear a request I cannot meet without hardship."[11] Turning the tables, examining how women today are often outsiders, refugees, insecure in their homes, unpropertied, or widowed, feminist care ethicists will also want to consider how hospitality could serve women in these predicaments, and in a broader sense proactively mitigate the need for hospitality as it currently exists. Although feminist care ethicists are prone to agree that hospitality should be understood as more than an optional virtue, and one that can play a crucial role in maintaining relations and meeting the basic needs of those who reside outside of household or homeland, they are likely to be more forceful in asking questions about precisely which people are benefited and burdened by current practices of hospitality, and in noting the precariousness with which many women exercise and receive hospitality. Telfer recognizes the significance of gender to the value of hospitality, but her observations, like those of other philosophers speaking on the subject, are cursory at best. While she rejects the understanding of hospitality as a special virtue of women, she fails to explore the very real ways in which these expectations nonetheless constrain the choices of women, and how, as Lisa Tessman describes, the virtues of the oppressed are "burdened" in the sense of not being conducive to the flourishing of the agents possessing them, despite being morally admirable.[12] Hospitality is one such burdened virtue in part because of how women traditionally have been deprived instruments more than recipients of welcoming practices.

Patriarchal Oppression and Deprivation in Hospitality Traditions

Before moving on to how the concept of reciprocity as developed by feminist care ethicists can salvage hospitality from patriarchal traditions, it is important to first identify common ways in which women and children are disadvantaged within these traditions and by ongoing norms of hospitality. In recent times, hospitality as a cosmopolitan and democratic ideal emerges strongly in the teachings of Emmanuel Levinas and Jacques Derrida. Neither of these philosophers do a very thorough job of exploring the intersections between hospitality and the subordination of women, but their work helps to frame this problem as one of unequal reciprocity. Both philosophers have high esteem of hospitality as a moral value, understood as an unconditional openness to strangers. For Levinas, to shelter the other in one's home, to tolerate the presence of the landless and homeless, is the "criterion of humanness."[13] As David Gauthier observes, "Levinas's analysis suggests that our status as moral beings stands or falls with our treatment of strangers," and as such, acts of hospitality are of profound ethical significance.[14] Alan Bleakly describes a Levinasian conception of hospitality as one that has no conditions attached, in which the giver must walk away without reciprocity, taking as a model, "a woman giving birth."[15] For Derrida also, there is an absolute quality to hospitality, requiring that "I open up my home and that I give not only to the foreigner, but the absolute unknown, anonymous other . . . without asking of them either reciprocity (entering into a pact) or even their names."[16]

Having said this, both Levinas and Derrida also highlight the importance of reciprocity in hospitality relations. For example, Derrida makes reference to, but without any specificity, the inevitable but avoidable "Laws of Hospitality," handwritten pages of Pierre Klossowski's *Uncle Octave*, framed and put high above the bed in the spare room, that serves to bind recipients of hospitality. For Derrida, the ideal of reciprocity imparts a paradoxical aspect to the law of hospitality in that its absolute and unconditional aspects break with hospitality "in the ordinary sense, with conditional hospitality, with the right to or pact of hospitality." Because hospitality is by nature gracious, it must not be approached as a duty like a Kantian categorical imperative, even as it is manifests as a duty.[17]

Leaving a gender analysis of hospitable duty aside for a moment, the paradox described by Derrida can be explained by understanding hospitality as a virtue that sometimes involves a sense of responsibility, and that as a practice has a moral dimension but is not exhausted by it. This approach allows us to recognize that not every offering of hospitality is motivated by a sense of moral duty, but also that a sense of response-ability, that is, an inclination and ability to help and respond, sometimes influences people to be hospitable.[18] Thus, in hotels and restaurants, workers typically offer hospitality to guests primarily not because they see it as their moral duty, but because they see it as part of their job description, and are motivated by the promise of money. As a moral practice, however, hospitality is performed best by people who are inclined toward being hospitable to those they meet, and who notice and respond to the needs of others, for reasons other than an expectation of monetary compensation. At different times such persons may be motivated more or less by a sense of duty or propriety, but will have consistent inclinations to be hospitable regardless. Thus, hospitable persons will not *always* feel obliged to feed or take in other persons into their homes, but they often will in the case of special relations, and as I shall argue especially in the case of women, there seems nothing wrong about acting from a sense of begrudging duty unless one capriciously or callously make guests aware of one's feelings. In many cases, it is appropriate to temper hospitable inclinations with an expectation of reciprocity on some level. For example, Sarah Holtman observes that it is legitimate for hosts/hostesses to take precautions against certain guests if there are reasons to suspect them of intent to harm, and like Green, notes that through hospitable exchanges guests and hosts ideally develop relationships of trust that carry future expectations and responsibilities.[19]

In practice, however, expectations about hospitality and reciprocity are not the same for women as for men. While Levinas and Derrida bolster the promise of hospitality as a means to strengthen social relationships by emphasizing the reciprocal nature of hospitality as a moral ideal, they only briefly acknowledge how these traditions are marred by checkered patriarchal histories that do not equally provide hospitality to women as men. Quoting Simon Critchley, Gauthier faults Levinas's account of hospitality for its emphasis on fraternalism, because this translates into "a relation between brothers, between free equals who also happen to be male," noting that this "is decidedly less attractive to those who stand outside of the circle of friendship," namely, women.[20] In a similar vein, Nancy Holland critiques Derrida for characterizing hospitality as a "family scene," but one in which it is, in his words, "the family despot, the father, the husband, and the boss, the master of the house who lays down the laws of hospitality."[21] Holland points out that Derrida acknowledges the oppression of women within traditions of hospitality, but fails to remark about how this trend can render hospitality an especially treacherous practice for women, or how it influences the paradox of hospitable duty that he outlines. Holland notes that Derrida ends "Of Hospitality" by uneasily recounting how in *Leviticus* Lot offers his virgin daughters for defilement by the Sodomites, and how in *Judges*, a concubine of a Levite guest is raped and dismembered, in the name of hospitality. But the fact that he takes this as an end point rather than a starting point for his analysis leads Holland to affirm that "Derrida closes his text to any redemptive feminist discourse, by concluding with descriptions of sexual abuse and mutilation of women that serve . . . as the mark of the tradition of hospitality that 'we' might be heirs."[22] Holland encourages feminists to be inhospitable to Derrida's account of hospitality because he acknowledges, but does not adequately redress the ways in which women are mistreated within hierarchically ordered hospitality traditions. The effect of such endorsements of hospitality absent concrete reformatory proposals threatens to reinforce certain gendered patterns of oppression.

Taking the subordination of women as a starting point for an analysis of hospitality requires non-essentialist awareness of how women are situated differently than men to associative ideals and practices of hospitality, as well as a posture of political resistance. Non-essentialism requires that we recognize that women are not uniformly or singularly disadvantaged by hospitality norms, even as certain general patterns are observed. In every culture, women who are privileged in various ways are more likely to be recipients and easy providers of hospitality than those disadvantaged by poverty and other factors. But at the same time, in nearly every society, it is more likely women and feminized, disempowered persons who serve as vehicles of hospitality, and more likely men and masculinized, empowered persons who are in a position to offer and receive hospitality. It is no coincidence, for example, that as a gift of hospitality and symbol of welcoming to all nations, the Statue of Liberty is the figure of a woman. In response, a posture of political resistance evokes goal oriented outrage against hospitable injustices, one of which is how women are often vehicles for hospitality rather than recipients.

For instance, such a posture invites outrage in response to the above Old Testament stories not only because of how the women in them are portrayed as nameless property, and their lives and well being are so clearly deemed of lesser value than those of men, but also because of how they themselves are denied hospitality even as guests and *in their own homes*. Whereas men are shown to be in need of hospitality because of the dangers of the world outside of the home, women are shown to have refuge nowhere, without condemnation. In a tradition that continues in many guises today, the mastering and offering of women, in the form of work, the creation of cozy ambiance, obedience, and commodified bodies, are integral parts and signs of hospitality. Derrida is at least to be commended for being troubled by this patriarchal aspect of Judaic hospitality traditions, unlike some commentators who use the story of Lot's daughters to merely underscore the modern value of hospitality—as if the great value of hospitality can somehow justify or explain away the brutal betrayal of intimate relationship depicted in the treatment of these women. Thus, Boisvert states that the very horror of Lot's offering is what yields the important lesson that hospitality is to be taken seriously and not to be treated as a dispensable minor virtue.[23] Yet he moves on with his analysis without pausing to instruct against the gifting, rape and murder of women, by known and unknown men, effectively denying women the very hospitality he promotes. Luckily for Lot's daughters they are not defiled, and perhaps receive their hospitality later in the form of divine absolution, when due to the lack of available men to marry after having fled Sodom, they intoxicate and seduce their own father in order to get pregnant. But however dramatic this turn of events, in fact, most girls and women are the *victims* of incest, and not *instigators* of it, another key way in which they are denied hospitality in their own homes by men to whom they are related. It is worth mentioning that honor killings, rape, sexual exploitation, and all of the others forms of domestic abuse to which women are subject, render women insecure in their homes, and permeate hospitality practices.

Neither is the outrage to these stories mitigated by the hope that (at least some) women today are no longer viewed as chattel or property, and are no longer forced against their will to be vehicles of hospitality from one man to another, because remnants of this tradition have evolved intact in both explicit and subtle fashions. One hopes that it is not a common or condoned practice for fathers or husbands to offer their daughters and wives as sexual gifts to male guests, but even in this literal sense it is not unheard of, reflected in the common question posed at weddings—"Who gives this woman?"[24] In recent history, one detects a similar trend in the establishment of brothels designed to service military men, as in the provision of "Comfort Women" in World War II to Japanese soldiers between 1939-1945. In this case it is difficult to identify who precisely was the "host," as "Comfort Women" were not offered by one nation to another, or one man to another, but rather were typically tricked or abducted from Korea and other occupied territories by Japanese forces, and forced into prostitution in service to the Japanese army. But the idea that these women were a gift, a sign of hospitality between the higher and lower ranks of the Japanese military, is not out of place. At least one army doctor characterized it as such, noting that more experienced Japanese prostitutes were less desirable than younger, inexperienced girls because they were more prone to sexually transmitted disease, concluding, "Care needs to be taken with the more jaded type of woman, whom I have repeatedly examined for syphilis and found clearly branded with a past history of venereal disease . . . These are really dubious as gifts to the Imperial Forces."[25] This case also reveals, though, that women are not related to hospitality in any uniform way, but are benefited and burdened differently according to myriad factors, including class, race, ethnicity, moral status, nationality, age, etc. Not only were non-Japanese women preferred as prostitutes because they were younger and less diseased, but also because their foreign status was less likely to cause Japanese soldiers concern that their own mothers or sisters potentially could be gifted in such ways.

Additionally, as indicated by the above cited passage from Khaled Hosseini's novel, *The Kite Runner*, women and children also suffer disproportionately from being deprived and neglected within hospitality traditions. One kind of deprivation is a failure to give credit where it is due, in the sense that the labor of disadvantaged women may be a large part of what makes an offering of hospitality possible, but the appreciation and acknowledgement is given not to these laborers, but to the one who visibly makes the offering. Because it is more often women disadvantaged by race, class, and ethnicity who fill the ranks of service work behind the scenes of formal hospitality industries and domestic spheres, they are more often deprived acknowledgment of their efforts. For example, in the scene described by Hosseini, the protagonist, Amir, has returned to Afghanistan from the United States after having moved away as a child, in order to rescue his half-brother's son who has been kidnapped by the Taliban. In need of food and a place to stay, he is brought to the house of Wahid, brother to his hired guide, Farid, where he is given temporary respite. Hosseini describes how Farid and Amir are brought bowls of steaming food by Wahid's unnamed wife and daughter, and are told that the family has already eaten, which he later finds out to be untrue. While this scene makes obvious a second kind of deprivation that women and children commonly suffer in the pursuit of hospitality— the expectation that they will not eat before guests are satiated— what is more subtle is how although it is Wahid's wife and daughter who have likely gathered and prepared the meal (as well as undoubtedly a bed), it is Wahid whom Amir later thanks for his hospitality.[26]

Returning to the second kind of hospitable deprivation portrayed in this novel, it is common across many cultures for women and children to eat only after guests and male heads of households have received their fill. This, combined with the expectation that mothers are centrally responsible for assuring that children are actually nourished (and not just provided with food), creates special conflicts of hospitality for women in times of scarcity. It is not only unfair that women are disproportionately expected to be hospitable in this way, but given these expectations, women face conflicts of motive in hospitality more so than men because they have practical obligations to more people of a direct sort. Women who are responsible for meeting the needs of proximate and vulnerable others such as their own children, as well as the stranger, experience conflicts of motive that are legitimate. But these motives seem flawed according to accounts of hospitality such as Telfer's, who counts an act as hospitable only when it is done from a pure giving motive. According to Telfer's analysis, Wahid's wife is not as fully hospitable as Wahid because she resents having to give the family's only food to a stranger instead of to her children. But Telfer overlooks how purity of motive is easier for those who face less conflict because of privileged irresponsibility and increased social privilege. Wahid's wife may be more concerned about the loss of the family's food because she is more acutely prone to see it as her responsibility to feed her children, and more likely to be proximate to their cries of hunger. Moreover, given a common social hierarchy whereby men and boys are given the lion's share of a meal, it is likely that her daughter and she will eat last and least when food is procured. Considering that as a mother her foremost responsibility is assigned to her children, Wahid's wife seems more, not less hospitable when, despite her reluctance, she sacrifices her children's (and her own!) only meal to a stranger from whom by tradition she can ask nor expect no reciprocity.

The deprivation that accompanies gendered hospitality roles can be seen in another widespread form in the tradition of paying gratuity to service workers. While it would be an error to claim that service industries are the exclusive domain of women, it is accurate to note that women disproportionately fill the ranks of food servers and hotel housekeepers, jobs that pay less than more traditionally masculine jobs, and that procure a primary source of pay from gratuities. Gratuities, by definition are financial offerings from guests that, while encouraged, are strictly gratuitous. This hospitality tradition introduces contingencies into the financial compensation of service workers, and subjects them to the capricious whims of those whom they serve. The fact that "pink collared jobs" are more prone to involve gratuity pay reflects the belief that hospitality work associated with women's work is not as worthy of guaranteed compensation as men's work, and is tied more directly to guest satisfaction.[27] While food servers and hotel housekeepers have the potential to exceed a minimum wage if their "guests" are generous and perceive them as competent and hospitable, it is also the case that they risk receiving little or no compensation if a guest is miserly or becomes disgruntled, even through the fault of some other, or for no good reason. This trend reflects the double homelessness of the woman hostess, who is not securely in possession of the safety of home as refuge from physical attack or poverty, and cannot always lay claim of ownership or entitlement to her own "personal provisions" which are to be offered to the guest. Just as the wife and child are often dependent upon the arbitrary and voluntary hospitality of the husband, Derrida's despot, so the gratuity worker is subject to the customer. Gratuity work also disproportionately benefits owners and managers, who make profit from the hospitality of service employees, but through gratuities are largely excused from having to reciprocally provide a standard or consistent minimum wage to these workers. These trends are more explicable in their correlation to gender than sex, in the sense that many men are food servers, but the gratuity-based wage afforded this job emerges from hospitality traditions that characterize the act of serving food (and cleaning rooms) as women's work, more so than greeting, cooking, and overseeing. But sex is still also relevant to the hospitality industry wage gap, in that when there is higher potential for making a very good living from gratuity work, such as in upscale restaurants, there is a higher likelihood that the jobs will be filled by men rather than women.

In these ways, although women have diverse relationships to hospitality as a moral practice, they collectively inherit traditions by which they are more likely to serve as deprived vehicles of hospitality than as recipients of it. This analysis also recommends using a more critical eye when it comes scrutinizing the relations between women and hospitality, and positing ways to counteract these trends. One way is to use a feminist care ethic to more clearly and emphatically stress the appropriateness of reciprocity in hospitality relations.

Hospitality and Care Ethical Reciprocity

Because the way in which women and others are disproportionately responsible for care work without having their own needs met, reciprocity, as a form of mutual exchange, is a concept of some significance for feminist care ethicists, and one that has evolved into an increasingly more broadly construed obligation. Early care theorists, like Noddings, highlighted the role of reciprocity in rejuvenating the care giver to provide yet more care, but did not always emphasize it as strategically aimed at meeting the care-givers' own needs for her own sake. For Noddings, the reciprocity that the cared-for offers to the care-giver is a responsiveness that discourages a care giver from withdrawing care, but one that is not owed, and cannot be demanded because manipulating the care receiver is incompatible with the goal of care to meet the other as a subject.[28] Focusing primarily on the care-giving relation between mother and child, Noddings affirms that genuine reciprocity is not an identity of gifts given and received, nor a reversal of the care-giving relation, but mere "response," "personal delight," or "happy growth." She finds that "what we seek in caring is not payment or reciprocity in kind, but the special reciprocity that connotes completion."[29] While this account of reciprocity may be appropriate for mother and child relations (and even this is questionable as children age), it is too thin to ground an adequate account of reciprocity for relations between adults who are more equal to one another in terms of ability, yet unequal in terms of privilege, including many relations characterized by ideals of hospitality. To some extent, a hostess receives reciprocity when guests respond and take delight in her offerings, but in many cases, such as those previously discussed, this kind of appreciation alone is not enough to assure that care is mutually given, or given under conditions of fairness. A thicker concept of reciprocity is thus required, and Derrida's "rule book for guests" must be spelled out more explicitly.

Eva Feder Kittay provides an account of reciprocity that gets closer to what is needed because she more forcefully promotes a sense of obligation to reciprocate care givers so that their needs are also met, but her account requires some adjustment because of how she imagines that reciprocity will be socially delivered.[30] On the one hand she recognizes that the paradigm case of care where there are extremely unequal levels of dependency, such as a mother and young child, is not always the norm. She cites common cases in which neither party is too incapacitated, or they are incapacitated in different ways, or they occupy a relation that unfolds over time, where care recipients have obligations to care givers, and care delivery moves in more mutual and shifting directions.[31] On the other hand, Kittay establishes her connection-based form of reciprocity as one in which a care giver need not be reciprocated by the same individuals she cares for, distinguishing this from "exchange reciprocity," which requires that the efforts that are exerted on behalf of X by Y is to be met by some equivalent exertion by X on behalf of Y at some future designated time. In a system of nested relations, the "dependency worker is entitled not to a reciprocity from the charge herself, but to a relationship that sustains her as she sustains her charge," provided by society through linking those who require help with those who are in a position to help more broadly, so that "what goes round comes round."[32] For Kittay, the larger society is obliged to treat a care worker herself as "some mother's child," worthy of treatment analogous to how a mother ideally treats her child.

Kittay's version of reciprocity allows us to focus more directly on the needs of women and children who are deprived vehicles within the practices of hospitality, and to stress that it is appropriate for them also to receive hospitality from those around them. However, in the case of hospitality, the allotment and scope of Kittay's reciprocal obligation is overly dispersed. Accepting Kittay's rejection of exchange based reciprocity, rather than modifying and making room for it as an informal limit on hospitality, commits us to the view that the obligation to return hospitality lies not with guests themselves, but with others in the larger society. No doubt this makes sense given that some forms of hospitality are needed because of unjust deprivation on national and international levels, and because those who offer and receive hospitality at times require the help of others. Kittay is correct that in the case of Lot's daughters, Japanese "Comfort Women," and the financial insecurity of gratuity work, it is clear that rectification requires massive social shifts in the way that women are treated in hospitality practices, and not just a reciprocal response or appreciation on the part of the guest. However, her analysis too quickly shuts to the idea that guests, as recipients of various forms of care, are obligated as individuals to reciprocate hospitality as they are able, especially in situations of great need and sacrifice, and when reciprocity is needed in the present rather than at some future time. This kind of direct reciprocity should not be passed over on the hope that society at large will reciprocate, not only because the obligation more squarely resides with the guest who is the recipient of the hospitality to varying degrees, but also because there may be times when there is good reason to expect that others in the larger society in fact will *not* see to it that hospitality is reciprocated. A better account of reciprocity in hospitality emphasizes also the ways in which guests are themselves responsible for virtuously receiving and returning hospitality. Although obligation applies in other forms within hospitality relations, (such as the mutual responsibilities between members of the same household) in the interest of brevity I will narrow my focus to that which is owed from a guest to a hostess.

What do recipients of hospitality owe to those who offer it? Some guidance is offered here from the four virtues of care—attention, response, respect, and competent completion. Even though these virtues are not entirely applicable to hospitality practices, and admit to situational variables such as the seriousness of need being met, they yield some general measures of propriety.[33] Taken together they are co-extensive, overlapping virtues that govern different stages of care as a goal oriented process. To begin, the virtue of attention suggests that guests ought strive to be sensitively aware of the needs of those who welcome them, assuring in the first place that as guests they are authentically invited and welcomed. A posture of attention minimally requires an absence of a blatant intention to conquer or harm the embedded relations from which hospitality emerges, and a willingness to establish trust, tell the truth, and honor difference.[34] Attentive participants in hospitable exchanges practice a kind of mutual adjustment, and sympathetic knowledge that transforms unknown others into known others.[35] Individuals should not be coerced into being hospitable, but should be able to consent, or to refuse to act hospitably when the sacrifice is great, or unfairly distributed, without being in danger. A prospective hostess should be given advance warning when possible so that preparations can be made. The virtue of attention also means being sensitively perceptive to cues that the guest is no longer welcomed, or is welcomed at a different time or fashion. It further requires that guests are perceptive of the immediate needs of the hostesses and her embedded relations, and how they might be able to help meet them, in ways that do not reiterate gender subordination. The nature and scope of the response to these needs is difficult to specify, but the virtue of attention is exhibited in Hosseini's novel by the character of Amir. After learning of the hunger suffered by Wahid's family, Amir realizes that his original response, which was to give his watch to one of Wahid's sons, has failed to meet the family's need for food. Amir reformulates his response, and exhibits attention again by perceptively hiding the money rather than offering it directly, in recognition that such a gift would likely be politely refused despite its need.

The second virtue of hospitable reciprocity is response. For care ethicists, response is the phase of care in which the work of care "gets done," in which a care giver moves from recognizing needs, to taking actions to meet these needs. Recipients of hospitality who exhibit the virtue of response will act in concrete ways to make relations amiable, show their appreciation, and ease the burdens of the hostess by offering to share labor, expenses, or responsibilities. Response means not only becoming aware of the "house preferences" of those who offer hospitality, but assuring that these preferences are honored. If those who offer hospitality report having no immediate or pressing needs, an appropriate response may be merely the expression of delight, the offering of a gift, a sincere thank you, and/or a parallel invitation. In some cases monetary compensation may be appropriate; at other times it will be an insulting expression of privilege that reinforces larger trends of exploitation and irresponsibility. Following from the virtue of response, it is important that a guest acts so as not to permit or encourage others to be made into deprived vehicles of hospitality, but to minimize these trends, and to performatively encourage gender reversals whereby men take greater responsibility for the labored provision of hospitable offerings, and women/children for hospitable reception.[36]

The third virtue of care is respect. According to Engster, respect involves accepting others on their own terms, listening to them, and being receptive to their point of view and articulation of need, rather than imposing one's own view. It is a virtue that balances general rules against an ongoing attentive and flexible negotiation with others presumed capable of expressing their own needs.[37] But because there are silences and sub-texts in dialogues of hospitality, respect can be a difficult virtue to exercise in these contexts. Women who are made vehicles of hospitality are often unable to speak. A hostesses' wishes may also be masked to the guest. A hostess may claim that a guest is not a burden, or that she does not require help, when it is suggested by her manner or state of mind that this is not the case. The virtue of respect benefits from open and honest dialogue, challenging the view that "guests should never feel that they are causing undue extra labor."[38] Because women especially are pressured to feign a welcoming attitude, even when there are legitimate reasons to be hesitant, respectful guests should tactfully read between the lines, and ask directly how they might assist. Respect also means deferring to the internal workings of a household, which may include schedule adjustments, trying food that one dislikes, or abiding more benign ideological conflicts or cultural differences.[39] A respectful guest does not manipulate those who welcome her, or ignore the fact that they have other projects and embedded relations. A respectful guest treats the ones who offer hospitality as subjects, and not as automated, degraded, or invisible objects of service. He does not exert gender or other forms of privilege at the expense of the one being hospitable, but seeks to avoid causing resentment and undue burden. Respectful recipients of hospitality are polite, and willing to accommodate, intruding lightly into the home of the other.

The final virtue of care is completion, which involves assuring that one's response to a perceived need adequately meets the need as judged by its intended recipient. This virtue involves assuring competence in following through on the prior virtues, seeing to it that a guest is successful in returning hospitality, as judged not by the guest, but the hostess. However, hospitality as a practice poses certain challenges for the exercise of this virtue in guests. In care ethics, completion is usually thought to be best accomplished when a care-giver personally observes and assesses the success of responsive action. But because hospitality typically ends with guests taking leave, this virtue seems somewhat out of place. For example, because he departs, Amir cannot be sure that leaving the money under the mattress successfully completes his effort to provide Wahid's family with food, and it is not clear even that he is under any obligation to do so in this case beyond making the initial solid effort. However, the virtue of completion in the context of hospitality relations can be understood, in part, as referring to the aspect of hospitality that involves leave-taking—a promise that, unless there is a mutually negotiated understanding of a longer stay or extenuating circumstances, the guest will leave at the proper time.[40] Ideally, a guest will not over-extend his stay, wear out his welcome, or leave behind damage or undue clutter. But in order for this to occur, guests need to have somewhere else to go. Completion thus also projects agents toward accomplishing change in social institutions and political and economic structures that unjustly render some the vehicles of hospitality, or homeless, in a position where they are able neither to receive nor offer hospitality. Additionally, completion involves assuring that sincere appreciation, and compensation when suitable, is received by all of those offering hospitality, not just those who are the "figure-heads" of such offerings. Special efforts are owed to concretely aid and/or recompense those made most vulnerable in current practices of hospitality. If a reversed invitation is in order, completion as a virtue encourages that action is taken to assure that all who labor to welcome guests are equally able to become guests.

Conclusion

Hospitality is an ancient value that continues to have relevance as long as humans are in need of gifts of food and shelter, needs on the rise in times of global economic struggle. The offering and reception of hospitality qualifies as a caring practice when it serves to meet the basic needs of others, but is one in which men and women are differently situated. I have argued that hospitality is a value not to be rejected by a feminist care ethic, but refined, as one that recommends scrutiny and reform of traditional practices that serve to make women and children into deprived vehicles of welcoming. Specifically, I have defended a normative expectation of reciprocity as one such remedy, understood as an obligation on the part of men, governments, and guests to meet the needs of those women and children deprived of or disadvantaged by hospitable offerings, and to reverse traditional arrangements so that women and children are as often likely to be receivers, as symbolic givers. This argument broadens Eva Feder

Kittay's account of reciprocity in encouraging some forms of exchange based mutuality between actual recipients of hospitality and their benefactors. It moves to inculcate a legitimate sense of expectation on behalf of disadvantaged hostesses, and duty in those who are privileged as hosts or guests. It further challenges both the idea that hospitality is rightly understood as a generic, open, and unconditional welcome to the other, pointing out how this endangers women and children, and the idea that women are inhospitable if they begrudge or feel conflicted in their welcome under certain conditions, such as in times of scarcity, coercive exploitation, or the deprivation of dependent others. The four virtues of care can guide reciprocity within relations of hospitable exchange, in terms of how guests may better attend, respectfully respond, and competently complete hospitable returns, in order to create conditions under which women are not unduly burdened in the name of hospitality. This account of reciprocal hospitality thus welcomes the welcomers, asking of women and children, and others disadvantaged by and omitted from hospitable offerings, "How may *we*, help *you*?"

Notes

1. Judith Green, "Building A Cosmopolitian World Community through Mutual Hospitality" in *Pragmatism and the Problem of Race*, ed. Bill E. Lawson (Bloomington: Indiana University Press, 2004), 211.

2. Emily Cook, "Hospitality is Biblical—And It's not Optional." *This Rock.* 2006. http://www.catholic.com/thisrock/2006/0602fea.2asp (accessed 9/15/2008).

3. Elizabeth Telfer, *Food for Thought: Philosophy and Food* (London: Routledge, 1996), 83-94; Elizabeth Telfer, "Hospitableness" *Philosophical Papers*, vol. 24, no. 3, (1995): 183-96, 183.

4. Telfer, "Hospitableness" 183, 187, 195.

5. For more discussion of the reasons for understanding care, and by extension, hospitality, as a practice more fundamentally than a virtue, sentiment, or attitude, see Sarah Ruddick, *Maternal Thinking: Toward A Politics of Peace*, New York: Ballantine Books, 1989, 61; Virginia Held, *The Ethics of Care: Personal, Political and Global.* Oxford: Oxford University Press, 2006, 19, 35; Maureen Sander-Staudt, "The Unhappy Marriage of Care Ethics and Virtue Ethics," *Hypatia*, Vol. 21, No. 4, Fall, 2006, 21-40.

6. The first definition of care is that of Joan Tronto and Bernice Fisher: Joan Tronto, *Moral Boundaries: A Political Argument for and Ethic of Care* (New York, NY: Routledge, 1994)103. The second definition is Daniel Engster's: Daniel Engster, *The Heart of Justice: Care Ethics and Political Theory* (Oxford: Oxford University Press, 2007) 29. It should be noted, however, that according to Diemut Bubeck, hospitality would not qualify as a caring practice when it serves to meet need of others who are capable of meeting these needs themselves. While I tend to favor Tronto and Engster's definition because it is inclusive of many caring industries, Bubeck's definition helps to clarify that displays of hospitality (such

as may occur at international events like the Olympics) do not meet any basic needs, and should not be understood as caring practice. By distinguishing between care and personal service, Bubeck also seeks to avoid conflating the paid labor that men may do within a profession, with the hands on applications of care more characteristically done by women. However, it seems to me more sound to agree with Engster that what distinguishes care from other work is not whether it is paid or unpaid, but whether it directly meets basic needs. See Diemut Bubeck, *Care, Gender, and Justice*. Oxford: Clarendon Press, 1994, 127-137.

7. Nel Noddings, *Caring: A Feminine Approach to Ethics and Moral Education* (Berkely, CA: University of CA Press, 1984) 46, 86.

8. The way in which immigration policies complicate ideals of hospitality is evident in the dispute over who is "at home." For example, in Southwest United States, groups such as "The Minutemen" are comprised of "citizens" who see themselves as defending their "homeland," while displaced Mexican "illegals" residing in the U.S. contend that "this is home." Similar disputes play out in the U.S. with the claims of Native Americans, and elsewhere in the world, such as the West Bank, Ireland, and other places with contested land rights. The association between gender and home, and military interventions aimed at protecting the homeland, is evident in that it is typically women and children (or mothering persons) who "keep the home fires burning." In terms of class and race, those with fewer economic resources are less likely to be in true ownership of their homes, reflected in the recent spate of homelessness in the U.S. among the working class due to foreclosures and evictions, which of all ethnic groups has hit Blacks the most hard. While my analysis suggests that even the homeless can reciprocate hospitality, they are certainly less well positioned to offer it in terms of the offering of a space. Again, women and children bear a different relationship to this trend, in that while more men have been initially laid off than women, joblessness and homelessness of women is on the rise in the U.S., complicated by the fact that women have a more difficult time accessing shelters, especially when they have custody of older male children.

9. The importance of asking questions about why hospitality is needed, and how to reduce the occasion in which people are in need of hospitality because of homelessness, persecution, etc., see Robert Mulvaney, "Hospitality and Its Discontents: A Response to Losito" *Proceedings of the South Atlantic Philosophy of Education Society*, vol. 36 (1991), 70-72.

10. Robert Boisvert, "Ethics is Hospitality" *Proceedings of the American Catholic Philosophical Association*, vol. 78 (2004) 289-300.

11. Noddings, *Caring*, 47.

12. Lisa Tessman, *Burdened Virtues: Virtue Ethics for Liberatory Struggles* (Oxford: Oxford University Press, 2005).

13. Emmanuel Levinas, "The Nation and Presence of Israel" *In the Times of the Nations*, trans. M.B. Smith (Bloomington, IN: Indiana University Press, 1994), 98.

14. David Gauthier, "Levinas and the Politics of Hospitality" *History of Political Thought*, 28, No. 1, (Spring 2007): 158-80, 163, 165.

15. Alan Bleakley "A Common Body of Care: The Ethics and Politics of Teamwork in the Operating Theatre" *Journal of Medicine and Philosophy*, 31, 2006, 315.

16. Jacques Derrida, *Of Hospitality: Anne Dufourmantelle invites Jacques Derrida to Respond*, trans. Rachel Bowlby (Stanford, CA: Stanford University Press, 2000).

17. Derrida, *Of Hospitality*, 25, 83.

18. Joan Tronto distinguishes responsibility from obligation as an implicit set of cultural practices and expectations, rather than as duties that arise from a set of formal rules or promises. Response-ability arises from different sources, but in the context of hospitality it often arises from recognition of need and a realization that "there is no other way that the need will be met except by our meeting it." See Tronto, *Moral Boundaries*, 131-2.

19. Sarah Holtman, "Civility and Hospitality: Justice and Social Practice in Trying Times" *Kantian Review*, 6, 2002, 102; Judith Green, "Building A Cosmopolitan World" 214.

20. Simon Critchley, "Five Problems in Levinas's View of Politics and a Sketch of the Solution to Them" *Political Theory*, 32, No. 2, 2004, 174.

21. Nancy Holland, "With Arms Wide Open: *Of Hospitality* and the Most Intimate Stranger" *Philosophy Today*, SPEP Supplement, 45, 2001, 133.

22. Holland, "With Arms Wide Open," 133.

23. Boisvert, "Ethics is Hospitality," 289.

24. The arranged exchange of women in marriage as a form of hospitality aimed at strengthening relations between families is less common in liberal societies today, but existent. For example, women who escaped enforced polygynous marriages within communities of the Fundamentalist Latter Day Saints, located in Canada, America, and Mexico, report that daughters are often gifted by their fathers to other men, in hopes of establishing or maintaining business and political relations. Bride gifting, especially of young girls, is not uncommon in India, Africa, and other countries.

25. George Hicks, *The Comfort Women: Japan's Brutal regime of Enforced Prostitution in the Second World War*, (New York, NY: W.W. Norton and Company, 1995) 34.

26. Hosseini, *The Kite Runner*, 241.

27. Hospitality as an industry often follows particular gendered patterns. In the typical franchise restaurant, for example, a standard is observable whereby a guest is first greeted and seated by a "hostess," who is very often a young and attractive female, is then served by a waitress or waiter who works for tips to supplement a menial wage, and has food prepared by a typically unseen cook, who is often a male wage earner, managed by salaried employees who are more often likely to be men as the salary increases. These patterns are duplicated in other areas of the hospitality industry, such as hotels, tourism, clubs, etc. There are also detectable racial patterns here also. One may observe these patterns at work in the Olympic games in China, where one attractive young girl was portrayed as singing during opening ceremonies, while a girl deemed less attractive supplied the actual voice.

28. Noddings, *Caring*, 48, 72.
29. Noddings, *Caring*, 74, 51.
30. Eva Feder Kittay, *Love's Labor: Essays on Women, Equality, and Dependency* (New York, NY: Routledge, 1999).
31. Kittay, *Love's Labor*, 32, 54.
32. Kittay, *Love's Labor*, 68, 107.
33. This emphasis on propriety is similar to that of Confucianism, which inculcates reciprocal hospitality in the youth: "The Master said, 'A youth, when at home, should be filial, and, abroad, respectful to his elders. He should be earnest and truthful. He should overflow in love to all, and cultivate the friendship of the good. When he has time and opportunity, after the performance of these things, he should employ them in polite studies.'" However, Confucius conspicuously addressed himself only to men, and indirectly endorsed the subservience of women through traditional hospitable offerings. See Confucius, The Analects, Complete On-Line Text, http://www.wright-house.com/religions/confucius/Analects.html
34. Mustafa Dikec, "Pera Peras Poros: Longings for Spaces of Hospitality" *Theory, Culture, and Society* 19, no. 1-2, (2006): 239; Green, "Building A Cosmopolitan World," 214.
35. Both Judith Green and Maurice Hamington offer more complete descriptions of attention and other caring virtues as inspired by Jane Addam's, cofounder of Hull House in Chicago, a social settlement committed to reciprocal caring relations between diverse people. These descriptions are particularly useful because they demonstrate how these virtues may take on both individual and social forms. See Maurice Hamington, *Embodied Care: Jane Addams, Maurice Merleau-Ponty, and Feminist Ethics* (Chicago, IL: University of Illinois Press, 2004), 98, and "An Inverted Home: Socializing Care at Hull House" in *Socializing Care*, ed. Maurice Hamington and Dorothy Miller (Boulder, CO: Rowman & Littlefield, 2006), 108; Green, "Building A Cosmopolitan World," 2004, 212.
36. For example, Chloe Taylor argues that a Levinasian account of hospitality could be reconcilable with a feminist care ethics like Tronto's, if the self who assumes an "infinite responsibility" for the other is posited as a male subject, and the recipient of hospitality (rather than the giver) is reconceptualized as a maternal subject. See Chloe Taylor, "Levinasian Ethics and Feminist Ethics of Care," *Symposium, Canadian Society for Hermeneutics and Postmodern Thought* 10, No. 2 (October, 2005): 222, 225.
37. Engster, *The Heart of Justice*, 31.
38. Cook, "Hospitality is Biblical—And It's not Optional"
39. This is not to say that there is no room for philosophical discussion within hospitality relations, indeed, my argument suggests that it is sometimes required. My claim is rather that a respectful guests should take care not to arbitrarily engage in discussions that may be threatening or disturbing to those who offer hospitality, or to push conversation when it seems futile that some good will come of it. The appropriateness of ideological or cultural confrontation also seems to depend in part upon whether the hospitality is being extended by family members or friends, and whether those engaged are chosen, easy deliberators, or unchosen, easily offended conversationalists. The degree of intimacy and

trust that has been established between hostess and guest, as well as the issue at hand, helps to set the context for judging the appropriateness of such debate.

40. Dikec, "Pera Peras Poros," 239.

Chapter 3

Hospitality: Agency, Ethics, and Gender

Helen Daley Schroepfer

A focus on the importance of hospitality faces some understandable objections, given the intersection of gender and class in the division of labor around serving as a host and preparing to entertain guests. Marguerite LaCaze, for example, argues that any understanding of the self/other relation as fundamentally asymmetrical undermines the self-respect crucial for human flourishing, particularly among groups that have born the burden of too much self sacrifice in attending to the needs and desires of others.[1] This paper will explore Jacques Derrida's understanding of hospitality and will then argue that work in contemporary developmental psychology lends support to his description of this phenomenon as it relates to the structure of the self-other relation. Far from undermining self-respect, I will argue that hospitality is a necessary part of the recipe for flourishing across the life span. Finally, I will explore how this understanding of hospitality can undermine gender and class divisions of labor, and can serve as an important supplement for both an ethic of care and an ethic of justice.

On Hospitality: Openness and Agency in Derrida

According to Derrida, openness to the other underlies human experience, in that the self is forged in and for hospitality. As Derrida highlights in *Speech and Phenomena*,

> The movement of différance is not something that happens to a transcendental subject. It produces the subject. Self-affection is not a modality of experience that characterizes a being that would already be itself (autos). It produces the same as self-relation with self-difference, it produces sameness as the non-identical.[2]

In order to understand this quite remarkable claim about the openness of the self, a brief review of several key Derridean concepts is necessary.

Beginning with his earliest work, Derrida points to the inescapable interplay between text and context, for any term in language can only be understood within its contextual field. By "trace," Derrida refers to this structure whereby without the "absent" other within the "present" same, the same could not appear as meaningful. Geoff Bennington notes that the implications of this insight are profound in that, "if every element of the system only gets its identity in its difference from the other elements, every element is in this way marked by all those it is not: it thus bears the trace of those other elements."[3] This "trace" thus throws into question the very distinction between presence and absence and any notion of a unitary origin unmarked by plurality.

Derrida broadens his understanding of text to speak of a generalized textuality. Institutions, traditions, cultures, sexuality and, most importantly for our purposes, self-experience are marked by this trace structure, coined "différance" by Derrida, in that all of these systems are inextricably intertwined in language. Indeed, Derrida argues that *all* thought is text-like since meaning and significance are possible only on the basis of sign, of text, of a kind of "writing."[4] There is thus a permanent disjuncture, a non-coincidence within the self belied by the very word "self-consciousness." This disjuncture enables and requires self-relation, a spacing that implicates every "I" into language in that anything I posit or think about myself must be repeatable because a purely idiomatic sign cannot carry meaning or significance. Much as the "trace" undermines the dichotomy between presence and absence, différance thus complicates any sharp dichotomy between self and other since the self is mediated via the dynamic, contested social world of language.

Moving to a consideration of other persons, Derrida insists (in step with many thinkers in modern and post-modern philosophy) that there is no pure access to or intuition of the other *as such*.[5] What is distinctive, however, is his insistence that the otherness of the other, the fact that the other eludes our grasp and appropriation, makes *relation* possible. According to Derrida, "The other is infinitely other because we never have any access to the other as such. That is why he/she is the other. This separation, this dissociation is not only a limit, but it is also the condition of the relation to the other, a non-relation as relation."[6] Just as it is only the mark of the non-presence of other words that allows for meaning to emerge, so here absence and disjunction are not the opposite of relation and joining for Derrida—they are their necessary element. Derrida thus argues that we are in an asymmetrical relationship of openness to and desire for an other that can never be given in the sense of appropriation or grasp. At the deepest level, then, the structure of conscious experience is always already engaged and responsive.

Derrida employs the structure of "the gift" to characterize this openness toward what eludes our grasp and appropriation. In French the word gift (*cadeau*) comes from *catena* or chain, an etymology that itself shows how a gift tends to form a circular economy, binding the giver and receiver in a system of gratitude and self congratulation. The very thing that makes the gift possible (actually giving the gift) renders it also impossible, because it initiates an exchange that tends to cancel it.

Derrida contrasts the gift with economy, by which he means the realm of what is foreseeable and calculable, the realm of exchange and transaction. Yet it is not a matter of choosing between the two, but rather of occupying the space between, recognizing the dependence of any economy on prior structures that elude it. Thus there can be no clear distinction between gift and economy, for "It is this exteriority that sets the circle going, it is this exteriority that puts the economy in motion. It is this exteriority that engages in the circle and makes it turn."[7] In other words, there is no access to this exteriority outside the give and take of exchange, yet this economy is put into play by the gift. Building from this understanding of the gift shared by Derrida and Levinas, Iris Marion Young notes that, "opening onto the other person is always a gift; the trust to communicate cannot await the other person's promise to reciprocate, or the conversation will never begin."[8]

Much as Derrida broadens the notion of text, here he notes that the structure of the gift points to something much more fundamental, namely that "there is something in excess of knowledge. We have a relation to the gift beyond the circle, the economic circle, and beyond the theoretical and phenomenological determination."[9] Every event has a paradoxical structure similar to that which operates in the gift: it is absolutely singular, but cannot appear as such, cannot *mean* anything, apart from the possibility of repetition, for again the purely idiomatic event cannot mean. According to Derrida, we reside in a world of "impossible" events in that we relate to an other that exceeds what can appear as such, yet without which experience is not possible.[10]

Derrida's discussion of the phenomenon of hospitality picks up on this notion of the gift, further illuminating and complicating the self-other relation. Derrida initially draws a distinction between conditional and unconditional hospitality, although the distinction will prove unstable and permeable in much the same way as the gift and economy. Unconditional hospitality, for Derrida, refers to an absolute openness to whatever or whoever may arrive. This absolute or unconditional openness, however, does not simply refer to a not-yet-realized ideal[11] because, on close inspection, it is structurally impossible. If hosts do not differentiate between who is invited and who is not, and provide no ground rules for the behavior of guests, they have renounced their responsibility for their own well being and that of their guests. However, this more conditional hospitality is bound to the unconditional in that rigid constructions of what guests may do or say nullify hospitality. Absent an exposure to the unpredictable which may well exceed and/or confound our plans and expectations, and the risks involved in this exposure, there is no hospitality worthy of the name, for "If I am sure that the newcomer that I welcome is perfectly harmless, innocent, that (s)he will be beneficial to me . . . it is not hospitality. When I open my door, I must be ready to take the greatest of risks."[12]

Another fruitful complication in the phenomenon of hospitality revolves around the issue of power and who is in charge. To welcome a guest presumes that the host is and remains in charge of the premises—to leave when the guests arrive or have no concern for their provision would be quite inhospitable. An unconditional welcome of another thus stands in tension with an equally necessary reserve. Central to hospitality, then, is the fact that it can never be purely self-sacrificial. The enactment of hospitality once the guests arrive, however, complicates this picture in that the host becomes the servant of the desires of the guest, a point that will become crucial as we look at various perversions of the phenomenon of hospitality in part three.

Broadening this reading of the ambiguities involved in hospitality even further, Derrida points to a "pre-originary" hospitality, arguing that "this being-'hostage' of the subject surely is not, any more than its being-'host,' some late attribute or accident that would supervene upon it. Like the being-host, the being-hostage is the subjectivity of the subject as 'responsibility for the Other.'"[13] Consciousness is itself an openness and responsiveness to the other, and thus the self is a product of a welcome that precedes any act of intentionality. This openness throws into question the very possibility of a self-possessive autonomy. In addition, any act of intentional hospitality holds the promise (and the danger) that the guest who arrives may fundamentally destabilize me—I may well be transformed in the encounter. Here too the stakes are high and the risks are great in that we are inescapably vulnerable; however, this openness and vulnerability is central to life and growth.

Hospitality thus offers an opportunity to see openness to others and concern for the agency and flourishing of the self as relational terms—not strict dichotomies. Without drawing boundaries and forging some agency and autonomy, the possibility of relation is undercut from the outset. In addition, we can come to own up to the exclusions by which we proceed as hosts, and strive to keep those exclusionary lines as fluid and open as possible. As Derrida claims,

> What is called non-narcissism is in general but the economy of a much more welcoming, hospitable narcissism, one that is much more open to the experience of the other as other. I believe that without a movement of narcissistic reappropriation, the relation to the other would be absolutely destroyed, it would be destroyed in advance.[14]

What is striking in Derrida is a fundamental affirmation implied in all of the above, for hospitality is not a cynical mask for power, nor do we give in order to bind the other in gratitude; rather, we really do strive toward both generosity and hospitality.[15] This typifies a central notion at the heart of all Derrida's work, for he tells us that:

> What I am interested in is the experience of the desire for the impossible. That is, the impossible as the condition of desire. Desire is not perhaps the best word. I mean this quest in which we want to give, even when we realize, when we agree, if we agree, that the gift, that giving, is impossible, that it is a process of reappropriation and self-destruction. Nevertheless, we do not give up the dream of the pure gift, in the same way that we do not give up the idea of pure hospitality.[16]

We strain against the limits of these impossibles not theoretically, but performatively, through acts of hospitality and generosity.

On Human Flourishing: Neo-Piagetian Developmental Theory

This reading of human experience might seem hopelessly naïve or simply mistaken for the image of the other as threat strikes many as beyond challenge, and we need no reminder that we are capable of violence and exploitation. However, attention to work being done in currents within developmental psychology provides robust support for the complex interplay between self-flourishing and openness to others. The particular current that we will follow is often referred to as relational or neo-Piagetian.[17] Since this work builds from Jean Piaget's underlying approach to human development, a brief review of several key concepts is important here.

Piaget came to his interest in cognitive development from a background in biology and philosophy. Of particular import in understanding Piaget is Kant's work in epistemology. According to Kant, we construct our world through basic categories that are a-priori (not based on experience) and are the same for all. Because of the contribution of these categories to any experience, the "noumena" (the things "in themselves") remain beyond our grasp.[18] In a similar manner, Piaget argues that knowledge is "a reconstitution of reality by the concepts of the subject, who, progressively and with all kinds of experimental probes, approaches the object without ever attaining it in itself."[19] According to Piaget, however, these structures by which we experience the world are *themselves* structured by the activity of the person via a process of development. One difficulty with philosophical epistemology, according to Piaget, is that it has tended to focus exclusively on the conceptual. His goal was to point out the fact that in all behavior there is underlying knowledge, and that conceptual knowledge is the product of a developmental process that is dependent on sensorimotor activity.[20] For Piaget, this development is characterized by a progressive restructuring of knowledge capacities as the person actively engages the world and finds current structures inadequate.

In outlining the dynamic nature of this development, Piaget and contemporary neo-Piagetians employ the language of assimilation and accommodation. By assimilation is meant the process of fitting experience to current means of organization. Accommodation, on the other hand, refers to the process of adapting to particular contents or events, reorganizing meaning-making structures to adjust to new experience. For Piaget, schemes are the structures whereby we assimilate experience and understand it in its *generality*. As such, they provide the basis for accommodation to new experience, which is always something *particular* because every event has some element of novelty. Our cognitive structures evolve over time and are conserved through their *functioning*. According to Piaget,

> these successive constructions always involve a decentering of the initial egocentric point of view in order to place it in an ever-broader coordination of relations and concepts, so that each new terminal grouping further integrates the subject's activity by adapting it to an ever-widening reality.[21]

A robust body of current research in developmental psychology supports this view of the process of development as one characterized by the inter-related emergence of a sense of self and other through activity and exploration. Michael Tomasello's extensive work on infant development is a case in point.[22] According to Tomasello, the infant comes to have a sense of self as agent through the active exploration and manipulation of objects. A more reflective sense of self as a social agent develops in interaction with other persons, behavior like joint attention and social referencing, which witnesses to a growing awareness of others as psychological beings. By 3-4 years of age, the child thus comes to understand others as having thoughts and beliefs, and begins to engage in efforts to actively influence them. At around age six, the child comes to appreciate the fact that others are also engaged in these "impression management" techniques. A growing body of research supports this overall understanding of the inherent interrelationship between self and other at the most fundamental level.[23] Building from the work of Hobson, Carpendale and Lewis observe that

> even in infancy, we need to conceptualize the individual's construction of events with the "relatedness" between the self, the other, and the items to which each refers. Indeed it is the very fact the infant comes to know that the world is "sharable" that drives him or her gradually to understand that others have unique perspectives on that world.[24]

Critical to this development is the much-researched phenomenon of joint attention, the capacity to coordinate attention with others. From following another's gaze as early as 6 months,[25] to the phenomena of social referencing which involves looking toward parents when faced with ambiguity,[26] joint attention appears crucial in allowing children to develop further capacities for social interaction. Importantly, this capacity appears central to language learning since,

> The meaning of words is not the object they map onto. The research on how children come to learn words appears to show that their very early use of words is tied up with specific contexts and then slowly generalizes to others . . . Learning to use words takes place within the context of the flow of interaction between infants, others, and events in the environment.[27]

Language, in turn, mediates further growth as children develop a number of progressively complex social skills. First, at around age 4 or so, the important ability to "pass" false belief tests, appreciating the fact that people with different experiences have different understandings.[28] Later, children come to grasp the interpretive nature of experience, coming to discern that people can have different understandings of the *same* experience.[29]

Research has pointed to a link between certain kinds of relationships and this process of development. For example, there appears a positive link with parental disciplinary styles that encourage children to reflect on the feelings of others[30] and with the existence of siblings.[31] The extent of peer interactions also appears crucial in that ongoing explanation to and arbitration with others is demanded more frequently in these kinds of relationships.[32]

Given this focus on relationships, neo-Piagetian theorists see cognitive development as one aspect of a much more holistic process of growth, placing more explicit focus on the importance of affect than did Piaget.[33] Robert Kegan argues, for instance, that development is marked by periods of instability and restoration of balance, experiences that may well be an important source of emotions. As an example, Kegan points to the fact that separation anxiety (which begins around 10 months) might best be understood as the affective dimension of the development of the initially fragile capacity to orient to objects, for the anxious behavior passes with the accomplishment of some sense of object permanence in children.[34]

In addition, contemporary neo-Piagetian theorists move beyond Piaget's focus on a certain closure in the process of development that comes with the achievement of formal thought. For Piaget, formal thought is characterized by a movement from embeddedness in the concrete toward the ability to think in the abstract, reason using analogy, and work with what might be possible. Contemporary theorist Michael Chandler moves beyond this closure in his work with adolescents, a period in life characterized by a growing appreciation that people differ in what they believe based on a host of social influences such as gender, culture, and class. As a result of this recognition, young adults exchange what he terms "retail doubt" for "wholesale doubt." Retail doubt entails the insight that different people can hold different beliefs about the same thing, for instance the meaning of a certain event. Wholesale doubt, on the other hand, is grounded in a more fundamental recognition that all knowledge is subject to a certain indeterminacy in that "facts" routinely support more than one interpretation. Coming to grips with the interpretive, perspectival nature of knowledge is the project of a lifetime, and Chandler points to research supporting a great deal of diversity and creativity in response to this inescapable epistemic uncertainty.[35]

What emerges clearly here is the fact that this entire process is rooted firmly in an openness and responsiveness to others that can aptly be described as hospitality in that it involves the movement through a succession of complex and dynamic renegotiated balances between self and other. In sharp contrast to the view that self/other ambiguity is fundamentally threatening, ambivalence is a profound factor in accounting for the dynamics of these changes in that difference and the ambiguities involved in the shifting articulation of self and other are a positive source of growth and development. Growth happens, not to return to stasis, but to bring a person into a coherence that can account for greater complexity. As Robert Kegan notes, "each qualitative change, hard won, is a response to the complexity of the world, a response in further recognition of how the world and I are yet again distinct—and thereby more related."[36] In sum, Neo-Piagetian developmental theory describes a multi-faceted structure of hospitality closely akin to that articulated by Derrida, and this active and ongoing articulation of the relationship between self and other is crucial in human flourishing.

Hospitality: Agency, Ethics and Gender

Derrida provides a strong and compelling case for the irreducibility of the relation between self and other, as well as for the trust and openness implied by the very nature of experience. Derrida specifically argues that we are not fundamentally driven by *threat*, but rather by a *desire* for that which is other. According to Derrida, this desire is not most appropriately read as lack or absence, but as affirmation and openness. Neo-Piagetian developmental theory lends robust support to this reading, providing evidence that our own development as persons is a function of our openness to others. In addition, we grow in our ability to recognize this openness in that we come, over time, to recognize that others have perspectives that are not our own, and we can be quite literally *transformed* by these differing viewpoints. What can we draw from this exploration of hospitality and its intersection with developmental theory?

First, we have here an interesting avenue into considering how self and other are relational terms—not strict dichotomies. As Iris Marion Young argues, however, it is important how we conceive of the structure of this relationship. Building from the work of Derrida, Levinas and Irigaray, she argues that we must avoid the pitfalls of seeing this structure as symmetrical in nature. For instance, generalizing from Irigaray's argument that conceiving of sexual difference as symmetrical serves to objectify women as a mirror image of the masculine subject, Young argues that viewing relations as symmetrical obscures real difference and can serve to solidify structural privilege and oppression through false projections onto others.[37]

Here it may be helpful to place this notion of the asymmetry of hospitality in juxtaposition with Lorraine Code's elaboration of the notion of "second persons." Code finds promise in this insight first developed by Annette Baier because "she shows that uniqueness, creativity, and moral accountability grow out of interdependence and continually turn back to it for *affirmation* and *continuation*."[38] Code goes on to argue that the paradigm of friendship as mediating second persons is more fruitful than the model of motherhood, given the dangers of essentializing the maternal role and the existence of unequal power relations between parent and child. Noting the more symmetrical possibilities in friendship, she argues that "Participants in a trusting, mutually sustaining friendship or alliance can effect and maintain a balance between separateness and appropriate interdependence."[39] It is here that the limitations of a symmetrical reading of this relation and the fruitfulness of the notion of hospitality comes sharply into focus in that there appears no room to be *challenged* by the other given this focus on affirmation, continuation and mutuality.

In *Why Ethics?* Robert Gibbs explicitly links this notion of the asymmetry of the self other relation with the emergence of a responsibility that opens me to growth in unveiling new and challenging possibilities.

> Responsibility cannot rest in my own relation to myself—because I cannot be my own teacher . . . Exposed to the other's questions, the other instigates new possibilities for me. My listening provides A SURPLUS OF CONSCIOUNESS, making me exceed my own capacities to think and to act. Only THE CALL OF THE OTHER can produce my ability to respond.[40]

Echoing the complexity of the structure of hospitality described above, Gibbs thus argues that it is the other that produces my agency, understood as an ability to respond to the call of the other.

Secondly, this ethics of hospitality might serve as an important corollary to both an ethics focused on justice and one focused more on care. In articulating aspects of what she terms feminist moral consciousness, Sheila Mullett argues that moral consciousness begins in moral sensitivity—an awareness of the suffering of others. This sensitivity then issues in ontological shock, the realization that the oppression and exploitation of others is not natural nor is it unchangeable. Finally, both of the above lead to praxis, wherein "We shift from seeing the world as an individual moral agent to seeing it through the eyes of a 'we.'"[41] Although not denying the validity and importance of what Mullett describes and of other currents in a feminist morality more focused on caring and responsiveness to need, there is danger afoot that "we" may presume to understand and know what's best without really *attending* to the other. An ethics of hospitality might well help foreclose this sort of presumptuousness.

One very familiar case in point revolves around the issue of female genital mutilation. For the most part, Western feminists have had a great deal of moral sensitivity around this issue; however, what was often sadly absent was any acknowledgment of how these practices were interpreted by the women involved. There has been a backlash against the condemnation of this practice, a backlash that might well have been avoided if an ethics of hospitality had been employed, opening us to the complex web of meanings associated with these practices. As Babatunde argued in his investigation of the Yoruba in Nigeria, "reducing the practice to a bizarre expression of male chauvinism just limits the wider cultural understanding needed to stop it. Cultural practices endure because they make sense to individuals in a society."[42] A similar point could be made about the practice of wearing Hijab among Muslim women and the rather monolithic condemnation of the practice as oppressive to women.[43]

An ethics of hospitality is also a useful corollary to what has been termed an ethics of justice, focused on autonomy in judgment and an impartial application of norms that can be universalized. As Derrida argues, there is danger in positing autonomous norms and principles, untroubled by an opening to the particularities of specific persons and situations. Law is always contaminated with violence in that necessary generalizations are made which marginalize the particularity and singularity of *concrete* relations with others. Derrida thus contrasts law with what he terms justice,[44] but not to indicate that one can or should be preferred over the other, for they are not simple opposites: laws ought to be just, and justice requires the force of law.[45] Law without the interruption of justice is purely violent, yet living without law is even more so. Just as there are degrees of narcissism and degrees of openness to the other, there are degrees in the economy of law. Justice is the unconditional attention to the singular other that must keep laws flexible and amendable, for every other is *wholly* other. However, respect for the other requires law because *every* other is wholly other.[46]

Derrida has never been opposed to working toward the kind of rational consensus required by law. However, he also holds that, if law were *fully* grounded on a social contract arrived at through a movement toward consensus, there would be no possibility of challenging it with questions of justice revolving around who or what is being excluded. For Derrida, any social contract must be *consistently* troubled by the asymmetry of the ethical relation, a respect for the other that impels us to constantly critique institutions, ideas, and the givens of our culture.[47] Iris Marion Young takes up a similar position in her discussion of the need for both equality and attentiveness to the particularities of the individual. She argues that, "While comparing the situation and desert of agents according to some standard of equality is ultimately necessary for theorizing justice, prior to such comparison there is a moment of respect for the particular embodied sensitivity of the person."[48]

Finally, to return to the concern raised at the outset about the intersection of gender and class in regard to the labor accompanying hospitality, Mireille Rosello's work is very pertinent. In her extensive treatment of gender and hospitality, she observes that,

> the more ambiguity exists between rituals of welcoming (gestures that generate prestige) and the taking care of guests (which tends to require humble forms of servitude), the more difficult it will be to distinguish between power and powerlessness, between the expression of mastery and of subservience. Conversely, if the definition of the host becomes less complex, less ambiguous, then forms of violence might creep into the system. Gender is the most obvious variable in this game, where dichotomies and the multiplication of roles shield some actors from the potentially humiliating features of hospitality.[49]

In our exploration of hospitality via Derrida and developmental theory, what she terms "humiliating" features can in fact be seen as central to the phenomenon. True hospitality is never possible from a position of powerlessness if guests are to be entertained, yet we have seen how the host then becomes subject to the desires of the guest. The flourishing of both the host and the guest requires a rich experience of this ambiguity involved in hospitality—a willingness to risk and tolerate vulnerability, an openness to the fragility of the permeable boundary between self and other, a wonder at what may well transform us. As Iris Marion Young argues, the presumption of simple autonomy and rigidity around remaining in charge of the situation stifles growth. On the contrary,

> Through such dialogue that recognizes the asymmetry of others . . . people can enlarge their thinking in at least two ways. Their own assumptions and point of view become relativized for them as they are set in relation to those of others. By learning from others how the world and the collective relations they have forged through interaction look to them, moreover, everyone can develop an enlarged understanding of that world and those relations that is unavailable to any of them from their own perspective alone.[50]

There has been a great deal of work done on how false projections have dire consequences for those who are subjected to them. For example, Claude Steele's important work on stereotype threat points to how easily performance is swayed by the threat of confirming false projections about a group with which one identifies.[51] What has not been as adequately explored or theorized is the effect on the *sources* of these projections, an effect that comes sharply into focus via this discussion of hospitality. Although it is certainly not the case that the risks here are equivalent, for those subject to the internalization of damaging ideologies are disproportionately vulnerable. However, in failing to attend to the hospitable welcome of others, we indeed foreclose a crucial opportunity to flourish and thrive. As we have seen in the foregoing, to extend the open hand of hospitality is to employ the hand in the serving/being served, and the touching/being-touched that continually remakes us as persons.

Notes

1. Marguerite LaCaze, "Seeing Oneself through the Eyes of the Other: Asymmetrical Reciprocity and Self-respect," *Hypatia* 23, no. 3 (July-September 2008): 118-35.
2. Jacques Derrida, *Speech and Phenomena and Other Essays on Husserl's Phenomenology* (Evanston, IL: Northwestern University Press, 1973), 24.
3. Geoffrey Bennington, *Derridabase* (Chicago: University of Chicago Press, 1993): 74-75.
4. Jacques Derrida, *Of Grammatology* (Baltimore: Johns Hopkins University Press, 1974).
5. Jacques Derrida, "Hospitality, Justice and Responsibility," in Richard Kearney & Mark Dooley, ed. *Questioning Ethics: Contemporary Debates in Philosophy* (New York: Routledge, 1999).
6. Jacques Derrida, "Hospitality, Justice and Responsibility," 71. Emmanuel Levinas also stresses the ethical relation as a relation *without* relation in the sense that one is in relation with something other, something that cannot be absorbed or comprehended within some larger totality. See Emmanuel Levinas, *Totality and Infinity: An Essay on Exteriority*, trans. Alphonso Lingis (Pittsburgh, PA: Duquesne University Press, 1969).
7. Jacques Derrida, *Given Time: I. Counterfeit Money*, trans. Peggy Kamuf (Chicago: University of Chicago Press, 1992), 30.
8. Iris Marion Young, *Intersecting Voices: Dilemmas of Gender, Political Philosophy, and Policy* (Princeton, NJ: Princeton University Press, 1997), 50.
9. Jacques Derrida, "On the Gift: A Discussion between Jacques Derrida and Jean-Luc Marion" in *God, the Gift and Postmodernism*, ed. John D. Caputo and Michael J. Scanlon (Bloomington: Indiana University Press, 1999), 60.
10. Derrida is very close to Hans Georg Gadamer in his understanding of experience. For Gadamer, we have genuine experience when something in the flow of perception catches us up short and confronts us as something unexpected. In this event, "experience" happens in that we become aware that there was something inadequate in our earlier relationship with the object of our experience. Insight is inherent in all experience because it "always involves an escape from something that had deceived us and held us captive." Hans Georg Gadamer, *Truth and Method*, 2nd ed. trans. J. Weinsheimer and D. Marshall (New York: Continuum, 1996), 356. For Derrida as well, experience is that which brings us up short, when we are exposed to something we did not see coming: an event of the impossible. For a discussion of Derrida's use of the term experience and his move away from placing the term "under erasure," see David Wood, "The Experience of the Ethical," in *Questioning Ethics*, ed. Richard Kearney and Mark Dooley (New York: Routledge, 1999), 105-19.
11. Martin Hagglund, "The Necessity of Discrimination: Disjoining Derrida and Levinas," *Diacritics* 34, no. 1 (Spring 2004), 63.
12. Jacques Derrida, "Débat: Une Hospitalité sans condition" as translated by Mireille Rosello in *Postcolonial Hospitality: The Immigrant as Guest* (Stanford University Press, 2001).
13. Jacques Derrida, *Adieu to Emmanuel Levinas* (Stanford, CA: Stanford University Press, 1999), 55.

14. Jacques Derrida, *Points . . . Interviews, 1974-1994*, ed. Elisabeth Weber (Stanford, CA: Stanford University Press, 1995), 199.

15. Derrida certainly recognizes that hospitality can be a mask for power and that hospitality can and does often give way to violence and hostility; however, with Levinas, he points to this as a perversion or repression of our fundamental openness to others.

16. Derrida, "On the Gift" in *God, the Gift and Postmodernism*, 72.

17. Clearly the field of developmental psychology is not monolithic. My interest in this current reflects its subtle and wide-ranging explanatory breadth. It is able to accommodate social learning theory and nativist accounts of development in that the importance of both experience and genetic/evolutionary factors are acknowledged. Robert Kegan notes the importance in that "Rather than locating the life force in the closed individual or the environmental press, it locates a prior context which continually elaborates the distinction between the individual and the environment in the first place." Robert Kegan, *The Evolving Self: Problem and Process in Human Development* (Cambridge: Harvard University Press, 1982), 43. For further discussion of this see *Cognitive Development: Neo-Piagetian Perspectives* by Sergio Morra, Camilla Gobbo, Zopita Marini and Ronald Sheese (Lawrence Erlbaum, 2007).

18. Immanuel Kant, *Critique of Pure Reason* in P. Guyer and A. Wood, eds. The Cambridge Edition of the Works of Immanuel Kant (Cambridge: The Cambridge University Press, 1998).

19. Jean Piaget as interviewed by Jean-Calude Brineuier in *Conversations with Jean Piaget*, trans. J Tomlinson and A. Tomlinson (Chicago: University of Chicago Press, 1980), 84.

20. Here at the outset Piaget's proximity to Heidegger is noteworthy in this stress on the derivative nature of the theoretical. See Martin Heidegger, *Being and Time*, trans. John Macquarrie & Edward Robinson (New York: Harper & Row, 1962). Of particular interest in this regard is recent work exploring how abstract thought is essentially tied via metaphor to sensorimotor experience. See M. Johnson, "Reason Incarnate" (paper presented at the annual meeting of the Jean Piaget Society, Philadelphia, PA, 2002).

21. Jean Piaget, *Structuralism*, trans. C. Maschler (New York: Harper and Row, 1970), 69.

22. Michael Tomasello, "Understanding the Self as Social Agent" in *The Self in Infancy: Theory and Research*, ed. P. Rochat (New York: Elsevier, 1995).

23. For excellent summaries of this research, see J. Flavell & P. Miller, "Social Cognition" in *Cognition, Perception and Language*, ed. E. Kuhn and R. Siegler, Vol 2, *The Handbook of Child Psychology*, ed. W. Damon (New York: John Wiley & sons, 1998) and P. Rochat, "Origins of Self-Concept" in G. Bremner & A. Fogel, eds. *The Blackwell Handbook of Infant Development* (Oxford: Blackwell, 2001), 191-212.

24. Jeremy Carpendale and Charlie Lewis, *How Children Develop Social Understanding* (Malden, MA: Blackwell, 2006), 246.

25. Mike Scaife and Jerome Bruner, "Capacity for Joint Visual Attention in the Infant," *Nature* 253 (1975), 256-66.

26. Tedra A. Walden and Tamra A. Ogan, "The Development of Social Referencing," *Child Development* 59 (1988), 1230-40.

27. Carpendale and Lewis, *How Children Develop Social Understanding*, 103. The researchers base this assertion on the research of D.A. Baldwin, who pointed out the fact that this interaction is the only way to explain how children avoid the massive mapping errors involved in simply presuming that the word they hear refers to the object they are currently attending to. See Dare A. Baldwin "Understanding the Link Between Joint Attention and Language" in Chris Moore and Philip J. Dunham eds. *Joint Attention: Its Origins and Role in Development* (Hillsdale, NJ: Lawrence Erlbaum Associates, 1995), 131-58.

28. Heinz Wimmer and Josef Perner, "Beliefs about Beliefs: Representation and Constraining Function of Wrong Beliefs in Young Children's Understanding of Deception," *Cognition,* 13 (1983), 103-28.

29. Jeremy I. Carpendale and Michael J. Chandler, "On the Distinction between False Belief Understanding and Subscribing to an Interpretive Theory of Mind," *Child Development*, 67 (1996), 1686-1706.

30. Ted Ruffman, Josef Perner and Lindsay Parkin, "How Parenting Style Affects False Belief Understanding" *Social Development* 8 (1999), 395-411.

31. Judy Dunn, Jane R. Brown and Lynn Beardsall, "Family Talk about Feeling States and Children's Later Understanding of Others' Emotions," *Developmental Psychology* 27 (1991), 448-55.

32. Jane R. Brown, Nancy Donelan-McCall and Judy Dunn, "Why Talk about Mental States? The Significance of Children's Conversations with Friends, Siblings, and Mothers," *Child Development* 67 (1996), 836-49.

33. Piaget did, however, stress the fact that "affectivity is always the incentive for the actions that ensue at each new stage of this progressive ascent, since affectivity assigns value to activities and distributes energy to them." See Jean Piaget, *Six Psychological Studies* (New York: Random House, 1967), 69.

34. It is noteworthy that this research significantly undermines any attempt to sharply distinguish between or isolate cognition and affect, blurring the feeling/thinking distinction.

35. Michael Chandler, "Beatify This: Late Arriving Miracles in the Succession of Children Developing Theories of Mind," (paper presented at the Annual Meeting of the Jean Piaget Society, Philadelphia, PA, 2002).

36. Kegan, *The Evolving Self: Problem and Process in Human Development*, 85.

37. Young, *Intersecting Voices*.

38. Lorraine Code, *What Can She Know? Feminist Theory and the Construction of Knowledge* (Ithaca, NY: Cornell, 1991), 82. Emphasis mine.

39. Lorraine Code, *What Can She Know?*, 95

40. Robert Gibbs, *Why Ethics? Signs of Responsibilities* (Princeton, NJ: Princeton University Press, 2000), 31. Emphasis in original text.

41. Sheila Mullett "Shifting Perspective: A New Approach to Ethics," in Judith Boss, ed. *Perspectives on Ethics, 2nd ed* (New York: McGraw-Hill, 2003), 19-23.

42. Emmanuel Babatunde, *Women's Rights versus Women's Rites: A Study of Circumcision among the KetuYoruba of South Western Nigeria* (Trenton: Africa World Press, 1998), 179-80.

43. For an excellent exploration of the assessment of Islamic revival movements by western feminists and an example of what this ethics of hospitality might offer in terms of a more fine grained analysis, see Saba Mahmood, *The Politics of Piety: The Islamic Revival and the Feminist Subject* (Princeton, NJ: Princeton University Press, 2005).

44. To avoid confusion here, what I refer to as an ethics of justice focused on generalized norms and principles is what Derrida refers to as law. Justice, for Derrida, is the opening to the particularity of the other person.

45. For an extended discussion of law and justice, see Jacques Derrida "The Force of Law: The 'Mystical Foundation of Authority,'" in *Deconstruction and the Possibility of Justice*, ed. Drucilla Cornell, Michel Rosenfeld and David Gray Carlson (New York: Routledge, 1992), 3-67.

46. Levinas describes something quite similar in his discussion of the third party. The asymmetry of the ethical relation provokes obligation, yet the other is also an equal at the same time. Levinas points to the double structure operative here, for there is equality among persons, yet it is based on an inegalitarian moment wherein the singular relation with the other calls me into question. See Emmanuel Levinas, *Otherwise Than Being Or Beyond Essence*, trans. Alphonso Lingis (Pittsburgh: Duquesne University Press, 1981).

47. Nancy Fraser criticizes Derrida for this discussion of law and violence arguing that, by concentrating his efforts on disclosing the necessary violence underlying all law, he never gets to a political critique of forms of violence that are not necessary. Seeing violence everywhere thus blinds him to real violence. See Nancy Fraser, "The Force of Law," in *Feminist Interpretations of Jacques Derrida (Re-reading the Canon)* (State College: Pennsylvania State University Press, 1997), 157-165. What Fraser seems to miss is what Derrida is getting at with this whole discussion: that it is knowing the violence of law in the face of the singularity of responsibility that impassions the desire for justice and opens up institutions to critique.

48. Iris Marion Young, *Intersecting Voices*, 50.

49. Mireille Rosello, *Postcolonial Hospitality: The Immigrant as Guest* (Stanford, CA: Stanford University Press, 2001), 135.

50. Iris Marion Young, *Intersecting Voices*, 59.

51. Claude Steele, *Whistling Vivaldi: And Other Clues to How Stereotypes Affect Us* (New York: W.W. Norton & Co, 2010).

Part II: Gender and Domestic Hospitality

Chapter 4

Shame in Feminine Hospitality

Daniel Haggerty

Hospitality has occupied a central place in Western religion and philosophy since antiquity.[1] It has also enjoyed renewed interest among contemporary philosophers, most notably in the work of Emmanuel Lévinas and Jacques Derrida. Attention to sexual difference, however, and to the role of the feminine in hospitality—the hostess— has been largely ignored. In this essay I want to address this neglect by uncovering an oppressive shame in feminine hospitality as it manifests in capitalist, patriarchal society.

The oppression of women in hospitality goes deeper than the gendered division of labor. To see how, we must notice a connection between women's embodiment and hospitality. This involves an intentional resonance of the woman's body in the dwelling-place of hospitality, her home-place. The body of the hostess and her home are, at once, a clearing in which the host/guest relationship develops. I call this feminine *body-dwelling*. This clearing involves a dialectic of shame and pride particular to women's embodiment. Shame, or the socially conditioned preoccupation with how things look and what people might say, discloses the feminine subject's "being-in-the-world" vis-à-vis her *body-dwelling*. This shame often surfaces as hostility and heightened self-consciousness in the hostess/guest relationship. In an attempt to explore feminine hospitality free from patriarchal control, I will consider ethical consequences of this situation from feminist perspectives.

Origins

Much is revealed by uncovering the Indo-European roots of hospitality. Émile Benveniste shows that hospitality has two primary roots: *hostis*—meaning "guest" or "host"—and *potis*, meaning "master."[2] The sense of mastery signified by *potis* includes domestic and social power, and also personal identity. As Tracy McNulty explains, "In the colloquial Latin, *ipsissimus* (from *i-pse*, "personal identity") indicates 'the master, the one in charge'; but more precisely, the man *himself*, the only person who matters. . . . The mastery or power of the *potis* is thus nothing other than ipseity, or identity as *self*-identity."[3] The noun *potis* has no feminine form.

The master of hospitality makes the laws in the home. As such, he is master of all his personal property, including the dependent women under his control. He is master of his own identity. He dwells not only in the home-place, but also within a well-established, recognized identity. This power and privilege is unique to the master. His domestic subordinates, having no power vis-à-vis property, cannot be masterful in the way of the *potis*. They lack identity. Masterful identity, then, is a condition for the possibility of offering patriarchal hospitality. In his home, the *potis* enjoys a plentitude of resources and abundance of being (identity) by virtue of which he is empowered to offer hospitality to the guest—to offer sustenance, rest, and protection to the stranger.

Hostis, the other primary root of hospitality, signifies reciprocity. This is why *hostis* means *both* host *and* guest. Thus the origin of the host/guest relationship designates compensatory expectations, reciprocal bonds of obligation between the one who offers and the one who receives hospitality. At the least, the guest is expected to reciprocate by confirming in word or deed the master's power, identity, and offering. This reciprocity functioned as a way to link together members of an extended human society.

As with *potis*, the noun *hostis* also has no feminine form. McNulty explains that "the modern word 'hostess' is not a feminine form of the Latin *hostis*, but a corrupted form of 'hostility.'"[4] To be sure, women have always been involved in the labor required of patriarchal hospitality. There are also archaic examples where women appear to offer hospitality independently of men (Penelope, Rebecca), but in such cases women typically offer in the name of the master of the home.[5] Thus we find that "the host is almost invariably male[;] . . . and even the many terms designating the host have no female equivalent. In these contexts, 'feminine hospitality' is almost an oxymoron, since women are rarely hostesses in their own right."[6]

Hospitality was man's work and man's reward. He could enjoy pride in his power and plentitude when he offered hospitality to another. For this reason, he could also suffer shame (the opposite of pride or self-respect). If his masterful identity were in some way impugned, if the guest were to usurp his power, for example, he might be exposed to shame, to that negative emotion of *self-assessment* wherein one's identity, or its value, goodness, or efficacy feels called into question or denounced.

Today, however, ordinary language in patriarchal society is more likely to associate hospitality with women's work. The cooking, the cleaning, the planning, and the pleasing of guests within the home reinforces the lopsided division of domestic labor that is expected of women. More than that, today a women's identity is more likely to be tied to the perceived success or failure of patriarchal hospitality. This situation exposes women to a kind of gender-based shame, a socially conditioned preoccupation with how things look and what people might say.

Unconditional Hospitality

Emmanuel Lévinas is the thinker of "radical alterity," of the "other of the other," of another kind of otherness. He aims to reveal how the other is experienced *beyond* totality, *before* conceptual, systematic, categorical thinking. The encounter with the other, as Lévinas describes it, is not a phenomenon. It is not something empirically present. It can never be present precisely because the content of the other is "absolutely transcendent." For this reason the relationship of the self to the other is not a totality, but infinity—a relation that reveals the limits of the self and its finitude. As such, the fundamental encounter with the other destroys the "ipseity of the 'I.'" Lévinas calls for a new understanding of the subject not as self-identity, but as "welcoming the Other, as hospitality."[7]

The ontology of *self*-identity, endemic to the Western philosophical tradition, has privileged a conception of the self-other relation that effaces the other's transcendence in the name of some totality. In an effort to reduce the shock of the radical alterity of the other, the ego attempts to "reduce the other to the same." Philosophy has posited an ontology of self-identity that reinforces this illegitimate, violent reduction. Lévinas seeks to reverse the priority of ontology over ethics by resisting language that would situate alterity in the domain of the identical, the same.

But Lévinas' critique is not wholly opposed to the above sketched genealogy of hospitality insofar as it upholds the notion that the ipseity of the host is a precondition for hospitality; that is, for shattering the ipseity of the host. This comes through in Lévinas' discussion of *sojourning*. Sojourning "is the way of the I against the 'other,'" which requires identifying and maintaining oneself by being "at home" in the world. As Lévinas writes, "The 'at home' is not a container, but a site where I *can*, where . . . I am . . . free. It is enough to walk, to *do*, in order to grasp anything, to take. In a sense everything is in the site . . . everything is at my disposal, even the stars if I reckon them. . . . Everything is here, everything belongs to me."[8] Sojourning is a mode of appropriation, a violence in which the other and the world are made to reflect the self. It is precisely this "being at home" which, according to Lévinas, is a precondition for hospitality, for ethics—for that which disrupts our "being at home."

In hospitality the host's *self*-concern is shattered. This directs his vision toward an other whose content is its transcendence. Seeing past a Hobbesian notion of the other as a locus of power, Lévinas sees in the other's vulnerability the self's obligations to the other. In this encounter, realizing his power over the guest, the host becomes an object to himself. For Lévinas, this is the source of ethical shame in hospitality. The self is shamed by the other, by the other's powerlessness, by the sublimity of the other's transcendence, by the other's vulnerability, and by the recognition of his power to kill the other.

Acknowledging his debt to Lévinas, Jacques Derrida goes on to stress the impossible, aporetical nature of the obligation of hospitality. For Derrida, unconditional hospitality demands welcoming whomever is in need, and thereby relinquishing all mastery and control, all claims to property and ipseity. Unconditional hospitality requires absolute care for the other, which requires, per impossible, integrating the foreigner into the home, into the self, while at the same time respecting and maintaining his identity as foreign. Unconditional hospitality thus contains and reveals an impossible limit: the maintenance of identity and its opening to what is non-identical to it.[9]

Derrida calls for thinking beyond common, conditional hospitality because he sees in unconditional hospitality—in its impossibility, in its interruption—the origin and locus of ethics. In *Adieu to Emmanuel Lévinas*, Derrida defines hospitality as "the whole or principle of ethics."[10] As Robert Bernasconi puts it, "the possibility of ethics is referred, not to its actuality, but to its impossibility."[11] In *Of Hospitality*, Derrida writes:

> To put it in different terms, absolute hospitality requires that I open up my home and that I give not only to the foreigner, but to the absolute, unknown, anonymous other, and that I *give place* to them, that I let them come, that I let them arrive, and take place in the place I offer them, without asking of them either reciprocity (entering into a pact) or even their names.[12]

In unconditional hospitality the host invites not in the sense of actively asking the guest to come, not by requesting the favor of his presence, but by "letting him come." The *inviting host* attracts the other independently of the host's desire, even unwillingly. Unintentionally bringing on the guest or encouraging him to come, the one who invites and induces becomes hostage.[13] Any other sort of invitation, the common sort, implies reciprocity and exchange, mutual expectation. For Derrida, this kind of invitation sets up "the most inhospitable exchange possible."[14]

Let us take a look at the work of Lévinas and Derrida on hospitality from a feminist perspective—that is, from the practical perspective of the movement to end sexism, sexist exploitation, and the oppression of women and girls.[15]

Derrida neglects the feminine in his analysis of hospitality. Insofar as he attempts to reveal the structure of any possible-impossible aporetic hospitality, he pays no attention to the embodied consciousnesses of hospitality-offering-subjects in specific social and historical locations. In particular, he ignores the embodied consciousness of the woman who invites and offers hospitality to the guest, to the foreigner, to the stranger—the woman who lets them come. He never asks how it would feel and what it would mean for women to be—and to feel they *should be*—unwillingly inviting to any and every would-be guest, to be made hostages in their homes. He does not consider how it would feel and what it would mean for women who are socialized feminine subjectivities in patriarchal society to undertake the possibility of the impossible in hospitality. For women, what is the affective quality of the Derridian imperative to *try and fail*?

Derrida posits and reinforces the impossibility of hospitality because he focuses on the abstract notion of absolute care. But care is never abstract; it is always embodied. In particular, the care of the hostess is an embodied hospitality. If we consider the lifeworld (the *Lebenswelt*) of hospitality in place of the abstract, absolute ideal, we find that most hospitality is not unlimited—it is *conditional*. In conditional hospitality the hostess actively invites her guests as opposed to passively letting them come. This empowers the hostess and values her desire. Moreover, insofar as feminine subjectivity in patriarchal culture does posit and reinforce the notion that feminine hospitality *should be* unconditional, that it *should* involve absolute care, the hostess who is destined to fail is subject to almost inevitable shame. Insofar as Derrida's absolute ideal hospitality neglects these considerations, insofar as it fails to consider how the "ideal" contributes to the oppression of women, it cannot, as he thinks it can, serve as the ethics par excellence.[16]

Unlike Derrida, Lévinas does not completely neglect the feminine in hospitality. But what he says is hardly feminist! Lévinas contends that "the other whose presence is discretely an absence, with which is accomplished the primary hospitable welcome which describes the field of intimacy, is the Woman."[17] Woman is more naturally hospitable than man, according to Lévinas, because her "receptivity" to the other and his alterity is less hemmed in by the masculine closure of ipseity (identity). "The woman," he writes, "is the condition for recollection, the interiority of the Home, and inhabitation."[18]

The problem here, as Tracy McNulty writes, is that,

> Lévinas tends to link . . . "feminine hospitality" to qualities supposedly innate in women, like maternal love, empathy, or care. He describes the maternal body, for example, as "pure renunciation, suffering for the Other." . . . The result is an often reductive understanding of femininity, supported by a gender ideology that makes woman no more than a welcoming vessel or a synecdoche of home.[19]

Beyond the obvious problems, from a feminist perspective, with Lévinas' essentializing language, with his reductive understanding of femininity and his attachment to "traditional" female traits, like Derrida he neglects to consider how it would feel and what it would mean for women to be seen as—and to feel they *should be* seen as—welcoming vessels.

In *Of Woman Born*, Adrienne Rich shows us how patriarchal descriptions of woman as vessel have been abstract and disembodied—disconnected from the reality that women are also vessel-makers, creators, and inventors. Because her words are powerful and central to my concerns in this essay, I quote her here at length:

> We can find some support for [the] hypothesis . . . that the deeply reverenced art of pottery-making was invented by women. . . . It does not seem unlikely that the woman potter molded, not simply vessels, but images of herself, the vessel of life, the transformer of blood into life and milk—that in doing so she was expressing, celebrating, and giving concrete form to her experience as a creative being possessed of indispensible powers.

But,

> Because of speculation like Erik Erikson's (wittily dissected by Kate Millet) as to the meaning and value of woman's "inner space," it is difficult to talk about women in connection with "containers" without evoking a negative if not derisive response. The old associations start pouring in: woman is "receptive," a "receptacle" . . . woman's place is in the "inner space" of the home; woman's anatomy lays on her an ethical imperative to be maternal in the sense of masochistic, patient, pacific; women without children are "unfulfilled," "barren," and "empty" women.

And finally:

My own negative associations with male derivations from female anatomy were so strong that for a long time I felt distaste, or profound ambivalence, when I looked at some of the early mother-goddess figures emphasizing breasts and belly. It took me a long time to get beyond patriarchally acquired responses and to connect with the power and integrity, the absolute nonfemininity, of posture and expression in those images. Bearing in mind, then, that we are talking not about "inner space" as some determinate of woman's proper social function, but about primordial clusters of association, we can see the extension of the woman/vessel association. (It must be also borne in mind that in primordial terms the vessel is anything but a "passive" receptacle: it is *transformative*—active, powerful).[20]

Lévinas considers the ethical shame of the male host who sees in the Other's vulnerability his own power to kill. But he does not see or consider the shame of reducing feminine hospitality and the woman's ability to create to "receptivity" and "inhabitation itself."

Shame and Hostility

Psychoanalytic theorist Helen Block Lewis reports that therapists and their patients find it difficult to distinguish guilt and shame empirically or introspectively.[21] Instead she provides a rudimentary conceptual analysis of the distinction: "The experience of shame is directly about the *self*, which is the focus of evaluation. In guilt, [however,] the self is not the central object of negative evaluation, but rather the *thing done* is the focus."[22] Recent work in empirical psychology seems to bear out Lewis' analysis. In *Shame and Guilt*, June Price Tangney and Ronda Dearing offer empirical findings that support Lewis' basic account: shame is directly about the self, while guilt is about actions and their consequences.[23] Here I offer a more thoroughgoing analysis of the structure of shame, building on the work of Lewis and others.

Shame involves beliefs about a real or imagined other. The subject experiences the "other" as a *watcher* or *witness*, perhaps an imago, intimately enmeshed in its own attitudes and behaviors. The watcher represents the experience of being seen inappropriately or under the wrong conditions by someone who feels close. The witness is similar to the watcher, but represents an "other" who records an accurate testament of the self's being seen under such conditions. Both may include feelings of being exposed, naked, ugly, or sexually vulnerable.[24]

The watcher or witness before whom we feel shame is not necessarily critical and punitive. Instead, the other may represent potentially affirming attitudes such as acceptance, admiration, respect, love, and resolve, as well as more painful ones such as disappointment, rejection, avoidance, or contempt. Nor is the watcher or witness experienced as an impersonal judge. With shame, we experience the (usually negative) appraisal *personally*. When we feel guilt we fear punishment at the hands of an impersonal other, but with shame we fear loss of love, honor, and respect in the eyes of our community. The threat involved in shame is not punishment, but rejection and abandonment.

Shame includes a desire to be seen as the self we feel we ought to be. It also includes a desire not to be seen as "falling short" or being "not good enough." If we are seen this way, we want forgiveness, acceptance, or *to be overlooked.* In shame desire to be forgiven or accepted often combines painfully with desire to be *not seen*—even the wish to disappear or vanish.

We can distinguish various types of shame. Stephen Pattison distinguishes acute, reactive shame, which is transient, occurring in particular circumstances, from chronic shame or shame-proneness, which is a more enduring character trait.[25] Sandra Lee Bartky introduces an important third type; namely, shame that is disclosive of its subject's "being-in-the-world," including the gender-based shame of women.[26] This is not a matter of individual character traits or dispositions, but of subjectivities' "character as selves and of the specific ways in which, as selves, they are inscribed within the social totality."[27]

I am concerned with revealing the gender-based shame of home-based hospitality in "advanced" patriarchal, capitalist culture. I recognize that most women do not live in such circumstances and that the diversity of women who do cannot be overstated. Thus, what I say about feminine hospitality is not meant to be true of all women in all times and places. Indeed, my focus is not on women—or Woman—directly, but on a certain activity and condition of a socially and historically constructed mode of femininity (viz., home-based hospitality). I am interested in advancing our understanding of the subjectivity of what Bartky calls "the 'chauvinized' woman . . . ashamed, eager to please, worried about her weight. . . . I sketch this woman . . . not only because there is so much of her in me and in many other women as well, but because her desire reflects the current social norms according to which female desire is, or is supposed to be, constituted."[28]

In addition to shame, feminine hospitality also involves pride. The form of pride here is not the well-deserved pleasure, close to the sense of joy, felt in relation to the self's goodness, success, or efficacy. Nor is it *hubris*—overconfidence based on unwarranted, over-valuation of the self. It is, rather, what Gershen Kaufman describes as pride bound by shame.[29] In women's performances of home-based hospitality, such pride—tied as it is to idealized/ inferiorized patriarchal femininity—manifests in rigid, sometimes obsessive compensatory fixation on perfecting the techniques and objects of hospitality and home (the right fork in the right place, the spotless kitchen, and the right way to serve). This pride is not joyous. It is another kind of self-obsession that manifests as arrogance and contempt for others, but which ultimately isolates the self.

Disclosing shame and pride as gender-based emotions in feminine hospitality is essential to feminist movement. As Bartky explains,

> The search for a feminist reconstruction of knowledge . . . must be augmented by a study of the most pervasive patterns of gendered emotion in their revelatory moment. Insofar as women are not just situated differently than men within the social ensemble, but are actively subordinated to them within it, this

project—the identification and description of these [emotional] attunements—will be at the same time a contribution to the phenomenology of oppression.[30]

Further, Helen Block Lewis identifies three ways in which shame might be phenomenologically present in people's lives, namely, as "overt shame," "overt, unidentified shame," and "by-passed shame." Overt shame connects with Pattison's acute shame. In these situations the self is highly conscious of shame affect as such. In overt, unidentified shame, shame affect is available to consciousness but the self experiencing it either will not or cannot identify it. Instead, the subject only knows "that he feels 'lousy,' or 'tense,' or 'blank.'"[31] With by-passed shame, the self is not aware of feeling shame affect at all: "the person is aware of the cognitive content of shame-connected events, but experiences only a 'wince,' 'blow,' or 'jolt.'"[32] The person does not experience the kind of disruption associated with acute, overt shame, but nevertheless there is "a peripheral, non-specific disturbance in awareness, which serves mainly to note the shame potential in the circumstance."[33] With by-passed shame, there may be little or none of the usual physiological marks of acute, overt shame (blushing, averting one's eyes), but the "ideation of by-passed shame involves doubt about the self's image from the 'other's' viewpoint. There is frequently an accompaniment of overt hostility along with this ideation, and sometimes clear retaliatory feeling."[34] Hostility and retaliatory feelings of by-passed shame may be directed at the self, at the real or imagined "other," or at both.

As a result of this analysis, we can categorize shame in feminine hospitality. First, it is shame of the type Bartky describes. It is a pattern of mood or feeling that tends to characterize women in hospitality more than men. It is an emotional attunement disclosive of women's being-in-the-world, of the total situation of patriarchal society in which feminine hospitality is located. This situation involves a familiar and dangerous "set-up": the technologies of femininity occur "against the background of a pervasive sense of bodily deficiency;" so that "virtually every woman who gives herself to it is destined in some degree to fail;" and this accounts for the often "compulsive or even ritualistic character" of the technologies of femininity.[35] Patriarchal capitalism manufactures a continuous array of products, services, images, information, and celebrity personages (Martha!) to produce and regulate femininity.[36] Women are "disciplined" to attempt to conceal and hide their deficiencies, their flaws. Focus on clothing and makeup, on the condition of the home, and on the body of the hostess are among the multifarious techniques for accomplishing—though never, ultimately, satisfactorily—an endless task of femininity: *aiming-to-please-while-concealing-flaws*. In this situation women are acutely susceptible to feeling flawed, imperfect, and ugly.

Second, shame in feminine hospitality is often by-passed shame. As such, it is felt as hostility. (Recall that the modern word "hostess" is not a feminine form of the Latin *hostis*; it is a corrupted form of "hostility"). Now, Derrida speaks of the "troubling analogy" between hospitality and hostility.[37] But for Derrida, the hostility that lurks in unconditional hospitality is a result of the fact that *hostis* includes the undesirable/enemy guest who has claim to absolute care. But this is not the hostility of shame in feminine hospitality, even if such shame does include the feeling of inevitably failing to meet the impossible expectations of absolute care. At the center of shame in feminine hospitality is the experience of heightened, tormenting self-consciousness in the situation of hospitality in patriarchal culture. Being by-passed, it is not felt as acute, transient shame affect—blushing, cowering, looking to hide. It is felt as hostility, even contempt, without knowing why. It may be experienced as a "cold" affect, which all the same feels excessive. There may be an impulse to break something, without knowing why. A mirror would feel like a suitable object! Finally, the shame in feminine hospitality involves a sense of being watched, of being (potentially) exposed, of being seen in the wrong way. As such it involves a threat to the self.

Surveillance and Doubling

Michele Foucault describes a variety of modern disciplinary techniques directed against the body. His work reveals the coercive influence of cultural forces, systems, and norms on living bodies—a "body politics."[38] As Foucault argues, the control of bodies requires relentless surveillance. Famously, he argues that the Panopticon captures the essence of modern, disciplinary society: the effect is "to induce . . . a state of conscious and permanent visibility that assures the automatic functioning of power."[39] With the new techniques of discipline and control aimed at living bodies,

> There is no need for arms, physical violence, material constraints. Just a gaze. An inspecting gaze, a gaze which each individual under its weight will end by interiorizing to the point that he is his own overseer, each individual thus exercising this surveillance over, and against, himself. A superb formula: power exercised continuously and for what turns out to be at minimal cost.[40]

The self-surveillance in Foucault's conceptualization of power connects to a central aspect of shame—the often internalized experience of being seen and being watched. It is also relevant to the more specific emotional attunement of shame and pride in feminine hospitality.

The feeling of scrutiny, of being under surveillance, "engenders a sense of heightened and tormenting *self-consciousness* and divided functioning."[41] As Helen Block Lewis explains, the experience of shame involves a feeling of being "split" between the "other" and the self.[42] This condition is accompanied by negative or hostile affect directed against the self, by the self. It may also be accompanied by a concurrence of the real or imagined "other's" negative or hostile affect. The result is an acute sense of "dividedness" or "doubling" in the self.[43] Helen Merrell Lynd adds that the acute self-consciousness is connected to a sense of *incongruity*.[44] "The person becomes aware that things are not as they thought, perhaps that the self is not as it was thought to be in relation to the world. . . . One's world and one's identity within that world appear to be jeopardized."[45]

Shame in feminine hospitality destabilizes the hostess's *self*-identity. It threatens her self. Can the masterful male host of the tradition experience such shame? No. To be sure, he may experience other kinds of shame; for example, by a guest usurping his power. But such scenarios would be the exception to the ipseity-conferring situation of traditional masculine hospitality—that is, the very opposite of shame-based, feminine hospitality. By way of self-surveillance and doubling, shame is disclosive of women's being-in-the-world vis-à-vis feminine hospitality. Oppressive feminine hospitality endangers the identity (the self-relation) of the hostess by force of shame. To see how, we must look more closely at the peculiar modes of self-surveillance and doubling in feminine subjectivity.

Recall that the heightened self-consciousness of shame in feminine hospitality is not idiosyncratic. It is embedded in the social world in which feminine subjectivity is constructed and performed. Along these lines, a number of feminist scholars have modified Foucault's insights about modern discipline.[46] Iris Marion Young, for one, details the phenomenological body politics that construct and constrict the embodied experiences of women and girls, not of "docile bodies" generally: "Insofar as we learn to live our existence in accordance with the definition that patriarchal culture assigns to us, we are physically inhibited, confined, positioned, and objectified." This goes together with the "ever present possibility that [a woman] will be gazed upon as a mere body, as shape and flesh that presents itself as the potential object of another subject's intentions and manipulations."[47]

Sandra Bartky commends Foucault's work on disciplinary practices that construct modern bodies, but objects that his analysis "treats the body . . . as if bodily experiences of men and women did not differ and as if men and women bore the same relationship to the characteristic institutions of modern life." She asks: "Where is the account of the disciplinary practices that engender the 'docile bodies' of women, bodies more docile than the bodies of men? . . . [Foucault] is blind to those disciplines that produce a modality of embodiment that is peculiarly feminine."[48]

Bartky describes femininity as a form of alienation. As such, femininity involves a fragmentation of the self and a prohibition of certain activities that constitute selfhood. Women, she argues, are subject to a special kind of fragmentation and prohibition *via* sexual alienation. On the one hand, women are alienated from their bodies as a result of being estranged from their own sexuality, while on the other hand women are estranged by being too closely identified with their bodies as sexual.[49]

> Sexual objectification typically involves two persons, one who objectifies and one who is objectified. But objectifier and objectified can be one and the same person: A woman can become a sex object for herself, taking toward her own person the attitude of the man. She will then take erotic satisfaction in her physical self, reveling in her body as a beautiful object to be gazed at and decorated. Such an attitude is typically called "narcissism."[50]

The total situation of female sexual objectification and the alienation it produces engenders feminine narcissism, wherein the feminine "self undergoes doubling: An Other, a 'stranger' who is at the same time myself, is subject for whom by bodily being is object."[51] The "Other" before whom women experience shame in feminine hospitality is the interiorized gaze of the patriarchal overseer. Thus, the body with which feminine narcissism is preoccupied is not the female self's real body, but the simultaneously idealized/inferiorized feminine body upon which the gaze is perpetually fixed.

The doubling that is a result of the surveillance of the feminine body produces shame in feminine hospitality—often experienced as hostility—which lies close to the center of the feminine condition itself. Bartky describes three "techniques of the self" that contribute to the construction and performance of femininity in patriarchy: deprivation, constriction, and ornamentation. These combine to "produce a body which in gesture and appearance is recognizably feminine" and reinforce a "disciplinary project of bodily perfection."[52] This brings us to another, even deeper, connection between women's embodiment and feminine hospitality. Shame in feminine hospitality, the socially conditioned preoccupation with how things look and what people might say, discloses the feminine subject's "being-in-the-world" vis-à-vis her *body-dwelling*. As I said at the outset, the body of the hostess and her home are, at once, the clearing in which the ethics of conditional host/guest relationships emerge.

Body-Dwelling

Phenomenology of architecture focuses on the corporeal resonance of building. Inspired by the work of Maurice Merleau-Ponty, this field of phenomenology sees building as a modality of the perceptual and embodied engagement of our being-in-the-world. As Timothy Casey explains,

> [Merleau-Ponty] uncovers a pre-personal sedimentation of meaning in the human body, in effect transferring the intentionality of consciousness to bodily activity. This sedimented meaning, so easily ignored in classical epistemology, consists of pre-predicative, intentional threads that "run out" beyond the body toward its surrounding situation.[53]

Architectural historian and phenomenologist Alberto Perez-Gomez underlines the significance of Merleau-Ponty's phenomenology of the lived body and the world of meaning it constitutes by identifying building with "the creation of an order resonant with the body's own."[54] Building, in the relevant sense—one connected with Heidegger's notion of dwelling—is an ontological event: "*Man dwells in that he builds* . . . Man is capable of such building only if he already builds in the sense of the poetic taking of measure."[55]

Phenomenology of architecture is interested in all forms of building. I am concerned here with domestic building. Building a home—not construction work, but building as dwelling, as in the sense of *building our lives together*—is world-making. In its spatial (and temporal) dimensions, world is an "openness" in which human beings dwell.[56] Building a home, home-making, clears a familiar and intimate mode of dwelling. Such building is always already more than an ontological event. Building as home-dwelling implies not only identity but *relation*—the possibility of relationships between lives lived together, and between host(ess)ing and guests.[57]

The home as dwelling is also a continuation of the woman's body. Home is the familiar and intimate site where intentional threads "run out" beyond her body toward its surrounding situation. If the embodied consciousness of woman could be made visible, if it could be lifted out of her being-in-the-world and given material form, that form would be her home and its contents. Elaine Scarry provides a beautiful example of what I mean by creating an image of intentional threads that "run out" from embodied movement:

> The chair is . . . the materialized structure of a perception; it is sentient awareness materialized into freestanding design. If one pictures the person in *the action* of making a chair . . . that is, if one pictures only the man and his embodied actions, what one at that moment has before one is *not* the *act of perception* (his seeing of another's discomfort and wishing it gone) but *the structure of the act of perception visibly enacted.* What was originally an invisible aspect of consciousness (compassion) has now been translated into the realm of visible but disappearing action. The interior moment of perceiving has been translated into a willed series of successive actions, as if it were a dance, a dance entitled "body weight begone."[58]

As she continues, she shows how the intentional threads that "run out" of this dance become sedimented in the production of an artifact, the chair:

> If, now, the tool is placed back in his hand and the wood placed beneath that tool, a second translation occurs, for the action, direction, and pressure of his dance move down across the tool and are recorded in the surface of the wood. . . . Thus in work, a perception is danced; in the chair, a danced-perception is sculpted.[59]

The home is not an image, reflection, or representation of the woman or her body. Rather, it is the dwelling where her embodiment performs what is most intimate and familiar in her life. Her performative dance makes waves of significance that are inscribed and recorded in the structure and the objects of her home—impressed upon the surfaces of furniture, on the images of photographs, and on the pages of her journal. In woman's *body-dwelling*, her perception is danced and her danced-perception is formed—arranged.

Patriarchal images of the feminine body, of the home, and of women's "inner space" evoke strong, negative associations. Therefore I want to make it clear that I am not talking about "home" as the determinate of woman's proper social function, nor about her "body" as a passive locus of feminine "inhabitation." Instead, with Adrienne Rich, I ask that we work to move beyond patriarchal responses to home and female body. We might connect instead with the power and integrity, the absolute nonfemininity, of women's embodiment and its creative continuation in home-dwelling. It is itself a resistance to patriarchy to see again the power and the beauty of women's *body-dwelling*.

We might wonder whether it is possible to have hostess/guest relationships without the shame and hostility I have described here. Fortunately, we can *feel* that this is not the case. We can feel it because we have experienced, or if not, at least we can imagine, the satisfaction, the gratification, the creativity, and the joy that sometimes accompanies women's home-making and hospitality. As bell hooks argues, the home-place often is and long has been a place of resistance to patriarchy.[60] We may overlook this if we focus too narrowly on the gendered division of labor in the home. The home-place can be an alternative to the shame and hostility women feel in *body-dwelling* and hospitality as a result of patriarchal domination. Instead, the building and maintaining of the home, and of women's *body-dwelling*, may clear joyful opportunities to create—freedom, *jouissance*.

Notes

1. Tracy McNulty, *The Hostess: Hospitality, Femininity, and the Expropriation of Identity* (Minneapolis, MN: University of Minnesota Press, 2007). McNulty provides an excellent account of the history of hospitality in Western religion and philosophy, as well as an inspired psychoanalytic critique of this tradition.
2. Émile Benveniste, "L'hospitalité," in *Le vocabulaire des institutions indo-européennes*, vol. 1 (Paris: Éditions de Minuit, 1969), 87-101. An account of Benveniste's work is provided by McNulty, *The Hostess*, ix-xii. I rely exclusively upon McNulty's translation and account of Benveniste's etymology.
3. McNulty, *The Hostess*, x.
4. McNulty, *The Hostess*, xliii.
5. McNulty, *The Hostess*, 240.
6. McNulty, *The Hostess*, xxvii.
7. Emmanuel Lévinas, *Totality and Infinity: An essay on exteriority*, trans. Alphonso Lingis (Boston: M. Nijhoff Publishers, 1979), 27.
8. Lévinas, *Totality and Infinity*, 37-8.
9. McNulty *The Hostess*, xiv.
10. Jacques Derrida, *Adieu to Emmanuel Lévinas*, trans. Pascale-Anne Brault and Michael Naas (Stanford: Stanford University Press, 1999), 50.
11. Robert Bernasconi, "Deconstruction and the Possibility of Ethics," in *Deconstruction and Philosophy*, ed. By John Sallis (Chicago: University of Chicago Press, 1988), 135.
12. Jacques Derrida, *Of Hospitality*, trans. Rachel Bowlby (Stanford: Stanford University Press, 2000), 25.
13. Derrida, *Of Hospitality*, 125. "So it is indeed the master, the one who invites, the inviting host, who becomes the hostage—and who really always has been. And the guest, the invited hostage, becomes the one who invites the one who invites, the master of the host. The guest becomes the host's host."
14. Jacques Derrida, "Hostipitality" in *Acts of Religion* (New York: Routledge, 2002), 364.
15. bell hooks, *Feminism is for Everybody: Passionate Politics* (Cambridge, MA: South End Press, 2000), vii.

16. Derrida made the argument that hospitality is not one ethics among others, but the ethics par excellence in his seminar at U.C. Irvine entitled "Hospitality and Hostility," April 3, 1996. See McNulty, *The Hostess*, xvii and endnote 10.

17. Lévinas, *Totality and Infinity*, 155.

18. Lévinas, *Totality and Infinity*, 155.

19. McNulty, *The Hostess*, xxv.

20. Adrienne Rich, *Of Woman Born: Motherhood as Experience and Institution* (New York: Bantam Books, 1977), 84-5.

21. Helen Block Lewis, *Shame and Guilt in Neurosis* (New York: International University Press, 1971).

22. Quoted in June Price Tangney and Ronda L. Dearing, *Shame and Guilt* (New York: The Guilford Press, 2002), 18.

23. Tangney and Dearing, *Shame and Guilt*.

24. See Sandra Bartky, *Femininity and Domination* (New York: Routledge, 1990), 85; Sigmund Freud, "Mourning and Melancholia" in *The Standard Edition of the Complete Psychological Works of Sigmund Freud*, Vol. 14, ed. J. Strachey (Hogarth: London, 1986), 248; Helen Block Lewis, *Shame and Guilt in Neurosis* (New York: International Universities Press, 1971), 60-68; Jean-Paul Sartre, *Being and Nothingness*, trans. Hazel E. Barnes (New York: Philosophical Library, 1956), 221-222; Gabriele Taylor, *Pride, Shame and Guilt: Emotions of Self-Assessment* (New York: Oxford University Press, 1985), 60-68; and Bernard Williams, *Shame and Necessity* (Berkeley, CA: University of California Press, 1993), 78, 82, and 219.

25. Stephen Pattison, *Shame: Theory, Therapy, Theology* (Cambridge, UK: Cambridge University Press, 2000), 83.

26. Bartky, *Femininity and Domination*, 84.

27. Bartky, *Femininity and Domination*, 84.

28. Bartky, *Femininity and Domination*, 8.

29. Gershen Kaufman, *The Psychology of Shame* (London: Routledge, 1993), 225.

30. Bartky, *Femininity and Domination*, 84.

31. Lewis, *Shame and Guilt in Neurosis*, 197.

32. Lewis, *Shame and Guilt in Neurosis*, 197.

33. Lewis, *Shame and Guilt in Neurosis*, 197.

34. Lewis, *Shame and Guilt in Neurosis*, 197.

35. Bartky, *Femininity and Domination*, 72.

36. Bartky, *Femininity and Domination*, 39.

37. Jacques Derrida, "Hostipitality," trans. Barry Stocker with Forbes Morlock, *Angelaki: Journal of Theoretical Humanities* 5.3 (2000): 3-18.

38. Michele Foucault, *Discipline and Punish* (New York: Vintage Books, 1977).

39. Foucault, *Discipline and Punish*, 201.

40. Michele Foucault, "The Eye of Power," in *Power/Knowledge: Selected Interviews and Other Writings, 1972-1977*, ed. Colin Gordon, trans. Colin Gordon et. Al. (New York: Pantheon, 1980), 155.

41. Pattison, *Shame*, 73.

42. Lewis, *Shame and Guilt in Neurosis*, 40.

43. Lewis, *Shame and Guilt in Neurosis*, 81.

44. Helen Merrell Lynd, *On Shame and the Search for Identity* (New York, NY: Harcourt Brace, 1958), 34.

45. The formulation is Pattison's, *Shame*, 73.

46. See *Feminism and Foucault* eds. Irene Diamond and Lee Quinby (Boston: Northeastern University Press, 1988); Jana Sawicki, *Disciplining Foucault* (New York: Routledge, 1991); Lois McNay, *Foucault and Feminism* (Boston: Northeastern University Press, 1992); and Susan Heckman, *Feminist Interpretations of Michele Foucault* (University Park, PA: Penn State University Press, 1996).

47. Iris Marion Young, "Throwing Like a Girl: A Phenomenology of Feminine Body Comportment, Motility, and Spatiality," in *The Thinking Muse*, ed. Allen and Young (Bloomington, IN 1989), 65-6.

48. Bartky, *Femininity and Domination*, 63-4.

49. Bartky, *Femininity and Domination*, 34-5.

50. Bartky, *Femininity and Domination*, 36.

51. Bartky, *Femininity and Domination*, 37.

52. Bartky, *Femininity and Domination*, 64 and 66, quoted in Monique Deveaux, "Feminism and Empowerment: A Critical Reading of Foucault" in *Feminist Interpretation of Michel Foucault*, ed. Susan J. Hekman (University Park, PA: Penn State University Press, 1996), 215.

53. Timothy Casey, "Architecture" in *Encyclopedia of Phenomenology*, eds. Lester Embree, et al. (Netherlands: Kluwer Academic Publishers, 1997), 26.

54. Alberto Perez-Gomez, "Introduction to Architecture and the Crisis of Modern Science," in *Architecture Theory since 1968*, ed. K. Michael Hays (Cambridge, MA: MIT, 2000), 466; quoted in Casey, "Architecture," 26.

55. Martin Heidegger, " . . . Poetically, Man Dwells . . ." trans. Albert Hofstadter in *Philosophical and Political Writings*, ed. Manfred Stassen (London: Continuum International, 2003), 276.

56. Casey, "Architecture," 27.

57. McNulty, *The Hostess*, xiv.

58. Elaine Scarry, *The Body in Pain The Making and Unmaking of the World* (New York: Oxford University Press, 1985), 290.

59. Scarry, *The Body in Pain*, 290.

60. bell hooks, "Homeplace: A Site of Resistance," in *Yearning: Race, Gender and Cultural Politics* (Boston: Southend Press, 1990).

Chapter 5

Domestic Hospitality: Self, Other, and Community

Jo-Ann Pilardi

In Memory of Iris Marion Young[1]

Hospitality's Two Faces

Hospitality has two faces, a public face and a private face. The subject of this essay is the latter, which I call "domestic" hospitality: the welcoming, generous work practiced in the home by the one(s) whose home it is, accomplished through activities like making and sharing meals, allowing the use of one's home to overnight guests, and bringing people together in small social groups to share time and conversation. Domestic hospitality is the much ignored stepsister of progressive theories of hospitality, most of which operate in either in a global/ international or a corporate context. Global theories of hospitality provide a forum for debates on immigration policy, while hospitality discourse connected to corporate environments ("the hospitality industry") provides a forum for critiques of capitalism. The gendered work in the home, i.e., "women's work," where domestic hospitality takes place, is often forgotten, ignored, or trivialized as less important, a mere echo of international or corporate hospitality. At best, commentators suggest that hospitality as an international (between nations) or cross-cultural activity mimics domestic hospitality.

It is my contention that through domestic hospitality, identified in the present era with women and what is called "women's culture"—though it is not limited to women, for both gay and straight men practice domestic hospitality—communities are created, i.e., "community" is created. In some cases these are short-lived communities of the moment. In other cases, longer-lasting communities are created, or a sense of community is fostered. By this connection and affiliation work women do through their homes, communities of people come into existence.

A stress on community does not equate necessarily to communitarianism. I don't intend here to provide a defense of communitarianism based in hospitality, nor to promote the creation of communities based in the theory that human beings are "social beings," though some feminist theorists have argued for communitarianism and its expansion to include ideals based in feminist theory.[2] Nor do I intend to defend the position that the values of local communities are to be respected (values that are sometimes healthy, but sometimes conformist or even dangerous). And though my focus is on the individual, "the self," my interest is not in the notion of the individual that classic liberalism holds, a being whose rights and freedom must be protected against government intrusion. I understand the individual to be a being in the world with others, one whose own being is achieved through this relationship with others. This approach is closest to existential-phenomenology, as my central sources will make clear.[3]

Women are not completely enfranchised within most societies, but where and when possible they use domestic hospitality to empower themselves and enable themselves to live a fuller life. In the modern era and especially since the industrial revolution and the separation of home from workplace in Western nations, the production of hospitality has been the responsibility of the "woman of the house" primarily.[4] Beginning with Beauvoir's study of women under patriarchy in *The Second Sex* (1949) and continuing through manifestoes, position papers, articles and books from the 1960s to the present, the feminist movement has negatively critiqued women's traditional roles, including the hospitality role. These critiques were essential correctives to patriarchal thinking, and there is still much to be done in this regard to achieve justice for women. But it has taken feminists longer to understand and properly value, i.e., to critique in a positive fashion, how women's traditional roles have served and even empowered women within patriarchal culture. Feminist theory did self-correct during the 1980s in regard to the role of motherhood; that subject became the focus of several brilliant works of theory and many commentaries on them.[5] Works of feminist theory on food and cooking have been published in recent years also, indicating that we may be reaching the stage where woman as home-maker, cook, and host(ess) are rediscovered for feminism.[6] And in 1986, in *A Passion for Friends*, Janice Raymond pleaded for re-valuing female community and friendship, epitomized by women's religious communities in the European Middle Ages, as "a basis of feminist purpose, passion, and politics"; such female community and friendship can be related to domestic hospitality.[7]

Domestic hospitality is often is employed to honor significant dates: holidays, anniversaries, and other celebrations with family and friends. But as civilization, at least in the North, has moved beyond a subsistence economy, a host there may engage in it just as often for no specific reason, or she may create new reasons for celebration.[8] Domestic hospitality is usually deeply personal, even intimate, unlike the public hospitality of diplomacy, of immigration policies, or of the hospitality industry's world of hotels and restaurants; it is different also from the ancient "law of hospitality," an unwritten contract for extending hospitality to foreigners. It arises in interpersonal practice, but the reason it arises at all is because there is an attitude of openness across the threshold of one's home, a welcoming attitude toward guests into one's dwelling, one's space. This open attitude must already be in place in the host's manner of being in the world, in order for her to achieve domestic hospitality.

Gender in Ancient Hospitality Stories

The roots of hospitality are buried in the deepest past of the human race; we are both a social and socializing race, yet also a race prone to creating borders—both qualities necessary components of hospitality. Ancient forms of hospitality in religious and historical documents fall into the class of what I call "public hospitality," i.e., a formal type of hospitality which is an aspect of social and political life, and which has enabled tribes or peoples to interact, providing safety and succor for "foreigners," people unknown previously to the hosts. Two notable stories of this appear in Genesis: Abraham's and Lot's. Neither story fits my definition of domestic hospitality, even though the acts took place in their homes, for these were offers of hospitality made to strangers, albeit Abraham and Lot both believed the strangers to be God's envoys.

The first is a report of Abraham's hospitality to three male guests who appear at his tent door; he understands these to be angels, messengers of the Lord, and he invites them in, offering them rest, water, and food. Most summaries of this famous story don't include his wife Sarah's part in Abraham's hospitality. As a woman, Sarah would not have had the right to *offer* hospitality, but we learn that it was she who actually produced the food the guests ate: "Abraham hastened into the tent unto Sarah, and said, Make ready quickly three measures of fine meal, knead it, and make cakes upon the hearth."[9] Without Sarah's work to produce something edible for the strangers, Abraham's hospitality would have been paltry indeed. The second hospitality story, appearing shortly after Abraham's, reports on Lot's hospitality to two angels who appear in the streets of Sodom; he begs them repeatedly to enter his house and partake of his hospitality, and finally they do. When the Sodomites demand that Lot turn over his guests, even boasting that they would "abuse" them, rather than break the contract of hospitality he had offered them, Lot strikes a quintessentially patriarchal and evil bargain. He offers up his daughters instead; not breaking the hospitality contract, he remains a good host to his male guests, though becoming a horrific father to his daughters.[10] What the story shows is what anthropologists and feminist theorists like Luce Irigaray have claimed: women were/are used as a "legitimate" means of exchange between men. As Irigaray put it, "The trade that organizes patriarchal societies takes place exclusively among men. Women, signs, goods, currency, all pass from one man to another."[11]

The ancient cultures of Greece and Rome held hospitality in high regard also; the "law of hospitality" (*ius hospitii*), an unwritten but binding law regulating how strangers should be treated, carried social, political, cultural, and intercultural power. In the first lines of his history of Rome, Livy reports that the Trojan Aeneas, Rome's founder (according to one story), was spared from execution by the victorious Greeks at the end of the Trojan War because he enjoyed "*vetusti iure hospitii*" (long-standing claims of hospitality).[12] An important element of social and political life in ancient Greece and Rome, the law of hospitality (*ius hospitii*) is seen by some as a critical element in the creation of civilization itself, and a precursor to notions of "brotherhood" and the golden rule, as well as Christianity.[13] Michel Serres points out that Livy's opening lines on the founding of Rome contrast two crucially important laws: the law of war (*ius belli*) and the law of hospitality (*ius hospitii*)—hospitality and war, both methods of interaction with foreigners. Serres believes that in setting up a stark contrast between *the law of hospitality* and *the law of war*, Livy signals hospitality's unique power: *ius hospitii* versus *ius belli*.[14] Here is one translation of the passage: "It is generally agreed that . . . two, Aeneas and Antenor, were spared all *the penalties of war* . . . owing to long-standing *claims of hospitality* and because they had always advocated peace and the giving back of Helen" (i.e., to the Greeks, for "Helen of Troy" was not "of Troy"; she was Greek).[15] Functioning as a means of exchange between men, Helen of Troy is the paradigmatic example of what Irigaray meant by saying that women were *"the goods."* Virtually all relationships between foreigners and natives of a place, whether invoking the law of hospitality, as in ancient Greece and Rome, or not, were conducted male to male. Though women surely played a critical role in the home and family, they were seldom if ever given direct power; the "family" was ruled by men ("family" both in its narrow meaning of blood relations, and in its broader meaning of household, i.e., *familia* in Latin, *oikos* in Greek).[16]

The English word "hospitality" has an etymology murkier than most, derived as it is from interrelated yet seemingly conflicting root meanings. The original form is "host," a word first appearing in written English in 1303 (earlier than the 1375 appearance of "hospitality"), and defined in the *Oxford English Dictionary* as "a man who lodges and entertains another in his house: the correlative of *guest*"; the *OED* traces "host" from the Italian *oste*, which originated in the Latin *hospit-em (hospes)*, a word carrying a variety of meanings: host, guest, stranger, foreigner.[17] Other closely-related forms are *ghostis* (stranger, guest) and *hostis* (stranger, enemy).[18] "Hospitality" is defined in the *OED* as "the act or practice of being hospitable; the reception and entertainment of guests, visitors, or strangers, with liberality and goodwill."[19] As does the *OED*, a contemporary dictionary's definition of hospitality, "the solicitous entertainment of guests," connotes a range of positive activities: care, friendliness, sheltering, welcoming, kindness.[20] Yet buried in the roots of the word lies the other side of hospitality: wariness at the potential danger which the *xenos* (foreigner) represents, i.e., xenophobia, the fear of strangers, for hospitality, the welcoming of guests, certainly includes the possibility that those guests may be strangers, possibly even enemies intent on harming the host. Hospitality is risky.[21]

The classical scholar L. J. Bolchazy notes that in ancient Rome there was no distinction made between guest (*hostis*) and enemy (*hostis*), though there was, in fact, a separate word for stranger/foreigner: *peregrinus*. Some foreigners were accorded a specific "right of hospitality" when they visited foreign countries, based either on their own actions, on an agreement between two countries, or because the right had been inherited from someone else.[22] But these travelers to foreign lands would most likely be males, not females. Bolchazy teases out seven categories within the so-called "law of hospitality" in ancient Rome, some expressing fear of, or the need to be separate from, foreigners.[23] But all refer to relationships with *strangers or foreigners*, not with members of one's own family or friendship group. What I call "domestic hospitality," however, is practiced by a host toward guests that are, for the most part, known to the host or, if not known prior to their entrance into the house, were invited voluntarily into it by the host.

The notion of international hospitality currently appearing in works of social and political theory, and being used to defend liberal immigration policies, including open borders, is a form of "public hospitality," the progeny of the ancient law of hospitality we read about in Genesis, Livy, and elsewhere; this *ius hospitii* is also akin to contemporary notions of international diplomacy. Valuable though it is, however, it cannot be equated with domestic hospitality; the former is hospitality defined as a set of laws (written or unwritten), practices, or public policies regulating interactions between strangers, i.e., foreigners. It should be clear that there is no contradiction between supporting liberal immigration policies, i.e., a progressive public hospitality, yet insisting on a radical, even essential, difference between public and private hospitality.

In the modern and post-modern era (i.e., industrial to present), the private form of hospitality has been under the purview of women for the most part, in heterosexual families or homes, providing them with one of their most empowering roles. In *Of Hospitality*, Jacques Derrida remarks that the "foreigner" in a sense disrupts local patriarchal power, "shakes up the dogmatism of the paternal *logos* . . . contesting the authority of the chief, the father . . . the 'master of the house.'"[24] His insight allows us to see how a guest may undermine patriarchy in some ways, but this reading of the power of the visiting stranger depicts public hospitality, the impersonal hospitality offered to strangers by strangers, much more common in times past, i.e., eras without postal services, telephones, or even organized societies. By contrast, domestic hospitality is offered by a host across the "border" of her own home to guests she has specifically invited (for the most part), people she welcomes into a place that is an extension of her self.

Celebration, Home, and Community

Hospitality has two faces, but it also has more than one dimension. Within it reside celebration, friendship, and community, elements that some, most notably the Epicureans, have argued are essential to living the good and pleasant life. To them happiness consisted in the joy produced in common (shared) pleasure: eating, drinking, sex, and friendship—what Jennifer Hecht labels "graceful life philosophy," in her offbeat cultural history, *The Happiness Myth*.[25] Domestic hospitality cannot be understood without seeing its place in the ongoing creation of a graceful life.[26] Patriarchal notions of gender roles may have constrained greatly women's ability to live such a life, but even in thoroughly patriarchal cultures like that of ancient Athens, where men ran the polis and held all economic and political power, and where women were confined to female quarters, women claimed a strong presence in many traditional celebrations. Hecht notes that women were central to the Greek festivals—and not only those identified specifically with women, such as the Thesmophoria. Originally, the Dionysian festival was restricted to women; one can see then why Hecht claims that "democracy was male; festival was female."[27]

Women's strong connection to celebration has continued and is embedded heavily in domestic hospitality; through celebratory activities that fall under domestic hospitality (i.e., not cultural, national, or religious festivals but idiosyncratic friendship "festivals" of varying sorts), women create friendship communities of both support and celebration. And new opportunities for community-building continually arise through the combination of friendship and domestic hospitality, for it often provides the foundation in which friendship develops and deepens. Hecht lavishly praises friendship and its frequent companion, the sharing of meals, and considers these necessary to survival, and she quotes Epicurus in support of this: "Of all the things that wisdom provides to help one live one's entire life in happiness, the greatest by far is the possession of friendship. Before you eat or drink anything, consider carefully whom you eat or drink with . . . not eating with a friend is the life of a lion or a wolf."[28]

Making a Home, a Self, a Community: Heidegger, Beauvoir, Young

Usually considered a paradigmatic exercise in generosity, domestic hospitality is also an important mode for the self-definition of the host through the sharing of her dwelling. As the host welcomes the guest into her home, she also indicates a proprietary border: "This place is mine and I welcome you to share it." So while willingly dissolving the border temporarily to share it, the host also affirms the existence of the border. An aggressive or self-inviting guest creates serious problems, problems not connected to the rights of property ownership but rather to this sense of self the host develops through her hospitality, a gift that must always be offered, never demanded. Derrida expresses perfectly the fear that results: "Anyone who encroaches on my 'at home,' on my ipseity, on my power of hospitality, on my sovereignty as host, I start to regard as an undesirable foreigner, and virtually as an enemy. This other becomes a hostile subject, and I resist becoming their hostage."[29]

In her essay "House and Home," Iris Marion Young took up the existential dimensions of domesticity by examining a number of theoretical discussions on home, from Heidegger's discussion of building and dwelling to twentieth-century feminist examinations (mostly rejections) of home and housework.[30] Young's comprehensive and provocative essay includes a study of Beauvoir's critique of housework, Irigaray's critique of male nostalgia for home and mother, and bell hooks' more positive reading of home as a place affording human beings the opportunity both to craft a material identity for themselves, and to provide themselves with safety.[31]

In "Building Dwelling Thinking," Heidegger asserted that the human being is a *dweller*, and because of that, s/he is a *builder*. But he makes a distinction between building as *constructing* (the raising of edifices) and building as *cultivating* (preservation, the care and nurturing of the earth and things that grow upon it).[32] Young critiques Heidegger's over-attention to building as constructing, a more male-identified activity than cultivating; she points out that, while he begins with the broader notion of building, he narrows it to focus on building as constructing: "Despite his claim that these moments are equally important, Heidegger nevertheless seems to privilege building as the world-founding of an active subject, and . . . this privileging is male-biased."[33] I found, on a rereading of "Building Dwelling Thinking," that while Heidegger's use of examples is tilted toward the building of edifices and other "built things," e.g., bridges, he still maintains the importance of both aspects of *bauen* (building): "the manner in which we humans are on the earth, is *Bauen*, dwelling . . . the old word *bauen*, which says that man *is* insofar as he *dwells* . . . *also* means . . . to cherish and protect, to preserve and care for, specifically to till the soil, to cultivate the vine. . . . building in the sense of preserving and nurturing is not making anything."[34] He adds this remark as well: "Cultivating and construction are building in the narrower sense. *Dwelling*, insofar as it keeps or secures the fourfold (earth and sky, divinities and mortals) in things is, as this keeping, a *building*."[35] So while Heidegger seems to emphasize the primacy of "building as constructing," he also insists that both types of building are important. His original German term for "dwelling" is *Wohnen*, which the noted Heidegger scholar and translator David Farrell Krell explains in this way: "to reside or stay, to dwell at peace, to be content . . . it is also related to words that mean to grow accustomed to, or feel at home in, a place . . . also tied to . . . 'delight,' *Wonne*; for Heidegger *to dwell* signified the way 'we human beings are on the earth.'"[36] English-speakers know that in English "building" can be used for broader, even ontological, activities (as in "building a good life" or "building a database"); it can be used as a noun (a building, an edifice), and also a verb (the constructing of a building). This is true in German also.

Domestic hospitality is a specific form of cultivation and nurturing that creates community, which not all cultivation, not all "dwelling/building," does. Through the act of domestic hospitality, one can create a community of the event, or a community of one night, or a community produced over a series of nights. One current example is the popular American phenomenon of book clubs; these clubs are primarily female, and meetings are hosted by one of the club members. When the host opens the door to her guests, she creates a community and also preserves (or resurrects) an already existing community, a society created specifically for the reading of books in common. As she opens the door, members are not only welcomed to a new "community of one night"; they are also reminded of their shared history as a community of those other nights they met, a community revived by the host's welcoming presence at the door.

There are two necessary elements to achieving domestic hospitality: place (location) and attitude. For women, that place, the home, is invested with patriarchal definitions and demands based in narrow, restricted views of women's capabilities and interests, views which can bind them to "woman's role," so that any subjective choices an individual makes to create *her* home, reflecting her self and empowering her as a subject, could be trivialized or rendered invisible, disappearing under the umbrella of "family" home, i.e., home of the proper (paternal) name, created and maintained by the woman, the "other" (Simone de Beauvoir's name for woman under patriarchy). It was this insight that provoked Beauvoir's groundbreaking discussion of woman's role in the home in *The Sec-*

ond Sex.[37] Women under patriarchy have been confined to a life of routine, never-ending toil, lack of appreciation, and lack of creativity. Beauvoir described domestic chores as repetitive, illogical, and without merit in and of themselves; they merely ("merely"?) reproduce and maintain the means needed for the continuation of the life of the human being. Defending the use of the home for the creation of an empowered female self is still fraught with difficulty and must be done with care.

Young agreed with Beauvoir that much of women's life in the home does involve "merely instrumental (actions) not invested with creativity or individuality" (changing diapers, sweeping floors), actions equated with the world of immanence (the being of things) rather than transcendence (the being of the human subject which chooses and creates itself). But there is another dimension to housework, Young noted: homemaking.[38] And what is homemaking, after all, but making a home? One creates a visible space that *materializes* one's self, that embodies a form of self identity. This process of materialization involves not only the collection, possession, and use of my belongings in my space, but also the process of their "sedimentation," for many of the things in one's home are invested with meaning and express the events and relationships of one's life.[39] This materialization reflects not only the values I espouse, but the significant events of my life.[40] In attending to these two aspects of homemaking—materialization and sedimentation, Iris Young created an elaboration of Heidegger's notion of "dwelling" that Heidegger never saw, while also critiquing and further developing Beauvoir's analysis of housework.

Making and Sharing Meals: Beauvoir's Kitchen and Mine

Achieving domestic hospitality without including at least the consumption of food and/or drink, or its offering to one's guests—deeds which usually also include the preparation of food—may be possible but would be difficult. The sharing of our material goods with others, a kind of socialism of the moment, is a necessary element of hospitality. And offering one's guests only what is easy and free is, at least in some cultures, not hospitality at all. My great-aunt Josephine, steeped in the food traditions of Italy's Abruzzo-Molise region, her birthplace, but living out her days in a mining town in western Pennsylvania, was offended once by her country neighbor's offer of a glass of water during a visit; to be offered water by one's host was offensive, a perfect example of the worst aspects of *Americani*.

Though Young's essay stopped short of a discussion of Beauvoir's ideas on cooking, I think that in Beauvoir's analysis of woman's life in the kitchen, as in her ideas about homemaking, Beauvoir was shortsighted and mistaken. (For this we may forgive her; she virtually never cooked.) In that place I call "Beauvoir's Kitchen" (i.e., in the discussion of cooking that appears in *The Second Sex*), women cooks are passive. Never exercising their creativity, they are the simple servants of two masters: patriarchy and the physical universe: "Each day the kitchen also teaches (woman) patience and passivity; here is alchemy; one must obey the fire, the water, wait for the sugar to melt, for the dough to rise . . . A syllogism is of no help in making a successful mayonnaise . . . masculine reasoning is quite inadequate to the reality with which (woman) deals."[41] While this passage may describe the experience of women who know little about cooking, it is an inaccurate description of many casual cooks and all *thoughtful* cooks. An experienced cook, like a scientist, understands cause and effect relations among ingredients, temperature, and time (though mistakes still may occur); the cook takes account of these causal relations, respects them as elements of the physical universe, and works within them, while also making choices: which dishes to prepare; which recipes to use; when to start the process; where to procure quality ingredients, etc., in order to make the process as much of what she intends as possible, within the physical world, a world whose limits define *all* human actions—e.g., driving a car, gardening, hiking, building bridges, etc., not only actions within the home. And Beauvoir was mistaken: a syllogism *does* help one make a mayonnaise, though most cookbooks don't complete the full syllogism in each recipe unfortunately, which is why cooking experience, including the knowledge of how foods interact, is so important. Amateur cooks ignore this at their peril, and bad cookbooks exclude too much of it. For *if* one uses the right ingredients, *if* one employs them in the correct proportions; *if* one blends them in the right order and at the right speed, *then* the blending will work and voila!—a mayonnaise appears.

The host's choices of food and her offering of it to her guests are extensions of domestic hospitality; through this and through other behavior, domestic hospitality happens. Even if she doesn't cook the food herself, she nevertheless makes choices through the selection of food she buys. Self identity is created as well ("have you tasted *my* coconut cake?"), and community is achieved at the same time, in one of the human race's oldest and most basic practices: the sharing of food: "Abraham . . . (said) unto Sarah, Make ready quickly three measures of fine meal, knead it, and make cakes upon the hearth."[42] Not merely a place filled with material things, even those inscribed with the sedimented meaning of the home's owner, a home is a place from which I choose to utilize those material things to interact with the larger world, a place where my values are lived out, extended out from the home into the world, as I create connections with others.

Hospitality and the Other: Levinas

There are strong connections between the home, the feminine/woman, hospitality, and generosity in the philosophy of Emmanuel Levinas.[43] The home, hospitality, and "the feminine" are significant aspects of Levinas's philosophy and his rejection of Heideggerian ontology, a system he calls a "Philosophy of the Neuter."[44] Levinas's discussion of the feminine is not unproblematic by any means, yet it does offer fruitful and largely unexplored paths for the discussion of domestic hospitality. Marked by the centrality of the relation of Self and

Other, his thought is deeply and purposively non-Hegelian and non-Heideggerian.[45] Levinas's "Other" is not the Hegelian Other (i.e., the negation of the Same). Nor is it the Beauvoirian Woman/Other, similar to the Hegelian Other (i.e., the negation of the Same). Beauvoir asserted that the "Same" or the "Essential" is male, and the Other is female; woman is the non-Essential within patriarchy. But Levinas's Other is the "absolute Other," actually the "master" of the self, a being radically different than the self and whose radical difference, defined as *alterity*—radical separateness—must be respected. In this analysis, generosity toward the Other, the one who is always "my master," is a fundamental quality of the ethical life.

Like that of Carol Gilligan, Julia Kristeva, and especially Luce Irigaray, in some respects Levinas's thought is identifiable as what American feminist theorists call "difference theory"; it claims the existence of a specific type of being (either of nature or nurture): "the feminine."[46] Beauvoir criticized Levinas for his notion of "the feminine," singling out his remark that "the feminine" was "a term of the same rank as consciousness but of opposite meaning."[47] Many feminist critiques of his notion of "the feminine" have been published since Beauvoir's, but there also have been defenses of him by feminist thinkers as important as Irigaray. The most serious objection is that he seems to exclude "the feminine" from full participation in ethical relations, asserting it is part of a relation of the "intimate Other" (the feminine presence in the home) to the absolute Other, though he does not equate it to a specific gender.[48] His ideas on "the feminine" are not easily understood nor categorized, and the controversy continues to the present. Levinas attempted to explain, even apologize for, some of his remarks about "the feminine" or "woman," since it became obvious they were continuing to receive negative commentary as feminist philosophy developed through the 1970s to the present.[49] One recent example (in an article published after his death) is Stella Sandford's remark that Levinas's notion of woman is "gratingly patriarchal," insofar as he claims woman is the "welcomer" and therefore the condition for another's "recollection" in the peace of the home, and that she is the "condition" for the ethical but is not part of it, since her relation is that of the "intimate Other," and not "Absolute Other."[50]

Levinas claimed consistently that "the feminine" did not refer to the empirical female, but rather was the term he chose to identify with a certain kind of presence, and that "the empirical absence of the human being of 'feminine sex' in a dwelling nowise affects the dimension of femininity which remains open there, as the very welcome of the dwelling."[51] Try as he might, his attempt at separating "the feminine" from "women" has not been convincing to many feminist thinkers. By contrast, Julia Kristeva's notion of "the semiotic" manages to avoid this problem and is an example of how a thinker successfully achieved such a separation, perhaps because she used a term not already loaded with contemporary meaning. "The semiotic" or "the semiotic *chora*" are Kristeva's terms for "the maternal" in poetic language, and that includes a list of qualities some feminists might find offensive: "A *chora*, receptacle, unnamable, improbable, hybrid, anterior to naming, to the One, to the father, and consequently, maternally connoted to such an extent that it merits 'not even the rank of syllable' . . . This signifying disposition . . . I have just named semiotic . . . (is) definitely heterogeneous to meaning but always in sight of it or in either a negative or surplus relationship to it."[52]

It is also important to remember that Beauvoir's analysis of woman relied on subject/object, self/other, dichotomies Hegel developed in *Phenomenology of Spirit*, ideas criticized repeatedly by Levinas, and also now the subject of feminist critiques, i.e., due to passages like this: "Things become clear if, following Hegel, we find in consciousness itself a fundamental hostility toward every other consciousness; the subject can be posed only in being opposed."[53] But ultimately this is irrelevant, since Beauvoir's Other and Hegel's Other are not Levinas's Other. And since Levinas rejected the notion that "feminine" means the presence of someone of a specific empirical manifestation or anatomy, i.e., a member of the "female sex," at least he should be credited with this, as Gilligan and other feminist theorists have been.[54]

One can use what is helpful in Levinas's thought about the home, the feminine, and hospitality, yet not accept all that he says about "woman," "the feminine," or the "intimate Other." In some places, his thought is underdeveloped and even sexist, but it reflects a serious attempt to give women's work its due, long before the feminist movement of the late twentieth century began. I take him at his word that he used "the feminine" to name a quality of existence that was radically different, not different in an ordinary way. His thinking on this resembles the conclusion reached by Carol Gilligan years later through her psychological research: there are two moral "voices"—one associated with women and one with men. Women's "voice" attends to responsibility and attachment, men's voice to rights and independence. Yet because these two voices are "modes of thought," not biological facts, they can appear in either gender; they are "characterized not by gender but theme," she says.[55]

For Levinas, the home is a place of intimacy, supporting and enabling us to move beyond it, while also localizing our generosity. "Woman" or "the feminine" is a presence that dwells in the home; it is "feminine alterity," where "alterity" indicates separation, i.e., exteriority: the quality of all ethical relationships to the Other, the absolute and radically different Other. Through the feminine, says Levinas, "separation is constituted as dwelling."[56] The feminine is the "intimate Other," which faces the (Absolute) Other, providing a welcoming presence to it, through the dwelling: "the Other who welcomes me in the home (is) the presence of the Feminine."[57] (And though he said the absence of a person of female anatomy in the home does not change the notion of "the feminine" as the welcoming presence in the dwelling, given the transgender sexuality theories developed from the 1990s to the present, we would now insist that terms like "female anatomy" be discussed more carefully).[58]

For Levinas, through the relation with the Other, specifically in generosity, the self comes into being, achieves reality as a human being and thereby also achieves morality: "It is only in approaching the Other that I attend to myself," he says, for in the "face to face" ethical relation, two things happen. First, I engage in language and expose myself to the questioning of the Other, so that I respond. That is, I become "responsible" literally; I am charged with making a "response." Understanding language in this enriched way, Levinas then claims famously: "the essence of language is friendship and hospitality" (Derrida uses this claim later in his discussion of hospitality).[59] Second, in approaching the Other I am attentive to the Other, as Other—i.e., not as the "like me" nor as its opposite (the negation of the Same), but as the "radically different than me,"[60] a being truly exterior, truly separate from me. This activity of attentiveness is hospitality, the welcome of the Other; it is not love nor the result of love, as might be assumed, but the result of generosity—of "service and hospitality," for in hospitality, understanding the being of the Other to be radically separate, I come to understand myself as well: "Speech is . . . instituted in . . . a world where it is necessary to aid and to give. It presupposes an I, an existence separated in its enjoyment, which does not welcome empty-handed the face and its voice coming from another shore."[61] Only a self, an I, is capable of this act, of responding to a face.[62]

Levinas's conception of the home is uncluttered by notions of ownership; the home is the place from which one practices hospitality, concretely realizes it. A home is not an object, a possession for which I strive, but is rather the place *from which* I begin my interactions with others, as I move from its intimacy out into the world. The home is "mine," but it is not an object I possess; if I treat it as object or property, its real being is forfeited.[63] My home allows me to create a world in common, a community, through my welcome and through my language, those ways in which I approach the other responsibly. In the home's intimacy I dwell, separated from the Other and aware of her/his radical Otherness. Far from being a disruption of its "private" nature, the welcome of others into my home is necessary to it: "the possibility for the home to open to the Other is as essential to (its) essence as closed doors and windows."[64] Profoundly unproprietary, my relation to my home is defined by the fact that it is a location; without a location, there is no "face to face," no ethics: "No face can be approached with empty hands and closed home. Recollection in a home open to the Other—hospitality—is the concrete and initial fact of human recollection and separation . . . The chosen home is the very opposite of a root."[65]

Heidegger claimed that death is "my ownmost possibility," in that it individualizes Dasein (human being). But more important to my life than the certainty of my death, a knowledge that undoubtedly affects my life, is *how* I live. Through my home and my actions there, more than my awareness of my ever-imminent death, I sense "my ownmost possibility," because the home individualizes the self. Through my hospitable presence in my home, I both acknowledge the radical separation between myself and the Other, and also engage with the Other "responsibly" in the response which is language, in *my* response, and in the service I give—*my* generosity, *my* hospitality. My engaged presence in my home, my response to the Other through language and service, humanizes me by providing a location from which the humanizing act of generosity can take place: the face to face, the self's relation to the Other, its master.

Hospitality's Antinomy: Derrida

What should be involved in acts of hospitable generosity, and should there be any limits? Jacques Derrida used an antinomy to investigate these questions about hospitality. Most notably used by Kant, "antinomy" refers to the existence of two contradictory propositions, a thesis and antithesis, both of which can be supported through valid arguments.[66] In *Of Hospitality*, Derrida claims that an insoluble antinomy arises within hospitality between its two *laws*: 1) the general, overarching, unconditional law of hospitality: *hospitality must be unlimited and infinite*; 2) the plurality of laws of hospitality, *its specific rights and duties, which are always limited and conditional*.[67] Still using a Kantian framework, but moving from Kant's metaphysics to his ethics, Derrida next claims that hospitality's overarching, unlimited law is a *categorical imperative* of hospitality, "the unique and singular and absolutely only great Law of hospitality, *the* law of hospitality."[68]

In later reflections captured in the post-9/11 publication, *Philosophy in a Time of Terror*, attempting to understand the challenges of globalization "in a time of terror," Derrida returned to Kantian ethical theory to discuss hospitality. Still using the antinomy that hospitality must not only be total and unconditional but must also take place through specific and limited actions, here he also claims pure hospitality cannot be done out of duty but rather is a gift. As a gift, it exceeds duty, i.e., the kind of duty espoused in Kantian ethics as the ultimate moral intention: "We must be dutiful beyond duty, we must go beyond law, tolerance, conditional hospitality, economy . . . (yet) to go beyond does not mean to discredit that which we exceed," Derrida says.[69] Yet that is precisely what his analysis does: it discredits the laws and limits of hospitality in two connected ways: first, it repeatedly subordinates conditional hospitality to unconditional hospitality; second, it ignores domestic hospitality for what I have called "public" hospitality. There is virtually no discussion of domestic hospitality in either of these two works. In *Of Hospitality*, it appears only in the context of the ancient stories of hospitality that are (as I discussed), proto-forms of public or societal hospitality, the sphere of men, so Derrida's analysis of hospitality is male-centered. Near the end of the text, he even critiques the basis upon which he selected his examples, saying it was "a conjugal model, paternal and phallogocentric (where) the familial despot, the father, the spouse, and the boss, the master of the house . . . lays down the laws of hospitality . . . represents them, submits to them, to submit the others to them in this violence of the power of hospitality."[70] But why use only the phallogocentric if one wants to escape it?

In *Philosophy in a Time of Terror*, Derrida once again splits hospitality into two kinds, echoing his analysis of the antinomy of hospitality: a hospitality of visitation (unconditional welcoming whoever arrives at one's door), and a hospitality of invitation (conditional welcoming of those who are invited).[71] He claims that a hospitality of visitation is the most authentic kind, because it poses no limits, makes no conditions, and always involves risks, whereas a hospitality of invitation sets limits (e.g., a guest list, a time and place, and perhaps even a purpose for the event): "Pure and unconditional hospitality, hospitality *itself*, opens or is in advance open to someone who is neither expected nor invited, to whomever arrives as an absolutely foreign *visitor*, as a new *arrival*, nonidentifiable and unforeseeable, in short, wholly other . . . (this is) a hospitality of *visitation* rather than *invitation*."[72] In this later assertion, he seems to be arguing that there is *no* antinomy, or only an apparent one, because in fact there is only one authentic hospitality. *Pure* hospitality is the hospitality of visitation, a welcoming offered to anyone who appears at the threshold at any time, whether that be the threshold of one's home or one's country. But in an effort to humanize and respect the guest, invited or not, under any circumstances, Derrida sacrifices the host, placing impossible demands on her, which he acknowledges: "An unconditional hospitality is . . . practically impossible to live; one cannot in any case, and by definition, organize it."[73] While we might find the notion of unconditional hospitality useful toward achieving the goals of cosmopolitanism and the ending of state sovereignty, for the home it would be unworkable. But his analysis overlooks the home and the host's (the woman's) role in the home, that home being an extension of herself, the person whose identity is to some extent connected deeply with the materiality of the home and its sedimented meanings. In Derrida's analysis, the host is truly "hostage" to the guest (a possibility he warned of, in *Of Hospitality*). The host's desires, motivations, and even inclinations are ignored; she is surrendered up to the guest. In his effort to give infinite respect to the guest through positing unconditional hospitality as the essence and goal of hospitable behavior, Derrida has failed to respect the host. He has defined hospitality so that it resembles Christian charity, with its obligatory demand of love, even though he specifically denies that hospitality is a form of charity.[74]

Derrida's claim that the host has no right to limit the use of the home and to claim it as her own is a serious problem for domestic hospitality, for one's generosity in welcoming the other into one's home is always accompanied by the sense that the guest should leave at some point; otherwise, host becomes hostage. In *Of Hospitality*, he acknowledged that hospitality is bound to personal actions and ethics, an indication that he understands there would be problems in opening one's own space unconditionally: "It is always about answering for a dwelling place, for one's identity, one's space, one's limits, for the *ethos* as abode, habitation, house, hearth, family, home."[75] In this remark, with its Levinasian echoes, Derrida indirectly affirms that being hospitable to any and all arriving at one's door would be not simply impractical; it also would be a depersonalized form of hospitality—and so, probably not hospitality at all.

Conclusion

I have argued that hospitality is a complex topic that includes at least two basic forms, domestic and public; that the distinction between the two types is important; and that domestic hospitality deserves a significant place in the contemporary discourse on hospitality. Domestic hospitality is the hospitality of the home practiced by the individual toward friends or acquaintances. Public hospitality is the welcome afforded to strangers or foreigners, and connected to ancient and largely unwritten laws of hospitality; many of the most significant events of these laws have been recorded in ancient texts and appear to be the forerunner to those agreements between nations we now call "diplomacy." Theorists asserting that a claim for international (or "global") hospitality is the basis for the humane treatment of immigrants and foreigners muddy the waters by not acknowledging that international hospitality is a form of public, not domestic, hospitality.

Understanding domestic hospitality from a feminist standpoint has been burdened with the important concern that, in valuing and re-valuing an activity traditionally identified with women, feminist theorists may encourage women to adopt traditional roles, leading again to the confinement of women in those roles. All feminist discussions of "women's culture" have faced this same problem. Iris Young made significant progress toward a feminist materialist interpretation of domesticity, namely homemaking, in her essay "House and Home." In it she used but also critiqued Heidegger's notion of dwelling and Beauvoir's notion of housekeeping. I have argued that we must append to Young's analysis of the home a further elaboration of the Heideggerian notion of dwelling and a feminist examination of the domestic task of meal preparation—cooking—not only to further assess Beauvoir's understanding of women's situation in the home, but because of the central role in domestic hospitality that both the cooking of meals and the sharing of them with guests play. But an additional and important dimension of homemaking and its virtue, domestic hospitality, is that when one offers to share one's home, one is sharing a deeply personal creation which is an extension of one's self and what, in Heideggerian language (and in opposition to his notion of being-toward-death), might be called "my ownmost possibility." Further, I claimed that one must include in discussions of domestic hospitality the dimension of celebration and the enjoyment of the good life which shared meals and all forms of domestic hospitality promote, since through these activities, friendship is encouraged and community is created. Domestic hospitality is not the sole way friendship and community are produced, but it is one of the most important ways, and we must begin to value it for these reasons.

I next argued that the content and limits of hospitality are imaginatively scrutinized by both Emmanuel Levinas and Jacques Derrida. Levinas's non-Heideggerian philosophy of the Other makes the claim that the only ethical relation is the face-to-face, through which one "responsibly" engages with and "responds" to the Other, i.e., the absolute and alterior Other. Though I and the Other are infinitely different, though what defines us is our "exteriority," we meet through the related phenomena of language, hospitality, and generosity. Levinas's thought allows us to complete our understanding of homemaking and domestic hospitality. I welcome the Other to my home, a metaphysical and non-proprietary dimension of my existence, an aspect of my being, not a form of property. Finally, I argued that Derrida's philosophy of hospitality, presented in two texts, including his assertion that two contradictory forms of it exist—unconditional and conditional—virtually ignores domestic hospitality, and when he notices it, he demands of it impractical and unrealizable tasks.

Domestic hospitality has been a significant factor in humanity's story, but like so many other aspects of the human story to which women's contributions have been central, it disappeared under the mantle of patriarchy. I'm hopeful that feminist theory is now ready and able to invite domestic hospitality into the feminist fold.

Notes

1. This paper was inspired by Iris Marion Young's essay, "House and Home: Feminist Variations on a Theme," in her book *Intersecting Voices* (Princeton, NJ: Princeton University Press, 1997), 134-64. Young's untimely death in 2006 deeply saddened her friends, colleagues, and the many people, near and far, who valued her work. Philosophy lost one of its liveliest and most brilliant voices. Social justice lost one of its champions.

2. See Marilyn Friedman, "Feminism and Modern Friendship," in *Applied Social and Political Philosophy*, ed. Elizabeth Smith and H. Gene Blocker (Englewood Cliffs, NJ: Prentice Hall, 1994), 233-40.

3. Communitarianism critiques classic liberalism's emphasis on the self in favor of an "anti-atomistic" emphasis on the community, claiming that liberalism has overlooked its importance. Some proponents of this view are Charles Taylor, Alasdair MacIntyre, Amitai Etzioni, Michael Sandel, and Michael Walzer. See Daniel A. Bell, "Communitarianism," Stanford Encyclopedia of Philosophy, http://plato.stanford.edu/entries/communitarianism/#PolCom (accessed May 20, 2009). For a fascinating anti-communitarian study of American civic organization, see Theda Skocpol, *Diminished Democracy: From Membership to Management in American Civic Life* (Norman, OK: University of Oklahoma Press, 2003).

4. If one used Thorstein Veblen's class analysis in his 1899 work, *The Theory of the Leisure Class*, hospitality would be seen as merely a function of the "conspicuous consumption" of women of "the leisure class," used to further their husband's power, the work of it being performed primarily by their servants.

5. Important works of feminist theory on motherhood of the late 1970s and 1980s include Nancy Chodorow's *The Reproduction of Mothering*, Adrienne Rich's *Of Woman Born: Motherhood as Experience and Institution*, and Mary O'Brien's *The Politics of Reproduction*.

6. *Cooking, Eating, Thinking: Transformative Philosophies of Food*, ed. Deane W. Curtin and Lisa M. Heldke (Bloomington, IN Indiana University Press, 1992) was one of the first of this type.

7. Janice Raymond, *A Passion for Friends: Toward a Philosophy of Female Affection*, (Boston: Beacon Press, 1986), 9.

8. I will use female pronouns or adjectives to refer to "host" and will not use the term "hostess," since I believe it both carries the stigma of being a diminutive and also has many traditional connotations within American society.

9. Genesis 18:1-6 and 19:1-8.

10. Both stories are quoted in Jacques Derrida *Of Hospitality: Anne Dufourmontelle Invites Jacques Derrida to Respond*, trans. Rachel Bowlby (Stanford, CA: Stanford University Press, 2000), 151-53. (The book replicates two lectures from Derrida's Paris Seminars of 1996.) The daughters were not acceptable substitutes, and what resulted from the incident was extreme: the destruction of Sodom and Gomorrah, the turning of Lot's wife into a pillar of salt, and the incestuous choice by his daughters to mate with him, to preserve his line.

11. Luce Irigaray, "When the Goods Get Together," (*Des marchandises entre elles*"), trans. Claudia Reeder (selection from *Ce sexe qui n'en est pas un*), *New French Feminisms: An Anthology*, ed. Elaine Marks and Isabelle de Courtivron (Amherst, MA: University of Massachusetts Press, 1980), 107.

12. Ladislaus J. Bolchazy, *Hospitality in Antiquity: Livy's Concept of Its Humanizing Force* (Chicago: Ares Publishers Inc., 1995; rev. ed. of 1977), i. Here is one translation of this passage in Livy's *History of Rome* (*Ab Urbe Condita*): "To begin with, it is generally admitted that after the capture of Troy, whilst the rest of the Trojans were massacred, against two of them—Aeneas and Antenor—the Achivi refused to exercise the rights of war, partly owing to old ties of hospitality." Titus Livius, *Ab Urbe Condita, Liber I*, trans. Rev. Canon Roberts, http://la.wikisource.org/wiki/Ab_Urbe_Condita/liber_I?match=en Wiki (accessed April 1, 2009). In another translation, the word "hospitality" disappears: "It is generally accept that after the fall of Troy the Greeks kept up hostilities against all the Trojans except Aeneas and Antenor. These two mean had worked consistently for peace and the restoration of Helen, and for that reason, added to certain personal connections of long standing, they were allowed to go unmolested." Livy, *The Early History of Rome*, trans. Aubrey de Sélincourt (London: Penguin Books Ltd., 1960), 31.

13. Bolchazy, *Hospitality in Antiquity*, i, and passim.

14. Michel Serres, *Rome: the Book of Foundations*, trans. Felicia McCarren (Stanford, CA: Stanford University Press, 1991), 139.

15. Serres, *Rome,* 139. Bolchazy quotes the whole passage: "Aeneae Antenorique, et vetusti *iure hospitii* et quia pacis reddendaeque Helenae sempter auctores fuerant, omne *ius belli* Achivos Abstinuisse." Bolchazy, *Hospitality in Antiquity*, 67-8, and n. 1 (emphasis added).

16. *Sexuality and Gender in the Classical World*, ed., Laura K. McClure (Oxford, UK: Blackwell, 2002), is just one work containing research on women's restricted role in the classical world. The word "domestic" is derived from the Latin "domus," house; "dominus" means "lord or master of the house," a term that, in Roman Catholic liturgy, is used for the Lord, i.e., God.

17. "host, *n.2*," *The Oxford English Dictionary*, 2nd ed., 1989, *OED Online*, Oxford University Press. http://dictionary.oed.com/ (accessed January 9, 2010).

18. *Webster's New World Dictionary of the American Language, Second College Edition* (New York: Prentice Hall Press, 1986).

19. "hospitality," *The Oxford English Dictionary*, 2nd ed., 1989, *OED Online*, Oxford University Press. http://dictionary.oed.com/ (accessed January 9, 2010).

20. *Webster's New World.*

21. "Hospitality" is related to two other words also, of later origin "hospice," a place of shelter, and "hospital," a place of care for the ill or infirm.

22. Bolchazy, *Hospitality in Antiquity*, 25. He relies on Cicero for some of this.

23. Bolchazy, *Hospitality in Antiquity*, 21.

24. Derrida, *Of Hospitality*, 5.

25. Jennifer Michael Hecht, *The Happiness Myth: the Historical Antidote to What Isn't Working Today* (New York: HarperCollins, 2007), 35.

26. Hecht, *The Happiness Myth*, 24.

27. Hecht, *The Happiness Myth*, 257-65.

28. Hecht, *The Happiness Myth*, 181.

29. Derrida, *Of Hospitality*, 53-55.

30. Iris Marion Young, "House and Home: Feminist Variations on a Theme," in Iris Marion Young, *Intersecting Voices: Dilemmas of Gender, Political Philosophy, and Policy* (Princeton N.J.: Princeton University Press), 1997.

31. Young, "House and Home: Feminist Variations on a Theme," 159, but also see the whole section, "Women as Nostalgic Home," 138-64.

32. Martin Heidegger, "Building Dwelling Thinking" (trans. of *"Bauen Wohnen Denken"*), in Martin Heidegger, *Poetry, Language, Thought*, trans. Albert Hofstadter (New York: Harper & Row, 1971), 147.

33. Young, "House and Home: Feminist Variations on a Theme," 134, and see 183, n.2.

34. Heidegger, "Building Dwelling Thinking," 147.

35. Heidegger, "Building Dwelling Thinking," 151, and see also 152.

36. David Farrell Krell, Introduction to "Building Dwelling Thinking" in Martin Heidegger, *Martin Heidegger: Basic Writings*, ed. David Farrell Krell (New York: Harper and Row, 1977), 321-22.

37. Simone de Beauvoir, *The Second Sex*, trans. H.M. Parshley (New York: Vintage Books, 1989). See especially Part V: "Situation," Chapters XVI, XVII, XVIII, and XXI in the English edition.

38. Young, "House and Home: Feminist Variations on a Theme," 147-49.

39. Young, "House and Home: Feminist Variations on a Theme," 149-51.

40. Young, "House and Home: Feminist Variations on a Theme," 149. Young incorporated ideas on home from D.J.Van Lennep and Edward Casey in this section of her essay.

41. Beauvoir, *The Second Sex*, 598-99.

42. See note 2.

43. Emmanuel Levinas (1906-1995) was a Lithuanian who became a French citizen in 1930; he wrote in French.

44. Emmanuel Levinas, *Totality and Infinity: An Essay on Exteriority*, trans. Alphonso Lingis (Pittsburgh, PA: Duquesne University Press, 1969), 298.

45. Levinas, *Totality and Infinity*, see the Preface and Section I especially.

46. Beauvoir, *The Second Sex*, xxii.

47. Beauvoir's criticism of Levinas (to quote her) refers to his "essai sur *le Temps et l'Autre*," but that title refers to a series of four lectures he gave in 1946-477, published as *Le temps et l'autre* (*Time and the Other* is the English translation by Richard A. Cohen). *Totality and Infinity*, Levinas's major work, was published in 1961.

48. For a study of Levinas's notion of "the feminine" that critiques it but also attempts to save it for feminism, see Tina Chanter, *Time, Death and the Feminine: Levinas with Heidegger* (Stanford, CA: Stanford University Press, 2001). Also see Luce Irigaray's "The Fecundity of the Caress," trans. Carolyn Burke, in *Face to Face with Levinas*, ed. Richard A. Cohen (Albany: State University of New York, 1986).

49. His "apology/explanation" appears in the preface to the 1979 edition of *Le temps et l'autre* (see note 42).

50. Stella Sandford, "Levinas, Feminism and the Feminine," in *The Cambridge Companion to Levinas*, ed. Simon Critchley and Robert Bernasconi (Cambridge, England: Cambridge University Press, 2002), 146-7.

51. Levinas, *Totality and Infinity*, 158.

52. Julia Kristeva, "From One Identity to an Other," in *Desire in Language: A Semiotic Approach to Literature and Art*, ed. Leon S. Roudiez, trans. Thomas Gora, Alice Jardine, Leon S. Roudiez (New York: Columbia University Press, 1980), 133.

53. Beauvoir, *The Second Sex*, xxii-xxiii.

54. See Carol Gilligan, *In a Different Voice: Psychological Theory and Women's Development* (Cambridge, MA: Harvard University Press, 1982) or Julia Kristeva, *Desire in Language: A Semiotic Approach to Literature and Art*, ed. Leon S. Roudiez (New York: Columbia University Press, 1980) for two very *different* examples of "difference theory."

55. Gilligan, *In a Different Voice*, 2.

56. Levinas, *Totality and Infinity*, 155.
57. Levinas, *Totality and Infinity*, 156, 158, 170.
58. Levinas, *Totality and Infinity*, 158.
59. Levinas, *Totality and Infinity*, 305. And see Derrida, *Of Hospitality*, 135.
60. Levinas, *Totality and Infinity*, 178, 202.
61. Levinas, *Totality and Infinity*, 216, and see 254 and 300.
62. Levinas, *Totality and Infinity*, 305.
63. Levinas, *Totality and Infinity*, 157-8.
64. Levinas, *Totality and Infinity*, 173.
65. Levinas, *Totality and Infinity*, 172.
66. Garrett Thomson, *On Kant* (Belmont, Ca: Wadsworth, 2000), 57.
67. Derrida, *Of Hospitality*, 77-81.
68. Derrida, *Of Hospitality*, 81.
69. Jacques Derrida in Giovanna Borradori, *Philosophy in a Time of Terror: Dialogues with Jürgen Habermas and Jacques Derrida* (Chicago: University of Chicago Press, 2003), 133.
70. Derrida, *Of Hospitality*, 149.
71. Derrida, *Philosophy in a Time of Terror*, 128-9.
72. Derrida, *Philosophy in a Time of Terror*, 128-9.
73. Derrida, *Philosophy in a Time of Terror*, 129.
74. Derrida, *Philosophy in a Time of Terror*, 127.
75. Derrida, *Of Hospitality*, 149-51. His counter-example for this becomes Lot and his daughters.

Chapter 6

From Saint Martha To Hurricane Katrina: A Feminist Theopolitical Ethic Of Hospitality

M. Christian Green

No inquiry into the possibility of a feminist ethic of hospitality should proceed without attention to a leading exemplar of hospitality in the Christian theological tradition—Saint Martha of Bethany, who received Jesus Christ into her home, was first witness to the coming resurrection, and is patroness saint of hospitality in the Christian pantheon. She is a hostess, but not sanguine or unreflective about her hospitable tasks. She is a hostess, but not a handmaid. Her example may inform both theological and secular ethics, particularly in situations that require freedom from fear and openness to the other.

Saint Martha is an ambivalent figure for a feminist ethic of hospitality—just as hospitality is an ambivalent posture and basis for feminist ethics. The domestic feminine roles with which Martha is associated tend to elicit a hermeneutic of suspicion from feminist theologians.[1] For even as hospitality affirms and valorizes traits and practices that have been seen to be distinctly feminine in many cultures, an ethic of hospitality also carries the possibility of naturalizing or essentializing those traits to women's detriment. At the same time, a feminist ethic of hospitality may also serve as a particularly powerful and transformative antidote to the ethos of fear that many see dominating many areas of public life in the United States today, often in areas that have a predominant and disproportionate effect on women's lives.

In this essay, I first examine the example of Saint Martha, as she has been received and interpreted in feminist theology, for the light that her story sheds on the promise and peril of hospitality. I then take up the topic of the political ethos of fear as a problem for hospitality that feminists have a particular stake in overcoming. As a practical application of these themes, I move to an analysis of some gendered dimensions of the recent natural, social, and political disaster of Hurricane Katrina, for the insights into gender and hospitality in the current sociopolitical context in the United States. Finally, I conclude by outlining some principles of hospitality as a feminist theological ethic.

Saint Martha of Bethany:
An Ambivalent Example of Feminist Hospitality

Martha first appears in the Christian Bible's New Testament in a key story of two sisters in the Gospel of Luke 10:38-42. In that text, Jesus arrives in the village of Bethany, where a woman named Martha welcomes him into her home. Martha lives with her younger sister Mary. Martha and Mary are the sisters of Lazarus, who is later raised from the dead in the Gospel of John. Competing traditions describe Martha as either a single woman or a widow. Her marital status remains uncertain, but she has generally been associated with single lay women in the church, which lends credence to the singleness theory. In the story in Luke, Martha is famously burdened by many domestic tasks of hospitality. When, instead of helping her sister with the preparations, Mary chooses instead to sit at the Jesus' feet to listen to his teachings, Martha grumbles to Jesus, "Lord, do you not care that my sister has left me to do all the work by myself? Tell her then to help me." In response, Jesus chides, "Martha, Martha, you are worried and distracted by many things, there is need of only one thing. Mary has chosen the better part, which will not be taken away from her."[2]

The story of Martha and Mary has most often been interpreted as depicting a division between the activity in this world and contemplation of the world to come. Such dualistic and intentionally hierarchical sibling dichotomies are found throughout the Bible—Cain and Abel, Jacob and Esau, Rachel and Leah—to contrast different character types and patterns in life and faith. Martha typically comes out badly in this interpretation, being mired in busy domesticity and the worries of the world.[3] Defenders of Martha have relished her feistiness, practicality, concern for justice, and inquisitive nature, over the apparently passive posture of Mary, who has no words in the story, but rather listens silently to Jesus' instruction. Nevertheless, the text and Jesus's affirmation of Mary's choice therein leave us with the conclusion that Mary has, indeed, to have chosen the "better part" in opting for a life of contemplation and learning. But is this really the case?

While this dualistic dichotomy between the sisters Martha and Mary is part of the received tradition surrounding their story and their saintliness, feminist interpreters and exegetes have proposed alternative possibilities. Alternative readings of Luke's account have seen the women as participating in two different, but no less equal, forms of *diakonia,* or service, to the Church—ministries of table service and ministries of teaching and preaching. Leading feminist New Testament scholar Elisabeth Schüssler Fiorenza, subjects the Martha and Mary story to feminist critical interpretation, objecting to "abstractionist interpretation" that "reduces the two sisters to theological principles and types."[4] She argues that these interpretations "not only dehistoricize the narrative but also make women historically invisible" and, further, serve to "obscure the androcentric dynamics of the text that uses women to make their point."[5] The dichotomization of Martha and Mary at the level of principled abstraction plays into the all too familiar real-world tendency to pit groups of women against one another. Such androcentric and patriarchal dualisms are the sort that feminist theologians are determined to debunk.

Even those interpretations that resist abstraction and deal with Martha and Mary concretely and historically fall into the similar tendencies toward dichotomy and polarization. Schüssler Fiorenza identifies three formulations of this more concrete good woman/bad woman polarization. The Catholic formulation distinguishes between women who serve God and women who serve men, leading to the conclusion that women are "either laywomen or nunwomen, secular or religious, serving their husbands or serving the lord."[6] The Protestant formulation folds these concerns into notions of the ideal "pastor's wife," in which women "have to fulfill their duties as housewives and hostesses of church suppers, but they should take some time out to 'listen, to pray, and to learn.'" The ideal pastor's wife is exhorted "to keep it simple so that she can fulfill her religious obligations,"[7] for beyond the obvious problem of women being relegated to a purely supporting role, one can imagine this ethic of hospitality becoming the occasion for excessive scrupulosity over domestic matters in a way that sets the bar too high. The imperatives of hospitality, simplicity, and balance can end up taking up quite a bit of women's time, becoming a new sort of patriarchal bind.

A third category of concrete interpretations consists in apologetic feminist interpretations that seek to reconcile women to religion and theology through a more charitable hermeneutic. In Schüssler Fiorenza's analysis, these interpretations "focus on Mary's rejection of the traditional housewife role and stress her option for theology" and Jesus' apparent vindication of her choice. Schüssler Fiorenza notes that, outside of the academy, particularly in the church pews:

> Many women greatly identify with Martha's plight. Traditionally, women have been told that our feminine vocation is to take care of men. Women do all the work in the house and in the kitchen, clean and shop, give dinner parties for the advancement of their husbands, and, at the same time, are supposed to be relaxed, entertaining, and well-groomed. In the church, they wash the altar linen, run the bingo, and hold bake sales, and they do all of this often without ever receiving a "thank you." Many women, therefore, identify with Martha who openly complains. They resent Jesus who seems to be ungrateful and unfair in taking Mary's side. But they repress this resentment and vent it against other women who, like Mary, have abandoned the traditional feminine role. The right-wing backlash in society and church feeds on this resentment.[8]

It thus becomes important to recognize both women's experience of resentment and the ways that this resentment may be coopted and exploited by conservative theological and sociopolitical forces. Resentment may give rise to grumbling, but it can also be the impetus to transformative action.

Schüssler Fiorenza's feminist critical analysis of the Martha and Mary story in terms of women's *diakonia*, or service, in the early Christian house churches illuminates, but does not settle, the ambivalence of the choices and conduct of Martha and Mary. Examining the way in which Luke's gospel account of Martha and Mary ends up silencing both women, Schüssler Fiorenza maintains, "Martha does not speak to Mary directly, but she appeals to Jesus as a little girl might run to her parents to tell on a sibling who misbehaves. . . . Mary who receives the positive approval is the *silent* woman, whereas Martha who argues for her interest is *silenced*."[9] Of the gospel account, Schüssler Fiorenza argues, "Its rhetorical interests are to silence women leaders of the house churches who, like Martha, might have protested and, at the same time, to extol the 'silent' and subordinate behavior of Mary. Such a reconstruction of women's struggles in the early church also shows why many women today can identify more with Martha than with Mary. It confirms women's 'suspicion' that in the Lucan account, Martha received a 'raw deal.'"[10] In the end, it is Martha's sense of justice and resisting the "raw deal" of traditional domesticity that makes Martha potentially an example of transformative agency and feminist hospitality.

There is a further argument for the value of Martha's ethic of hospitality that comes in reading the account of Martha in the Gospel of Luke along with the Gospel of John, the other place where Martha is referenced in the New Testament. If Mary's theological stature in the gospel of Luke comes from being a disciple who studied at the feet of Jesus, Martha's theological role in the gospel of John is no less significant, particularly when the story of Martha in the gospel of Luke is read along with the account of her activities in the gospel of John.[11] In John, Martha is again troubled, in this case by the death of her brother, Lazarus. Initially she seems to be deeply in the grips of grief, as well as a crisis of faith. She appears to blame Jesus for her brother's death, suggesting that he might have saved Lazarus had he arrived sooner. She requests Jesus' intercession with God for a life-restoring favor on her brother's behalf. When Jesus assures her that her brother will rise again, Martha provides the first statement of faith in the resurrection, saying "I know that he will rise again in the resurrection at the last day." Jesus then proclaims to her, "I am the resurrection and the life; he who believes in me, though he die, yet shall he live, and whoever lives and believes in me shall never die." When Jesus asks Martha whether she believes this, Martha responds, "Yes, I believe that you are the Christ, the Son of God, he who is coming into the world." Immediately thereafter in John's account, there is a moment of apparent reconciliation between the sisters, when Martha, rather than disparaging Mary's desire to study with Jesus, calls out to Mary, "The Teacher is here and is calling for you."

Thus, Martha is transformed from a grumbling servant in Luke to pillar of faith in John. She is transformed through an expansive form of hospitality, an attitude of welcome and openness to persons, ideas, and experiences that seem alien, strange, and other. Martha, first witness to Christ as the redeemer, and Mary Magdalene, first witness to the resurrection and messenger of the good news to the male disciples, along with other women present at the crucifixion and resurrection were, in fact, Christ's first disciples in terms of pure faith. In these instances, women were open, receptive, and hospitable witnesses to the messiah, in contrast to the masculine triad of Peter, Thomas, and Judas, all disciples who variously denied, doubted, or betrayed Jesus before the news of the resurrection was revealed. While lifting up openness, receptiveness, and hospitality as feminine traits may risk the twin perils of naturalization and essentialization, it may also suggest something about hospitality as the basis of a positive and transformative feminist ethic.

The Inward Curve, Circles of Fear, and Openness to the Other: The Ethos of Fear as a Problem for Hospitality

The opposite of hospitality is fear, which has also been the subject of political and theological attention in recent years, particularly in the aftermath of the terrorist attacks of September 11, 2001. Characterization of the political landscape in the United States as being dominated by a "politics of fear" has made fear an important topic for theology and ethics.[12] The ethical concern is that fear has a constraining or distorting effect on our capacity for right and ethical behavior. Fear has also become a topic of scientific speculation, as neuroscientists and behavioral biologists have sought to understand fear's biological basis and social effects.[13] Social psychologists, in particular, have recently articulated "terror management" theories in which those who have experienced a heightened sense of danger or threat to their existence in connection with acts of terror cognitively engage in a process of "worldview support" by which they exclude and justify the exclusion of those who are perceived to represent a threat.[14] The dichotomization of these "others" may be based simply on differences in appearance, behavior, and racial/ethnic/national origin, but these distinctions, conscious or unconscious, become the basis of a construction and support of a worldview that reinforces categories of good and evil, neighbor and stranger, and just and unjust response, in order to make terror and its aftermath meaningful and manageable.

These perspectives on fear from the biological and social sciences have a long pedigree in Christian theology and ethics. Late medieval theologian Thomas Aquinas categorized fear as a state of being suspended between hope and despair.[15] The theological challenge is to avoid despair and to move in the direction of hope. Hope is an appetitive power of desire that moves us toward the good and ultimately to God. Those who possess hope are said to be "full of spirit," such that their "heart expands."[16] But even as hope moves toward the good, despair causes us to withdraw, especially in circumstances of fear. We either fear the loss of a good that we love or that we will fail to obtain what we hope for.[17] Rather than a movement of outward expansion, fear is a movement of inward contraction. Aquinas describes this contraction in very physical terms as a "bodily transmutation,"[18] such that the "weaker a power is, the fewer the things to which it extends."[19] Fear, further, renders the fearful person "inclined to run away" and "makes its subject speechless."[20]

Aquinas's remarks on fear leading to contraction and withdrawal resonate with a number of contemporary issues—ranging from the "war on terror," to internationalism and isolationism in foreign policy, to immigration policy along our nation's borders, to how we relate to one another in public debate and civil society. Far from inspiring transformation and change, fear is a reactive and conservative phenomenon hearkening back to an idealized past or seeking to preserve the status quo in a time of chaos. Flight and speechlessness are far from helpful when the goal is transformation and change, especially when the retreat is an inward one that hinders engagement with one's neighbors and society. In Christian theological terms, such withdrawal and breaking off of relations to God and neighbor, is not only a failure of love and justice, but also the essence of sin. Aquinas's language of circular contraction builds on Augustine's conception of sin as the self's inward curve.

Another way to think of fear and sin is to conceive of them as failures of hospitality. In an article titled "Practicing Hospitality in a Time of Backlash,"[21] theologian Letty M. Russell takes up these themes from a feminist theological perspective. Writing in the mid-1990s, she observed, "We are in an age where those already marginal to the power structure of the society are being disempowered and blamed for their own victimization, with constant pressure to create laws that exclude and punish the weak."[22] Addressing primarily the problematic doctrines of predestination and divine election within her Presbyterian Calvinist tradition, Russell ends up saying quite a bit about the importance of "hospitality in diversity" for a feminist ethic. The problem, as Russell sees it, is that "Diversity has to do with difference. It represents a description of the differences of race, culture, gender, sexual orientation, age, abilities, economic and political status, and much more that are parts of the world in which we live. Many differences are God-given acts of creation and lend beauty and excitement to our world. Yet the connotation of difference seems to be that persons and groups who are not like us cause threat and discord to our way of life and our particular community."[23] A key part of Russell's feminist reconstruction of the doctrine of election entails taking the perspective of those labeled outsiders in our communities. As she notes, "Those who see themselves elected with Christ through faith are called to take up his lifestyle of compassion and hospitality to neighbors in need.... If God has extended a welcome to all 'outsiders,' including ourselves, then we are called to practice hospitality by being for others, standing with them in their struggles, and understanding election from their perspective."[24] This is a particular challenge for Christian churches, for Russell maintains, "Jesus' willingness to change models for all of us what it means to face the contradictions of our lives that serve to exclude our brothers and sisters. ... The stranger needs to be welcomed by a community that is able to practice hospitality. If a Christian community has not sense of its identity in Christ as the center of its life, it will not have a great deal of generosity and compassion to share with others. Just as persons cannot give themselves away if they have no sense of self-worth to share, churches with no sense of identity and worth have little to share. It is our identity in Christ who welcomes the stranger that leads us to join in the task of hospitality."[25]

In the last years of her life, Russell again took up the topic of hospitality—framed this time in an even more urgent context of terror. In a lecture, titled "Encountering the 'Other' in a World of Difference and Danger" in the spring of 2006,[26] Russell directed her audience's attention to the alternatives of hospitality or a process of "othering" in the aftermath of 9/11 and in the current context of globalization and pluralism. Analogizing the current situation to her experience as a white, middle-class, Protestant aspiring minister in an urban church in East Harlem in the 1950s, Russell proclaims:

> We saw the need for new ways of living out the gospel if it were to come alive for those who had been abandoned by the church and the city around them. We found ourselves with new questions from the perspective of the "other." We were no longer looking for a *gracious God* as in the time of the Reformation, or a *gracious neighbor* as in the era of capitalist expansion and industrialization, but for a *gracious stranger* in a world of alienation. In the last fifty years this reality of encounter with the "other" has become a universal problem as globalization and pluralism create a world that is "other."[27]

Even in identifying this situation of otherness, Russell initially resists the term "other," arguing, "In my perspective there are no 'others,' for all are created by God and no one is an *other*. Yet if we look at our postcolonial world we see a constant process going on of what I would call *othering*: social structures and interactions that divide the world into subjects and objects often demean, disgrace or destroy the ones who are objects or *others*."[28] And, of course, much of the "othering" is driven by fear, for as Russell so keenly observes:

> This othering works through the internalization of fear: fear of being other, or being seen as other; fear for one's own identity and the need to conform to the dominant paradigm of those who fit in a culture. Those declared "other" because of their nationality, skin color, gender, sexual orientation, or any dissimilarity to the dominant political economic and social norm are forced to internalize this need to conform in order to avoid being *othered*. In the same way, those from dominant groups also internalize the norms so that they will fit in and refuse to associate with those who are different.[29]

This process of "othering" is, in Russell's view, tied up with the "misuse of difference."[30]

But the misuse of difference need not be the last word in our encounters with others, for Russell maintains, "There is a process at work among us in our nation and around the world . . . that may assist us in resisting this dualistic divide and conquer pattern. . . . Mixtures of culture, race, religion, language, and just about everything are becoming a norm in a globalized society."[31] Drawing on the biblical story of the Tower of Babel, Russell calls for recognition of a "world of riotous difference," arguing, "Differences of race, gender, sexual orientation, language or culture are not problems to be solved and controlled by a dominant group, rather they are important ways of assuring that God's gift of riotous diversity in all creation will continue. . . . If difference is a gift which helps to prevent domination, surely it is *not* something to be overcome."[32] The solution to the problem of difference is not erasure, but community—a relationship that Russell conceives as crucially entailing a sense and a reality of *just hospitality*—in which "those who risk openness to the process of hybridity will have the advantage of moving beyond the old dualistic stereotypes of oppressor and oppressed."[33] Citing the "practice of hospitality or welcoming of the stranger" as an important aspect of Jewish, Muslim, and Christian spirituality, Russell returns to her initial insight from her urban ministry work to argue, "In a world so full of danger and fear it becomes apparent that our search for a gracious God and a gracious neighbor needs to be expanded to a search for a gracious stranger."[34] Rather than *xenophobia*, we need *philoxenia*. In the end, as Russell puts it, "Hospitality is not *the* answer to difference, but it is a challenge to us, pointing us to a future that God intends where riotous difference is welcomed! Hospitality will not *make us safe,* but it will lead us to risk joining in the work of mending the creation without requiring those who are different to become like us."[35]

There is an important connection to be made between these theological discussions of fear, difference, and hospitality and the story of Martha. While Martha might have remained mired in worries and resentment over her domestic duties, invidious comparison to her sister, or her brother's ill health, Jesus' admonition that she pay heed to the "one thing" created a space of openness in her life that allowed her to welcome and be transformed by Christ's coming resurrection and the possibility of her own redemption. Ethical challenges arise and ethical decisions are often made in such spaces of openness, even those that emerge from the chaotic aftermath of a storm.

Hurricane Katrina: Gender, Race, Injustice, and the Challenge of Hospitality

The response to Hurricane Katrina, which devastated the Gulf Coasts of Louisiana and Mississippi and particularly the city of New Orleans in the late summer of 2005, is an excellent case study for the application and ethics of hospitality, as it exemplifies both hospitality's promise and its potential perils. In the minds of many in the United States, New Orleans and the Gulf Coast are part of the "Deep South," a popular term for the region that is suggestive of strangeness and remoteness. This exoticism was amplified by media coverage of the disaster, including remarks by news reporters and commentators that the pictures coming out of the disaster looked like they were from Haiti or some other "Third World" country. The ensuing diaspora of those fleeing Katrina's devastation demanded no small amount of hospitality from Americans. By and large, Americans rose to the challenge, feeding, sheltering, and welcoming victims of the storm—variously referred to as "refugees" and "evacuees"—in one of the greatest outpourings of hospitality that the nation has ever seen.

The very debate over how to refer to those displaced by the storm indicates a significant dimension of the hospitality challenges presented by Katrina. Many observers, particularly the Reverend Al Sharpton of New York, challenged the use of the term "refugee," arguing that it connoted statelessness, a lack of political identity and rights, a people with no government charged with meeting their basic needs and providing for their health, welfare, and common defense. Others embraced the term, at least rhetorically, to suggest precisely that these *were* people with political and human rights, however ill-respected and poorly addressed by their government officials before, during, and after the disaster. The "refugee" debate raised the question of whether some segments of the population can be so disenfranchised and disempowered by race, class, gender, or other status that they come to be refugees in their own country. This was an idea broached famously decades before by anti-poverty writer and activist, Michael Harrington, who described the poor as "internal aliens" in his landmark study of poverty in *The Other America*.[36]

The concepts of aliens and alienation are suggestive of the image of strangeness and otherness of Katrina's victims cultivated by the media. Insofar as the suffering throngs in the streets and public buildings of New Orleans were portrayed as alien to mainstream America, the tasks of community, solidarity, and hospitality were that much harder to achieve. Further, there was a peculiar dynamic of mirror-like reciprocity among the seers and seen, the witnesses and the witnessed, in the media presentation. Theologian Michael Eric Dyson, in his book-length discussion of Katrina's implications for theology, race, and politics, describes it well:

> It is not all about *what we saw*—which, after all, may be a perverse narcissism that makes their plight ultimately about our failure and what we must learn at their great expense. It is also about *what they, the poor, saw in us, or didn't see there*, especially the government that didn't find or feed them until it was late—too late for thousands of them. It is their surprise, not ours, that should most concern and inform us. Perhaps it is their anger, too, that is uninspiring, since the outrage of the black survivors proved their tenacious loyalty to a country that hasn't often earned it. As Michael Ignatieff argues, the poor blacks struggling to survive Katrina's backlash saw more clearly than most others "what the contract of American citizenship entails."[37]

Many Americans viewed the helplessness of the poor in New Orleans with horror and were forced to confront their consciences and their complicity, but those poor New Orleanians also saw a reflection of themselves *as they were seen* by mainstream America. As we know from Letty Russell's account of *othering*, both *being other* and *being seen as other* matter in a context of fear of difference. The latter may be worse than the former if it serves to further diminish the moral agency and the moral capabilities of the already disempowered.

There were also distinctly gendered dimensions to these problems of fear, difference, and hospitality in Katrina and the aftermath. One story that dominated early media coverage concerned allegations of the rape of women and children at the Superdome and the Convention Center in downtown New Orleans. These allegations remain poorly substantiated to this day, but they were given considerable—some would say disproportionate—attention by the media.[38] Despite important concerns that the rape story was media hype motivated by racial prejudice and a history of portraying the sexuality of African American men as violent, uncontrolled, and alien to mainstream sexual mores, feminist commentator Lucinda Marshall situated the alleged rapes amid a range of gender disadvantages that women typically suffer in times of disaster. On this point, she observed, "In the wake of Hurricane Katrina, women whose lives were disrupted by the storm face numerous gender-specific vulnerabilities that commonly occur with disasters of this magnitude. . . . [W]omen and children are more likely to die in disasters than men. . . . Female victims of catastrophic events are more likely to lack mobility and resources as well as having caretaking responsibilities that make it more difficult to flee. Pregnant women and mothers of newborns in particular face greatly increased health risks."[39] These vulnerabilities are seemingly universal and cross-cultural, occurring over and over in numerous locales and contexts, as attested to by those who have studied gender and disaster.[40] In light of the significant parallels between Katrina and other natural disasters and political conflicts, the possibility that women suffered rape and other assaults does not seem improbable.

Media portrayals of the Katrina disaster also raised questions about the feminization of poverty and family structures that deviate from the nuclear family norm. Conservative scholars, social commentators, and political pundits pointed to the apparent prevalence of father-absent families in the African American population affected by Katrina as confirming the importance of fatherhood and the special vulnerabilities of single-mother families. Sociologist James Q. Wilson wrote, "New Orleans is not simply a city of poor people—it is a city that has left its black population untaught, unguarded, and unmarried. . . . We do not know who the looters were, but among black thieves, I imagine that most came from single-parent families."[41] To Wilson and others, these families seemed very strange and alien, indeed. By contrast, Lillian Poats, a professor of education and a scholar of social and racial diversity, argues that the African American family and its strengths have been rendered invisible in contemporary media and research. In her view, "There is an increasing buzz in American society about the 'collapse' of the Black family. . . . But that belief has a hard time explaining what we all saw on our televisions after Hurricane Katrina decimated New Orleans and the Gulf Coast region. . . . There was very little, if any, coverage given to the challenges for families, yet it was clear to me that many of the people survived only because of the strength of the family."[42] As one Katrina evacuee quoted by Poats proclaimed, "There were four generations of us in that water."[43] "Strange" or not, these families were clearly survivors.

The government's response to Katrina, when it came, was of a heavily militarized nature, suggestive of the concerns about the aforementioned "politics of fear" said to prevail in post-9/11 America. On this point, feminist activist, Loretta Ross observes, "The concept of peace and security was dreadfully misused during the crisis to impose a police state. The reality is that women live in a borderland of insecurity all the time, yet the needs of women are invisible in discussions on security preoccupied with criminals and terrorists. Poverty, hunger, and deprivation are real threats to security because security is determined by the extent to which people have their basic needs met and can live in freedom and safety, not by number of armed occupiers in their communities."[44] A truly hospitable ethic and response to disaster, reflecting the imperative of the Hebrew Bible to take special care of the strangers and aliens among us must be one that does not sow the seeds fear and otherness, but rather recognizes the distinct needs of those who are vulnerable in our communities, while also nurturing and empowering their capacities for resilience.

One fascinating insight from cross-cultural studies of gender and disaster is that, while women may suffer unique vulnerabilities during a disaster, once the heavy lifting of immediate response and repair is complete, women become the major forces of relief and recovery. Whereas the heroic activities of mostly male first responders garner much initial media attention, it is women who become the resilient sustainers of the recovery over time. But even in the outpouring of generosity after Katrina these relief and recovery efforts were not always without ethical issues.

Many communities received Katrina evacuees into their own communities, though sometimes with ethically ambiguous results. One church group in Kalamazoo, Michigan, undertook to welcome and provide for a family relocated from New Orleans.[45] At one point, the church women sponsoring the group experienced consternation when the sponsored family used church-provided gift cards to purchase a portable stereo system, rather than basic necessities. One of the church women remarked, "I just didn't think their first item should be a gigantic boom box."[46] By contrast, another woman maintained, "I think, when you give, you give freely. And you cannot have an expectation over what you give."[47] Disputes rose to such a pitch among the church women that some of the women ended up withdrawing from the project and the family ultimately moved out of the church-bought house as soon as they were financially able.

As in some interpretations of the Martha and Mary story, women were pitted against one another in the Kalamazoo tale. Hurricane Katrina raised many classic theological concerns of neighbor-love, charity, and welcoming the stranger. But it also raised concerns of race, class, gender and justice that feminists in particular cannot and should not ignore. The story of the Kalamazoo church women is an important cautionary note about differences of race, class, and status between women and the potential for domination, despite the best of intentions.

Principles of a Feminist Theological Ethic of Hospitality

The figure of Martha in Christian theology attests to an ethic of hospitality that is active and contemplative, public and private, practical and theoretical. It is an ethic which, when released from fear and anxiety, is open to the most radical and strange of possibilities—resurrection and salvation through the risen Christ. Yet as feminist theologians have recognized, it has secular as well as spiritual implications, particularly in the way that we relate to those who are "other" to us in some sense. Through that relationship, there is the potential for community and solidarity. What are some specific principles that we learn from the Marthine tradition of hospitality in relation to such contemporary challenges as the social and political disaster spawned by Hurricane Katrina? Here are some preliminary possibilities.

Welcome the strange and alien. One of the oldest biblical injunctions regarding justice, repeated over and over in the Hebrew Bible and predating the

New Testament and the story of Martha, is to welcome the stranger and the alien. In the desert and highly interdependent nomadic environment inhabited by the Hebrew people, failure to provide hospitality and shelter to a passing stranger could have lethal consequences for strangers turned away. The Exodus command "You shall not wrong a stranger or oppress him, for you were strangers in the land of Egypt" became central to the identity of the Hebrew people, and later to Christians who considered themselves strangers and sojourners, "in but not of" this world. In the gospel of Luke, Martha welcomes Jesus, though not without worry and distraction. In the gospel of John, she welcomes the strangeness of Jesus's coming resurrection with confidence and faith.

In response to the sluggish efforts of their government, Americans were called upon to extend hospitality to strangers in the aftermath of Hurricane Katrina. In so doing, they were also challenged to confront the poverty and racism that exacerbated the hurricane's effects for many of the storm's victims. For many Americans, that reality was strange—the "strange fruit" of decades of inattention and neglect based on race. That there might be gendered dimensions and implications of the disaster also seemed strange in the context of the unity experience and response that is so often demanded as part of the "Americans coming together" narratives of solidarity that so often follow catastrophic and traumatic events. Such solidarity narratives have their place, but they risk diverting us from confrontation of strange and uncomfortable realities about our society. Feminist ethics, an ethics of care often practiced from the margins, is well placed to address both the need to welcome and the dignity of the stranger and to call for the transformation of unjust social structures that diminish that dignity.

Hope, not fear. There has lately been abundant talk of hope on the American political scene. Thomas Aquinas conceptualizes fear as the circular trap that is produced when we curve and contract inward upon ourselves. Such a posture precludes all forms of hospitality. In such circumstances, hope is fear's opposite and remedy. In the aftermath of 9/11, there was a line of feminist commentary that noted a way in which America's sense of invulnerability, coded as masculine, was rendered subject to a kind of fear and vulnerability that many women experience everyday. But far from wallowing in vulnerability and victimhood, feminist theory and praxis empower resistance as an act of agency and hope.

Hope is prophetic in its orientation toward the future—optimistic, but also realistic, in its aims. Commenting on the work of Dorothy Day, founder of the Catholic Worker movement with its eponymous newspaper and "Houses of Hospitality" that continue to serve the poor and needy, Tom Frary writes, "The prophetic person addresses a possible future that demands action in the present for which the present offers little credibility."[48] Day was a charismatic and at times enigmatic figure—an anarchist, pacifist, devout Catholic convert, who had two common-law marriages, an abortion, and yet has been recommended for sainthood in the Roman Catholic Church. With her "Houses of Hospitality," Day was a twentieth-century Martha. Indeed, there is a notable connection to Martha-style table service in the very origins of these houses. As Day recounts, "Our first house of hospitality came into being very shortly after *The Catholic Worker* did ... A young woman, an unemployed textile work about to have a baby, took charge of the kitchen and busied herself preparing meals for the homeless men who had already begun drifting in. It wasn't long before we were all eating in shifts."[49] A feminist ethic of hospitality depends on perceiving such open doors of opportunity and in meeting challenging and often fearful realities with prophetic optimism.

Embrace otherness. Perceptions of the "other" are frequently occasions of fear, or at least anxiety. Today, otherness frequently manifests itself when borders of gender, race, nationality, and class are traversed through technology. Communication, media, the internet, forces of economic and cultural globalization put us in touch with others as never before. We continually confront our diversity and plurality. Feminist theory now shapes many academic disciplines, political practices, and social justice movements, but this was not always so. For much of its history, feminism has been considered other, radical, marginal. If anything, feminism today risks being uncritically mainstreamed and "domesticated" unless it retains its own critical stance of otherness, while also taking notice of the otherness in its own ranks.

In this connection, it is significant that some of the most significant appropriations of the Martha story today are being done by feminist theologians of color around the world.[50] Korean feminist theologian, Sook Ja Chung, makes connections between problematic interpretations of Jesus' admonition to Martha and the exploitation of women in globalization, arguing, "Under the influence of globalization, Martha's role is now played by the urban poor, young girls from farms and migrant workers. This is a consequence of the degradation of Martha's role that follows the questionable interpretation of Jesus' saying."[51] Satako Yamaguchi connects the Martha story to the difficulties that women ministers in the Asian churches and its usefulness in the "struggle to stop all kinds of discrimination against 'women ministers' in our church and to build up better conditions for women ministers to work to their full potential."[52] The resonance of the Martha story with feminists of different racial, ethnic, and national identities is an example of the power of hospitality, and stories of hospitality, to overcome boundaries of otherness.

Hospitality, not homophily. Social scientists in the United States have recently been analyzing and reporting a disturbing trend toward "homophily," literally "love of the same," or the tendency to associate and bond with others similar to oneself. The term has been used to describe social phenomena ranging from the Red State/Blue State divide in American politics, to assortative residential patterns and the rise of the gated community, to consumer culture and the commodification of identity in "individual" choices that become remarkably homogeneous across social groups.[53] The *New York Times* declared homophily to be one of its "ideas of the year" in a recent year-end list of trends.[54]

Hospitality is the antidote to homophily. It is an ethic of deliberative and transformative receptivity and welcome that is open to the other, inclusive of the alien, and unafraid of the strange. Far from being a "natural" or "essential" attribute of one gender, it is a humanist ethic that must be actively cultivated by all of us, over and against those forces that would turn us inward upon ourselves and away from others. It must recognize the concrete and diverse needs of others, particularly in times of chaos. In particular, hospitality must overcome fear.

Outside of the bible, the best known tradition associated with Saint Martha comes from the medieval French legend that, following the events recounted in the gospel, Martha journeyed with her siblings Mary and Lazarus to the south of France. There she saved the people of the village of Tarascon from a dragon, not by killing it—which would certainly be most inhospitable—but by boldly confronting it and leading it away from the town with the sash of her dress. This example of hospitality boldly confronting fear and otherness makes Saint Martha a prime resource for a feminist ethic of hospitality.

Notes

1. Feminist New Testament Scholar, Elisabeth Schüssler Fiorenza, has proposed a four-part feminist critical hermeneutical method for the interpretation of biblical texts that involves a hermeneutic of suspicion, a hermeneutic of proclamation, a hermeneutic of remembrance and a hermeneutic of reconstruction. See Elisabeth Schüssler Fiorenza, *In Memory of Her: A Feminist Theological Reconstruction of Christian Origins*, 10th anniv. ed. (Crossroads, 1994).

2. Bible, Revised Standard Edition, Luke: 10:38-42.

3. Popular Christian devotional literature, particularly of a traditional or conservative bent, bears out this theme, as seen a recent book which proposes to help women manage time and stress to the end of greater intimacy with God. See Joanna Weaver, Having a Mary Heart in a Martha World: Finding Intimacy with God in the Business of Life (WaterBrook Press, 2002). This author has recently continued the Mary/Martha theme with a sequel titled, Having a Mary Spirit: Allowing God to Change Us from the Inside Out (WaterBrook Press, 2006).

4. Elisabeth Schüssler Fiorenza, Theological Criteria and Historical Reconstruction: Martha and Mary: Luke 10:38-42 (Berkeley, CA: Center for Hermeneutical Studies in Hellenistic and Modern Culture, 1986), 4. See also Elisabeth Schüssler Fiorenza, "A Feminist Critical Interpretation for Liberation: Martha and Mary: Lk. 10:38-42," Religion & Intellectual Life 3:2 (1986): 21-36. 5. *Theological Criteria and Historical Reconstruction*, 5.

6. *Theological Criteria and Historical Reconstruction*.

7. *Theological Criteria and Historical Reconstruction*.

8. *Theological Criteria and Historical Reconstruction*, 4.

9. *Theological Criteria and Historical Reconstruction*, 7.

10. *Theological Criteria and Historical Reconstruction*, 9.

11. Bible, Revised Standard Version, John 11:17-27.

12. See Scott Bader-Saye, Following Jesus in a Culture of Fear (Grand Rapids, MI: Brazos Press, 2007); Forrest Church, Freedom from Fear: Finding the Courage to Love, Act, and Be (New York: St. Martin's Press, 2004). For an excellent political intellectual history of fear, see Corey Robin, Fear: The History of a Political Idea (New York: Oxford University Press, 2005).

13. See Marc Siegel, *False Alarm: The Truth About the Epidemic of Fear* (Hoboken, NJ: John Wiley & Sons, 2005).

14. See Tom Pyszczynski, "What Are We So Afraid Of?: A Terror Management Perspective on the Politics of Fear," Social Research 71:4 (Winter 2004): 827-48; Young-Ok Yum and William Schenck-Hamlin, "Reactions to 9/11 as a Function of Terror Management and Perspective Taking," Journal of Social Psychology 145:3 (June 2005): 265-86.
15. Thomas Aquinas, Summa Theologica, I-II, Q. 40, a. 1.
16. Aquinas, Summa Theologica, Q. 40, a. 6.
17. Aquinas, Summa Theologica, Q. 43, a. 1.
18. Aquinas, Summa Theologica, Q. 41, a.1; Aquinas, Summa Theologica, Q. 44, a.1.
19. Aquinas, Summa Theologica, Q. 44, a. 1.
20. Aquinas, Summa Theologica, Q. 44, a. 2.
21. Letty M. Russell, "Practicing Hospitality in a Time of Backlash," Theology Today 52 (January 1996): 476-84.
22. Russell, "Practicing Hospitality in a Time of Backlash," 476.
23. Russell, "Practicing Hospitality in a Time of Backlash," 478.
24. Russell, "Practicing Hospitality in a Time of Backlash," 482.
25. Russell, "Practicing Hospitality in a Time of Backlash," 484.
26. Letty M. Russell, "Encountering the 'Other' in a World of Difference and Danger," Harvard Theological Review 99:4 (2006): 457-68. The article is the text of Russell's Paul Tillich Lecture delivered at Harvard Divinity School, Cambridge, MA, May 9, 2006, and is audible online at http://www.hds.harvard.edu/news_online/tillich_2006.html
27. Russell, "Encountering the 'Other' in a World of Difference and Danger," 458.
28. Russell, "Encountering the 'Other' in a World of Difference and Danger," 459.
29. Russell, "Encountering the 'Other' in a World of Difference and Danger," 459.
30. Russell, "Encountering the 'Other' in a World of Difference and Danger," 459.
31. Russell, "Encountering the 'Other' in a World of Difference and Danger," 461.
32. Russell, "Encountering the 'Other' in a World of Difference and Danger," 463.
33. Russell, "Encountering the 'Other' in a World of Difference and Danger," 464.
34. Russell, "Encountering the 'Other' in a World of Difference and Danger," 465.
35. Russell, "Encountering the 'Other' in a World of Difference and Danger," 468. Similar insights seem lately to be motivating theologians, particularly women, to reexamine hospitality as central to both Christian theology and to a broader theopolitical ethic. See Christine D. Pohl, Making Room: Recovering Hospitality and a Christian Tradition (Grand Rapids, MI: Eerdmans, 1999); Elizabeth Newman, Untamed Hospitality: Welcoming God and Other Strangers (Grand Rapids, MI: Brazos Press 2007).
36. Michael Harrington, The Other America: Poverty in the United States (New York: Macmillan, 1962).
37. Michael Eric Dyson, Come Hell or High Water: Hurricane Katrina and the Color of Disaster (New York: Basic Books, 2006) (emphases added). See also Michael Ignatieff, "The Broken Contract," The New York Times, September 5, 2005.
38. Lucinda Marshall, "Were Women Raped in New Orleans?: Addressing the Human Rights of Women in Times of Crisis," 35(9/10) Off Our Backs (September/October 2005): 15.
39. Marshall, "Were Women Raped in New Orleans?" 14.
40. See, Elaine Enarson and Betty Hearn Morrow, The Gendered Terrain of Disaster: Through Women's Eyes (Westport, CT: Praeger, 1998).
41. James Q. Wilson, "American Dilemma," National Review (December 19, 2005): 61-2.
42. Lillian Poats, "The Invisibility of the Black Family During Hurricane Katrina," 23:3 Diverse: Issues in Higher Education (March 23, 2006).
43. Poats, "The Invisibility of the Black Family During Hurricane Katrina."

44. Loretta J. Ross, "A Feminist Perspective on Hurricane Katrina," *Off Our Backs* (September/October 2005): 11. See also Joni Seager, "Noticing Gender (or Not) in Disasters," *Social Policy* 36:2 (Winter 2005/2006): Ibid., 12. This idea that women live in a pervasive posture of fear was also heard in the aftermath of 9/11 by feminists commenting on how the terrorist attacks seem to have particularly shaken men's sense of masculine security and immunity from harm in ways that may have led to an excessively hasty military response. For an excellent, earlier account of the role of fear in women's lives, particularly fears connected with the possibility of rape, see Margaret T. Gordon and Stephanie Riger, *The Female Fear: The Social Cost of Rape* (New York: Free Press, 1989). Feminist journalist and commentator Susan Faludi has recently written compellingly about fear-driven backlash in gender roles following 9/11 in *The Terror Dream: Fear and Fantasy in Post-9/11 America* (Metropolitan Books, 2007).

45. Jonathan Cohn, "The Golden Ticket," *The New Republic*, August 14 and 21, 2006, 13-17.

46. Cohn, "The Golden Ticket," 13.47. Cohn, "The Golden Ticket," 17.

47. Cohn, "The Golden Ticket," 17.

48. Tom Frary, "Thy Kingdom Come: The Theory of Dorothy Day," *Commonweal* 127 (November 11, 1972): 387.

49. Dorothy Day, *Loaves and Fishes* (New York: Harper & Row, 1963), 28.

50. See Mitzi J. Smith, "A Tale of Two Sisters: Am I My Sister's Keeper?" *Journal of Religious Thought*, 52-53:1-2 (1996): 69-75; Sook Ja Chung, "Bible Study: Women's Ways of Doing Mission in the Story of Mary and Martha," *International Review of Mission*, 93:368 (2004): 91-16; Satako Yamaguchi, "Christianity and Women in Japan," *Japanese Journal of Religious Studies* 30:3-4 (2003): 315-38.

51. Chung, "Bible Study," 13.

52. Yamaguchi, "Christianity and Women in Japan," 335.

53. Shankar Vedantam, "Why Everyone You Know Thinks the Same as You," *The Washington Post* (October 16, 2006); Shankar Vedantam, "Why the Ideological Melting Pot Is Getting So Lumpy," *The Washington Post* (January 19, 2009).

54. Aaron Retica, "Homophily," (The Sixth Annual Year in Ideas) *The New York Times Magazine* (December 10, 2006).

Part III: International Explorations of Feminism and Hospitality

Chapter 7

Welcoming Courtyards: Hospitality, Spirituality, and Gender

Fauzia Erfan Ahmed

Extravagant, spontaneous, and, at times, overwhelming, hospitality is taken for granted in Bangladesh. As essential as speech, hospitality is an ever present priority in daily life. Indeed, it is difficult to imagine how society would work without it. Yet, the ways in which indigenous meanings of hospitality enable the creation of a strong civil society and shape social structure are overlooked in gender and development studies.

What comprises social structure and what constitutes social change are central to debates in development circles. In the over three decades since Bangladesh gained independence, the gender and development effort has shown remarkable progress. The fertility rate has decreased from 6.1 to 3;[1] girls' enrolment in primary school has increased so that for every 100 boys there are 104 girls;[2] and women's entrepreneurial activities have increased female mobility and the household income.[3] It is widely acknowledged that a strong civil society based on a cohesive women's movement has overcome patriarchal religion to achieve these impressive social change indicators. But the role that hospitality continues to play in this social transformation has not been researched in the vast literature on gender and development in Bangladesh.

These achievements have not been easy. Patriarchal interpretations of Islam posed a formidable challenge: right wing religious extremists opposed family planning, which enabled women to have control over their bodies and work opportunities which took them outside the home. Gender and development scholars and activists used feminist interpretations of Islam to counter the Islamicist premise. Progressive as they are, these interpretations are based solely on the Quran and the Hadith (sayings of Prophet Muhammad), key Islamic texts. Muslim feminist scholars also need to explore ways in which a syncretic Islam which is the fusion of Hinduism, Islam, and folk wisdom provides a base of spiritual resistance.[4]

Based on a continuing ethnographic study, I argue that hospitality is an important expression of this spirituality. But exploring what hospitality means is central to understanding constituent elements of village society: As Goethe said there is no outward act of politeness that does not have a profound moral significance.[5] In this chapter, I explore the nexus of gender, syncretic Islam, and hospitality.

I investigate the following questions: What does hospitality mean to the villagers themselves? What is the link between spirituality and hospitality? How does hospitality facilitate social change? The literature review section, which is a critique of the economist model and alternate feminist paradigms, is followed by a contextual overview of Bangladeshi rural society. Since ways of knowing influence what one comes to know, the methods section precedes the findings.

The Economist Model and Alternate Feminist Paradigms

Hospitality lies at the frontiers of scholarship on alternate paradigms to patriarchal capitalism. The economist model, with its emphasis on individuation, commodification, and the market has been contested by feminist scholars. Since economics necessarily deals with what is tangible, quantifiable, and measurable, an economist vantage point does not include hospitality; instead it focuses on the gift as the good that is given. Gift giving as embedded in the moral economy,[6] as an aspect of a maternal economic logic,[7] and the ethics of care theory[8] have been presented as alternate paradigms. It is useful to outline the economist model prior to analyzing these feminist paradigms.

The gift which is a good in this model is explained in terms of identity, value, and exchange. Economic theory is based on *homos economicus* or the maximizing individual who always and only seeks to maximize his or her self interest; this alienable identity is atomistic. It follows that society consists of individuals who know exactly what they want, try to get it at least cost to themselves, and for themselves alone.[9] Not surprisingly, in such a scenario the value of the gift is its price. More profoundly, value is measured by how much the host or giver is willing to sacrifice it order to give or buy it. The willingness to give is measured by the cost of the good and the likelihood of receiving an equivalent or greater benefit in return. Rational exchange is, therefore, an integral assumption of the economic theory of the gift. In reality, what appears as altruism only seems so. It happens only because a reward, which can also take the form of power, prestige or social approval, is expected.[10] Purposive and predictive gift giving, therefore, is part of the inevitable societal quid pro quo.

Gift Giving and the Moral Economy

Vaughn's critique of economism challenges the economist notion of identity, value, and exchange.[11] She argues it is the patriarchal capitalistic nature of certain societies, which mutates the human being into a self-centered isolated individual. In contrast to the maximizing individual, gift giving can lead to a human identity which seeks to connect to others because the gift is given to fulfill someone else's need. Unlike the calculated cost benefit ratio, the nature of the gift giving is creative and, therefore, beyond measure or price. Based on the creative impulse of the giver and the receiver, gift giving as an alternate paradigm creates a relationship of inclusion. According to Vaughn[12] any theory based on the gift as a rational exchange can never value the receiver or other people in general. Exchange produces division; gift giving inspires community.

The picture of a different identity under a gift giving paradigm is clear, but few, if any, details of how this paradigm would work in real life are provided. I argue that gift giving cannot be understood unless it is viewed in a larger theoretical context. In order for this paradigm to be sustainable, the maternal economic logic that Vaughn[13] mentions needs to be developed and amplified as broader theoretical context.

The notion of a moral economy is based on system of socially desirable transactions.[14] Cheal uses rational transfers theory to construct the underlying basis of the gift economy: the rational redistribution of resources when a distributive imbalance occurs in society. He cogently argues that even in a capitalist society, not everything is acquired through a rational process. But his concept of the gift economy is still an attempt to legitimize the gift in economic terms. The gift is still defined as a transaction, even though he does make a distinction between transactions such as waged payment which are confined to a narrow definition of societal relations and the "free floating" presence of gifts within the moral economy of interpersonal relations.[15] Clearly, the moral economy, presumably as opposed to a market economy, is the alternative contextual paradigm. But again, Cheal does not develop what this "free floating" context means and how it works in the everyday lives of ordinary people.[16]

The Ethics of Care Theory

The ethics of care theory is far more compelling as an alternate paradigm because it provides a developed moral context.[17, 18] It is based on the universal experience of children who can claim the requirement to be cared for by parents. The ethics of care theory emphasizes the societal need for human beings to have interdependent caring relationships with each other.[19] In contrast to the rational self-interested individual, it underscores human beings as having sympathy and moral concern for each other. Both as a value and as practice the ethics of care has been applied to a variety of socioeconomic and political contexts: as an attitude which focuses on the needs of others[20] as labor[21] as relational labor[22] and as based on face to face interaction.[23] The need to care has been defined as something intuitive and instinctively fundamental.[24] Indeed the ethics of care theory has developed as an alternative framework of social relationships which meet human needs in a contextual and ethical manner.

However, as Cheal points out, there are key lacunae: caring is ill-defined; what people actually do when they care for others remain contextually vague; and why we should care for each other is not convincingly explained.[25] In response, he posits the caring theory of obligation, which illustrates that caring is not just an emotion; it is also rational to care for others. I agree with his critique of the ethics of care theory, but I do not find his inclusion of rationality to be persuasive as an alternate model. Even though care theory emphasizes people's belief in each other to behave in accordance with an overarching morality, why this belief should persist (not just exist) or what this collective morality means in everyday life remains indeterminate. What do we do when we care for each other? Why should we care? Religion, as a unifying reason, has been dismissed by the ethics of care theorists.[26] But, I think an exploration of what feminist theologians have written about hospitality indicates answers to these compelling questions.

Hospitality and Religion

Clearly, any viable theory of hospitality must explain why it exists and how it works. What it is, or the nature of hospitality itself, is inextricably linked to its abstraction and practice. In order to build a theory of hospitality, I investigate what hospitality means in the ancient Hindu philosophical tradition and in the present day syncretic Islam of rural Bangladesh.

Hospitality and the Hindu Cosmic Order

In an attempt to highlight the status of Hindu womanhood in the Vedas (Hindu religious texts), Findly analyzes religious meanings of hospitality within the Hindu cosmic order. Hinduism prescribes four stages of life necessary to maintain this order: *brahmacarya* or celibate studenthood; *shongshari* or householder; *sannyasin* (ascetic); and *vanaprasth* (forest dweller).[27] Findly focuses on ways in which *brahmacarya*, or Vedic student, and *sannyasin* or ascetic are distinguished by *bhiksha* or alms seeking.[28] Unlike the student who lives with his teacher, the *sannyasin* who has renounced a home wanders from village to village seeking alms. The peripatetic nature of his lifestyle also means that he has to accept alms without eagerness and as the bare minimum needed for sustenance. In the idealized form, he is not even supposed to ask for food. Since the renunciate cannot exist without the provision of cooked food, the obligation, therefore, rests on the housemistress to give him food. Hindu philosophy describes the guest as Agni, the God of Fire. The responsibility to give and to receive food is not only a matter of host-guest etiquette.

The identity of both the host and the guest shapes the ritual of the threshold encounter between the mendicant and the household mistress. Though some orders require that alms be sought from family members, others forbid it. But it cannot be denied that caste, which remains an important feature of identity in the Hindu tradition, shapes the threshold encounter. A *brahmacaryin* is forbidden to seek alms from the lowest castes. The threshold encounter ensures the maintenance of caste purity and social boundaries even as it heightens student's awareness of various classes and castes.

This threshold encounter is a "ritual of tremendous sacramental character"[29] based on *danadharma*, which literally means the dharma or moral law of giving. In order to emphasize the role of the householder's wife in the maintenance of the cosmic order in Hindu religious philosophy, she emphasizes *danadharma*, as the duty of the gift of food. In my opinion, Findly's emphasis on food is somewhat narrow.[30] Clearly, *danadharma* necessarily extends beyond edibles. This ritual is also governed by *atithya* or (Vedic) hospitality, which is the primary principle of the threshold encounter. The form which *atithya* takes in present day Bangladesh, a predominantly Muslim country, has not been studied.

Hospitality and Syncretic Islam

What hospitality means today in the everyday lives of villagers cannot be explored without a sense of historical context. As Islam spread from its birthplace in Saudi Arabia to other countries, the various religious and cultural traditions it encountered changed its original character. In Bangladesh, extant Hindu, and other traditions and religious philosophies impacted the nature of Islam. Not surprisingly, new converts retained prior cultural customs even as they converted to the new religion. Thus a syncretic Islam, which is the amalgam of Hinduism, Islam and folk wisdom, was created when local inhabitants embraced Islam and made it part of their heritage and culture.

In his masterful book, Roy stresses spirituality in his analysis of the way in religious traditions blended with each other in Bengal.[31] He emphasizes syncretic Islam as a blend of Sufic and Vaishnav spirituality. Indeed the theme of love as the primary connection between the devotee (*bhakta*) and the Divine is common to both Hindu (Vaishnava) and Muslim (Sufic) spirituality in Bengal. Feminist Muslim scholar Kassam describes spirituality as the "hidden backbone" of Islam, and as the Feminine in the concept of Allah. More research needs to be carried out on the ways in which this spirituality is expressed in the quotidian by the beliefs of ordinary people and their activities.[32]

Recent scholarship indicates that villagers consider spiritual achievements as important as material outcomes in their vision of a good life and that women use Muslim spirituality as a positive ideology in their struggle to overcome poverty.[33] *Shongshare shanti* (peace at home) and *shonman rekhe chola* (to walk with dignity) are as imperative as material assets and a permanent job.[34] Syncretic Islam helps Muslim women distinguish between outward piety as reflected in religious ritual and the everyday expression of love which can only come from inner faith. In direct repudiation of a punitive patriarchal Allah, village women believe in a compassionate loving Allah. Village women regaled me with stories of Rabia al Adawiya, the Sufi Muslim saint who was the first to preach the doctrine of Divine Love, as a role model.

Bangladesh: The Sociocultural Context

Even at first glance, this country of 151 million appears as a landscape rife with contradiction. The Prime Minister is a widow; so is the leader of the opposition. Yet in the village in which I lived, widows face the specter of destitution. On December 29, 2008, Bangladeshis voted overwhelmingly for a secular government. But in rural areas, social pressures, created by the religious right wing, compel women to wear *burkhas* (outer garments which covers their bodies). Despite the impressive social change indicators, patriarchal gender norms remain a challenge for gender and development programs and women's rights activists.

Samaj needs to be understood in all its dimensions. In daily life it means "society" or "association" whereas in etymological terms it signifies "going together."[35] In an abstract sense, it denotes belonging. *Samaj* is also a symbol. It is its "representation as a model of community, of the shape social life into which a member of a human *Jat* (race) is gradually modeled" that is more important than its territorial or structural status.[36] Community beyond the extended family is created through *samaj*, the collective sanction of which is ever present in daily existence. Expressions like *shobai bole* (everybody says) or the negative *manshe mondo koy* (people will speak badly) reverberate through the interstices of village discourse.[37] Clearly, belonging to *samaj* is conditional. Men, particular *matubors*, (who are also the rich men) create and define *samaj* while women have to conform to its rules to belong. *Samaj* is an important tool since the very anticipation of its disapproval or worse still, exclusion from *samaj* is sufficient to maintain the status quo.

The persistent efforts of the women's movement, state, and non state actors, which resulted in the dramatic national achievements, challenge the very foundations of *samaj*, which controls Bangladeshi women of all classes through a definition of marriage and family formation that is patrilocal. Women used to have many pregnancies in order to have a son. The government's family planning program, which has dramatically reduced the fertility rate, has contested this patriarchal son preference. Girls used to be married off after the onset of menarche. Now the 100 percent national primary school enrollment rate has broken this pattern; girls want to finish high school and then go on to college. The strong women's movement has created a flourishing civil society at the grass roots level which enables women to analyze and debate their status in society. The fact that both the Prime Minister and the leader of the opposition are women inspires rural women to run for public office. Clearly a new meaning of *samaj* has emerged with these structural changes.

However, these accomplishments, tangible as they are, cannot be a reason for complacency. Patriarchal gender norms remain an obstacle for gender and development programs and women's rights activists. Gendered identities are still defined by *purdah* (veil), a complex social system that secludes women and divides the world into male and female spaces. Villagers live in a *bari* (homestead) system and several *baris* constitute *paras* (neighborhoods) which, in turn comprise a *gram* (village). Women who leave their neighborhood to go to work can still be chastized by *samaj*. "Respectable" work opportunities, therefore, remain restricted to the homestead.

Though as an institution, *purdah* confines women's activities, ironically the homestead allows the creation and sustenance of woman-space. The *bari* comprises dwellings around a *uthan* (central courtyard), which is woman's space. This courtyard is where women thresh grain, watch their children, and plant kitchen gardens. It is also where women can meet and discuss issues of common concern. It is also where hospitality takes place.

Method

My research design has three important distinguishing characteristics. First, it is a continuing ethnographic study which started in 1999 in Tala union (a geographic unit) which expanded to include Debhata, an adjacent union in 2009. An extending study is necessary given my overarching research goal of investigating the relationship of gendered identity, society and development. I have continued to interview the same families in Tala, having added another geographic unit recently.

Second, I chose to live with the villagers. Indeed, the findings of this field-based multi-method study are based on three ethnographic techniques: participant observation, five videotaped focus groups consisting of approximately thirty villagers each in four different neighborhoods, and eighty-five interviews. The subset of eighty-five male and female interviewees was drawn from a larger sample of 215 villagers. The sample was chosen through snowballing, a standard anthropological technique, and theoretical sampling, the basis of grounded theory in sociology.

Ways of knowing influence what one comes to know. Participant observation, the standard technical term in anthropological research, means to learn about something as one lives it. I learned about hospitality even as I was giving and receiving it. For example, I learned about the creation of women's space as my bedroom on the second floor of my house became transformed into a women's courtyard in which women felt free to talk about problems, resistance, and change.

Third, Kulia, the village in Debhata, is my ancestral home. Reflexivity is fundamental to ethnography; the researcher is the data instrument in qualitative research. I came with an inherited identity to the Muslim *para* (neighborhood) which gave me acceptability and access. But what did it mean for me as an Americanized, Bangladeshi Muslim to try to cross Hindu Muslim boundaries? The exploration of this multifaceted question deserves a separate chapter in and of itself. Suffice it to say that the most important thing was to gain permission to enter the emotional landscape of the Hindu *para*. As Kumar, also discovered, I found that adoption helped.[38]

Creating kin, however, can never be contrived. I was adopted by a Hindu (Swarnakar) family in Gopalpur; this happened because Ma, the eighty-year-old grandmother reminded me of my great-grandmother to whom I was very close. Like her, Ma was a midwife. Spunky and determined, Ma had raised four children as a Hindu widow. I thought that she was simply terrific, and I think that she also liked me a lot. I loved to recline on the bed in their veranda and listen to her stories about Hindu gods and goddesses. It seemed very natural that we should adopt each other, but I was also aware that this was the first time that a Muslim had ever eaten with them.

Two Vignettes of Hospitality

In this section, I describe two vignettes which illustrate what people actually do and what happens when they engage in hospitality. In the first scenario, I was an unexpected guest when I returned to visit Ma in the Hindu neighborhood of Gopalpur. I was accompanied by my Muslim cousins. This unexpected visit serves as a cameo of hospitality in its classic idealized form. In the second account, I was the hostess in my ancestral home in Kulia, situated in the Muslim neighborhood. Here I was able to observe how hospitality facilitates social change.

As Guest

Lush bamboo groves arched over the entrance to the Hindu *para* in Gopalpur, the most beautiful of all the neighborhoods. Even before the car stopped, people came out to greet me. I was welcomed by the excited chatter of relatives and friends.

Ma and Boro Bou (elder daughter-in-law) were sleeping in the veranda of their home in the heat of the noonday sun when I arrived. After the initial hugs, everyone became very busy in a flurry of excitement: Ma immediately got up and started slicing the mangoes for us on a *dao* (large curved knife) in the bedroom; out of the corner of my eye I saw Boro Bou having a whispered conversation with a niece about lunch; Choto Dada (younger brother) climbed a tree to get *dab* (fresh coconut) for us to drink. Choto Bou (younger daughter-in law) took me to her house and gave me a sari, petticoat, and a blouse to change into. It certainly was a relief to change out of my sweat-stained clothes. Mejo Bou (middle daughter-in-law) put oil in my hair and combed it carefully.

Two of the sons jumped into the pond to catch fish for lunch, preparations for which were already underway. At first, two medium size fish were caught. They were thrown back. My nephews wanted to catch a big fish for their *pishci* (paternal aunt). Indeed, the fish head was presented to me ceremoniously as the guest of honor. After a delicious meal, we were treated to several desserts in different homes in the *bari* (homestead). I felt embraced by a loving space as I wandered in and out of the homes. The shared sense of joy had a timeless quality to it.

The news of my visit spread. Everyone came to see me and to examine my gifts. I had brought gifts: saris for all my sisters-in-law and shirts and *lungis* (sarongs worn by men) for my brothers. They were given in the middle of great excitement. I gave Ma a white sari. I was then told to present the sari that I had brought for my eldest sister-in-law. Her sari design was more intricate than the saris for the junior sisters-in-law, a sign of respect for hierarchy, which was commented on appreciatively. Ma gave me a big jackfruit and asked me to take it all the way to America! I left with a big bag consisting of five coconuts, lots of *jamrul* (a fruit) and the jack fruit, which was carried ceremoniously to the car by Choto Dada on his head.

As Host

From the very first day that I set foot in my ancestral home in Kulia, women came to visit me in the upstairs bedroom of the second floor of my house. They came unexpectedly: sometimes alone; sometimes in pairs; and sometimes with the entire extended family in tow. They usually came at sunset. The veranda was surrounded by huge palm trees; the slim minarets of the nearby mosque were silhouetted against a pink sky. It was in this lush setting that I gave and received gifts. I offered saris from Dhaka; they brought fruits from their trees. I served them whatever food I had: *muri* (puffed rice); *jalabi* (a sweet snack); and tea. But food was not foremost.

Before I even realized it, my bedroom and the adjoining veranda became a welcoming courtyard, a women's space where village women were free to come and go as they pleased. Most importantly, it was in this hospitable space, cloistered by the trees and the doves that flew in and around them, that women felt that they could discuss their problems. Secure in the belief that they would not be interrupted nor overheard, they claimed the bedroom and the veranda as their own. Just as women are restricted from entering male spaces, men cannot always enter the courtyard with impunity. As a result women can analyze and debate vital issues without fear of male intervention. Women told me their stories: how they were compelled to wear *burkha* (outer garment worn over the sari) for protection immediately after widowhood and how another woman had acid thrown at her because she refused an unsuitable marriage proposal. There in the shadow of the mosque, they told me how much they despised the hypocrisy of the religious right wing and how they had created alternate organizations in their homes. As the canopy of night descended, women sang songs that only women sing. In this way, hospitality created a protected space for women in my house.

Hospitality (*Aapayon*), Gender, and Spirituality

Practiced by Hindus and Muslims today, *aapayon*, as hospitality is known in rural Bangladesh, is an expression of syncretic Islam. But, hospitality is an inadequate translation of what *aapayon* really means. Clearly, the threshold encounter, even though it is based on *atithya* or (Vedic) hospitality of the threshold encounter in Hindu philosophy is a narrow and incomplete definition of *aapayon* or the hospitality of the loving embrace that I encountered in Gopalpur.[39]

Whenever I entered a *para*, I was greeted by a chorus of voices saying "*Ashun Ashun* (Come in Come in)." *Aapayon* is an ambiance, a state of readiness for the grace of an unexpected visitor. Village narratives abound with myths of the host who jumped into the pond to get fish for the surprise guest who arrived at midnight. These extremes to which hospitality can be carried, despite all protestations of the guest, indicates a spirit not only of extravagant generosity but an ability to give oneself totally to a concept of whom one should be. In rural Bangladesh, I found that standards of hospitality created the ideal social form for village society and flowed from the sphere of the mythic to actual life. Far more profound than the stark quid pro quo of the exchange transaction or the economy of gift giving, it is the moral order that helps humans observe, evaluate, and understand each other. Hospitality is context.

Hospitality as Peoples' Religion

> God approves of hospitality to other human beings. Actually what is God? Hospitality to human beings is religion. If I can love you very much, if you are the kind of person who can inspire love, then there is God within you.
> —Manik, Hindu (Kayasth) man

In the above-mentioned quote, Manik describes *aapayon* as the peoples' religion. In so doing, he also expands the meaning of religion to a way of life and separate from established formal religion, which emanates from the mosque or the temple. This indigenous concept of religion is much broader than Findly's analysis of almsgiving as hospitality in the Vedic philosophy.[40] Contrary to popular belief, many villagers do not always fulfill the formal religious requirements every day; but to shirk hospitality is unthinkable. Ashok, the rickshaw puller who drove me around, did not always observe all the Hindu *pujas*, especially those which required fasting for the whole day, and many Muslim women do not pray five times a day, but hospitality was never violated. While women complained about daily chores and the lack of male assistance, they never complained about the work that hospitality necessitated. If what is sacred is something that must never be defiled, then as Manik says, hospitality is indeed the peoples' religion.

Hospitality (*aapayon*) is part of syncretic Islam because it infuses *atithya* (Vedic hospitality) with Divine Love. Manik describes divinity and love as the basis of hospitality, which is more reminiscent of Sufic and Vaishnav spirituality.[41] Unlike formal religion, be it Islam or Hinduism, this spirituality is based on the twin concepts of the in-dwelling Divine and the theme of love as the primary connection between devotee (*bhakta*) and the Deity. The concept of the Divine in *aapayon* (hospitality) is the spiritual bridge between Hinduism and Islam in rural Bangladesh. Perhaps, this hospitality, therefore, is the loving moral and social context that Hamington describes as a key challenge of the feminist vision.[42] *Aapayon* (hospitality) in abstract is a moral responsibility, and it is in this context that its practice, such as giving clothes, food, and shelter, has not only a sacramental ritualized character but also establish a joyous unity between the host, the guest, and the Divine.

Also implied in Manik's quote is the distinction between religion and spirituality, a difference that proponents of care ethics theory do not make.[43] It is this distinction that makes hospitality sustainable as a moral paradigm, as a way of being. It can legitimately be argued, and as this study shows, even if religion carries "universal baggage," spirituality based on love carries universal appeal.[44] I argue that in abstract, *aapayon* means love in syncretic Islam in contrast to the ritualized *atithya* (Vedic hospitality) of Hinduism.

The ethics of care theory is built on the premise of the receiver or the child, the raison d'etre being that one must do the right thing for one's child. It is in the moral universe of *aapayon* that we can find a compelling answer to the why of caring for others. In contrast to the ethics of care theory which emphasizes the needs of the person who is cared for, *aapayon* also emphasizes the host.[45] If the guest is God, then it is the host who is blessed and honored.

Hospitality, Femininity, and Masculinity

The praxis of hospitality enhances notions of womanhood and manhood in distinctive ways. Ways in which hospitality is a symbol of traditional femininity are obvious. During my visit Ma cut mangoes on the *dao* (a large curved knife, which takes practice to use) to serve them to us. Ma also cleaned fish that had been caught from the pond and Boro Bou (oldest daughter-in-law) cooked it. Another granddaughter cooked the vegetables. Choto Bou (youngest daughter-in-law) also massaged my hair with coconut oil and combed it very carefully. Various hospitality activities were assigned according to female hierarchy within the extended family. Women also derive great pleasure from hospitality as a display of a femininity, which not only glories in traditional skills of making special and intricate dishes for the guest, but also in activities that create physical intimacy and warmth.

Though my study revealed at least four different types of masculinities, ranging from the high-minded to the abusive in Bangladesh, traditional masculinity is viewed as uniformly oppressive.[46] But hospitality as a performance of South Asian masculinities, which has not been investigated in Chopra, Osella, and Osella's book, reveals that traditional masculinity is a more complex phenomenon.[47]

As my visit to Gopalpur indicates, there are specific hospitality activities which embellish traditional notions of manhood. One of Ma's grandsons was immediately dispatched to do the bazaar (food shopping) for lunch; and yet another gave a *lungi* (sarong) to my male cousin who had accompanied me, to change into. Demonstrated physical effort to procure food for the host is an emblem of traditional manhood. Two other grandsons jumped into the pond to catch fish for my lunch. Another climbed a tree to present me with *dab* (fresh coconut). Finally it was Choto Dada (younger brother) who put all the gifts of fruits and vegetables in a bag and carried them on his head to the car which was going to take me to the airport. When I returned to Dhaka, Sanjay, the eldest grandson repeatedly called inviting me back, saying that he would hire a taxi and meet me at the airport. Clearly, these hospitality activities are a performance of male physical strength, agility, and social status but they are also an expression of paternal and fraternal love, an aspect that is neglected in studies of hospitality.

Hospitality as Social Change: Opportunities and Challenges

The women's movement is a pillar of civil society in Bangladesh; multiclass solidarity has been noted as its signal achievement.[48] But the ways in which *aapayon* (hospitality) created this solidarity since the very inception of this country have not been researched. The Pakistani military crackdown, which took place on March 25, 1971, compelled urban families to flee and take shelter in the villages. The flight was imperative for young women, since the Pakistan army had also embarked on a pogrom of pillage and rape. Personal narratives reveal that villagers welcomed them, giving them shelter and food. This hospitality creates a mutuality among women of different classes: upper and middle class women were able to understand the troubles of low-income rural women because they lived with them. Village women realized that rich women also had problems. The bonds that were formed through hospitality endure to the present day. Hospitality strengthens the women's movement by creating women's spaces and unity. However, ways in which societal identity impacts it remains a challenge.

Women's Courtyard as Metaphor

> All I hear from the mosque is: "Don't do this; don't do that. Don't go out of the house to work; don't educate your daughters." Is Allah a long list of don'ts? I believe Allah is Love. "If you love human beings, then Allah will love you."
> —Qulsum, Muslim woman

Aapayon (hospitality) does not only take place in the women's courtyard; it creates woman's space as metaphor. In this sense, and as the above quote indicates, the women's courtyard is a counterpoint to the mosque establishment. Unwelcoming to women, often openly hostile, the mosque establishment is a bastion of right wing patriarchal Islam in Bangladesh. In violation of the Quran and Hadith, women are forbidden to pray in the mosque. I was not allowed to pray in the village mosque even though it had been built by my great grandfather. Men gather to pray there at least five times everyday; but much more than prayers takes place in the mosque. Well funded, spacious, and airy, the mosque provides a free space for the homeless and travelers as well as leadership development and political organizing. It is a designated male space.

Women have no such physical arena. In the absence of a space, lack of resources, and in the face of the mosque network, why is the women's movement so strong? What sustains it? My research reveals that hospitality provides an answer to these important questions. My bedroom, and the adjoining veranda became the courtyard of hospitality, a women's space. Custom dictated that men could not enter; indeed it would be shameful for them to do so. The courtyard is safe. Central to women's culture, it develops women's unity and leadership.

Clearly, solidarity gives women voice and, therefore, is key to the success of the women's movement. In this way, it facilitates freedom of speech, which persisted even during the martial law. The most important lever in the empowerment process it has been extensively researched.[49] The courtyard allows women leaders to create and sustain women's unity with tangible improvements in national and social indicators;[50] indeed, it enabled the national family planning program. Unity among women gives abused women resilience to cope with the everyday. Through the exercise of compassion in the courtyard, women's hospitality mitigates domestic violence, a serious threat to women's safety. Women gather around the victim to provide relief, be it moral support or medicine.

The courtyard sustains women's culture in Bangladesh. Subterranean but age old, this culture revels in women's household managing skills, and in female sexual and reproductive powers. If the proverb is the formalized expression of male culture, songs, stories, and jokes are symbols of traditional women's culture, as Raheja and Gold discovered in their wonderful study of North Indian women.[51] I noted songs protesting domestic violence, and stories about how thrifty women rescued their households (i.e., from men who do not know how to make ends meet), and woman-only jokes, which made fun of men. What is important to note is that women saw these songs and jokes as empowering and as resistance to the male culture with its public display of bravado. Women sang not just as individuals enraptured with the beauty of the songs, but as a group conscious of its subordination and how it can use power to circumvent this subordination. The songs united women; they also enabled women's leadership development.

Hospitality and the Challenge of Societal Division

Given Islam's message of spiritual equality, one would expect *aapayon* (hospitality) to be entirely free of caste class and other barriers. But this is not true. Vestiges of the brahminical tradition which ensured caste purity in the threshold encounter combined with increased income inequality and commodification impact the host guest relationship.[52] As Feldman argues, market values threaten the traditional respect for "reciprocity, obligation, and community solidarity."[53] Caste, class, and hospitality intersect to define how villagers exist in their own as well as in the social imagination.

Hospitality can become socially divisive. A social ideal, hospitality also inextricably linked to identity and self worth. Perhaps the statement that "you are who you eat with" is an over simplification. But it is not far from the truth. Eating also means status. Who eats with whom is a way of establishing social hierarchy and making it very transparent at the same time. The older landed families only ate with each other. Sometimes they would condescend to eat with someone lower down in the social hierarchy, but this was noblesse oblige. The refusal of hospitality is, therefore, a calculated insult tantamount to spiritual rejection. It means that the welcoming household is unworthy. In rural Bangladesh, people express anger by refusing hospitality.

The need to define who one eats with is also the need for identity. As Sarah Lamb says, "People who eat the same food together at the same time and in the same location (as in persons served in the same row at a feast) also share substantial qualities with each other."[54] When I invited a Kayasth (upper caste) woman to eat with Ma, she told me "*ami oder shathe khai na*" (I don't eat with them). She was woman with a husband who was too sick to work, a blind mother-in-law, and, two daughters to marry off. Despite her poverty, this statement was made with determination and pride. Her high caste gave her a superior identity because the neighbors though better off were lower caste. Yet, the refusal to eat, based as it was on a definition of identity, prevented solidarity. Such a definition of hospitality threatens women's solidarity, so critical to all pathways of empowerment.

Conclusion

Village women and men make the critical distinction between the outward piety of ritualized religion and the inner conviction of syncretic faith. It is in the theoretical interstices of this distinction, that I discovered *aapayon* (hospitality) as a living indigenous paradigm, an alternative code of ethics. Indeed, it exists in various forms as theory and praxis all over South Asia which is home to over a billion people. Rooted in ancient spiritual tradition, hospitality (*aapayon*) is the sacred in everyday life in rural Bangladesh.

In the theory of *aapayon* (hospitality), the guest as Deity provides a compelling spiritual rationale; specific hospitality activities reveal its myriad meanings and shape gendered identities. A bulwark against rightwing Islam, a feminist tool and strategy, hospitality continues to sustain the women's movement. Despite a history of purging Islam of "foreign" elements, as local religious traditions were called, *aapayon* (hospitality) has survived.[55] The decades since Liberation have been those of remarkable social change, but a society of equality and justice, has yet to be attained in Bangladesh. Serious obstacles which include societal division, increasing inequality; and an emerging consumer identity, exist. But these challenges are not insurmountable. As my experience of hospitality in a Hindu family reveals, communal and other barriers can be contested. The women's movement needs to be conscious of hospitality (*aapayon*) as a theory, strategy, and social institution. Only then will the glow of this everyday sacrament, create a just society in which life is lived with purpose, love, and zest.

Notes

1. Rounaq Jahan and Adrienne Germain, "Mobilizing Support to Sustain Political Will is the Key to Progress in Reproductive Health." *Lancet* 364 (2004): 742-4.
2. Human Development Report, (Oxford: United Nations Development Programme 2005), 46.

3. Mark Pitt, Shahidur Khandker, and Jennifer Cartwright, "Empowering Women with Micro finance: Evidence from Bangladesh" *Economic Development and Cultural Change* 54, no 3 (2006):791-831.
4. Fauzia Erfan Ahmed, "Microcredit, Men, and Masculinity" *National Association of Women's Studies Journal* 20, no 2 (Summer 2008): 122-55.
5. John Huizinga, *The Waning of the Middle Ages* (New York: Doubleday, 1954), 46.
6. David Cheal, *Towards an Anthropological Theory of Value: The False Coin of our Dreams*. (Palgrave: New York, 2001).
7. Genevieve Vaughn, *Women and the Gift Economy: A Radically Different Worldview* (Toronto, Canada: Ianna Publications, 2007).
8. Virgina Held, *The Ethics of Care: Personal, Political, Global* (Oxford: Oxford University Press, 2006).
9. Cheal, *Towards an Anthropological Theory of Value*.
10. Cheal, *Towards an Anthropological Theory of Value*.
11. Vaughn, *Women and the Gift Economy*.
12. Vaughn, *Women and the Gift Economy*.
13. Vaughn, *Women and the Gift Economy*.
14. Cheal, *Towards an Anthropological Theory of Value*.
15. Cheal, *Towards an Anthropological Theory of Value*.
16. Cheal, *Towards an Anthropological Theory of Value*.
17. Nel Noddings, *Caring: A Feminist Approach to Ethics and Moral Education* (Berkeley: University of California Press, 1986).
18. Carol Gilligan, *In a Different Voice: Psychological Theory and Women's Development* (Cambridge, Mass: Harvard University Press, 1982).
19. Held, *The Ethics of Care*.
20. Nel Noddings, *Starting at Home: Caring and Social Policy* (Berkeley: University of California Press, 2002).
21. Berenice Fisher and Joan C. Tronto, "Towards a Feminist Theory of Caring" in *Circles of Care*, E. Abel and M. Nelson, ed., (Albany, New York SUNY Press, 1990).
22. Sara Ruddick "Care as Labor and Relationship" in Mark S. Halfor and Joram C. Haber, eds., *Norms and Values: Essays on the Work of Virginia Held*. (Lanham MD; Rowman and Littlefield, 1998).
23. Diemut Bubeck, *Care, Gender, and Justice* (Oxford University Press: Oxford, 1995).
24. Peta Bowden, *Caring: Gender Sensitive Ethics* (London: Routledge, 1997).
25. Cheal, *Toward Anthropological*. Rounaq Jahan, *The Elusive Agenda: Mainstreaming Women in Development* (London: Zed Books, 1995).
26. Held *Ethics of Care*.
27. Ellison Banks Findly, "The Housemistress at the Door: Vedic and Buddhist perspectives on the Mendicant Encounter" in Lauri L. Patton, ed., *Jewels of Authority: Women in the Textual Tradition* (Oxford, UK: Oxford University Press, 2002).
28. Findly, "The Housemistress at the Door."
29. Findly, "The Housemistress at the Door," 13.
30. Findly, "The Housemistress at the Door."
31. Asim Roy, *The Islamic Syncretic Tradition in Bengal* (Princeton University Press: NewYork, 1983).
32. Tazeen Kassam,"Response" *Journal of Feminist Studies in Religion* 22:1(2006):59-66.
33. Fauzia Erfan Ahmed, "Microcredit, Men, and Masculinity," *National Association of Women's Studies Journal* 20: 2 (Summer 2008): 122-55.

34. Fauzia Erfan Ahmed, "Hidden Opportunities: Grassroots Muslim Feminism, Masculinity, and the Grameen Bank" *International Journal of Feminist Politics* 10:4 (Fall 2008): 542-562.

35. Jitta Kotalova, "Belonging to Others: Cultural Construction of Womanhood among Muslims in a Village in Bangladesh. Uppsala Studies," *Cultural Anthropology* 19 (1990), 88.

36. Kotalova, "Belonging to Others," 87.

37. Kotalova, "Belonging to Others," 41.

38. Nita Kumar, *Friends, Brothers, and Informants: Fieldwork Memoirs of Banaras.* (Berkeley: University of California Press, 1992).

39. Findly, "The Housemistress at the Door."

40. Findly, "The Housemistress at the Door."

41. Roy, *Islamic Syncretic*.

42. Maurice Hamington, *Embodied Care: Jane Addams, Maurice Merleau-Ponty and Feminist Ethics* (Urbana, Il: University of Illinois Press, 2004).

43. Held, *Ethics of Care*.

44. Held, *Ethics of Care*, 1.

45. Held, *Ethics of Care*.

46. Ahmed, "Microcredit, Men, and Masculinity."

47. Radhika Chopra, Caroline Osella, and Filippo Osella, *South Asian Masculinities: Context of Change, Sites of Continuity*, (New Delhi: Kali for Women, 2004).

48. Rounaq Jahan, *The Elusive Agenda: Mainstreaming Women in Development* (London: Zed Books, 1995).

49. Marilyn Carr, Martha Chen, and Renana Jhabvala, eds. *Speaking Out: Women's Economic Empowerment in South Asia*. (UK: Intermediate Technology Publications Ltd, 1996).

50. Fauzia Erfan Ahmed, "Women, Gender, and Reproductive Health: South Asia" in *The Encyclopedia of Women and Islamic Cultures* (Netherlands: Brill Academic Publishers, 2006), Vol. III no 3.041i. (31-4).

51. Gloria Goodwin Raheja and Ann Grodzins Gold, *Listen to the Heron's Words.* (Berkeley: University of California Press. Ltd, 1994.)

52. Findly, "The Housemistress at the Door."

53. Shelly Feldman, "NGOs and Civil Society: (Un)stated Contradictions," *Annals of the American Academy of Political Science* 554 (1997): 46-65, 3.

54. Sarah Lamb, *White Saris and Sweet Mangoes: Aging, Gender, and Body in North India* (Berkeley: University of California Press, 2000), 33.

55. Roy, *Islamic Syncretic*.

Chapter 8

Feminism, Hospitality, and Women in Exile

Ileana F. Szymanski

Exile is as complex a problem as it is common. It is an experience that affects millions of people[1] every day mostly in a negative way in the form of loss of identity, uncertainty about the future, lack of prospects, financial hardship, lack of community support, racism, etc.[2] As a consequence, knowing more about and finding alternative, more complete ways of approaching exile, makes it a worthy subject of enquiry. In particular, it is a worthy subject from a feminist perspective for at least two reasons. First, feminism understood as an equality-seeking movement aims at ending instances of power imbalance. As we shall see below, when the exiled person is understood as a guest of a new country (her host), this relationship is understood as fixed and static; the host is conceived as the only one with agency, and the guest as being entirely passive. As a consequence, the exile is confined to exchanges where she has no power to act, and this leaves her in a greatly disadvantaged position. Ending all forms of unjust power imbalance is a feminist concern. Second, the experience of exile is, in many cases, one that facilitates the empowerment of women who, before being exiled, did not conceive of themselves as fully empowered, or self-confident; yet, after their exile they became empowered and self-confident. Since feminism is also a movement that seeks to facilitate the empowerment of women and other disadvantaged groups, it can benefit from looking at the experience of exile to see which channels may be further explored to advance towards the goal of the empowerment of the disadvantaged.

Displacement, its awareness, and that of being an other are what make someone an exile.[3] But how does an exile deal with this? How does she begin approaching this new crossroads of specific times and places in and with an other where she now finds herself? I would like to offer an approach to dealing with these questions by looking at the relationship that the exile has with her new community. This relationship is in many cases framed in terms of the relationship between a guest and a host and, thus, questions about whether and how hospitality is offered and received are pertinent. In most cases, as was mentioned above, it is understood that the exile is the guest, i.e. the one that has left home behind, and now looks for a new home; the host, by contrast, is the inhabitant of the exile's new home, the one that will receive the guest. This understanding is, on many occasions, coupled with the idea that exiles are guests that are handed something out and, consequently, they are expected to behave as polite guests; namely, to take what is given to them, be grateful, and leave promptly.[4] This description of the relationship between the exile as a guest and her new community as a host is partial and dissatisfactory; it does not address the situation in its multiplicity and richness. On the one hand, not all relationships of exiled persons and their new communities are negative and, thus, we need not encase all guests and hosts in the model described above. On the other hand, the relationship of guest and host needs to be understood as if the roles of guest and host could be or should be multiplied and exchanged amongst the interested parties. In other words, both the exile and her new community can be guests and hosts of one another. It is my contention that this alternate understanding of roles may lead to a greater possibility for a fulfilling and peaceful cohabitation of the exile and her new community.

I would like to show this by taking the case of women that have been physically and/or culturally exiled. In the first part of this chapter, I will discuss what I mean by exile and I will distinguish it from other related terms, namely refugee, diaspora, nomad, expatriate, and émigré. I will also discuss differences between kinds of exile (physical, cultural, and internal). In the second part I will discuss a variety of experiences that women exiles undergo (the most important of these experiences is having to grapple with a problem of knowing or securing their personal identity); I will do this by referring to accounts that women exiles have given to interviewers. In the third and last part, I will propose how the relationship of the exile with her new community can be fleshed into the relationship of guest and host, and how the alternate understanding of these roles proves fulfilling and beneficial for both parties, and also for their common bond as there is less of a power imbalance in the relationship. It is my view that this alternate understanding of roles serves the feminist project broadly understood as an equality-seeking movement. Moreover, in many cases, women exiles experience empowerment and independence, and they embrace a new participatory role in their adoptive community; this also serves the feminist project insofar as it is a movement that fights oppression and that can learn new strategies from the women who have become empowered, at least partly, because of their exile.

Exile And Related Terms

In order to start the discussion of the relationship of guest and host that can help us describe and frame the experience that an exile has with her new community we need to clarify what it means to be exiled. To be exiled is a kind of being displaced, and there are many ways in which one can be displaced: physically, spiritually, intellectually, culturally, alone, with others, because of war, because of lack of job opportunities, because of political persecution, voluntarily, forcibly, etc. In all cases, this displacement implies being positioned at a new crossroads of identity: a person's what/who/where/why shifts in a way that awareness of going at a different tempo than most everyone else becomes palpable, both by the person who is exiled, and by those that will become the exile's new community. However, not all cases of displacement are necessarily cases of exile. Let us, then, distinguish exile from terms directly associated with it.

Exile is closely related to other experiences of displacement such as being a refugee, a nomad, and expatriate, an émigré, and the diaspora, and it is not always easy to distinguish one from the other. They all have in common *leaving* a certain place—but whether this place is physical or not, what the circumstances are that would make one leave it, or whether one plans on returning to it is not clear unless we look at each term specifically. I will first discuss Edward Said's understanding of the expatriate and the émigré. Afterward, I will refer to the concepts of exile, diaspora, refugee and nomad following Halleh Ghorashi's work; this will include a brief mention of the term "home," which grounds all experiences of displacement.

The first two terms that need to be addressed are "expatriate" and "émigré." According to Edward Said,

> Expatriates voluntarily live in another country, usually for personal or social reasons... Expatriates may share in the solitude and estrangement of exile, but they do not suffer under its rigid prescriptions. Émigrés enjoy an ambiguous status. Technically, an émigré is anyone who emigrates to a new country. Choice in the matter is certainly a possibility.[5]

The category of "émigré," then, is the root category that signifies that en experience of displacement has taken place. If the displacement is voluntary and, in general terms, not associated with political issues, we can refer to the émigré as an expatriate. There are, of course, cases when the displacement is not voluntary and/or it is connected to political reasons. Moreover, one can be displaced in a physical and/or a non-physical sense. We thus turn to Halleh Ghorashi and her work *Ways to Survive, Battles to Win: Iranian Women Exiles in the Netherlands and the United States*.[6]

In this piece, Ghorashi distinguishes the general notions of exile and diaspora by alluding to the different understandings that a person has of her homeland. What the homeland is, however, is not an easy question to answer. For example, in *Feminism without Borders* Chandra Talpade Mohanty says,

> I have been asked the "home" question (when are you going home?) periodically for twenty years now. Leaving aside the subtle racist implications of the question (go home, you don't belong), I am still not satisfied with my response. What is home? The place where I was born? Where I grew up? Where my parents live? Where I live and work as an adult? Where I locate my community, my people? Who are "my people"? Is home a geographical space, a historical space, an emotional, sensory space?[7]

The homeland, according to Ghorashi, becomes a physical space when someone goes into exile, and a non-physical site in the case of diaspora:

> Within exilic discourse home is considered as a space that has to be physically claimed, and it is where people do not live at present... By diasporic understanding of homeland, being at home is not linked to a physical space of the past but to a domain where the past and the present are mediated through present choices and networks.[8]

Nevertheless, Ghorashi recognizes that one and the same person may have exilic *and* diasporic experiences, and thus she believes that the distinction between such experiences "is not a strict one but should serve as an analytical tool to understand the variety of the life of displaced people in general."[9]

Ghorashi also distinguishes between being a nomad and a refugee. In this case the distinction is expressed not in an understanding of the homeland, but in the *causes* of displacement, and the attitude taken towards it:

> A nomad has no home, but at the same time has many different homes. This term is similar to exile and diaspora insofar as it leaves space for simultaneous existence and articulation of different worlds . . . Real nomads move from one place to another on a voluntary basis for economic or political reasons. By contrast, refugees have left their country mainly because of various forms of violence.[10]

We have now seen four terms that allude to different experiences of leaving one's place of origin: exile, diaspora, nomad, and refugee. Nomads and refugees are distinguished on the basis of *why* they left their place of origin. Exile and diaspora are distinguished on the basis of an understanding of the *homeland*. The question that arises next is, how are these four terms (exile, diaspora, nomad, and refugee) related to each other? All of these terms signify some part of an experience of leaving "home" behind (at least partly), and it is clear that in all of the experiences mentioned there is a crossroads of perspectives (spatial, temporal, psychical, spiritual, etc.) that is new for the person that undergoes it. As we will see in the next section, this complex experience may have long-lasting and hurtful consequences in the displaced person, but it may also bring about, in addition, pleasures and advantages that will be treasured.

Said's understanding of the expatriate seems to run parallel to Ghorashi's understanding of the nomad because of the voluntariness of their displacement, and the non-violence associated with it. The root category of a displaced person is what seems to be denoted by Said's idea of the émigrés. Taking Said and Ghorashi together, we can see a gamut of experiences of displacement, i.e. experiences of being an émigré(e): some undergone by choice, others by force, some with hopes to return to a physical home, others where home is not immediately or primarily associated with a physical place, some where more than one world coexist, others where there is a resistance to let these worlds mingle.

Of all of these experiences I am most concerned with that of exile. I agree with Everett and Wagstaff when they say that "the concepts of exile and displacement . . . resist and reject any form of polarization or neat definition."[11] Their position is that what is common to different kinds of exilic displacement is "the impact on individual human lives of a movement away from a fixed and trusted centre and into a fractured and disorientating world."[12] It is on this very ground that I would also like to concentrate, namely, the experience of the displacement of the cluster of experiences that make up someone's identity, the crossroads of different aspects of a person's being, which are challenged by the experience of exile in the construction of a new identity.

In general terms, I characterize exile as a kind of displacement that carries with it at least some negative experiences of different ranges and that, more often than not, has taken place because of external pressures such as political repression, exploitation, etc. One possible way in which to subdivide the broad category of exile is by parsing it as physical, cultural, and internal exile.

Ghorashi's view of exile mentioned above points especially to *physical* exile, where there is a physical homeland geographically located in the world that is left behind. This notion is too narrow to capture other kinds of exilic experiences, i.e. to other kinds of experiences of displacement caused by violence and/or political repression. Thus, we need to expand the notion of exile that Ghorashi offers us so that we are able to address the exilic experience in its complexity.

Gabriella Gutiérrez y Muhs tells us about a kind of exile, which she, inspired by Argentinean writer Julio Cortázar, names "*cultural* exile".[13] This kind of exile refers to the experience of a group or a person excluded from mainstream culture; there is no immediate connection to a geographically located home; rather, the "location" where the person experiences displacement is her culture. In this way, she who is culturally exiled may, in addition, be physically exiled, but this is not a precondition to be culturally exiled.

The third kind of exile is named "*internal* exile";[14] this excludes by necessity the physical displacement of a person, but implies that such person, while remaining in her geographically-located home, does not have access to outlets for her work and may be forced to physically hide from the authorities because of her political views.[15]

Cultural exile, then, may be lived in one's country *or* in a different place; and this is why it is different from *internal* exile, which is always lived in one's country. People that live under an oppressive regime, which cuts down their freedoms and power, and who decide to stay in their country and all the while protest (verbally or not) about how they are being treated by their won government are internal exiles. If they experience, on top of this, clear persecution of their creative work, they would be cultural exiles in addition to being internal exiles. If the oppressed people decide to leave their country and go to a place where they can live with more freedom, they become physical exiles. It is possible that someone who has experienced physical exile will also experience cultural exile in her new residence.[16]

For instance, some Chilean and Mexican writers who are exiled in the United States are culturally exiled because of the lack of opportunities to publish in Spanish in an English-speaking country. Other Chilean writers who remained in Chile through the Pinochet regime were culturally exiled because freedoms were significantly reduced throughout the nation, and publication opportunities for creative writers were almost non-existent. Nevertheless, only the latter group of exiles is considered as having experienced *internal* exile since they remained *in their home* while their cultural exile took place.[17]

We have now explored three kinds of exile: physical, cultural, and internal. There are, doubtless, other ways of categorizing exile (for example, insofar as it is received positively or negatively by those who live it, or as it affects different areas of one's life: beliefs, values, religion, finances, political ideology, profession, etc.).

Nevertheless, all kinds of exile partake of a common characteristic. Exile, just as identity construction, is a *relational* experience. This means that exile is not only a personal experience, i.e. an individual or closed experience. It is rather lived in and with others: others are there to other me, and I other myself with respect to those very others.[18] The self is not just what it declares itself to be, it is also what others see it as being, and their attitudes and responses elicit yet another response from the self they judge and observe; this response, however, will be decoded on the basis of who *they* think she is. For example, Norma E. Cantú tells us

> I am who I am where I want to go. However, having said that, every place you go your identity is shaped by that. For example, I'm a writer but I'm also a professor ... the way people would see me as a Chicana when I'm in here at talks and they would see me as a *pocha* when I'm in Mexico, and how they would see me in Spain as a *norteamericana* ... so they have these identities that they put on me. I call myself Chicana in all of those situations but the way they're seeing me is identifying it or defining that identity for me.[19]

There is a double othering, which is a displacement of identity, and it is neither static nor expressed in a single aspect of one's life. The tag of "exile" is not only a marker of one's political status in a country, it may also be a marker of being a victim, or someone that is uneducated, or that is taking advantage of the system, etc. Exile always implies a multiplicity of participants to bring it to life; there cannot be exile in solipsism. And, also, there cannot be exile in one isolated aspect of identity, as if someone's identity could be split into incommunicable cells (a political self, a social self, a family self, etc.). On the contrary, exile is lived *in community*, and the experience pervades one's *whole* identity, which is, in itself, multiple and changing. There is thus a double play of shifting components: first, the interplay of the self and other; secondly, the interplay of the multiple dimensions of each self. While there is constant exchange between self and others in anyone's life regardless of whether the person is exiled, the exilic experience happens when the experience of displacement is, at best, novel for the person who lives it and, at worst, traumatic and disabling for her.

Regardless of which kind of exile one is talking about (cultural, physical, or internal, etc.), being exiled and experiencing this novel shift of identity is a complex situation on at least three counts. First, the awareness of a difference in one's identity is not always welcomed, pleasant, or expected, and thus it may be problematic to locate it, confront it, reflect on it, disclose it, and grapple with it. There are cases, however, where exile is welcome as a way out to freedom, or safety and, also, as a way out to self-empowerment. Secondly, constructing one's identity is a relational task, which implies the presence of an other who is sometimes fully unknown. Thirdly, being an exile implies the experience of liminality, i.e. of being "between and betwixt" worlds. In what follows, I will explain each of these three angles of exile.

Let us first deal with the awareness of difference. Awareness comes once the difference is manifest—even if it is not manifest to the person living it, it will be manifest to others; for example, one may not notice there has been a change in one's personality, or in one's ways of approaching problems, but this may be perfectly apparent to others, as when parents watch their children grow into adults and take ownership of their actions, and yet the daughter or son have not noticed those changes themselves; or, for instance, when several friends realize that one of their group members has changed towards them because of new acquaintances, experiences, environment, and the friend has no notion of behaving any differently towards her peers. The difference, indeed, is noticed by others, even if not by the agent herself. The experiences undergone in exile are, of course, of a different caliber, but there is nevertheless an awareness of difference that may or may not be acknowledged by the agent.

The awareness of difference, then, may have different guises according to who becomes aware of the difference in the other. It may have an *internal* guise, such as when the exile recognizes herself as an exile: she is not who she was a moment ago, i.e. a lawyer, a doctor, a cabinet minister, a housewife, a teacher, but an exile. It may have an *external* guise, when others make the exile known she is an exile: she is not a lawyer that has won all her cases or a doctor that is personable and knowledgeable and would surely qualify for a certain position in the new country, she is rather the exile that has an accent, wears strange clothes, and she is looked at with suspicion, perhaps even with fear; she is not a citizen, she is the target of jokes, of snarls, of comments whispered on people's ears, of people refusing to serve her at a restaurant. She may also be perceived as the one that needs help, the one that needs to be saved, the one that needs to be liberated, taken in, cared for. In all of these cases, the exile has to realize she is not only who *she* thinks she was; her being has changed, and it has changed because her status has changed: from not being an exile now she is one; and this brings with it a large number of consequences for many aspects of her life—consequences that will have to be met and overcome in order to find peace and, if possible, fulfillment.

As was mentioned above, the particular shift in someone's identity as a result of exile makes it evident that one's identity is always constructed *in relation to others* and, in this case, these are others who are mostly or completely unknown to the exile, which adds to the complexity of the experience because we do not know how our behavior, expectations, history, etc. will be received by others. When the others who judge the exile are a different community, with different institutions, practices, perhaps even a different language and different economic and/or educational opportunities, and who hold some kind of power over the exile, the rift between who a person thinks she is and who others think she is may be experienced so suddenly and be so difficult to grapple with that the experience crosses over from sudden to shocking, from unexpected to oppressive, and from momentarily puzzling to permanently dislocating; the less knowledge there is of the new community, the more difficult it is to deal with it.

Finally, the experience of exile as a shift in one's identity is complex because of the condition of liminality (being "between and betwixt" worlds) that exists in the life of the exile. As Edward Said puts it,

> Most people are principally aware of one culture, one setting, one home; exiles are aware of at least two, and this plurality of vision gives rise to an awareness of simultaneous dimensions, an awareness that—to borrow a phrase from music—is *contrapuntal*.[20]

This contrapuntal awareness brings a sense of feeling divided. Several women interviewed by Mahnaz Afkhami in her book *Women in Exile*[21] speak about this experience. Azar Salamat, an Iranian exile, found herself in the United States while she awaited the news of her husband's execution back home; the liminality she felt as an exile was heightened at that moment.

> People were eating and watching the Superbowl on television. The whole place was feverish with excitement. I felt so alien. The world with which my life was interwoven and the world in which I found myself were far apart.[22]

The experience of liminality may be felt at particular, identifiable moments such as the one described above, but it may also signal a more permanent condition that accompanies the exile everywhere. Hala Deeb Jabbour frames her experience of liminality as follows: "During bad times, I am an alien in both [cultures], during good days, I am a native in both. Exile is a no man's land, where one fully belongs nowhere."[23] This experience of feeling as if one does not *belong* anywhere, and is not *located* completely anywhere is echoed in María Teresa Tula, who survived beatings, rape, torture, and imprisonment in her native El Salvador before she was able to take residence in the United States. As we shall see, her experience of feeling divided was accompanied by a need to pay attention to what was urgent, thus eliminating the possibility of unhurried reflection. She speaks about her exile as follows:

> I was torn between the feeling of relief to be safely away with my youngest children, but aware that with every move I was getting farther away from my oldest children and from my country. But the need to survive did not allow me to think much about the future or about the meaning of every act or every event.[24]

Alicia Partnoy, an Argentine writer exiled in the United States, recounted to Afkhami her experience of liminality in the following terms:

> I know I am neither an Argentine nor an American. I am between two worlds. When I go back and I look at my people through the distance one gains in exile, I feel an outsider to my own culture as I am in this culture. Yet it is not all negative. I sometimes feel I have gained a new window on the world. I have said it in my poem, "When they cut off my voice, I grew a second voice." I feel that I have another language now to express myself in and to relate to a new world. So in a sense I belong to both places.[25]

In the experiences of Salamat, Jabbour, Tula, and Partnoy we can see a sense of being neither here nor there, or belonging neither here nor there, or belonging everywhere—an experience that puts the idea of home in a different light.[26] Now that some of the ways in which exile is a complex phenomenon have been shown, the question whether exile is an experience lived by men and women in different ways must be raised.

Experiences Of Women Exiles

Do women live exile differently than men? Does the experience of displacement affect one group differently than the other? This section will attempt to provide an answer to these questions, and to explain how women and men live exile differently due to their previous roles in patriarchy. I want to acknowledge first that the questions posed above need to be framed in a specific context so as not to be misunderstood. I do not want to imply that I believe *all* women or *all* men could experience *anything* as being "the same;" in other words, as if the whole group of women or men were homogeneous. Each man and each woman is a crossroads of nationality, personal and cultural history, sexuality, gender, education, abilities, etc. It would thus be unhelpful to imagine that these differences should be *erased* in order to give place to a simplistic binary split of the subjects that undergo the experience of exile.

However, there is a case to be made for women as a group experiencing exile in a different way than men. This stems from women being a disadvantaged and oppressed group. This recognition does not erase the differences that exist among women; rather, it focuses on one thing that all women have in common, and this is their gender. The differences that exist among women will, evidently, not be disengaged from their experience of exile; but the focus is on experiences that are lived by women and that would, most probably, not be there if they were men. While it is true that not all women are oppressed, and that not all women are oppressed to the same degree and, also, that not all women are oppressed by men only, many women, for the simple reason of being women have experienced, continue to experience, and will continue to experience oppression of different kinds (e.g. physical, psychological, social, political, religious, etc.) and in different degrees.

Patriarchal values imply that women as a class can or should be oppressed without impunity. If because of patriarchal values women are both portrayed and conceived of as being *a certain kind of person* (e.g. weak, in need of protection, not intelligent, promiscuous, in need of supervision and control, superficial, immature, that can be manipulated, that is undeserving, etc.), then *any* woman who faces those values will face the superstructure that keeps them in place, namely, the political and social institutions that will attempt to prevent her from reaching empowerment and equality: political parties, religious associations, social practices, regulations, prohibitions, etc. It is in this respect that it may be said that women and men *do* live the experience of exile differently. As we said above, exile is a relational experience; it is not only the private understanding of one's geographical or cultural position, it is the interaction of the multiple aspects of our self with the way in which those same aspects are seen by others. Thus, we need to keep in mind this double dimension of women and exile: on the one hand, women are, in general, a disadvantaged and oppressed group; on the other hand, the disadvantage is not experienced in the same way by all women because of their personal histories, geographical locations, religious affiliations, political views, educational opportunities, personal character, social stakes, friendships, social networks, commitments, etc. If the question is, "do women experience exile differently than men?", the answer is "yes, but with qualification." This is the same answer we can give when a similar question is posed about any experience that can be lived by both men and women: do they experience professional success in the same way? Do they have the same feelings when witnessing an unjust act? In a way, yes; in a way, no. And, what does this mean? It is means that one will experience it as being part of the advantaged group, and the other one will experience it as being part of the disadvantaged one; this is the difference that favors better salaries, more medical research, a more secure social standing, better educational opportunities, etc. for one group, and not the other. If the answer is clear, then, why should we introduce a qualification? Why not say that women and men *categorically* experience things differently? In a nutshell, this is because women and men are not reduced to their gender. While gender may be at the crux of our being, so is our class, ethnicity, physical ability, sexual orientation, skills, habits, etc. All of these aspects are connected and partly inform people's experiences of exile; the other part, of course, is supplied to those who witness the exile and form its context.

If then, the reason why women are said to experience exile differently from men is patriarchy, we need to explain how this happens. Gina Buijs believes that this may happen because the experience of exile is one where the life roles of women change less than those of men. On the one hand, when men become exiles they suddenly find themselves in a position of subordination, rather than superiority, which would have been the status given to them by a patriarchal society. On the other hand, women in exile are likely to continue their previous routine of minding their home, which allows them more stability in their agency. This is not the case for men as, if they cannot find a job, their condition of unemployed (and, perhaps, unemployable because of lack of language skills or relevant experience) proves to be more taxing.[27]

If men experience a lack of social mobility when in exile, this allows them to spend more time in their home.[28] However, this is sometimes a double-edged sword for women. While women may have less trouble adapting to the experience of being exiles, they may also find themselves restricted in more ways than before they were exiles because men will attempt to exert stricter control over their lives, and will have the time and opportunity to do it. Speaking about Palestinian exiles living in refugee camps in Berlin, Buijs notes:

> Male household heads lost their roles of provider for the family and their continual presence in the home restricted the movement of unmarried girls, as well as the opportunity of wives to visit other women. The domestic arena became a means . . . to increase control over women and to enhance the ideology of gender relations.[29]

The lack of social mobility that exiled men are faced with may also be manifested in violence against women. Speaking about Vietnamese refugees in Hong Kong, Buijs tells us,

Once they arrived in the camps in Hong Kong, the women found themselves subject to an authoritarian regime which looked favourably on passivity and compliance as female attributes. Conversely, the want of work for Vietnamese men in the camps and their inability to be responsible for their families led to an increase in violence directed against women, arising from the men's sense of powerlessness and lack of what they assumed to be their male roles.[30]

Aspects of the exiles' lives such as personal history, educational, and cultural background play an important role in determining whether women's status of power will improve in their new situation. Nevertheless, some women do believe that women in general experience exile differently than men.

Hala Deeb Jabbour, a former businesswoman from Palestine exiled in the United States, refers to the contrast of the experience of her exile with that of her husband:

> I began to feel unencumbered. I had a voice with which to express my thoughts and feelings. My mind filled with stories I wanted to tell, I needed to tell. I began writing. For my husband, it was much more difficult. Being a man and a Lebanese meant that he would suffer a harrowing experience . . . Being a man, he had a more vested interest in the status quo and gained less in the transition. I have come now to consider myself an American of Arab origin. I have reconciled myself to living here as a citizen. My husband is an Arab living in America. There is a great difference.[31]

Women witness their strength and that of other women in sustaining their identity, and helping others (their male kin included) in this process. For example, Azar Salamat, an Iranian with a Berkeley University education, says in reference to her exile of eleven years,

> During this time I have learned and grown and found a new identity for myself . . . I have seen my women friends become the pillars that hold up the other members of their families, lending support to their husbands' search for a new identity while restructuring their own.[32]

Sima Wali, former Peace Corps worker from Afghanistan, and founder of the Refugee Women in Development Association, echoes these experiences:

> I have to be culturally sensitive to the heightened vulnerability of men who are living in exile. They have lost their status, they are afraid, and their women are faring better than they are. The women are the pillars of support in their community.[33]

Samnang Wu, a Cambodian refugee, is a former Red Cross worker exiled in the United States where she has worked as a translator; she also comments on this point using her and her husband's experience in exile as a departure point.

> [A]ll in all I think women can cope better with the disruptions caused by exile. They can gather up strength and push forward, all the time trying to find some joy within the family or in friendship or in their discoveries. In my own case

even though I have suffered, I have not lost my sense of adventure or capacity for fun. My husband finds it impossible to relate to this society . . . He is so sad . . . I feel sad for him knowing there will never be happiness in his life. He simply cannot deal with the new world . . . Some women suffer more than others. But it is all the same pain and sorrow. Cambodian women are at first so afraid to go outside by themselves. They have no education. But it is a joy to see them break out and try to help themselves.[34]

Marjorie Agosín, a well-known Chilean writer, also sees women as pillars in their community, and points to what, in her experience, signals a greater investment in relationships in the part of women:

I have learned that women are deeper, stronger than men in their relationships. They are capable of intimacy without too much preparation, too much hedging and insurance. During the period of exile, the women who had never worked, never supported a family, women with little education picked up the pieces of their lives and started building. They were the pillars of the family structure. They held everything together.[35]

Marita Eastmond, in speaking of Chilean refugees in the United States, gives us a slightly different perspective on the way in which men and women experience exile. She tells us that women and men believed they *lost different things*; men felt their loss concentrated on the political aspect and their social role of providers; women, by contrast, felt their loss in the community that used to be central in their lives at home:

[T]he sense of loss and concern for the future had a somewhat different focus for men and for women. The men tended to center on the political defeat and the ordeal they had suffered in prison. After the coup men were displaced from their roles as political actors and breadwinners, both important bases for male identity and self-esteem. The women, on the other hand, grieved the loss of their social world, the network that made up their daily life in the *barrio*.[36]

The accounts reproduced above help us identify two aspects in which women live their exile in a different way than men. One is that men, in becoming exiles, lose their past role of breadwinners; another is that men are not used to being subordinates, and in their new position as exiles, the rift between past and present, superiority and subordination, is not easily breached. A third aspect, perhaps, is that in some cases men have had experiences of torture that women have not had. This latter line, however, is, in my opinion, not very strong as there are plenty of examples available of women that have undergone torture, rape, mutilation, and other unspeakable acts of violence.[37] Their exile, in fact, is almost secondary to those experiences, as they may well have undergone them not at the hands of enemies of war from whom they fled into exile, but at the hands of their own families.[38]

Some of the most common experiences that women have in exile hinge on what is common to every exile, and this is displacement, the awareness of one's difference with the rest of the world, the upheaval in one's world, and one's identity. Others have to do with uncertainty about the future, lack of prospects, financial hardship, lack of community support, and racism. While both men and women are susceptible to being affected negatively in these experiences, I will be dealing only with women exiles and, thus, taking into account their experiences form the point of view of being oppressed by patriarchal values.

Forging a new identity is a theme that is repeated in several interviews conducted by Mahnaz Afkhami in her aforementioned book *Women in Exile*.[39] Thinking of her own experience as an exile, Afkhami recounts how she asked herself, "Who am I going to be now that I am no longer who I was a few hours ago?"[40] She adds, "my identity was already becoming blurred. The 'I' of me no longer had clear outlines, no longer cast a definite shadow."[41] This loss of identity comes from a dislocation of time and place, of language, habits, and social practices, where the past and the present meet and cause a discontinuity in the exile's experiences. Edward Said explains that, "exile, unlike nationalism, is fundamentally a *discontinuous* state of being. Exiles are cut off from their roots, their land, their past."[42] Being "cut off," however, is not a fixed or clearly delineated state that is separable from other aspects of someone's life; on the contrary, the life that is cut off is so only partially as it continues into an inescapable present that makes its immediacy felt; thus the past becomes more and more distant from the present.[43] Ghorashi says, "When there is a rift between the experiences of the past and the present, and the trajectory of life does not go smoothly, the future becomes vague and scary."[44] However, as frightening as the present is, it must be faced.

Financial hardship is one of the things that many exiles have to face and live with constantly. Even when in the exile's country of origin she may have enjoyed a life free of financial worries, her condition of exile rarely continues in the same trajectory.[45] Ge Yang, an exile in the United States of Chinese origin, speaks about the economic hardship she lives as an exile: "I feel the pressure of not having enough money and not knowing what will happen tomorrow . . . If I were to live in China I would have a house, a job, a car, and no material worries. But I live here, with very little."[46]

Financial hardship, of course, is preferred to a life of persecution, or of restricted freedom. However, it is rarely financial hardship on its own that exiles have to suffer. One of the things that some exiles in North America find difficult to deal with is the way in which society is organized: as opposed to being community-oriented, it is individual-oriented. For example, Alicia Partnoy says,

> Americans do not seem to relate to collective experiences and collective tragedies.[47] They have to relate to you as an individual to be able to sympathize. Once that happens, they understand the rest. We come from Third World countries where collective experience weighs more heavily on the individual than in the "developed world."[48]

The collective experience of community members is lived in some cultures right from the start, without the need for a collective event to bring it together: daily existence is seen as collective.[49] Sima Wali points at how community support was the norm for both men and women in her native Afghanistan, and how it is experienced differently by these exiles in the United States:

> The women, feeling frustrated, isolated, and terrified in an alien culture and without comfort from their immediate family, turn to fundamentalist religious beliefs. The men have the relief of their own groups and the socializing opportunities with those groups. They hang out together and drink and talk. Women don't have that. They have to work. And then they come home to their second job as wife and mother. Back home they had the support system of household help or extended family. The women are experiencing an internal turmoil for which they have no outlet. They haven't been able to discuss their problems as women in exile. They just don't have the opportunity to come together.[50]

Dima Abdulrahim mentions a similar phenomenon when exploring the lives of Palestinian refugees in Berlin.

> The communal living of the older women, characteristic of life in the [refugee] camps they had left in Lebanon, was transformed [in the camps of Berlin]. The economic inactivity of men also affected their movements in West Berlin and made contact between them more difficult. The presence of the man in the household made it more difficult for his wife to visit other women or be visited by them . . . Women's domestic activity was also subject to transformation. First and foremost, they lost much of the help they had from other women—especially kin—in domestic and child rearing . . . Despite men's inactivity, their unemployment did not result in any important contribution to domestic work.[51]

Racism is another experience common to many exiles. An example is mentioned by Sonya Rosario; she was born in San Antonio to Mexican parents; she is now the founder and Executive Director of the Women of Color Alliance. As a teenager she grew up on a military base in the Netherlands with her parents, and she says that she never realized there was racism in the base until she experienced it first hand from a military G.I.: "I was asked to get out of line in buying a movie ticket . . . I was called a dirty squaw and I was told to get out of line and they wouldn't sell me a movie ticket."[52]

When women become exiles they experience a change in their circumstances insofar as they are affected by patriarchy. If a woman is exiled in a place where there is less control over women's lives, bodies, and sexuality, her relocation can have a great impact on her life. On the one hand it is possible that she feels liberated and decides to challenge and change some of the patriarchal structures that previously made her life uncomfortable, frustrating, or tormented. As we have seen in the accounts above, she may learn to work outside the home, nd derive a sense of empowerment from it, she may become more independent, learn a new language, and realize that she is doing things for herself that she had not even thought were possible (e.g. joining organizations, developing skills, dealing with figures of authority outside the home on a more or less equal basis, making business transactions, going to school, organizing groups and meetings, etc.); it thus may become pleasurable to see how she contributes to the development and fulfillment of her own life feeling at the same time safe, and (to a point)[53] at peace with herself.[54] On the other hand, if a woman is exiled with or into a community that does not agree to these challenges to patriarchy (especially if there is a mass exile and she is in a refugee camp such as the Vietnamese women in Hong Kong,[55] or the Palestinian women in Berlin[56]), the challenges to patriarchy may be muted, postponed, or even shied away from so as to hold on to what is familiar and appears stable and, thus, trustworthy for continuing social relations with her kin. Yet, even in these cases one can see challenges to patriarchy in their offspring. Speaking about the offspring of Palestinian refugees in Berlin, Abdulrahim reports that adolescent women, through education, are being exposed to German culture and thus challenging the norms imposed by their parents, such as the prohibition to associate with males, even when there is no sexual undertone to the relationship.[57] While the young women also feel guilty about this challenge, in some cases it leads to an exposure to a different kind of life, which they may choose for themselves.[58] She states,

> [I]t has been noticeable that girls and adolescent women showed more interest in education and performed better in schools than boys. Education gave women a legitimate reason to justify their presence in unsegregated German public areas: technical colleges and universities, and established an alternative to early marriages. The newly found possibility of further education posed a potential source of conflict within the household between young women and their parents. A small number of young women enrolled in technical colleges and universities; for them education will also have personal and social importance. Very few though they are, they will make a social precedent.[59]

The option of continuing the same lifestyle as their parents is available to the young exiled women; however, the more exposure they have to alternative ways of living, and the more freedom they have to make those choices, the more authenticity there is in the choice of lifestyle and, as a result of this authenticity, there is more investment and fulfillment in their lives.

It might be tempting to think that women who live in societies where patriarchal values are not only pervasive but also blatantly backed up by the law[60] have absolutely no agency and no freedom to choose; the consequences of this, it might be thought, are (1) that if and when they find themselves in a society where they would be much less subject to external control of their lives they may be unable to want to *embrace* the lack of strict supervision of their activities, and (2) that in their present circumstances (i.e. before moving to a less restricted environment) they are unable to *critique* the way in which they currently live, or are made to live. Uma Narayan refers to these as "specters of the other woman;"[61] one she calls the "prisoner of patriarchy," which is believed to have "various forms of patriarchal oppression imposed on her *entirely against her will and consent*—similar to how a prisoner is subject to constraints in liberty."[62] The other one is called the "dupe of patriarchy," who supposedly self-imposes patriarchal violence "because she is imagined to completely subscribe to the patriarchal norms and practices of her culture. Her attitudes are envisioned as completely shaped by the dominant patriarchal values of her cultural context."[63]

These "specters" are simplistic and do not reflect the "*variety* of responses that shape their [i.e. the women's] lives."[64]

We cannot expect women who have been exiled from places where patriarchy is deeply embedded to *all* have the same reaction to the possibility of a different life; this could be a life that is less repressed, or repressed in other ways. That women become empowered to search for options, and embrace those options, in many cases comes with a price; sometimes this means being rejected by their own community, or being restricted in other areas where there was no restriction before; in other cases it means doing away with a set of values that are meaningful to them. For example, the Sufi Pirzada women from Old Delhi, according to Narayan, both criticize and agree with (to different degrees) the practice of veiling themselves with a burqua. Among the reasons for wearing a burqua, women believe that it is a sign of their modesty and propriety, that it is part of their identity, that it will allow them to have a good marriage and, surprisingly, that it is convenient as it allows women the invisibility needed to "go out in a hurry without changing the old clothes they were wearing for housework, or ... sneak off to the cinema with a friend ... the husbands being none the wiser even if they pass them on the street."[65] What would happen if it were made obligatory for women to *not* veil themselves? Some of them may surely feel more comfortable, and freer in their body movements, perhaps render them more able to express themselves in their physical appearance and obtain approval or recognition from other groups. However, these new practices may have consequences that extend well beyond comfort, physical movement, and expression; just as women may build some social ties by refusing to wear a burqua, they may also break other ties by engaging in the same action; they may end up with a deflated morale, and seeing that they are subjects to constraints of other kinds that will prevent them from engaging in other behaviors that, before, under the veil, they could get away with, such as wearing old clothes or making a go for a spontaneous movie afternoon.

Narayan's findings are important for the purposes of this essay in three very important respects. First, they provide a more complete version of the lives of women, one that is less influenced by colonialist remnants in the Western mind, i.e. one more open to looking at women not as dupes or prisoners of patriarchy. Secondly, Narayan's findings are helpful insofar as they illustrate the interconnectedness of practices and, therefore, of the many aspects of a person's life: a stance for the freedom of someone's physical movement is connected to her social standing in the community, and this with possibilities for a future, and this, in turn, with educational and employment opportunities, etc. Thirdly, what Narayan has showed allows us to make a claim for the guest-host relationship in which exiled women are involved. If the host society expects its guests to assimilate to its practices, or to agree without any mixed feelings to a complete transformation of their identities, there is something wrong—this is not, clearly, the alternate understanding of the guest/host relation that will provide opportunities for true, i.e. freely-chosen, empowerment of women.

It is possible to imagine 'empowering practices' being *imposed* on women and, as a consequence, many times feared, or even rejected. From one perspective, it may seem inconceivable that anyone would reject empowerment as well as more opportunities for independence and a wider gamut of choices for life paths. This incredulity, as was said above, is accompanied by the lack of acknowledgment that what seem to be practices of empowerment are so *in a determinate context*, and their implementation will affect other areas of that context. Iran and France are two countries where legislation against women veiling themselves has been passed at some point. On June 22, 2009, French president Nicolas Sarkozy declared that the burqua was not welcome in France. The full veil "is not a religious sign, it is a sign of subservience, it is a sign of debasement" of women.[66] France is the only country in Europe to have legally forbidden, in 2004, wearing the Islamic scarf (which covers only the head) in school after a passionate debate.[67] There will be an inquiry to see whether a law should be passed against the wearing of the burqua as a possible infringement of France's commitment to secularization and gender equality.[68]

What seems to be an act of protection of citizens that are oppressed by their families, cultures, and/or religion, is interpreted as such only in a determinate context—this being the context of those that, while more than likely well-intentioned, experience on a daily basis many other freedoms that would not be compromised by this decree. Sarkozy, from a position of power and privilege, seems to see only the good aspects that his comment would bring: empowerment, freedom, perhaps even the fuller interaction of members in the larger society, and the benefit of the French nation at large by being more cohesive. However, it is necessary to acknowledge that these purported benefits would, if at all, spur in a context that would not allow them to be enjoyed evenly, and that would, potentially, bring about other negative situations that may result in harm for the same people that the practices are designed to help. As we mentioned before, Narayan showed how the practice of veiling provides women with freedoms they would not otherwise have, such as being invisible in places where it would not be advantageous for them to be recognized.

It might be argued that the fact that some women have to hide in order to take advantage of innocent forms of entertainment should be changed. In the specific case mentioned by Narayan of women escaping to a movie, the idea would be that women would not have to lie to their husbands about going to the cinema with a friend. It could even be argued that in order to change the patriarchal values that keep these practices in place one has to start somewhere and, perhaps, the way to start is to forbid the use of the burqua with the hope that, in the future, the rest of the freedoms that would make it enticing to not use the burqua would follow. The latter is, however, an optimistic prediction or hope that cannot be guaranteed. And, most importantly, it ignores the autonomy of choice of women: some women agree to wearing a burqua and want the advantages it brings them—most of these advantages being of a social nature. If a woman feels naked without her burqua,[69] will she go out in public, or will she rather not go out at all out of fear? Ridiculing this behavior, or calling it childish or backward does not solve the problem, and does not address the failure to understand how the practice of wearing the burqua inheres in some women's *identities*, not only in their clothing habits. If a woman feels that by not wearing her burqua she will not be able to find a husband, or keep some of her friendships, or continue the relationship to her parents, will she agree to not wear it and go on living life as if nothing had changed except her clothes? If a woman feels as an immoral person for not wearing her burqua, why would she want to go out in public where she may feel her immorality is exposed, or condoned by a society that is itself, in her eyes, immoral? Again, one could push the agenda that women should *not* feel that their morality and identity depends on them not showing their body, face, or hair. However, these are ideas that cannot be changed simply by removing the burqua, and it is not desirable that these ideas be changed by force; not to mention that one would have to face the problem of dealing with the idea that women's identity *depends* on them showing their body, face, or hair.

In Part II, chapter 49, of the novel of *Don Quixote De la Mancha*, Sancho Panza wants to jail a youth and yells to his guard, "Ho there! Lay hold of him and take him off; I'll make him sleep there [viz., in jail] to-night without air." To which the young man responds: "your worship will make me sleep in gaol just as soon as make me king." Sancho is puzzled about this, and believes the young man is challenging his authority and power to jail him. After a brief exchange, the young is finally able to clarify what he meant,

> Now, señor governor . . . let us be reasonable and come to the point. Granted your worship may order me to be taken to prison, and to have irons and chains put on me, and to be shut up in a cell, and may lay heavy penalties on the gaoler if he lets me out, and that he obeys your orders; still, if I don't choose to sleep, and choose to remain awake all night without closing an eye, will your worship with all your power be able to make me sleep if I don't choose?[70]

Sancho, as an authority figure, has overlooked the extent of his powers. The young man corrects him, reminding him that, while Sancho has authority over where he will spend the night, whether he sleeps or not is up to the discretion of the jailed man, and not of Sancho. The young man in this story has asserted his autonomy. This story reflects the autonomy of choice that we all have about the ideas that we espouse. Sarkozy may forbid women to wear the burqua, but he cannot impose that they change their minds about what the burqua means to them, and he cannot force women to go *out* when they know they cannot wear their burqua.

What in the West we may see as advantages, or 'civilized' actions need not be wanted by others. If women do not agree that not wearing a burqua will make them more liberated, or if they do not want the purported liberation, this does not necessarily imply that they are dupes or prisoners of ideas (patriarchal ideas in this case); it may be because those same practices bring other advantages that we cannot see because we are ignorant of the context in which they arise, and the same goes for other practices that women in exile may choose to not adopt.[71] Their context as exiles is indeed multifarious, even though in most cases it is effectively reduced to one of its manifestations: the condition of displacement. Being displaced is pervasive throughout a person's identity: it extends beyond her passport, and beyond the stereotypes associated with displacement. Alicia Partnoy speaks about these stereotypes of women exiles:

> we are sometimes called "innocent," which meant not guilty of being involved in politics. We were seen as mothers, or daughters, or wives of political activists who were targeted and our predicament defined as an extension of theirs. Or we are seen as the opposite, women who are very outspoken and aggressive. Sometimes we are seen as illiterate peasants who come here seeking better material conditions or highly educated intellectuals who don't have a sense of the realities of our people's condition.[72]

These stereotypes are born out of what Rubén Martínez identifies as "paternalistic" conduct. He reinforces Partnoy's point when he says:

> refugees are most often treated paternalistically by their host countries. They are perceived as victims, and they are treated as such. In the popular consciousness, the very word "refugee" brings to mind impoverished, passive victims of brutality—nameless peasants, not restaurateurs or petrochemical engineers ... The expectations of the adopted country's "hosts" are low, because it is impossible for the American middle-class to imagine a Third World middle-class victim. Perhaps they cannot imagine a Third World middle-class at all.[73]

Moreover, we need to note that some of the practices that we may see as "liberating" need not be exempt of patriarchal remnants. As Narayan points out, how many women in the West would feel comfortable going out on the street showing unshaved legs?[74] We may be able to wear garments that show our legs and that we feel are esthetically pleasing and complimentary to us, but, are we not slaves of the pre-conditions (e.g. shaved legs, good skin, no scars, beauty, status, the myth of eternal youth) for that to happen? It is a matter of choice and a matter of what we consider valuable.

Ge Yang, for example, says that she prefers living in the United States to living in China even if in the United States she is poor—she prefers her freedom of expression and the fact that she can challenge the government in a public way, and there is a trade-off that she has accepted and brings her peace.[75] Trade-offs, negotiations, exchanges, all of these become the life of the exile: there is a trade-off in what one considers valuable, a negotiation of one's identity, and an exchange of contexts. When this is addressed from the point of view of *assimilation* to another culture, when the host community says to the exile, "you either become like us or you leave," the host culture does not welcome the exile with openness or respect. This lack of openness may mean that the host culture believes it cannot be enriched by others, or should not be challenged or critiqued by others, as if they held all the cards, or as if their vision could not be given more depth. What this means for the exile is that values and systems are being imposed on her, even if these are supposedly "liberating." If one will indeed promote "liberty, equality, and brotherhood," the value of autonomy should be respected in all equally, even when they are not "brothers," but "sisters."

In the next section I will flesh out the relationship of guest/host in the experiences of women in exile. While it is anticipated that the benefits of thinking about the exilic experience using the guest/host model will be of service to all exiles (not only women exiles), I will continue to focus on the experiences of exiled women, and the solutions they have found to empower themselves through exile.

Fleshing Out The Guest/Host Relationship For Women In Exile

I have thus far explored conclusions that apply to internal, cultural, and physical exile. In this section I want to pay particular attention to women who have overcome physical exile, which is, in many cases, accompanied by some kind of cultural exile. The reason for why I want to flesh out the relationship of guest and host insofar as an exile and a new country is that this seems to be the most extreme case of exile. Using this kind of exile as a model, conclusions applicable to other kinds of exile may follow.

Let us begin, first, by clarifying what we mean by "guest" and "host." These are terms that are not alien in conversations about exiles; as has been pointed out before, it seems that the most immediate way of piecing together the ideas of exile, new country, guest, and host is by relating them in pairs: the exile is the guest, and the new country is the host. In a way, this arrangement is supported by the fact of displacement lived by the exile: before she was at home, and now that she has moved to a new country where other people are established and have *their* home, she is their guest. In other words, the exile leaves a community to enter another one that has formed seemingly without her help, input, or contributions. When the exile steps into this community and is received by it, she occupies the position of receiving something: a physical space and opportunities for interaction with others.

This is, of course, a simplistic way of putting the situation: "interaction with others" might mean a safe, respectful, and fulfilling exchange with community members, or it might mean an intimidating, racist, and debasing encounter with them. A new "physical space" might mean a house, a hotel room, a refugee camp, an interrogation room, or a prison cell. The blanks are filled by the personal histories of the exiled: did they arrive at their new country in a raft that was picked up by the Navy? Did they arrive after walking miles under the beating sun almost without food or water? Did they have money, identity papers, family heirlooms, family members or friends accompanying them? Do they have skills that will be valuable for their new community? Are they from a place that is feared and hated, or respected and loved? Do they speak the language, have education, professional credentials, and work experience? Are they young, strong, and healthy, or are they illiterate, sick, maimed, disabled, or mentally unstable as a result of previous imprisonment and torture?

The physical space and interactions exiles can have with their new country is based a great deal on the considerations mentioned above. What we can see is that posing questions such as the ones I just asked implies there is, on the one hand, a questioner and, on the other hand, one who is questioned; a judge and one who is judged; a host and a guest; and, with them, a power imbalance.

There are certain expectations that follow the understanding of an exile exclusively as a "guest" of her new country, the most important one of these is that the guest will be gracious, and not overstep her boundaries and, perhaps, that the guest will leave after a time of hospitality from the part of the host.[76] This expectation leaves the host in control of the situation, and it prevents the guest from making any contribution to the culture or country where she is because she is not seen as capable of contributing anything. The exile is, then, effectively reduced to a passive state where only the host acts, only the host questions, judges, oversees, and expects. It appears, then, as if the guest were powerless and, if we were to follow this line of reasoning, we would conclude that, qua guest, she cannot or should not have any expectations about her new situation; after all she is the one that came and requested to be admitted into a country, and not vice versa, so she should take whatever is given to her, it does not matter if that is not what she wants or needs; all she should be worried about is how to fulfill her role of guest as best as possible, and the host will make sure of this.

This understanding of the relationship between an exile and her new country is preposterous; it reduces the exile to a role that is partly imposed on her, and it reduces the new country to playing a part in a play that turns out to be a monologue, where it must close avenues of communication and growth to itself and to others. Is this all there is to the relationship that an exile has with her new country, with the place and the people that live where she will, perhaps, find a home too? In other words, is there another way of piecing together the ideas of exile, new country, guest, and host that does not end in an unjust power imbalance, and in seeing the guest as a victim, or as someone incapable of agency and self-determination?

I believe there is a lot more to the relationship of an exile with her new country, and that there is indeed an alternate way to piece together the ideas of exile, new country, guest, and host so that a peaceful and beneficial relationship with less power imbalance exists. This alternate way that I propose here is a strategy of multiplying and reversing the roles of guest and host so that the guest becomes not only a guest but also a host and, in turn, the host becomes also a guest. This is in fact the state of affairs which we usually reduce to a relationship between *one* guest and *one* host. I propose a revision of this, an expansion of our line of vision so that we can realize that the country that will house the exile is not *the* host by decree, it plays the role of host just as much as it plays the role of guest, and it also plays other roles (mediator, negotiator, facilitator, etc.). The exile, in turn, is not *the* designated guest; being a guest is only *part* of who she is (she too will be mediator, negotiator, facilitator, etc.), but we need to highlight both roles (guest/host) and not only one of them.

The basis for this alternate understanding of relating an exile and her new country to the terms "guest" and "host" is the recognition that both entities supersede the roles of "guest" and "host" that they are usually encased in. In other words, the exile is more than a guest, and the new country is more than a host. Yet, what does this "more" mean? What can it mean for a guest to be *also* or *more than* a host, and for a host to be *also* or *more than* a guest? The roles of guest and host are both inherent in the exile and in the new country where she will live, both roles coexist and are not mutually exclusive: while the guest is a guest it is, at the same time, also a host, and vice versa. Seen from this point of view, the exile is not only someone who receives whatever the host gives, she is also someone who gives to the host what she has to offer, she is an agent, not just a passive recipient. The host, in turn, is not only the one who transmits its agency but is the recipient of the agency of the guest, and it is changed by it. The country where the exile now resides is not equivalent to a rigid receptacle that gets filled with whatever is thrown into it while keeping its distinctive shape (much like an acrylic box would be if we threw items of different shapes and sizes into it). Thinking of a community as a "receptacle" we need to see that it is not stiff but malleable; it changes with what is put into it, and this is because it is not only a receptacle or something that receives, it is an envelope, something that coats and that is shaped by what it coats; it does not receive exclusively in its own terms, but, rather, whatever it receives affects it too.

Neither the receiver nor the received are at any point stable and unchanging entities; each is a multiplicity of aspects like axes whose points of contact slide continuously. The exile and the community are both receiver and received, and in these roles they are never static. It is perhaps very clear how the exile receives and is received in the old scheme: the exile is a receiver (of help, of asylum, of opportunities), and she is received (as a problem, a nuisance, as someone to be exploited, as someone to be helped, as a potential employee, or friend). Thus, class, race, financial situation, personal history, etc. continuously shift; in this shifting sometimes we will see her role as host highlighted and, at other times, it will be her role as guest. The exile *receives* the community and what the community gives her, and she is received into the community—the important thing to note is that this does not only happen one time, namely, when the exile crosses the border, but that it happens continuously. Every time the exile rehearses a phrase in a new language, every time she takes a bite of *Wonderbread* and compares it to the bread from her lost home, every time she hears a racial slur, or she gets a hand-me down dress to go to a job interview she experiences being a receiver and, at the same time, being received.

How does this happen on the side of the host country? That is to say, how is the new country or community both a receiver and received by its guest? It is easy to see how the host country is *received* insofar as it was, in most cases, chosen as a destination; and, in any case, it dictates the terms in which the exile is accepted, so it is received as a figure of authority. The new community, however, also *receives* as it is the recipient of physical bodies into its physical borders. But, is this all there is to be received? What about the person that is partly expressed in and through a physical body? Is that being received into the border as well? Who is indeed this person partly expressed in and through a physical body? She is a cluster of sliding and interconnected crossroads: culture, time, place, language, religion, habits, social practices, likes and dislikes, fears, hopes, abilities, skills, in a word, identity. How are the identities of diverse people received? How open are we to see they are valuable, and not simply some exotic curiosity? And, also, how open are the exiles to sharing their identity? There is no one answer to this: if you feel ashamed of who you are, of where you come from, what can you think you could possibly contribute?[77] Or, if you do believe you have something to give, how can this contribution be invited? And, if invited, and successfully understood as invited, how can we promote that it be offered in response to that invitation? Should we, in fact, *promote* that it be offered, or is this a kind of tampering with the scale in our favor? A fundamental question remains: how do we promote that the party that holds all the power, shares it? Is this not the quintessential feminist question? How do we convince the one that benefits from the exploitation of others that sharing power does not mean defeat, but rather that doors are open to something positive to be gained on all sides? And, what is this that can be gained? It is not money, or more power, but fulfillment; this is an eudaimonic quest.

This quest for happiness and fulfillment is grounded on an understanding of the relationship between an exile and her new country that takes into account that each is more than the role they are tagged with ("exile" and "new country," "guest" and "host"). The exile is a person with a unique history, abilities, skills, etc. that can enrich the life of the new country where she will live, for example, with her work and the taxes she will contribute, with her example to other exiles and to natives of that country, with her presence as a reminder of the multiplicity of backgrounds and experiences that affect people (some of which we cause or contribute to cause ourselves), with her history and experiences of empowerment that may inspire women and men across the board. The exile can be a link to other geographical places, to other cultures, languages, perspectives on life and happiness; she may be an active member of the community that will allow it to grow in tolerance, diversity, and provide an opportunity for dialogue: she may create or help run associations that point to problems in the community and offers ways to help them, she may provide relief, companionship, friendship, professional resources, educational opportunities, etc., and she may also play a role where, in a quiet way, by the mere fact that she exists and that she exists *there*, even if she does not play a highly visible, political or controversial role, she will be a testimony to the work that has to be done in the improving of life throughout the world *beginning at home with ourselves*. If her presence makes us uncomfortable or afraid this is an opportunity to ask *why* this is, and to challenge our own views of the world, our beliefs, superstitions, predictions and, in general, the ideas we have about who *we* are, and not only or even primarily, who *she* is. All of this is what is to be gained, received, by the so-called "host" country: a critical reflection that will lead to a self-transformation and, in consequence, transformative practice that may help bring about fulfillment and justice.

But to achieve even the notion of transformative practice being something positive and worth engaging in, it is required that we exhibit a respectful openness to the other, and an awareness that the other, the exile, can bring about a beneficial change in her new community; this implies, de facto, a recognition of our own incompleteness, our own vulnerability, and the possibility of egalitarian cooperation with others, which is a form of generosity and gentleness. According to Judith M. Green, this idea has been explored before in some Eastern traditions: "[t]he traditional Taoist, Confucian, and Buddhist emphasis on 'softness' and 'responsiveness' expresses a . . . relational awareness and openness to receive the other, and perhaps to be beneficially altered in one's way of being thereby."[78]

In her article "Building a Cosmopolitan World Community through Mutual Hospitality,"[79] Green proposes that we look at hospitality as a *mutual* endeavor; in other words, one that implicates the key participation of all parties involved so that they all give hospitality to each other. Green bets on a "'rebinding' of our lives together as neighbors, nations, and world citizens guided by shared cosmopolitan hopes that our spirit of unity amidst valued diversity will make possible a more inclusive, more just, and thus more peaceful future for our children's children."[80] This understanding of mutual hospitality is akin to the alternative interpretation of the guest/host relationship present in the exile and her new country that I propose. I agree with Green in the involvement of all parties in the practice of hospitality, so that it is not only one community working as a host or guest of another but rather all the communities involved working as guests and hosts of one another; I echo her ideas of the value placed on diversity, and the shared hopes for lasting fulfillment, which is the object of the eudaimonic quest I mentioned above.

One of the theories that Green uses to support her understanding of mutual hospitality is that of W.E.B. Du Bois' understanding of "race" as being a cultural rather than a genetic construct, and lived in community. The communities that Du Bois proposes as forming "race" are based on shared practices and outlooks. As Green points out, this understanding of "race" allows for a meeting point where communities are mutually benefitting.

> Du Bois argued that these real, affinity-based "racial" communities . . . have the potential to turn their collaborative energies and their developed institutions toward the building up of remarkable individuals and towards the shared pursuit of excellence and insight that will allow them to fulfill the highest levels of human potentials, to meet other "races" as equals on the world stage, and to contribute there the highly developed cultural gifts and goods that can help shape a new, cosmopolitan world civilization that celebrates both common humanity and the distinctive contributions of diverse racial-cultural groups."[81]

The proposal that Green makes is that mutual hospitality will not erase differences of cultures, i.e. it will not be a welcoming of the other that erases who the other is; rather, there will be a coexistence of diversity that will be advantageous to all. There is a hinge that allows hospitality to be mutual among different groups, and this is what the groups have in common; namely, that the groups are human, and, together, they make the world diverse. It is not only one of them that contributes to this and is, therefore, dominant or dominated; rather, all groups contribute to the diversity of our world and, consequently, they are on equal footing.

Nevertheless, we know that power imbalances are lived whenever "we" and "they" appear, i.e. whenever the other qua other makes an appearance. Therefore, how can diverse groups work together so as to not rehearse a dynamic of power imbalance? Green answers that, in order for the "would-be benefactor" to recognize this, there needs to be *respect for the other*, which will lead to a reflection on one's practices and values.

> [H]ospitality can fulfill its aim of meeting the needs of its intended recipients at the same time positively transforms the would-be benefactor in important ways through a growth of knowledge-based respect for the other that sheds light on her own assumptions and habits, as these interactively influence a now shared situation."[82]

Fleshing this with the ideas of guest/host, exile/new country, one can see that the host can undergo a transformation that is beneficial to itself, but that this will occur if and only if there is respect for the other, for the exile and the exile also needs to respond in this way to her new country to make the transformation happen. The agency of both parties is needed: the exile cannot change the community if it does not want to be changed, and the community cannot be changed by the exile if she does not want to contribute to this change.

Once respect is in place the event of an encounter between the exile and her new country or community can spur and, afterward, the mutual responsiveness of hospitality can be recognized as a *shared* experience, where the weight of responsibility for the event, its agency, and the benefits that it will produce are shared between the exile and her new country. It is usually the exile who extends to her new country, but this does not always happen. As Said says,

> Clutching difference like a weapon to be used with stiffened will, the exile jealously insists on his or her right to refuse to belong . . . Willfulness, exaggeration, overstatement: these are characteristic styles of being an exile, methods for compelling the world to accept your vision—which you make more unacceptable because you are in fact unwilling to have it accepted. It is yours, after all.[83]

Indeed, the exile in many cases has lost everything: from a home, to family members, friends, political protection, personality traits, her ability to make herself understood in her own terms, etc., and the loss of these affects her identity profoundly. If there is anything left that can be said is *hers* and hers alone, something that was not *given* to her but *achieved* by her own person, why trade it for what someone else can supply? Doing so would be like letting go of the last shred of dignity and identity, and cooperating with open eyes to a complete and systematic reorganization of her self that, to top it all, is being imposed on her.

Eva Hoffman, in her piece "Exile," illustrates eloquently her experience with loss and the imposition of another culture on her. In this first excerpt, the loss of identity and the problems ensuing are made evident:

> The worst losses come at night. As I lie down in a strange bed in a strange house . . . I wait for that spontaneous flow of inner language which used to be my nighttime talk with myself . . . Nothing comes. Polish, in a short time, has atrophied, shriveled from sheer uselessness. Its words don't apply to my new

experiences; they're not coeval with any of the objects, or faces, or the very air I breathe in the daytime. In English words have not penetrated to those layers of my psyche from which a private conversation could proceed . . . those images through which we assimilate the external world, through which we take it in, love it, make it our won—become blurred too . . . What has happened to me in this new world? . . . I have only a memory of fullness to anguish me with the knowledge that, in this dark and empty state, I don't really exist.[84]

The time of her life that Hoffman is describing is when she was a teenager, exiled with her parents in Canada. An older Polish woman who she names Mrs. Lieberman takes her under her wing without even asking her ("she has simply taken it upon herself to teach me how things are done here"[85]). As a young exiled teenager, Hoffman had to deal with pressures both typical and atypical for teenagers (peer pressure, wanting to belong, feeling embarrassed because of her poverty, etc.)—typical because most teenagers have to face these issues and, atypical because she was an exiled teenager that had to deal with her typical problems while not being able to make perfect sense of what was her way to deal with them, and not only insofar as her personality was being formed, but insofar as she was experiencing a fragmentation in her very self due to her displacement. Another Polish exile, Mrs. Steiner, also takes Eva under her wing (she "has semiadopted me, and I spend whole days and weekends in her house, where I'm half exiled princess, half Cinderella"[86]). Reflecting as an adult on her relationship with Mrs. Steiner and her family, Hoffman says, "They were more generous towards me than I was towards them; but then, a sense of disadvantage and inferiority is not a position from which one can feel the lightheartedness of true generosity."[87] It is this last statement that I would like to explore now.

Hoffman claims there was generosity on both the part of her hosts, and herself; however, after time had passed, she realized that the generosity of her hosts had exceeded hers, and for good reasons: her sense of being disadvantaged and inferior to them. An exile comes into a new country usually in a position of disadvantage: economic, cultural, social and, especially, political—she is not part of the community of citizens or residents, she does not know "how things are done here," she does not get to vote, and have her say. Generosity is required from the part of the community that will receive her; the one that is in power needs to start the ball rolling so that the exchange and transformation can happen. Yet, the precondition for a successful exchange is respect—generosity needs to be respectful of the other. It is a type of generosity that needs to be suggested, it needs to wait for an invitation before it acts, it cannot be imposed. It rather needs to be a generosity divested of its power, one ready to be transformed at the point of contact with the exile into humility; it needs to be a generosity coupled with vulnerability. Whoever is generous in that way needs to want, from the beginning, to embrace the possibility of change through an other.

It is this kind of generosity and respectful openness to the other that allows the new community to not see exiled women—to use Narayan's terms—as "dupes" or "prisoners" of patriarchy. And, while this generosity coupled with vulnerability to receive the other and be transformed by the other needs to start from the part of the one seemingly holding all the cards (i.e. the non exile), it is also needed as a response from the exile. And this is because, on the one hand, she will extend herself to her new community and, on the other hand, she will not close herself to the multiplicity and complexity of her circumstances—she will not deny the turmoil that she lives, the history and the past that used to be her present and that has been already irremediably altered; she will work through it all realizing that who she thought she was has changed, and that this change can bring about something good.

This is, without a doubt, easier said than done. The fragility and precariousness of the exilic condition make the exile vulnerable to turn against everything and everyone, including herself. How do we prevent this from happening? How do we assuage the fears of the exile so that she lets us in? It is not an easy task, and one best carried, perhaps, by others who have gone through the same thing because they—if they have reflected on their experiences critically and with a spirit of openness—may know best what needs to be understood between the exile and her new community from the start, may act as listeners and sounding boards, may have organizations and procedures in place for this, and may be able to act as role models, as proof that it can be done, that a mutual hospitality *is* possible.[88]

For mutual hospitality to begin, I have said above, we need respect for the other, and generosity coupled with vulnerability. This implies recognizing that the intentions of the new community may not be able to be grasped clearly by the exile; thus this new community needs to find a way to communicate with the exile. I believe one way of doing this is to yield authority to the exiles the new country has harbored and that have integrated into the community. They can guide the rest towards the exile; they can serve as a bridge between two entities that may be completely foreign to each other. But, again, it is necessary to remember that this bridge can be built by invitation only; it cannot be imposed on the exile as the *only* or *best* way to pass through.

In the particular case of women exiles, many of them have found this bridge in other women exiles. As Afkhami tells us, "the similarities between their lives as women and as women in exile supersede every other experience they have encountered as members of different countries, classes, cultures, professions, and religions."[89] Marjorie Agosín has lived this experience and has responded to the call of helping others and, as a result, has realized she was being helped all along herself. She acted as a bridge between exiles and their new community, and realized that, in so doing, she was not only performing a service for others, but she was also being transformed in a constructive way.

> Women have always been profoundly real in my life. Working with them during exile was a source of strength and stability. During this period I saw my own role as someone who could build a bridge of understanding and communication, someone who could help bring the cases of these women and their suffering to the consciousness of the Americans. Having language as my main tool, I used it in the service of a cause that has now become my cause. Exile became a positive thing for me.[90]

A community of women who experience exile can act as a bridge also by being inspirational, being mentors and role models for new generations. Demetria Martínez refers to this community as her

> group of powerful over-fifty mentors who have raised their kids, are involved in raising their grandkids, and who hide refugees on the side. Who are able to put together a pot of beans and chili at the last minute, and who have a profound sense of humor . . . I've always been exposed to that, and it has had a really important effect on me, to see this generation of mothers for whom private life was not separate from political or public life.[91]

In certain other cases, the communities that build bridges with exiles are their cultural[92] or professional communities.[93] In some cases, these communities establish contact with organizations where being an exile or belonging to a certain culture may not be the common denominator, but that are interested in the promotion of fulfillment across the board in their country. By providing outlets and spaces for discourse, bridges start being built between exiles and the larger community. Alicia Partnoy was part and parcel of such efforts.

> There was a group of refugees from Argentina in Seattle. We all had the support of the churches and of Amnesty International. They helped with medical and psychological checkups. More important (sic.), they provided a forum for us to speak. They arranged a number of speaking tours for me to talk about my experiences. I discovered the healing effect of talking about what I had gone through. I talked to anyone who would listen, at conferences, to audiences, to the bus driver, the cashier at the supermarket. I talked and talked, telling everybody my story. In a sense this is what I have been doing since I came into exile . . . That's the way to make people understand.[94]

Besides finding ways into the community, an important tool for the exile is to be able to redescribe her situation, and use her creativity to find new ways of being, and to develop the skills that she needs to deal both with her new identity as an exile, and with the experiences that ensue from that new identity—experiences which will more than likely, last a lifetime.[95] It is thus important that there be opportunities for her to develop her creativity (e.g. work on creative writing, or organizing groups, meetings, activities with others, etc.). These exercises will nourish her creative development as a whole, and will thus nourish possibilities for grappling with exile. In other words, once exile happens and there is a shift in one's identity, this very experience can be used to combat itself: exile impels us to find new solutions, and by being creative in one area we stimulate the production of solutions in other areas. Helena María Viramontes, professor of Creative Writing at Cornell University, discusses the importance of creativity development for exiles as the creative process is

> a real space of empowerment because if you can tap into your creative mind it's like the universe, it's limitless. So you can reimagine your world, you can reimagine solutions to problems now. So that's why I feel that writers, especially Chicano and Chicana writers have to be visionaries, they have to, they have no

other choice, we cannot afford not to use our imagination because our communities are under siege at any given time, we can not afford to write without that as an inspiration.[96]

Writer and exile Marjorie Agosín also makes mention how her experiences in exile and her writing are connected:

> Out of my own marginality in exile, I began to understand and communicate with "Women of Smoke," beggars, women in mental hospitals, disappeared women, veiled women. I made poetry out of such horrible things, but the words grew out of complete identification, direct association, and empathy . . . I write when I am in pain, when I am sad—I write to feel safe. Writing brings me closer to the language which is my inner self, my reality, my identity. I think life in exile has sharpened my feeling for and my appreciation of the Spanish language. Things become sharper because one uses one's memory and imagination more.[97]

Traversing exile is one way out of its pain, and taking ownership of this realization can bring empowerment and even pleasure. Hala Deeb Jabbour, in an interview with Mahnaz Afkhami, explained it in the following terms:

> The pain of exile is palpable and long-lasting. But there are pleasures also. The greatest joy is the potential to break through the structures, rules, regulations, written and unwritten, that bind a woman and take her real voice and her true identity. Breaking out of those structures is painful, but the pain can be the signal of a rebirth. I grew as a human being during exile. I felt an expansiveness inside of me. It was something I had always yearned for but could not achieve.[98]

These women's understanding of their exile, and the way in which they chose to combat the negative experiences it brought need not be applicable in the same way to all women exiles. Some women find, in fact, that talking about their experience and thus educating others is taxing and frustrating.[99] However, the important thing to keep in mind is that bridges are being built—not all of them have to lead to the same place, or look exactly the same; this fecundity of options is, indeed, part of the complexity of the interaction between the exile and her new country. Yet, clearly, the more one is able to interact rather than close oneself off, the better results there are for the exile and her new community.

Ways in which bridges can be built are, for example, talking to one's community members (other exiles, other women exiles, others of a certain profession, religion, culture, etc.), talking to other community members, availing oneself of opportunities to learn the language of the place where one currently is, joining and/or founding associations, workshops, informal clubs, interest groups, advocacy centers, going to school, writing, obtaining (and putting the social and political mechanisms in place so that this can happen) a more prominent and visible role in the new country, etc. The exile and her new community will be faced with another in these and other ways that will spur from their respectful, egalitarian, and generous interaction. Both parties have a responsibility to engage in this interaction in a respectful way in order to better the living conditions of people *in* that community and *abroad*. This is a feminist concern, and the same one that guides this essay. The ideas of writer Pía Barros echo this.

> I became a feminist because I dreamed of a better world for all people . . . It is a world in which no one is left out . . . I became a feminist to empower myself, but to empower myself in order to deliver a dissertation, and to share, and to teach. It is something fundamental. I became a feminist because I wanted a better world where no one would be left out, a world where all people were indispensable, where we would all fit.[100]

A world where no one is left out is a feminist world, a communal world—one where neither the exile nor her new community feel superior to the other, but they rather share power to work through their differences, growth, and adaptation to the twists and turns that their co-existence brings. As Fatima Ahmed Ibrahim says, "[l]earning from past mistakes should help us work toward a world in which there is an equitable distribution of the necessities of life, full participation of the people in determining their destiny, and justice and the rule of law."[101]

A feminist world is by no means a world free of conflict where justice and law are not needed—that would be a post-feminist world. What is needed right now are ways in which to bring about a feminist world to both reduce the suffering of exiles and that of their new community. Suffering exists not only when something is taken away, but also when one lacks what one does not even know is not there; the potential members of our community are the ones we currently miss; we miss their stories, their skills, their presence. And we do not miss them because if we had them we could make a profit by exploiting their labor; rather, we miss them because they are agents in the constant and critical revision of our pre-suppositions, and only by working through them can we in fact claim that we are engaged in the quest for what we all say we seek, namely, happiness.

In this essay I have explored the issues of feminism, hospitality, and women in exile.

The basic characteristic of exile is to have to leave one's home or place behind—the definition of "home" or "place" is, of course, multiple and changing, and this is the first reason why exile is a complex problem. "Home" or "place" need not be understood as physical, i.e. as one's place of origin, the place where one lives, the place where one was born; "home" or "place" can be understood also as one's convictions, a cluster of thoughts, principles, values, habits, behaviors, practices, etc. that help someone define who she is. Leaving one's home or place, then, can be forged in different ways. There is physical exile, and also cultural or internal exile. After exploring these different kinds of exile, I proposed that the common thread that joins them is the experience of displacement and changing of identity. Then, I focused on how women live exile differently from men pointing at their differences insofar as women are a group oppressed by patriarchy (albeit to different degrees and in different ways depending on the person). I explored some of the common experiences lived by most women that are exiled physically and/or culturally, and these are: displacement, the awareness of one's difference with the rest of the world, the upheaval in one's world, and one's identity, uncertainty about the future, lack of prospects, financial hardship, lack of community support, and racism. I then fleshed out the relationship between the exile and her new country/community using the terms "guest" and "host" and proposed that, in order to draw benefit and fulfillment from this relationship, one needs to use a strategy of multiplying and reversing these roles. This will be possible only in a foundation of respect and generosity towards the other that is joined with awareness and disclosure of vulnerability. Building bridges between the exile and her new community on this foundation will allow us to effectively create a feminist world. The practical means to doing this include the collaboration of exiles and organized groups (cultural, professional, religious, etc.), which will provide ways in which the pain of exile can be invited to heal: speaking forums, conferences, workshops, associations, safe spaces, medical attention, ways to keep in touch with their community, etc. This will allow exiles to effectively participate in their new community using their self-determined agency being not only guests but also hosts.

Notes

1. The UNHCR reported in a press release that "[t]he number of people forcibly uprooted by conflict and persecution worldwide stood at 42 million at the end of last year [2008]" UNHCR press releases, June 16, 2009, "UNHCR Annual Report shows 42 million people uprooted worldwide," UNHCR, http://www.unhcr.org/4a2fd52412d.html (accessed January 9, 2010). The same organization lists 6,572,167 'stateless' persons world wide at the end of 2008, these exclude stateless refugees and stateless asylum-seekers. Cf. UNHCR, "Frequently Requested Statistics," UNHCR, http://www.unhcr.org/pages/4a0174156.html (accessed January 9, 2010).

2. Specific examples of how these experiences are lived by exiles will be given below.

3. See, e.g. Marjorie Agosín's comment on this issue: "If you dress unusually, have an accent, look at the world in a different way, you are made to feel your otherness . . . I am not sure which was the cause and which the effect—whether my strong involvement with Chile kept me from being fully integrated into this society or my lack of attachment here drove me to even closer ties with my home country." Mahnaz Afkhami, *Women In Exile* (Charlottesville: University Press of Virginia, 1994), 143.

4. Halleh Ghorashi provides us with a clear example of this when she examines the traditional view of migration in the Netherlands: "In the Netherlands, the most important effect of migration linked to return is that it is seen as mainly temporary, not as a kind of settlement. This image was initially present in the case of the Indo-Dutch and later reinforced by patterns of migration among guest laborers and refugees . . . The idea that migrants should return, which implies that they are seen as guests, was especially high during the 1970s, when the name 'guest workers' was used both by the migrants themselves and the host country. In the 1980s when the term 'guest workers' changed to (im)migrants, this did not mean that the understanding of return and its link to migration was also adapted. At the end of the 1990s, the debates among politicians and in the media were concentrated around the return of those refugees refused legal status. Efforts were exerted to stimulate the repatriation of first- and second-generation immigrants to their

country in 2000." Halle Ghorashi, *Ways to Survive, Battles to Win Iranian Women Exiles in the Netherlands and United States* (New York: Nova Science Publishers, Inc. 2002), 119.

5. Edward Said, *Reflections on Exile and Other Essays* (Cambridge: Harvard University Press 2000), 181.

6. Halleh Ghorashi, *Ways to Survive, Battles to Win.*

7. Chandra Talpade Mohanty, *Feminism Without Borders*, (United States of America: Duke University Press, 2003), 126.

8. Ghorashi, *Ways to Survive, Battles to Win*, 106.

9. Ghorashi, *Ways to Survive, Battles to Win*, 107.

10. Ghorashi, *Ways to Survive, Battles to Win*, 107. Ghorashi's understanding of refugee echoes the definition that the UNHCR offers. According to this definition a refugee is "every person who, owing to well-founded fear of being persecuted for reasons of race, religion, nationality, membership of a particular social group or political opinion, is outside the country of his nationality and is unable or, owing to such fear, is unwilling to avail himself of the protection of that country, or who, not having a nationality and being outside the country of his former habitual residence as a result of such events is unable or, owing to such fear, is unwilling to return to it . . . [and] every person who owing to external aggression, occupation, foreign domination or events seriously disturbing public order in either part or the whole of his country of origin or nationality, is compelled to leave his place of habitual residence in order to seek refuge in another place outside his country of origin or nationality." Heads of African State and Government at Addis Ababa, September 10, 1969, "OAU Convention Governing the Specific Aspects of Refugee Problems in Africa, Art. I (1,2)," http://www.africauion.org/Official_documents/Treaties_%20Conventions_%20Protocols/Refugee_Convention.pdf African Union (accessed January 9, 2010).

11. Wendy Everett and Peter Wagstaff, eds., *Cultures of Exile: Images of Displacement* (New York: Berghahn Books, 2004), xviii-xix. I differ from Everett and Wagstaff in that I do not believe anyone has a "fixed" center of identity; I do believe, however, that many people *think* they have a fixed identity, and feel secure because of it.

12. Everett and Wagstaff, eds., *Cultures of Exile*, x.

13. "Initially it was Julio Cortázar who used the term 'cultural exile' to denote his exclusion from his country by the institutional banning of his books. I use this term . . . as a specific phenomenon, as a category of exile." Gabriela Gutiérrez y Muhs, *Communal Feminisms: Chicanas, Chilenas, and Cultural Exile* (Lanham: Lexington Books, 2007), xxxii.

14. Internal exile is also sometimes referred to as "insile." Sosnowski and Popkin, *Repression, Exile, and Democracy: Uruguayan Culture* (Durham: Duke University Press), 2, 5, 6.

15. Cf. Gutiérrez y Muhs, *Communal Feminisms*, xxxii-xxxiii.

16. Gabriella Gutiérrez y Muhs and Norma E. Cantú, who have experienced cultural and physical exile, discuss their experiences trying to publish their work in the United States in an interview: "G.G.M.: . . . I have this other project that I am working on, *Las Otras: Chicana Writers in the Dim Light*, and it's always amazing to me how there's, what is it, thirty five million Latinos in the United States, and how there's basically four or five writers, one Chicana that has been published . . . by a major house. . . . N.E.C.: . . . The alienation comes from not having your place or your position validated or acknowledged as equally valid. . . . N.E.C.: . . . For example, this book is in both English and Spanish. I don't have a publisher, because nobody wants to publish something in both. They want just in English or just in Spanish. And I'm writing in both, I have to have the authenticity of those voices." Gutiérrez y Muhs, *Communal Feminisms*, 32-3.

Feminism, Hospitality, and Women in Exile   157

17. Pía Barros is someone that has experienced internal and cultural exile. In speaking about this it becomes clear that, even in her own country, the outlets for her creativity were almost totally out of reach because of the politics of the time. She tells us, "I published seven books. The first was in 85, during a time when you could not publish in Chile . . . . Nothing was published without censorship. We writers began to publish around 1980, books that were circulated by hand . . . .. Everyone was interested in reading everything that came out that had something to do with the opposition, or what in reality we did *without being part of the official culture.*" Ibid., 3-4, emphasis mine. A similar experience is recounted by Alejandra Basualto, another Chilean writer, who says that in the 80s, "[e]veryone was an internal exile . . . a cultural exile because there were no books to buy since no literature was coming into Chile . . . we were disconnected from the world." Gutiérrez y Muhs, *Communal Feminisms,* 108.

18. See the previously quoted passage of Marjorie Agosín in Afkhami, *Women In Exile,* 143.

19. Gutiérrez y Muhs, *Communal Feminisms,* 37.

20. Said, *Reflections on Exile and Other Essays,* 186.

21. Afkhami, *Women In Exile.*

22. Afkhami, *Women In Exile,* 97.

23. Afkhami, *Women In Exile,* 59.

24. Afkhami, *Women In Exile,* 48.

25. Afkhami, *Women In Exile,* 108.

26. Florence M. Simfukwe, Sima Wali, Marjorie Agosín, and Tatyana Mamonova also express similar accounts of liminality in her interviews with Afkhami. Cf. Afkhami, *Women In Exile,* 117, 123, 138, 144-4, 161. Women exiles interviewed by Halleh Ghorashi also express feelings of liminality. See, e.g., Ghorashi, *Ways to Survive, Battles to Win,* 154-5.

27. Buijs tells us that it is said women may have less trouble adapting to exile: "because they have the responsibility for maintaining household routines which provide them with occupation, and also that they are less conscious of status deprivation associated with the failure to find positions comparable to those they left." Gina Buijs, ed., *Migrant Women: Crossing Boundaries and Changing Identities* (Oxford: Berg, 1993), 4-5.

28. Not all men, however, experience this lack of social mobility. Some are able to continue socializing with other men even when they do not have a job. This does not mean that they allow or encourage women to also get together with other women (or other men) and socialize. See Afkhami, *Women In Exile,* 136.

29. Afkhami, *Women In Exile,* 5.

30. Buijs, *Migrant Women,* 8.

31. Afkhami, *Women In Exile,* 58.

32. Afkhami, *Women In Exile,* 98.

33. Afkhami, *Women In Exile,* 135.

34. Afkhami, *Women In Exile,* 188-9.

35. Afkhami, *Women In Exile,* 149.

36. Marita Eastmond, "Reconstructing Life: Chilean Refugee Women and the Dilemmas of Exile." In Afkhami, *Women In Exile,* 46.

37. There are many examples one could cite about this, but see, e.g. the testimonials of Ana Guadalupe Martínez, María Tila Uribe, Gloria Bonilla and Claribel Alegría in Alicia Partnoy, *You Can't Drown the Fire, Latin American Women Writing in Exile* (Pittsburgh: Cleis Press, 1988).

38. The examples one could cite of crimes committed against women all over the world go by the trillions throughout history and all over the world. One particularly compelling work that deals with issues of violence against women is Ayaan Hirsi Ali's autobiography *Infidel*. There, she recalls her own female circumcision and that of her sister (orchestrated by their grandmother), the terrible yet regular beatings she and her sister underwent at the hands of their own mother, and her knowledge of similar experiences and other issues (such as honor killings) happening to migrant women in Europe. Ayaan Hirsi Ali, *Infidel* (New York: Free Press, 2007).

39. See e.g. Afkhami, *Women In Exile*, 57-8, 98-9, 109, 122-3, 133-4, 137-8.

40. Afkhami, *Women In Exile*, 2.

41. Afkhami, *Women In Exile*, 2-3.

42. Said, *Reflections on Exile and Other Essays*, 177, emphasis mine.

43. Edward Said locates what he calls the "pathos of exile" "in the loss of contact with the solidity and satisfaction of earth: homecoming is out of the question." Said, *Reflections on Exile and Other Essays*, 179.

44. Ghorashi, *Ways to Survive, Battles to Win*, 163.

45. An exception to this would be many (but not all) of the Iranian exiles living in Los Angeles—they especially live in rich areas such as Beverly Hills, and they are so popular that the region is often referred to as "Irangeles." See Ghorashi, *Ways to Survive, Battles to Win*, 142 ff.

46. Afkhami, *Women In Exile*, 76-7.

47. This idea was expressed before the tragedy of September 11, which, I would argue, would show that Americans are integrating the idea of relating to a collectivity in a significant way into their culture.

48. Afkhami, *Women In Exile*, 105.

49. See also the passage quoted above where Marita Eastmond speaks about the loss of the social world of women exiles from Chile (Eastmond, "Reconstructing Life: Chilean Refugee Women and the Dilemmas of Exile," 46).

50. Afkhami, *Women In Exile*, 136.

51. Dima Abdulrahim, "Defining Gender in a Second Exile: Palestinian Women in West Berlin," in Gina Buijs, ed., *Migrant Women: Crossing Boundaries and Changing Identities* (Oxford: Berg, 1993), 64-5.

52. Gutiérrez y Muhs, *Communal Feminisms*, 160.

53. I say "to a point" because, for many exiles, there are feelings of guilt for having left, or for having accepted a different kind of life, which resurface time and again. For example, Fatima Ahmed Ibrahim, an activist of Sudanese origin exiled in England, says, "I yearn for news of my country, and when I hear of the scarcity of food and see the drawn faces of the starving children on television, I am filled with guilt. Food sticks in my throat and I am unable to swallow. I cannot sleep at night. I lie down in bed but my mind travels home. I am not anxious for the dawn" (Afkhami, *Women In Exile* 207). See also Afkhami, *Women In Exile* 61, and Abdulrahim, "Defining Gender in a Second Exile: Palestinian Women in West Berlin," 69.

54. In some cases, guilt is finally displaced and done away with. Ge Yang speaks of this experience: "Now I have come to terms with myself. I think I have suffered so much that I have paid for all that . . . I feel no guilt. I am at peace with my past" (Afkhami, *Women In Exile*, 76). Alicia Partnoy echoes similar sentiments; see Afkhami, *Women In Exile*, 106.

55. Linda Hitchcox, "Vietnamese Refugees in Hong Kong: Behaviour and Control," in Gina Buijs, ed., *Migrant Women: Crossing Boundaries and Changing Identities* (Oxford: Berg, 1993), 145-60.

56. Abdulrahim, "Defining Gender in a Second Exile: Palestinian Women in West Berlin," 55-82.
57. Abdulrahim, "Defining Gender in a Second Exile: Palestinian Women in West Berlin," 68.
58. Abdulrahim, "Defining Gender in a Second Exile: Palestinian Women in West Berlin," 69-70.
59. Abdulrahim, "Defining Gender in a Second Exile: Palestinian Women in West Berlin," 77.
60. For example, the Afghan government has recently had to review a law commonly referred to as "rape law" that allows Shiite husbands to rape their wives. See CNN "Afghanistan to change controversial "rape' law," CNN,http://www.cnn.com/2009/WORLD/asiapcf/04/16/afghanistan.law.karzai/ (accessed July 2, 2009). Also, the so-called 'honor killings' are infamous for having no repercussions for the perpetrators. See, e.g., Ayaan Hirsi Ali's discussion of honor killings in Holland (Hirsi Ali, *Infidel*, 295-6). See also Amnesty International, "Trapped by Violence—Women in Iraq," http://www.amnesty.org/en/news-and-updates/feature-stories/trapped-violence-women-iraq-2 0090420 (accessed July 2, 2009).
61. Uma Narayan, "Minds of Their Own: Choices, Autonomy, Cultural Practices, and Other Women," in *A Mind of One's Own*, Louise M. Antony and Charlotte E. Witt, eds. (U.S.A.: Westview, 2002), 418.
62. Narayan, "Minds of Their Own: Choices, Autonomy, Cultural Practices, and Other Women," 418.
63. Narayan, "Minds of Their Own: Choices, Autonomy, Cultural Practices, and Other Women," 419.
64. Narayan, "Minds of Their Own: Choices, Autonomy, Cultural Practices, and Other Women."
65. Narayan, "Minds of Their Own: Choices, Autonomy, Cultural Practices, and Other Women," 420.
66. AFP, "Al Quaeda menace de se venger de la France," La Libre.be, http://www.lalibre.be/actu/international/article/512995/burqa-al-qaeda-menace-de-se-venger-de-la-france.html, my translation (accessed January 23, 2010).
67. In a speech to the French Armed Forces in Kabul, a propos of a tragic ambush in Uzbeen where ten French soldiers died, Nicolas Sarkozy said, "thanks to you one does not see anymore those images of barbarians gathered in a stadium in order to stone a supposedly adulterous woman, to cut the hand of a little girl that put on nail polish, to forbid the schooling of little girls, or to condemn women to live behind a prison called the burqua. It is thanks to you that people can live normally . . . the French Nation is proud of you." Présidence de la République, "Allocution de M. Le Président de la République, Kaboul—Mercredi 20 aout, 2008," Présidence de la République, http://www.elysee.fr/download/?mode=press&filename=20.08_Kaboul.pdf, my translation (accessed June 30, 2009).
68. See Angelique Chrisafis, "Nicolas Sarkozy says Isalmic veils are not welcome in France," Guardian.co.uk, http://www.guardian.co.uk/world/2009/jun/22/islamic-veils-sarkozy-speech-france (accessed July 2, 2009).
69. Cf. Narayan, "Minds of Their Own: Choices, Autonomy, Cultural Practices, and Other Women," 420.
70. Miguel de Cervantes Saavedra, *The Ingenious Gentelman Don Quixote de la Mancha*, Spanish Arts.com, trans., http://www.spanish-books.net/quijote/2chapter49.htm (accessed July 2, 2009).

71. Another side of this issue that is sometimes brought up is the potential danger that exists in a society when some or many of its members are fully veiled; indeed, in encountering someone that is fully veiled one cannot read the person's facial expression, and ignores whether the person is hiding a weapon underneath the veil. For example, Rita Manchanda tells us, "In Kashmir, the *burqa*, which was expected to protect women, made them even more vulnerable to security forces . . . [They] were convinced that one in every three *burqa* clad persons was a militant . . . Women wearing *burqas* suffered humiliation and sexual harassment as the security forces lifted their *burqa* to search for weapons and ammunition." Rita Manchanda, "Guns and *Burqa*: Women in the Kashmir Conflict," in *Women, War, and Peace in South Asia*, Rita Manchanda, ed. (New Delhi: Sage Publications, 2001), 59-60. While the use of the burqua to conceal items (weaponry or items of other kinds) is a possibility, this does not make the burqua stand alone as dangerous. Indeed, the veil is not the only thing that can prevent us from reading someone's facial expression, as sunglasses, hoods, and caps may sometimes prevent us from doing the same thing. Also, weapons can be concealed under many kinds of clothing and accessories that are commonly used in societies that do not espouse the burqua. Examples of such items are trench coats, sweatshirts, baggy sweaters and pants, priestly robes, Halloween and advertisement costumes, purses, wigs, hats, etc. In one of the recent terrorist attacks in the United States (Northwest Airlines Flight 253 on December 25, 2009), Umar Farouk Abdulmutallab, a 23-year old Nigerian male, concealed explosive materials in his underwear.

72. Afkhami, *Women In Exile*, 106. See also Gutiérrez y Muhs, *Communal Feminisms*, 65.

73. Rubén Martínez, *The New Americans* (New York: The New Press, 2004), 69. The idea that the third world is inhabited only by people in poverty is explored by Uma Narayan and Radhika Balakrishnan in their article "Combining Justice with Development: Rethinking Rights and Responsibilities in the Context of World Hunger and Poverty" (*World Hunger and Morality*, Aiken, W., and LaFollette, H., eds. Upper Saddle River: Prentice Hall, 1996, 230-47).

74. Narayan, "Combining Justice with Development," 421.

75. Afkhami, *Women In Exile*, 77.

76. See Ghorashi, *Ways to Survive, Battles to Win*, 139-40, and Mohanty, *Feminism Without Borders*, 126.

77. Rubén Martínez speaks eloquently about the sense of embarrassment he felt in grade school at being of Mexican and Salvadorian descent. His interaction with a Mexican child then recently incorporated into his school is telling about his feelings, and the auto-repression his attitude towards his classmate caused. In describing him, he says, "He wore polyester to our American cotton, responded to our consonant-heavy English in the lyrical vowels of Spanish . . . He was an innocent deep-brown-skinned boy from the Mexican provinces, representing everything both sides of my family had hoped to banish from our future: the look, the smell, the very idea of poverty, and more than that, of the past . . . he reminded me and all the white kids and smattering of Asians at school of my ignominious origins. Seen through American eyes, Mexico was dusty, dirty, lazy; the vanquished Indian empire of the South. Me, I wanted to be a cowboy . . . I treated that boy terribly, denying him what I denied in myself: history. Initially ecstatic at having a Spanish-speaker to commune with, the poor kid's gregarious manner quickly gave way to a morose silence" (Martínez, *The New Americans*, 9). On the issue of seeing a culture in a negative way from the perspective of a different, dominant culture see Ghorashi, *Ways to*

Survive, Battles to Win, 139 and Rodríguez, *What Women Lose: Exile and the Construction of Imaginary Homelands in Novels by Caribbean Writers* (New York: Peter Lang, 2005), 11. See also Chávez, *A Taco Testimony* (Tucson: Rio Nuevo Publishers, 2006), 174.

78. Judith Green, "Building a Cosmopolitan World Community through Mutual Hospitality," in *Pragmatism and the Problem of Race*, Bill E. Lawson and Donald F. Koch, eds. (Bloomington: Indiana University Press, 2004), 208.

79. Green, "Building a Cosmopolitan World Community through Mutual Hospitality."

80. "Building a Cosmopolitan World Community through Mutual Hospitality," 221.

81. "Building a Cosmopolitan World Community through Mutual Hospitality," 209-10.

82. "Building a Cosmopolitan World Community through Mutual Hospitality," 213.

83. Said, *Reflections on Exile and Other Essays*, 182.

84. Eva Hoffman, "Exile," in *A Map of Hope*, Marjorie Agosín, ed. (New Brunswick: Rutgers University Press, 1999), 202-3.

85. Hoffman, "Exile," 203.

86. Hoffman, "Exile," 204.

87. Hoffman, "Exile," 208.

88. In some cases, however, first-generation exiles are the hardest on other exiles. As Said says, "Exile is a jealous state. What you achieve is precisely what you have no wish to share, and it is in the drawing of lines around you and your compatriots that the least attractive aspects of being in exile emerge: an exaggerated sense of group solidarity, and a passionate hostility to outsiders, *even those who may in fact be in the same predicament as you*" (Said, *Reflections on Exile and Other Essays,* 178, emphasis mine). Rubén Martínez also refers to this making special mention of first-generation immigrants in opposition to second- or third-generation ones, see Martínez, *You Can't Drown the Fire,* 14. This is also lived in cases of repatriation. In these cases, the exile returns home to find herself a foreigner once again, and, in addition, viewed in a space where "[a]fter an initial period of mutual celebration, doubt and suspicion set in" (Hugo Achugar, "Postdictatorship, Democracy, and Culture in the Uruguay of the Eighties," in Saúl Sosnowski and Louis B. Popkin, eds., *Repression, Exile, and Democracy: Uruguayan Culture* [Durham: Duke University Press], 229). Susana Sanchez Bravo knew when she returned home that nobody could understand what she had gone through: "I have a wonderful family, but when I went in exile for fifteen years and returned, no one asked me if at any point I was cold, if at any time I became depressed, if I cried. No one asked me about the emotions that inundated me during this period of my life. It is as if I had gone on a long trip around the world and had returned" (Gutiérrez y Muhs, *Communal Feminisms,* 49).

89. Afkhami, *Women In Exile,* 12.

90. Afkhami, *Women In Exile,* 144.

91. Gutiérrez y Muhs, *Communal Feminisms,* 57.

92. See Afkhami, *Women In Exile,* 82.

93. See Gutiérrez y Muhs, *Communal Feminisms,* xxx, 30, 35.

94. Afkhami, *Women In Exile,* 105.

95. Gutiérrez y Muhs, a Chicana writer currently living in the United States, also indicates the possibilities of creativity as a way to deal with exile: "I came back from Europe to Mexico, attempting to survive the pain of being an exile. Because from afar I was aware of the cultural rejection into which both countries sandwiched me, *I could strategize a recovery*. The question became how to recreate a nationalism that fit my heart, the heart of those like me, its ethics, culture of rejection, my portability and that of my belongings and culture" (Gutiérrez y Muhs, *Communal Feminisms*, xviii, emphasis mine).

96. Gutiérrez y Muhs, *Communal Feminisms*, 132-3.
97. Afkhami, *Women In Exile*, 147.
98. Afkhami, *Women In Exile*, 63.
99. See Ghorashi, *Ways to Survive, Battles to Win,* 139-40.
100. Gutiérrez y Muhs, *Communal Feminisms*, 17.
101. Afkhami, *Women In Exile*, 206-7.

Chapter 9

Hospitality and European Muslims

Meyda Yeğenoğlu

Migration, displacement of people, as well as the decline of the force and power of the nation-state as preeminent tendencies associated with processes of globalization have accentuated discussions in the field of hospitality, giving the topos of hospitality a new salience and relevance. Most importantly, hospitality has become an important motif to discuss the gesture by which the identity and mastery of the host—be it self, culture or nation—is constituted and/or dispossessed. In this essay, it is from this perspective that I will discuss the nature of the hospitality offered to the European Muslim population. In addressing the nature of the relation between the European host and Muslim immigrant as a relation of host/guest, I will particularly focus on Julia Kristeva's and Seyla Benhabib's texts, and more specifically the position they take with regards to the Muslim woman's headscarf.[1] I focus on their discourse as revealing the ways in which Muslim presence in Europe is responded to. I take these two texts as symptomatic of a certain gesture of hospitality which ends up endorsing the means of reaffirming the European subject as a soverign and self identitical entity: a subject whose "at home-ness" of identity is managed not to be disturbed or destabilized in its relation with Otherness. The Muslim foreigner presence in Europe, revealed in the response given to the headscarf issue, does not call for Europe as a subject of unconditional hospitality. On the contrary: Europe as foreign or not identical to itself is opposed surreptitiously. Any introduction of foreignness into the European home, which entails dispossesion of European sovereign identity or openness to the uncannyness of Otherness is evaded in a subtle way both by Kristeva and Benhabib. It is the nature of this evasion that my reading aims to reveal.

It is possible to talk about two positions on the issue of hospitality. One approach, exemplified in Immanuel Kant's essay "To Perpetual Peace: A Philosophical Sketch" casts hospitality as question of universal right, as a stranger's right of visit that should be regulated and institutionalized under the sign of a formalizable and legislatable law.[2] In so far as the question of hospitality is limited to a question of law, it upholds the hosts's sovereignty over the ethical relation and hence is in favor of a relation that reinforces rather than challenges the dispossession of the masterful position of the host. In the Kantian understanding of hospitality, no room is left for an accidental encounter and therefore what is endorsed is a hospitality of *invitation* not a hospitality of *visitation*, to put it in Derrida's terminology. The other approach, exemplified in Emmanuel Levinas's (1969) understanding of ethics, casts hospitality not simply as one particular ethic but the name of ethicity as such or as the very basis of ethics.[3] This Levinasian understanding of hospitality achieves a different sense in Jacques Derrida's (1999) reading of Levinas's assesment of ethics.[4] Derrida, by recasting the ethical with the political, shows how absolute or unconditional hospitality requires not only the welcoming of the stranger to one's own home but involves calling into question the ownership of home and hence entails its dispossession. In this reading, the ethical encounter with Otherness is about calling into question the *Chez soi* into question.

It is Derrida's reading of the Levinasian ethical relation with Otherness that shapes and guides my thinking of Europe's encounter with its Muslim population. Seyla Benhabib's (2002; 2004; 2006) discussion of the notion of hospitality is also situated in the context of Europe and its relation with the Muslim immigrants and their rights claims.[5] However, in Benhabib's discussion, hospitality, like cosmopolitanism, receives a different reading than that of Derrida's. Below, I focus on Kristeva's and Benhabib's position on the issue of the headscarf and the kind of hospitality that is implied in their respective positions.

Allergic Reaction To Islam

Any discussion of hospitality in Europe needs to understand what is that allows the permissive circulation and marking of European Muslims (as I refrain to call them "immigrants") in the parlance of European public sphere today as an internal enemy of Europe and therefore as a demographic, cultural and civilizational threat to its integrity. The historical constitution of Islam as the archetypal external enemy certainly plays an important role in this marking. The making of the enemy is undoubtedly a discursive operation. Certainly, the discourse of enmity, as it pertains to Islam/Muslims, show variation in different historical episodes in the European history. The different modalities by which Islam stands as an enemy to Europe, to Christianity, and to secular Europe attests to how Islam is an adversary to Europe in multiple ways. But analysis of this multiplicity is beyond the purpose and scope of my analysis in this essay.

A particular spatial imaginary participates vitally in the positioning of Europeans as national subjects and the Muslim groups as strangers/enemies. The making of the stranger or an internal enemy takes place through a multitude of social, legal, as well as spatial arrangements. In his inspiring book, *White Nation*,[6] Ghassan Hage points to the dimension of territorial and more generally spatial power in the formation of racist imaginary and violence. Critiquing the understanding of racism as something either to be reserved for traditional biological forms of racism or as a system of beliefs, thereby limiting it to an issue of mental phenomenon, Hage suggests that racist practices need to be conceived as nationalist practices as they always assume a national space and an image of the nationalist himself/herself as master of this national space while at the same time imagining an ethnic or racial other as an object in this space.[7] So, space is never a neutral space; it is always imagined, lived and experienced in a particular form. One's imagination of oneself as the "owner" of a particular space is always about claiming an exclusive power to manage and regulate that space. This is about declaring oneself as having the privilege and right to inhabit that space, and concomitantly, the others as external and in many cases as a threat to the unity and integrity of that space. Such is the nationalist imagining himself/ herself as the sole possessor of a particular space. Hage calls a nationalist someone "with a managerial capacity over this national space."[8] The imagination of oneself with this managerial capacity is at the same time the condition of seeing others as being "too many."[9] The category, "undesirable," is somewhat meaningless without the imagination of oneself as the sole owner of that space and hence the feeling of being invaded by the undesirables is symptomatic of this managerial power. The German notion of *"Uberfremdung"* (understood as over-foreignization[10]), for example, is a reflection of this aggressive defense of a territory and the power of the nation-state to control its territory when the so-called outsiders have leaked in, thus threatening its homogeneity and integrity. As Michel de Certau notes, ethnic confrontation is a violent allergic reaction by the natives to the "foreign" ways of using the natives' space.[11] Such a reaction regards the different uses of the so-called native territory "as 'errors' or 'barbarism' committed by immigrants."[12]

Who and what can be regarded as a demographic threat so comfortably? What is it that enables the discourse which registers Muslim Europeans as an internal menace and strangers to European culture to become a sanctioned knowledge in the life-world of the European subject? For example, how can someone like Le Pen threaten the French public with the idea of over-Islamization and put forward the possibility of being surrounded by mosques as a threat to Frenchness? What is it that enables the representation of Muslims as "intolerant of freedom of speech" when cartoons of Mohammed printed in the Danish *Jylland-Posten* were clearly racist and demonizing? What explains the currency of the "Dutch values of tolerance" which shows not much tolerance for the immigrant Muslim ways of life within its borders? What is that enables such discourses to be sanctioned as rightful? This is certainly part of a gesture which enables some to imagine themselves as European and hence as the sole and legitimate inhabitants of the space called Europe, a space which is understood to be first and foremost Christian.

The very naming and marking of a space called Europe is to imagine it in some sense as a unified entity. The most recent figuration of the entity called Europe is secured, among other things, *via* the creation of the figure "European citizen": a category, which is legally, economically, politically, and culturally managed. Involved in the idea of the "European citizen" is not only an imagination of a unified territorial space, but as a necessary by product of this, an operation of bifurcation that separates the political, cultural and economic spaces of the strangers and natives. The imagination of a sense of European unity and the land that belongs to European citizens is not independent of the institution of borders and frontiers of Europe. Borders are not neutral demarcating lines; they are processes of territorialization and as they territorialize they contribute to the "absolutization and sacralization of borders."[13] The institution of borders and the concomitant institutional segregation in Europe is now such that it compels Balibar to call it "European apartheid."[14] As a political and economic entity, Europe is waged at its borders as well as territories, and by frontier wars which takes place along racial lines.[15] To quote from Balibar "It is not the existence of borders which produces or gives way to wars, but increasingly the endemic social war which 'territorializes' and 'spatializes' itself through the institution and the localization of borders."[16] The creation of borders is thus a by-product of a certain social regime, which while producing borders simultaneously creates the stranger or the internal enemy.

The language of "clash of civilizations" and "war of cultures" and the violent exclusion this language engenders partakes in a robust way in the constitution and maintenance of borders which in turn results in the marking of the European Muslims as the internal enemy. The language of culture wars not only institutes borders that separate the European citizen from the stranger but also shapes the very meaning of who the foreign and strange is. What is now first and foremost foreign to the European culture is the non-secular ways of life lived on European soil, exemplified by the European Muslim culture. But what are the constituents of the allergy that is experienced *vis-à-vis* the Muslim immigrant culture in Europe, an allergy that turns them into strangers of a presumably unified European culture and to internal enemies—enemies of the secular? As Zygmunt Bauman states: "all societies produce strangers but each kind of society produces its own kind of strangers, and produces them in its inimitable way."[17] How do we discern the unique ways and the specific modalities in which the strangeness of the Muslim groups is constituted? The bluntly and the matter-of-factly presumed menace that Islam (which is represented internally by European Muslim groups and externally by Turkey trying to become a member of the EU) constitutes for the secular and modern European way of life is certainly not independent of the history of the modern European Christian discourse on religion which is simultaneously a discourse of secularization as well as a discourse of othering of Islam. Any attempt to understand the place Islam occupies today in the imaginary of Europeans has to address the manner in which Islam has historically been cast as the religion of fanaticism and the geo-political significance the Islamic rule has historically played for the European Christendom. But this is beyond the scope of this essay.

A central question that needs to be asked is whether the Muslim presence in Europe will be allowed to transform what the hegemonic definition of Europe is and the way it has managed to define the nature of its public domain or will Islamophobia win and therefore whether the myth of Europe founded on Judeo-Christian values be reinforced and Muslims will remain external and alien in a "Christocentric Europe," to use Gabriella Marranci's term.[18] The ethico-political question that awaits Europe is whether it will be capable of opening itself to Otherness which will enable Muslim presence to call into question the *chez soi* of Europe into question? Or are they going to continue to be treated as the enemies within? From Huntington's thesis of clash of civilizations, to Gisgard d'Estaing's description of Europe as a Christian club, to the Dutch media presenter Pim Fortuyn's book entitled *Against Islamization of Our Culture*, to Le Pen's presentation of himself as the last defense against Islamization of Europe and France, to the Somali immigrant Hirsi Ali's authentic narratives about the dangers of Islam for women, an Islamophobic culture is well and alive. The fear of Islam, that is, the fear of being invaded by Muslims and the resultant Islamization of Europe is indeed about the fear of multiculturalism. As Marranci (2004) suggests, Islamophobia is a phobia of multiculturalism.[19]

In various occasions Derrida has addressed the question of Europe. The rethinking of Europe Derrida suggests can be understood with what he considers a "paleonym," an old word with a new meaning grafted onto it. With this we actively attend to a new Europe that is yet undetermined. Derrida (1992) suggests that Europe must go beyond jumping to the other heading and recall ourselves to the other of the heading.[20] The attempt to redefine Europe or the grafting of the new Europe onto the old one requires that we attend to the European memory, its inheritance, and its legacy by breaking its Western monopoly and control. So, if the European identity has to be rethought and renewed differently from the previous European programs, the "today" of Europe has to be thought differently. Derrida suggests that if the "today" of Europe is going to be questioned, altered and thought differently, then Europe will have to distance itself from the assumption that today's Europe can refer to a single, undivided experience of the present. The present Europe can be thought anew only when its presence to itself is regarded as not entirely present to itself. European identity needs to be understood as inhabited by its yesterday and tomorrow. This requires the opening of Europe to Otherness or responsibility to the Other and a new Europe will emerge precisely in not closing itself off in its own identity but by advancing itself toward what it is not.

One very obvious instance where Europe's relation with Otherness reveal itself is the question of the Muslim woman's headscarf. It is believed that the protection of individual liberties in France is secured when the interference of religion and religious practices into public life and institutions is disallowed. But ironically, the suggestion that the state should legally intervene and regulate the expression of religious practices in public is not framed as an issue of protection of individual liberties. It is interesting to note that the interference of coercive state regulations is deemed preferable to the so-called interference of religion in public life. What does this preference tell us about the antinomies of liberalism? What happens when religion is seen as something to be conquered, subjugated, regulated or encapsulated in the domain of the private life in every instance that it dares to articulate itself publicly? What I am interested in exploring here is the language used in regulating the headscarf. This language poses interesting and revealing contradictions about liberalism when it attempts to rejuvenate and reinstate its sovereignty when it perceives a threat to it.

The headscarf issue has doubly metamorphosed itself: first, it became a question of defending the secular principles upon which the French nation was built. Concomitantly, this issue has been linked to a concern over the troubles caused by the integration of Muslim immigrants into French culture. Thus the concern with the headscarf, regarded nothing but as an *ostentatious* religious sign, has been displaced to a concern over Muslim immigrants' lack of respect for the secular principle of their host society and their simultaneous refusal to integrate into French culture. It is certainly noteworthy that neither the crucifixes worn around the neck nor the yarmulkes are declared to be ostentatious by any school administrator or court.[21] However, my concern is not to sort out which religious sign is ostentatious or for that matter engage in the exercise of computation of the degree of ostentaiousness of different religious signs. Rather, I am interested in exploring the nature of irritation with certain religious signs that results in the attribution of *ostentatioussnes* to them and what this irritation tell us about the subject who is irritated and the psychoanalytical dynamics behind this irritation. The objection to the use of headscarves in schools on the grounds that they are ostentatious is more telling about the allergic and hostile reaction shown when the Muslim Other makes its presence visible in public, rather than the religious sign itself. The attribution of an *ostentatious* quality implies that the eye that looks at the headscarf sees an excessive *visibility*, *theatricality*, and *performativity* in it. At least, the choice of the term to describe it tells us that an excessiveness was seen in it. Whatever may be the sociological reasons behind the use of headscarf (i.e. immigrants are becoming more religious; they are using religion as way of refusing to integrate into the culture they are inhabiting and hence the use of headscarf a sign of their recalcitrance; headscarf is their way of making connection to their homeland and hence a reinvigoration of an undesired nationalism[22]; a sign of politicization of a religious belonging; Islamic identification provides immigrants with a transnational identity when racism interrupts their identification with Europeanness; it is their way of affirming their belonging to a community) it is perceived to be articulating and making visible the alterity of the Muslim Other in public space. But what does it mean to see excessiveness in the headscarf? What is it excessiveness of? It is by way of transforming the presence of Christianity and its multifarious symbols (the fact that the calendar is Christian, the school schedule is arranged according to Catholic religious practice) in the organization of everyday life into some sort invisibility that the signs of Islam can be deemed excessive, conspicuous, pretentious, flashy, spectacular, splashy and theatrical. As Auslander puts it: "the requirement that people bear no distinctive sign of religious belonging and yet that they inhabit an everyday life that is rythmed by the Christian calendar forces observant Muslims and Jews to make a choice. They can be either good French citizens and bad Muslims or bad Jews, or vice versa. This fundamental inequality is, however, invisible to most French social commentators, politicians, teachers, and school administrators. The calendar is not justified on the grounds of majority rule, it is simply not noticed."[23] Thus it is only Islam's public presence that is regarded as excessive. When belonging to either Christianity or for that matter to Judaism, and the use of various signs to communicate this adherence are not deemed threatening for the integrity of the foundations of the French nation and culture (i.e. not to regard their use of them as excessive) then it does not require much astuteness to infer that the irritation is not simply about the use of any religious sign *per se*, but is about religious signs that are presumed to belong to immigrants and hence to the alienness of the culture that threatens to leak through them. This is what makes their presence and their use of certain religious symbols excessive. Consequently the European Muslims' excessive visibility (the Western eye sees it in the ostentatiousness of the religious sign) and hence their troubling presence is traced in their continuing attachment to their national culture, which can be conveniently traced in the use of the headscarf by women. This is what troubles Julia Kristeva in *Nations Without Nationalism*. It is worth examining Kristeva's cosmopolitan anxieties concerning the continuing attachment of the immigrants' to their nation and motherland, which is symbolized, what she calls, in the "Muslim scarf."

Kristeva's Attachment To Europe

In her attempt to uphold cosmopolitanism against nationalism, Julia Kristeva sees in immigrants, who in their willingness to emigrate from their original homes, a potential for cosmopolitanism. But unfortunately, due to the worshipping of their national language, native soil and motherland the immigrants (her examples are Muslim immigrants) in France are incapable of developing that kind of healthy detachment from their motherland.[24] I will dwell on this point further, but allow me to draw attention to one point that should not be overlooked before I proceed. Kristeva's discourse also participates in the now fashionable gesture of turning the immigrant to the metaphor of cosmopolitanism and thereby the attributing a certain sort of liberatory potential to the mobility entailed in immigration. I will not dwell on this issue in detail here. I have discussed elsewhere the problems of privileging mobility and migration as conducive to the attainment of liberation from the shackles of nationalism in the long march for cosmopolitanism.[25] Gayatri Spivak's criticism of the privileging of the metaphor of the migrant is pertinent here.[26] In her critique of Derrida's *Specters of Marx*, Spivak notes that, in comparing Marx to a clandestine immigrant, Derrida privileges migrancy as a metaphor. But for her "the privileging of the metaphorics (and axiomatics) of migrancy by well-established migrants helps to occlude precisely the struggles of those who are forcibly displaced, or those who slowly perish in their place as a result of sustained exploitation: globality."[27] The turning of the migrant into a metaphor, this time into a metaphor of cosmopolitanism, applies well to Kristeva herself.[28] Kristeva, being the well-established migrant that she is, describes herself as a "rare species, perhaps even on the verge of extinction in a time of renewed nationalism. I am a cosmopolitan."[29]

As a concerned cosmopolitan, Kristeva is unhappy about the "twofold humiliation" that the French population is subjected to.[30] If one source of humiliation results from the "exterior impact of tomorrow's broadened Europe," the second source of the humiliation stems from the impact of immigration.[31] The demands coming from the immigrants make French society feel as if "it had to give up traditional values, including the values of freedom and culture"[32] whereas for Kristeva, these values were "obtained at the cost of long and painful struggles (why accept [that daughters of Maghrebian immigrants wear] the Muslim scarf [to school]? Why change spelling?"[33] For Kristeva, the nature of assimilation drive of immigrants is such that it only wants "to enjoy the social benefits and does not at all involve giving up their own typical, behavioral, religious, cultural, or even linguistic features. What sort of common life and what degree of mixing remain possible under such conditions?"[34] While the immigrants' insistence on the use of their linguistic, cultural, religious, and behavioral features is a source of humiliation for France, the French secular tradition "asserts women's freedom and it is proud of an education system that gives one access to the linguistic subtleties of Moliere and Proust."[35] In Kristeva's cosmopolitan framework, the desire to maintain Maghrebi customs of wearing the headscarf, linguistic, cultural, religious and behavioral features is disdained while the French linguistic, cultural, educational, intellectual features are overvalued. Kristeva is not only disturbed with the insistence on the use of the Magrebi customs of wearing the headscarf and other nationalistic forms of attachments, but she is also troubled with the two responses to the immigrants' presence in France. The one response, that comes from the left-intellectuals, is based on a misunderstood cosmopolitanism and has the "tendency to sell off French national values, including and often mainly the values of the Enlightenment, considered once more—and wrongly so—to be too French or too unaware of the particularities of others."[36] She warns these left-intellectuals to "not be ashamed of European and particularly French culture, for it is by developing it critically that we have a chance to have foreigners recognize us as being foreigners all, with the same right of mutual respect."[37] One then wonders what is entailed in the kind of cosmopolitanism Kristeva is fond of. But then Kristeva does not forget to add a disclaimer: "far be it form me to claim a cultural hierarchy and much less so the supremacy of one over the others. Nonetheless, we must note that as far as recognizing the other is concerned—the other as different, as foreign—Western culture has, with its Greek, Jewish, and Christian components, traveled as road as difficult, as strewn with risks and pitfalls, error and crimes."[38] The other response, one that comes from Le Pen's nationalism, is too nationalistic for Kristeva's taste either.

For Kristeva, insofar as immigrants remain attached to the particular cultures of their home countries, they remain within the limits of the nation. The endurance of their attachment to their homeland and culture leads them to reject the French citizenship. At best, they relate to it in instrumental terms, enjoy social benefits without giving up their own. For her, in the much-needed transition from nationalism to cosmopolitanism, the headscarf stands as a fetish object, indicating the immature attachment to an object and an inability to achieve detachment from a nation. This detachment is necessary because "'abstract' advantages of a French universalism may prove to be superior to the 'concrete' benefits of a Muslim scarf."[39] The idea of the nation that Kristeva is fond of is a transitional one, which, while offering an identifying space that is transitive and transitory, it is not one that inhibits and leaves open and creative space for its subjects.[40] It is Montesquieu's thoughts that enable Kristeva to sort out the proper format of the nation: "'If I knew something useful to myself and detrimental to my family, I would reject it from my mind. If I knew something useful to my family but not to my homeland, I would try to forget it. If I knew something useful to my homeland and detrimental to Europe, or else useful to Europe and detrimental to Mankind, I would consider it a crime' refers indeed to a series of sets that, from the individual to the family, from the country to Europe and to the world, respects the particular if, and only if, it is integrated into another particular, of greater magnitude."[41]

A nation that is transitional demands that particular rights are highlighted while giving "way before the 'general interest,' the *espirit* general favored by Montesquie."[42] It would be a nation that is open-ended and is willing to acknowledge another general interest, that is, "the general interest of Europe and of the world."[43] The French national idea is endowed with this quality as it is prepared to "be potentially stripped of the sacral aspects of its totality to the advantage of the greatest growth of its members."[44] As such, it does not have the fear that the nation will be weakened. French nation's defining feature is its transitional character.[45] On the other hand, an interpretation that regards the nation's transitional logic as a sign of its weakening is a nostalgic and melancholic interpretation.

The attachment of immigrants to their nation does not have this sort of healthy, transitional and open-ended character. In their form of attachment, the serial logic of harmony is interrupted and the nation is turned into an absolute object. National pride is privileged and this becomes comparable to the narcissistic image the child receives from its mother. Home, native soil, motherland, national language are all worshipped and they arose "a feeling of revenge and narcissistic satisfaction in a number of women, who are otherwise sexually, professionally, and politically humiliated and frustrated."[46] Kristeva warns us about the dangers of the possible symbiosis between nationalism and "feminism," at least a certain conformist "maternalism" that can turn women into accomplice of religious fundamentalism. For this reason Kristeva believes that the "*abstract advantages of French universalism are preferable to the 'concrete' benefits of a Muslim scarf*" (italics mine).[47] It is the figure of the scarf wearing Muslim schoolgirls, which enables her to evoke an unhealthy and immature attachment to the motherland, origin and home. In other words, the Muslim scarf, unlike the nation, is not a healthy object of attachment but is essentially a fetish object (47) and is indicative of a melancholic connection to the nation.[48]

Bonnie Honig's reading of Kristeva is very illuminating. She suggests that Kristeva seems to have the Muslim scarf in mind when she says that "there are mothers (as well as 'motherlands' and 'fatherlands') who prevent the creation of a transitional object."[49] Attachment to an object such as the Muslim scarf is regarded not a healthy one, because it is taken as indicative of continuation of the attachment to motherland/tradition/homeland. For Kristeva, it signifies the immigrant's inability to develop a mature transition to the French society/nation, let alone developing cosmopolitan forms of attachment to Europe. As an unhealthy object of transition, the headscarf pinpoints to the "melancholy of nationalism."[50] Honig suggests that in the linear and progressive sequence of transition from self to family to homeland to Europe and Mankind (each operates as a transitional object for the next), Kristeva successfully avoids any possible conflict among them. Nor she designates the specifically Frenchness of the affiliation she is talking about by using the abstract term homeland for that set. Her call for identification with Europe is posited without questioning either the asymmetrical or contradictory attachment of the French and the immigrants to cosmopolitanism nor with any vigilance about cultural supremacy and Eurocentricism the position she takes.[51] On the contrary: Kristeva straightforwardly conflates the idea of Europe with values and ideals of Frenchness, and then suggests their universal embracement as a sign of cosmopolitanism. While seeing the immigrants having continuity with home and the nation-state as something to be abandoned, Kristeva sees no predicament in maintaining the attachment to the nation-state of France. Nor the desire to reinstate Europe as a home is subjected to any political quandary.

The reasons attributed to the use of headscarf by Kristeva seems to be challenged in the framework developed by French sociologists Gaspard and Khosrokhavar.[52] However, they, like Kristeva, reiterate the same problematic of seeing the issue within a teleological and linear temporal framework of transition from tradition to modernity (in Kristeva's case the terminology changes from family to nation to Europe and mankind (sic!)—note the interesting choice of terminology for a feminist like Kristeva). Their argument differs from Kristeva's only marginally in the sense that Kristeva sees a continuation of attachment to home (which is seen as identical to tradition), whereas Gaspard and Khosrokhavar attribute to it a discontinuity under the pretext of tradition. For them what is being reiterated by the use of headscarf is not a simple tradition but an indication of transition to modernity and modern forms of belonging to a new world they inhabit.[53]

> [The veil] mirrors in the eyes of the parents and the grandparents the illusions of continuity whereas it is a factor of discontinuity; it makes possible the transition to otherness (modernity), under the pretext of identity (tradition); it creates the sentiment of identity with the society of origin whereas its meaning is inscribed within the dynamic of relations with the receiving society... it is the vehicle of the passage to modernity within a promiscuity which confounds traditional distinctions, of an access to the public sphere which was forbidden to traditional women as a space of action and the constitution of individual autonomy.[54]

Honig suggests that Kristeva sees a possibility of a different relation to the French nation. If the re-signification of the French nation is a possibility, asks Honig, then why doesn't Kristeva see that possibility in the use of headscarf? She suggests that Leila Ahmed's evaluation of the headscarf use among professional women in contemporary Egypt leaves room for such a possible re-inscription of the headscarf as it enables women to make a transition from a familiar rural to an alien and sexually integrated and hence uncomfortable social reality. I am not particularly interested in exploring the ways in how the headscarf has resulted in the re-signification either of the nation or of women. This is an issue that is also addressed by Benhabib in *Rights of Others*. Rather, here, I am interested in understanding whether the use of the headscarf and the discourses that surround its use pose a possible interruption to the sovereign constitution of the European self or not.

Kristeva's recognition of a possibility of a healthy potential attachment, especially in terms of achieving a transition to cosmopolitan forms of attachment, in the use of headscarf can at best be described as a limited political gesture. Honig also rightfully states that Kristeva's problem is not simply her not being able to see the healthy transitional potentiality of the headscarf, but her inability to engage with Otherness. This reflects itself in her inability to engage in self-interrogation and to rush to provide answers rather than ask questions in a conversation. For this reason, Kristeva's cosmopolitanism "risks becoming another form of domination, particularly when it confronts an Other that resist assimilation to it, an Other that is unwilling to perform for 'us' the wonder of our conversation to world (or French) citizenship."[55] Honig argues that democratic cosmopolitanism is about an ethical renewal in the engagement with foreigners. But this energy for renewal will not come from the foreigner's affirmation of our existing categories and forgiveness of our past "blunders and crimes."[56] Instead, as Honig rightfully suggests, this renewal of cosmopolitanism will come from its engagements with foreigners.[57] I suggest that unconditional hospitality and openness for a renewal of European identity, which is the basis of a democratic re-definition of Europe, needs to involve this kind of openness to Otherness.

However, the current context in Europe is just the opposite. Islam evokes an axiety in Europe. Muslim groups are registered as an *unassimilable alterity* or *difference* within Europe. However, this unassimilable and irreducible alterity necessarily opens up that community called Europe to something that exceeds it and thereby threatens its sovereignty. Hospitality as ethics is the means by which Derrida suggests rethinking the identity of the nation-state, body, national spaces, political institutions as well as individuals in non-identical terms. Hospitality as ethics enables us to grasp how any identifiable sovereign entity is made possible by a continual reinscription, which is made possible by its sovereignty being perpetually threatened or undermined. The renunciation of sovereignty implied in unconditional hospitality in fact "evokes the powerlessness, vulnerability, dependence and instability of every self or autos."[58] Thus the very gesture of the assertion of a sovereign community called Europe inescapably opens itself to something other than itself, to an "otherness within," an otherness that in turn keeps the community alive.

It is such an ethical hospitable welcoming of Muslim Otherness that can perhaps facilitate the undermining of the sovereign, self-identical constitution of Europe. In fact, that fictive, autonomous, independent and stable identity of Europe has never been possible but nevertheless has always been posed, asserted, and staged. But perhaps Europe's renunciation of its sovereignty is an inevitable process. This is so because Europe is trying more than ever not only to maintain it. But while it is extending and expanding its sovereignty, it is becoming more vulnerable as a sovereign community for this is a process that entails its opening itself up to the counter-sovereignty of the other, thus compromising Europe, perhaps undoing itself by becoming vulnerable in its sovereignty as Europe. Hence ethical hospitality becomes the condition of thinking a democratic Europe because whenever the sovereign tries to make its power an all-expansive one and extend its scope, it inevitably opens itself to the counter-sovereignties and thus compromises and autoimmunizes itself.[59] Precisely for this reason, that is, due to its aporetic nature that is built into the autoimmunity itself that pure sovereignty of a nation-state or a community of Europe does not exist. Its every positing of itself implies its own denunciation and undermining of its sovereignty, for Europe can only exist in that act that is shared, compromised and partitioned by the participation of something other than itself. Counter-sovereignty is thus built into the very sovereign identity of Europe. In *Rogues,* Derrida connects the aporetic nature of the autoimmune character of the positing of the nation-state to democracy that is beyond the nation-state and citizenship:

> To confer sense or meaning on sovereignty, to justify it, to find a reason for it, is already to compromise its deciding exceptionality, to subject it to rules, to a code of law, to some general law, to concepts. It is thus to divide it, to subject it to portioning, to participation, to being shared. It is to take into account the part played by sovereignty. And to take that part or share into account is to turn sovereignty against itself, to compromise its immunity. This happens as soon as one speaks of it in order to give it or find in it some sense or meaning. But in the process of positing itself by refuting itself, by denying or disavowing itself; it is always in the process of autoimmunizing itself, of betraying itself, by betraying the democracy, beyond the nation-state and beyond citizenship.[60]

Perhaps Kristeva should be reminded that calling home into question or dispossesing it due to the encounter with a stranger is not the name of a complete malice or ailment. By making possible the exposure to the Otherness of the other, by enabling the opening and exposure of the ipseity to otherness, dispossession enables an event to take place and thus interrupts the stability of an enduring self of the auto. In this respect, the presence of European Muslims has to be regarded as Europe's chance to open itself to something beyond itself, to maintain a relation to something that is beyond the European self. Islam, embodied in its Muslim immigrants, is now Europe's chance for a *self-destructive conservation of Europe,* for a relation to something beyond the European self. The threat of the alien Islam that is built into the very constitution of the community called Europe is indeed Europe's chance or opportunity for a democratic iteration of Europe. But what Derrida calls democracy, which can be described with the term "constitutive autoimmunity" reveals itself in the aporias or double injunctions of hospitality.[61] It is the arrival of the guest who puts the host into crisis as it threatens to inhabit the immune system of the host with all its alienness and transform the host's capacity to sustain its auto condition.

But can such openness to the voices of the past and the encounter with the memory of Islam as Europe's earlier external enemy assures a hospitable welcoming of the European Muslims today? Certainly not. Why does the demand by the European Muslims to be welcomed in the space of Europe provoke hostility? Following Derrida's understanding of hospitality, we can imagine how such an encounter inevitably entails an aporetic structure. Conditioned by indeterminacy, such an encounter is therefore marked by both hospitality and hostility. As Hent de Vries suggests "hostility, that is, the very postulation of the enemy is contingent upon the historical emergence of a public sphere that defines, constitutes, and orients the political, together with the primary division between friend and foe."[62] It would be a mistake to assume that friends receive hospitality and enemies receive hospitality. Rather than a strict division of hospitality and hostility into two distinct and opposed binary pairs where enemies receive hostility and friends receive hospitality, Derrida's understanding of hostility and hospitality implies ambiguity and paradoxical conditions. Given that hospitality and hostility are mutually implicated in each other, any right to grant hospitality to a European Muslim is unavoidably caught up in its opposite, i.e. hostility. So, it is not simply the presence of a European Muslim as a stranger that provokes hostility; it is the Muslim immigrant, the stranger, who claims equal rights, who by inhabiting our space (which was presumed to solely belong to us) claiming and demanding hospitality is what triggers hostility. In Anidjar's terms, it is the stranger who is "recognized as enjoying equal rights" who triggers hostility.[63] So, it is the invitation offered to the European Muslim as a guest which, aporetically and paradoxically, offers hospitality and lays down a threshold, limiting the acceptance of the other's visitation.[64]

Benhabib's Conditional Hospitality

Unlike the cosmopolitan ideals of Kristeva, Benhabib's cosmopolitanism sees in the *L'affair du Foulard* an articulation of issues and dilemmas about French identity, multiculturalism, democratic citizenship, how to retain French traditions of *laicite* and so on. In between the lines of Benhabib's analysis is the attribution of an affirmative quality to the public presence of headscarf because she thinks that through its use, an articulation between modern French and traditional patriarchal norms are achieved. The problem Benhabib designates is that "the girls' voices have not been heard . . . Had their voices been heard and listened to, it would have become clear that the meaning of wearing the scarf itself was changing from being a religious act to one of cultural defiance and increasing politicization . . . ironically, it was the very egalitarian norms of the French public educational system that brought these girls out of the patriarchal structures of the home and into the French public sphere, and gave them the confidence and the ability to *resignify* the wearing of the headscarf."[65] Note that according to Benhabib, patriarchal structure belongs to home and by extension to tradition, and egalitarian norms belong to French society. What makes the use of headscarf positive in Benhabib's eyes is not that an exiled religious signifier finds place in public sphere and hence interrupts the sacralized secularist anxieties, but that through the use of headscarf in public sphere its meaning is changed from being a religious act to one of cultural defiance. It is this resignification, the change in its meaning that matters for Benhabib, not the presence and articulation of an excluded identity marker. In this respect, Benhabib and Kristeva's analysis attribute radically different potentialities to the headscarf. Kristeva sees in the Muslim scarf the stalling of the transition from *nationalism* to *cosmopolitanism (only if it is eventually abandoned)* and Benhabib sees in it a process of democratic iteration and cultural re-signification. This might be the reason why Benhabib sees it as the emergence of a "moderate French Islam," "despite the harshness of recent events and confrontations between religious

Islamic groups and the authorities"[66] while Kristeva sees nothing but the surfacing of religious fundamentalism in the headscarf. In either case, our allergy to Islam continues. We do not want Islam as Islam (whatever that means!) in the midst of our public sphere (let alone its fundamentalized versions) but a moderate (whatever that means) or Protestanized version of Islam is acceptable.

Benhabib states that her interest is not simply to think of schemes of *just distribution* but she aims to incorporate a vision of a *just membership* on a global scale through a cosmopolitan theory of justice. She believes that through people's critical examination and reflexive acts of *democratic iteration*, the practices of exclusion that institute a distinction between the citizens and aliens can be altered or at least can be made fluid and negotiable. This, she believes, is the condition of making a "postmetahpysical and postnational conception of cosmopolitan solidarity which increasingly brings all human beings, by virtue of their humanity alone, under the net of universal rights, while chipping away at the exclusionary privileges of membership."[67] She suggests that with the emergence of subnational and supranational formations, citizenship is becoming disaggregated which is making conditions more conducive for democratic attachments. But the disaggregation of the unitary model of citizenship is not necessarily a democratic citizenship for Benhabib. She accepts the fact that non-nationals are integrated into the rights regimes and thus national citizenship no longer functions as the sole basis of attribution of rights. But she diagnoses a contradictory development in the transformation of citizenship in Europe: on the one hand, there is a minimization of the distinction between the legal status of the citizen and aliens; on the other hand, there is an affirmation of the significance of national citizenship. However, the uncoupling of political identities from national membership that people like Yasemin Soysal have applauded is not necessarily indicative of a democratic citizenship for Benhabib. Here I don't disagree with Benhabib, as the privileging of the postnational forms of citizenship as harbingers of a democratic opening as well as the celebrations of the dismantling of the sovereignty of the nation-state certainly needs to be approached with more caution. Neither the nation-state's sovereignty is dismantled nor the postnational forms of citizenship, which we witness in the case of Europe, can be taken as indicators of a more democratic Europe or the opening of Europe for a democracy to come. It might be the case that individual European nation-states no longer have exclusive grip or sovereign claims on certain issues that pertain to immigration and various other issues, but this does not mean that European sovereignty is not reinstituted even more firmly while citizenship is denationalized.

Just membership, for Benhabib, entails the recognition of the moral claims of refugees and asylees, implying a regime of more porous borders for immigrants, injunctions against denationalization and the loss of citizenship rights, vindication of the right to every person to be a legal person. Most important of all, "just membership entails the right to citizenship on the part of the alien who has *fulfilled certain conditions*" (emphasis mine).[68] In Benhabib's neo-Kantian framework, there can be no reason that can deny any individual membership permanently (does this mean that a temporary denial is acceptable? But my point is besides this). However, if certain provisions are demanded (such as demonstration of certain qualifications, marketable skills, language competence, certain proof of civic literacy, demonstration of material resources to become a member) then these are acceptable and tolerable since they do not imply a denial of the communicative freedom to those from whom such stipulations are demanded.

It is here, in the introduction of conditionality, that the limitations inherent in the Kantian tradition of thinking hospitality reveal themselves and indicate how those limitations also constrain Benhabib's analysis. She suggests that the Kantian question of hospitality is not a question of philanthropy, but of rights.[69] For Benhabib, hospitality is a right, a right that belongs to all human beings and "it occupies the space between human rights and civil and political rights, between rights of humanity in our person and the rights that accrue to us in so far as we are citizens of specific republics."[70] Adhering strictly to the legacy of Kantian cosmopolitanism in her understanding of hospitality, Benhabib insists that concepts such as "right to universal hospitality" is about creating quasi-legally binding obligations as well as generation of enforceable norms not only for individuals but for states and governments. The right to universal hospitality entails an obligation on the political sovereign and hence prohibits states from denying asylum and refuge status to those who have peaceful intentions.

Benhabib's normative theory standpoint and her adherence to the legacy of Kantian thinking evoke all the problems associated with that of the conditional hospitality. This framework prevents Benhabib framing the question of hospitality beyond the opposition of *philanthropy* versus *legal rights*. The model of rights she subscribes to, leads her to limit hospitality to a question of legal, political and ethical norms and regulations, and thereby prevents her from engaging with the remainder left by the hospitable regulation of rights, invitations, or as Honig's reading suggests, how hospitality is haunted by hostility.[71] Benhabib sees no problem in introducing certain qualifications (as I listed them above), which can easily be translated into the language of conditionality in hospitality. Such conditionality is in accordance with the *democratic iterations* that she desires to be installed but it needs to be questioned whether this would have the potential to result in a *democratic interruption of Europe*. It is important to mention, in passing that, Benhabib's use of Derrida's notion of iterability, like her use of the notion of hospitality is a misguided one. With the term she refers to the processes of "public argument, deliberation, and learning through which universalist right claims are contested and contextualized, invoked and revoked."[72] She claims that she borrows the term from Derrida and notes that although there is really no "originary" source of meaning or an "original" to which subsequent forms must conform. Nevertheless she suggests that this would be more valid when applied to language as such and "it may not be so ill placed in conjunction with documents such as the law and institutional norms."[73] Following this disclaimer, she then suggests that every act of iteration involves the authoritative original's repositioning and re-signification, indicating that the original meaning is enhanced, transformed, and creatively appropriated. By this way, the original loses its authority. Referring to the use of headscarf by women in Europe, she thinks that the right claims of these women indicate their reappropriation, resignification, and transformation of the meaning of it. Benhabib overlooks that Derrida's notion iterability is related with his notion of generalized writing. Iteration is not just a different interpretation allowed by the absence of origin. It involves loss, chance, contingency, disappropriation, erring, or simply put, uncontrollable otherness to and of what is iterated. What Benhabib calls iteration would itself be subjected to all of these. Hence, the notion of iteration in Benhabib's use does not indicate anything different than "interpretation" and is not capable of conveying the understanding that repetition is the basis of identification as well as alteration.[75]

A similar misreading is valid for her use of the notion of hospitality. Moreover, to be able to think the notion of hospitality together with democratic interruption perhaps we need to liberate the notion of hospitality from the grips of this neo-Kantian framework. Such a task entails first of all attending to the two discontinuous and radically heterogeneous orders that hospitality belongs to: conditional and unconditional. It is not a question of choosing between the conditional and the unconditional. As Derrida in numerous places makes it clear, the relationship between conditional and unconditional hospitality is that they are discontinuous and heterogeneous and yet they are inseparable. Existing in a paradoxical and aporetic relation to one another, they attest to the mutual implication of hospitality and hostility.[76] This is where the essence of the radically different understanding of hospitality in Kant's and Derrida's frameworks lies. Kant, (so does Benhabib) limits hospitality to a question rights, formal law and state's regulatory mechanisms. By doing so, Benhabib introduces the circles of conditionality thereby limits the hospitality offered to the other in the model of rights and formal law of the nation-state and citizenship, and as such it brings into fore the teleology of the regulative framework of rights. In other words, in Benhabib's framework hospitality holds a future. But this future, unlike the future anterior in Derrida's understanding, thinks of future in linear and progressive terms. As Honig also notes, the model of rights adjudication that Benhabib subscribes to presupposes a certain linear progressive temporality, for there is a sense in Benhabib's account that the "trajectory of rights will take us to a desirable democratic outcome."[77] Note here the similaity between Kristeva's linear and progressive sequence of transition from self to family to homeland to Europe and to Mankind. However, I must underline that there is no such linear temporal aspect in Derrida's understanding of unconditional hospitality because it is not a question of transformation hospitality into a regulative idea, law, theme or thematization.

The democratic iteration which Benhabib's analysis is fond of is only capable of installing a change in the foreigner's (who is marked by particularity) relation to the European universality. Honig suggests that this framework leaves intact the universalist categories themselves as the particular continues to be marked with particularity and the universality of European remains intact. It is only through the foreigner's relation to the existing universalistic categories that the democratic iteration changes. In Benhabib's framework, there is a sense in which hostility is identified with one singular principle, that is, state nationalism or republican self-determination and hospitality with another, that of Enlightenment universalism.[78]

Conditional hospitality is one that belongs to the order of laws, regulations, and norms and is based on calculable claims. This difference between the Kantian and Derridean problematic is essential as they have radically different ethico-political implications. For Derrida, hospitality is impossible but the impossibility of the unconditional hospitality is not for nothing, as Derrida puts it:

> I have always, consistently and insistently, held *unconditional hospitality*, as *impossible*, to be *heterogeneous* to the *political*, the *juridical*, and even the *ethical*. But the impossible is not nothing. It is even that which happens, which comes, by definition . . . There are, it is true, paradoxical and aporetic relations between the two concepts that are at once *heterogeneous* and *inseparable*, *unconditional* hospitality and *conditional* hospitality (that is the only one, let me repeat it, that belongs to the order of laws, rules and norms—whether ethical, juridical or political—at a national or international level. (emphasis original)[79]

The opposite of what it wants to do is inscribed in hospitality: it immobilizes itself on the threshold. The aporetic paralysis of hospitality on the threshold must be overcome. In other words, what must be overcome is this impossibility. But this impossibility for Derrida is something that:

> must be overcome <it is the impossibility which must be overcome where it is possible to become impossible. It is necessary to do the impossible. If there is hospitality, the impossibility must be done>, this "is" being in order that, beyond hospitality, in deciding to let it come, overcoming the hospitality that paralyzes itself on the threshold which it is. . . . In this sense hospitality is always to come [*a venier*], but a "to come" that does not and will never present itself as such, in the present <and a future-a future without horizon>. To think hospitality from the future—this future that does not present itself or will only present itself when it is not awaited as a present or presentable—is to think hospitality from death no less than from birth.[80]

Following this Derridean insight, I suggest, that Europe's re-constitution of itself as a sovereign entity takes place through the waging of new thresholds, borders and frontiers. This strange war of thresholds and borders occurs through the regulation of the mobility and management of migrants. The war on the threshold or border which re-constitutes and re-news Europe's sovereignty is waged both inside and outside the territory of Europe by staging a new imaginary of Europe in which strangers figure as internal enemies. The creation and transformation of strangers and more specifically Muslim immigrants as internal enemies cannot be understood independent of the figuration of an external enemy that has long functioned as Europe's quintessential Other, namely the Oriental/Muslim Other. By examining this strange dynamic which transforms the Muslim migrant to a magical double of an external Oriental enemy and how this reversal is staged on the threshold, I would suggest thinking that the very hospitality offered to the Muslim immigrant is the condition of its disruption, namely the institution of hostility. Migrants were offered conditional hospitality, say as "gasterbeiters" but their permanency (we invited labor but human beings have arrived!) resulted in turning this hospitality into hostility, as theirs became a demand of hospitality of the *visitation,* not of hospitality of the *invitation.* In distinguishing the two, Derrida states that conditional hospitality,

> To which I—I won't say "oppose"—but in contrast to which I try to think pure and unconditional hospitality, the idea of a pure welcoming of the unexpected guest, the unexpected arriving one. From that point of view I would distinguish between the hospitality of the invitation and the hospitality of the *visitation.* In the *invitation,* the master remains master at home, *chez soi,* and the host remains the host and the guest remains the guest, the invited guest—"Please, come in, you're invited"—but of course as invited guest you won't disturb too seriously the order of the house, you're going to speak our language, eat the way we et cetera et cetera et cetera. To this invitation, to this hospitality of invitation, I would oppose—or not oppose but rather distinguish from it—the hospitality of visitation. The visitor is not an invited guest, the visitor is the unexpected one who arrives and to whom a pure host should open his house without asking questions such as: who are you? What are you coming for? Will you work with us? Do you have a passport? Do you have a visa? and so on so forth—that's unconditional hospitality. (emphasis mine)[81]

Talking about doors and thresholds that limit hospitality, Derrida addresses the gap between the hospitality of *visitation* and the hospitality of *invitation*:

> if there is a threshold, there is no longer hospitality. This is the difference, the gap, between the hospitality of invitation and the hospitality of visitation. In visitation there is no door. Anyone can come at any time and can come in without needing a key for the door. There are no customs checks with a visitation. But there are customs and police checks with an invitation. Hospitality thus becomes the threshold or the door.[82]

By Way of Conclusion

We can read the dynamics operating behind the European liberal tolerance suddenly going awry and looking askance to the practice of Muslim women's use of headscarf in public. The subtext of liberating Muslim women from the imposition of patriarchal communalist oppression and eliminating the threat posed to the European secular tradition is the desire to purify the European public sphere from the trace of Otherness. It is indeed an indication of the unwelcoming of the arrival of the different, unrecognizable and alien. The European subject, in desiring to protect the public sphere from the threat of its Islamization, indeed resists a relation with the unlike, with the unrecognizable and the dissimilar and hence evades responding and being responsible to the other. In refusing to acknowledge the arrival of something other than itself, the European subject abjures the experience of an *interruption* to its self-presence and thereby reinstates its mastery and control. Such a gesture, in the name of protecting the domain of publicness, eradicates it, as the other becomes tolerable only in so far as it resembles the self. As Jacques Derrida suggests that "pure ethics, begins with the respectable dignity of the other as the absolute unlike, recognized as unrecognizable, indeed unrecognizable beyond all knowledge, all cognition and all recognition. . . . The neighbor as like or as resembling, as looking alike spells the end or ruin of such an ethics, if there is any."[83] Here Derrida alludes to the paradox of democracy, always wanting two incompatible things: on the one hand, it offers welcome only to those who are citizens, brothers and compeers. On the other hand, it always wants to open itself to all those excluded and offer hospitality. But the problem here is that the hospitality offered remains conditional and limited and hence is far from enabling a democratic opening. When we think that public space is the space of unlikes as well as semblances, then the current European desire to limit the public to those who are recognizable and likes only ends up eradicating the publicness of public space in Europe.

From the moment hospitality is instituted and formalized its effect is disrupted and threatened by its opposite, namely by hostility as its ethical impact is curbed. It is this transformation in the European attitude that explains how hospitality becomes imbued with hostility. Derrida suggests that hospitality always in some way does the opposite of what it pretends to do, as there is almost a self-contradiction in the law of hospitality, which limiting itself at its very beginning remains forever on the threshold. But if there is a threshold, there is no longer hospitality. Derrida takes up the figure of the door. Threshold or door is that figure which is necessary for hospitality to exist. But if there is a door then there is no hospitality because it implies that someone has the key to the door and thus controls the conditions of hospitality.

We need to consider the process of the eradication of the publicness in the European context in conjunction with the demise of multiculturalism, which is heightened by the so-called war on terror. Popular opposition to immigration in conjunction with nationalist and xenophobic sentiments is abundant. It has become humdrum to hear complaints regretting multiculturalist days as diversity is thought to have been responsible in the current chaotic condition that Europe is undergoing. As Paul Gilroy notes, "difficulties arising from what is now seen as the unrealistic or unwelcome obligation to dwell peaceably with aliens and strangers somehow confirm the justice of these sorry developments."[84] The rhetoric that celebrates the downfall of multiculturalism is indeed a political gesture. And this political gesture is based on the denunciation of what Gilroy calls "conviviality." Although conviviality does not describe absence of racism or unconditional tolerance, it nevertheless has the potential to open up the publicity that I was trying to describe above. Conviviality or publicity, implying the welcoming of Otherness is indeed the very minimum condition of multiculturalism whose death has now been announced and celebrated by right wing xenophobic groups.

The immigrant Muslim woman, whose oppression is symbolized in her headscarf, is almost a test case of European tolerance that is used as the defining characteristic of European civilization. As Gail Lewis suggests, the nonalignment between the self-defined womanhood and the figure of the immigrant woman inscribed in the imaginary of Europe exposes the limits of liberal tolerance precisely because her visibility is to be erased. The dilemma becomes one of whether the immigrant Muslim woman will be "divested of her visibility as an 'immigrant' woman by processes of assimilation. . . . Or is she to be 'allowed' to demonstrate her difference and . . . abjection and thus 'display' the contamination in our midst—in which case Europe's civilizing mission is undermined. Either way, the figure of the 'immigrant woman' both bespells and exposes the limits of Europe."[85]

Notes

1. Julia Kristeva, *Nations Without Nationalism*, trans. Leon S. Roudiez (New York: Columbia University Press, 1993); and, Seyla Benhabib, *The Rights of Others: Aliens, Residents and Citizens* (Cambridge: Cambrdige University Press, 2004).
2. Immanuel Kant, "To Perpetual Peace: A Philosophical Sketch" in *Perpetual Peace and Other Essays*, trans. Ted Humphrey (Indianapolis: Hackett Publishing Company, 1983).
3. Emmanuel Levinas, *Totality and Infinity*, trans. Alfonso Lingis (Pittsburg: Duquesne University Press, 1969).
4. Jacques Derrida, *Adieu to Emmanuel Levinas*, trans. Pascale-Anne Blunt and Michael Naas (Stanford: Stanford University Press, 1999).
5. Seyla Benhabib, "Democratic Iterations: The Local, the National, and the Global," in *Another Cosmopolitanism: The Berkeley Tanner Lectures*, ed. Robert Post (Oxford: Oxford Universty Press, 2006), 45-80; Benhabib, *The Rights of Others*; and, Seyla Benhabib, "In Search of Europe's Borders" *Dissent*, (Fall, 2002) http://www.dissentmagazine.org/article/?article=559 (accessed March 16, 2010).
6. Ghassan Hage, *White Nation: Fantasies of White Supremacy in Multicultural Society* (New York and London: Routledge, 2000).
7. Hage, *White Nation*, 28.
8. Hage, *White Nation*, 42.
9. Hage, *White Nation*, 37.
10. Ruth Mandel, *Cosmopolitan Anxieties: Turkish Challenges to Citizenship and Belonging in Germany* (Durham and London: Duke University Press, 2008), 10.
11. *Culture in the Plural*, trans. Tom Conley (Minneapolis: University of Minnesota Press, 1997).
12. Michel De Certeau, quoted in Mandel, *Cosmopolitan Anxieties*, 10-11.
13. Etienne Balibar, "Europe as Borderland: Models of Transnational Citizenship," The Alexander von Humboldt Lecture in Human Geography, University of Nijmegen, November 10, 2004.
14. Etienne Balibar, "Strangers as Enemies: Further Reflections on the Aporias of Transnational Citizenship," *Globalization and Autonomy Online Compendium*, May 9, 2006. http://www.globalautonomy.ca/global1/article.jsp?index=RA_Balibar_Strangers.xml (accessed March 16, 2010).
15. Balibar, "Strangers as Enemies."
16. Balibar, "Strangers as Enemies."

17. Zygmunt Bauman, *Postmodernity and its Discontents* (Cambrdige: Polity Press, 1997), 17.

18. Gabriel Marranci, "Multiculturalism, Islam and the Clash of Civilizations Theory: Rethinking Islamophobia," *Culture and Religion*, 5:1 (2004): 105-17.

19. Marranci, "Multiculturalism, Islam and the Clash of Civilizations Theory."

20. Jacques Derrida, *The Other Heading: Reflections on Today's Europe*, trans. Pascale-Anne Brault and Michale B. Naas (Bloomington and Indianapolis: Indiana University Press, 1992).

21. Leora Auslander, "Bavarian Crucifixes and French Headscarves: Religious Signs and the Postmodern European State," *Cultural Dynamics* 12:30 (2000): 291.

22. Kristeva, *Nations Without Nationalism*.

23. Auslander, "Bavarian Crucifixes and French Headscarves," 288.

24. Kristeva, *Nations Without Nationalism*, 33-4.

25. See my "Cosmopolitanism and Nationalism in a Globalized Age," where I also criticize the taken-for-grantedness of the complete disregard for a necessity of a different sort of nationalism and national attachment for the subaltern strata of the Third World.

26. Chakravorty Gayatri Spivak, "Ghostwriting," *Diacritics* 25:2 (Summer 1995): 65-84.

27. Spivak, "Ghostwriting," 71.

28. Kristeva, *Nations Without Nationalism*.

29. Kristeva, *Nations Without Nationalism*, 15.

30. Kristeva, *Nations Without Nationalism*, 35.

31. Kristeva, *Nations Without Nationalism*, 36.

32. Kristeva, *Nations Without Nationalism*, 26.

33. Kristeva, *Nations Without Nationalism*, 36.

34. Kristeva, *Nations Without Nationalism*, 7-8.

35. Kristeva, *Nations Without Nationalism*, 36.

36. Kristeva, *Nations Without Nationalism*, 37.

37. Kristeva, *Nations Without Nationalism*, 38.

38. Kristeva, *Nations Without Nationalism*, 38.

39. Kristeva, *Nations Without Nationalism*, 47.

40. Kristeva, *Nations Without Nationalism*, 42.

41. Montesquieu quoted in Kristeva, *Nations Without Nationalism*, 40-41.

42. Kristeva, *Nations Without Nationalism*, 41.

43. Kristeva, *Nations Without Nationalism*, 41.

44. Kristeva, *Nations Without Nationalism*, 43.

45. So claims Kristeva, but the debates about the French national integrity over the headscarf issue attests just to the opposite where the secular French nation is sacralized.

46. Kristeva, *Nations Without Nationalism*, 33-34.

47. Kristeva, *Nations Without Nationalism*, 47.

48. Kristeva, *Nations Without Nationalism*, 47.

49. Bonnie Honig, "Ruth, the Model Émigré: Mourning and Symbolic Politics and Immigration," in eds., Phegh Cheah and Bruce Robbins, *Cosmopolitics: Thinking and Feeling Beyond the Nation* (Minnesota: University of Minnesota Press, 1998), 204.

50. Kristeva, *Nations Without Nationalism*, 43.

51. Honig, "Ruth, the Model Émigré," 204.

52. Francoise Gaspard and Farhad Khosrokhavar, *Le Foulard et la Republique* (La Decouverte, Paris, 1995).

53. A similar understanding regarding the articulation of modernity with Islam can be found in Nilufer Gole's (1991) sociological study of the use of headscarf by Muslim women in Turkey. Nilufer Gole, *Modern Mahrem: Medeniyet ve Ortunme* (Istanbul: Metis, 1991).

54. Gaspard and Khosrokhavar, *Le Foulard et la Republique*, 44-5.

55. Honig, "Ruth, the Model Émigré," 205.

56. Kristeva, *Nations Without Nationalism*, 46.

57. Honig, "Ruth, the Model Émigré," 206.

58. Michael Naas, "'One Nation . . . Indivisible': Jacques Derrida on the Autoimmunity of Democracy and the Sovereignty of God," *Research in Phenomenology* 36 (2006): 19.

59. One needs to engage in a fuller discussion of Derrida's understanding of autoimmunity to develop this point further. However it is beyond the scope of this essay.

60. Jacques Derrida, *Rogues: Two Essays on Reason*, trans. P.A. Brault and M. Naas, (Stanford: Stanford University Press, 2005).

61. Naas, "One Nation . . . Indivisible," 28.

62. Hent De Vries, "Hospitable Thought: Before and Beyond Cosmopolitanism" in *Religion and Violence: Philosophical Perspectives from Kant to Derrida*. (Baltimore and London: the Johns Hopkins University Press, 2001), 356.

63. Gil Anidjar, "Secularism and the Theologicao-Political: An interview with Gil Anidjar," conducted by Nerman Shaik, *Asia Source*, January 28, 2008. http://www.asiasource.org/news/special_reports/anidjar1.cfm (accessed March 16, 2010).

64. The limits of conditional hospitality are discussed in MeydaYegenoglu, "Liberalism and Multiculturalism in a Globalized World," *Postmodern Culture*, 13:12 (January).

65. Benhabib, *The Rights of Others*, 191.

66. Benhabib, *The Rights of Others*, 193.

67. Benhabib, *The Rights of Others*, 21.

68. Benhabib, *The Rights of Others*, 3.

69. It is important to emphasize that the question is not one of philanthropy because many invested mis-readings of Derrida also tend to frame his understanding of hospitality as a question of "good will."

70. Benhabib, *The Rights of Others*, 22.

71. Bonnie Honig, "Another Cosmopolitanism?: Law and Politics in the New Europe," in *Another Cosmopolitanism: The Berkeley Tanner Lectures*, ed. Robert Post (Oxford: Oxford Universty Press, 2006), 102-127.

72. Benhabib, "In Search of Europe's Borders."

73. Benhabib, *The Rights of Others*, 179-80.

74. Benhabib, *The Rights of Others*, 209.

75. I would like to thank Mahmut Mutman for bringing this point to my attention and for his suggestive comments helping me sort this point out.

76. Derrida, *Rogues*, 172-173, note 12. In "Another Cosmopolitanism?" Honig offers a succinct and well-argued commentary on Benhabib's reading of Derrida's hospitality. I am in full agreement with Honig's criticisms.

77. Benhabib, *The Rights of Others*, 111.

78. Honig, "Another Cosmopolitanism?" 106.

79. Derrida, *Rogues*, 172-173, note 12.

80. Jacques Derrida, "Hostipitality," trans. Barry Stocker with Forbes Morlock. Angelaki, 5:3 (December 2000), 14.

81. Jacques Derrida, "A Discussion with Jacques Derrida" with Paul Patton. *Theory and Event*, 5 (2001), 12-13.

82. Derrida, "Hostipitality," 14.

83. Derrida, *Rogues*, 60.
84. Paul Gilroy, *Postcolonial Melancholia* (New York: Columbia University Press, 2005), 1.
85. Gail Lewis, "Imaginaries of Europe: Technologies of Gender, Economics of Power." *European Journal of Women's Studies*, 13:2 (2006), 95.

Chapter 10
Caring Hospitality and Mexican "Illegal" Immigrants
Maurice Hamington

The universal right to hospitality which is due to every human person imposes upon us an *imperfect moral duty* to help and offer shelter to those whole life, limb, and well-being are endangered.
—Seyla Benhabib, Eugene Meyer Professor of Political Science and Philosophy, Yale University

Public and political rhetoric regarding undocumented immigrants from Mexico is decidedly one-sided: immigrants, and more specifically *Mexican illegal immigrants,* are conceived of as problems and popular sentiment is that the United States government needs to do more to stop it.[1] Recommendations have ranged from greater Mexican-American border security (including building a wall), new legislation regarding citizen rights, interior enforcement of employment laws, and changing citizenship laws to prevent the practice of giving birth to "anchor babies."[2] Although different responses to the perceived problem exist on both the right and the left, the common belief across the political spectrum is that illegal immigration is a serious concern and threatens the United States culturally and economically. The widespread perception of an illegal immigration crisis in the United States is so strong that commentators can assume popular assent without providing justification. For example, on his website, former CNN pundit Lou Dobbs, claims, "Our government turns a blind eye to the thousands of people who illegally cross our borders."[3] Note that Dobbs does not have to argue for the negative nature of migration as he can take for granted that everyone who reads his words will automatically find the influx of undocumented immigrants problematic. The anti-immigrant fervor in the United States, an ongoing source of controversy, has taken on a fever pitch after the events of September 11, 2001. Organizations such as Minutemen who patrol the U.S.-Mexico Border, Save Our State, and Mothers Against Illegal Aliens paint a picture of Mexican immigrants as out to cheat Americans of their resources and undermine U.S. cultural heritage.

In a number of academic disciplines, including political theory, the ancient concept of hospitality has reemerged as an important topic of theoretical and policy consideration. The unprecedented rate of modern global movement makes intellectual inquiry into the nature of modern hospitality appropriate. Yet, there is a disconnection between scholarly pursuits and public discussions of hospitality, particularly for immigrants. As Mireille Rosello describes, "There is no sign that our supposedly global village has started thinking about a global yet diverse law of hospitality."[4] Immigrants are often conceived as unwelcome "guests" to nation-state "hosts." In public rhetoric, the term "guest" with its kind and welcoming connotation is seldom extended to Mexican immigrants in the

United States, particularly if they are not officially sanctioned immigrants. However, the metaphor of host/guest hospitality is a supple one and even if it is not explicitly applied to Mexican immigrants, a privileged-based hospitality, which I discuss in this chapter, instantiates the power and resources of the U.S. over its southern neighbors, is implicitly operant.

Addressing contemporary U.S. discourse around immigrants from Mexico, this chapter suggests that feminist care ethics can enrich and reframe the language and metaphor of host/guest relations in ways that complement traditional rule-based and consequence-based moral approaches to political theory. One dominant image applied to Mexican immigrants today is that of supplicant: a *"guest" who is too needy*. Pat Buchanan exemplifies this rhetoric:

> Half the 100 million Mexicans are still mired in poverty. Tens of millions are unemployed or underemployed. Because of devaluations, real wages are below what they were in 1993. Thus the great migration north continues. Some 1.5 million are apprehended every year on our southern border breaking into the United States. Of the perhaps 500,000 who make it, one-third head for Mexifornia, where their claims on Medicaid, schools, courts, prisons, and welfare have tipped the Golden State toward bankruptcy and induced millions of native-born Americans to flee in the great exodus to Nevada, Idaho, Arizona, and Colorado. Ten years after NAFTA, Mexico's leading export to America is still—Mexicans. America is becoming Mexamerica.[5]

Another pervasive image is that of the Mexican undocumented immigrant as unfair competition for work. As pundit Rob Sanchez claims, "Increased joblessness in the U.S. is directly attributable to the large influxes of immigrants who compete for jobs."[6] Here, the undocumented worker is the *"guest" who doesn't know their place*. Accordingly, the United States is the wealthy and powerful host. The relationship is portrayed as unidirectional in terms of benefits with immigrants *gaining* and the U.S. *giving* to the point of detriment to American society and economy. The discourse is reductionist and alienating: immigrants, particular "illegal" immigrants are portrayed as problems to be solved rather than as human beings. The discourse has such a powerful hold that political rhetoric assumes the conclusiveness of the immigration problem despite evidence to the contrary. Because the epistemological aspect of care ethics emphasizes voice, respect, and humility in the context of reciprocal relationships, it has the potential to reinvigorate hospitality in our relationship with Mexican visitors, travelers, and employment seekers.

This chapter has two purposes: one theoretical and one political. On a theoretical level, I integrate feminist care ethics into how we think about the host/guest relationship of hospitality to frame a "flatter," reciprocal, and inquiry-based notion of *caring hospitality*. Rather than replace legal frameworks for hospitality, caring hospitality describes an intellectual and affective disposition that supports legal or policy ethical scaffolding (i.e. laws, rules, policies) at the interpersonal level. In other words, policies that are more tolerant of illegal immigration cannot entirely fulfill the moral spirit of hospitality when individuals confront one another. The second purpose of this chapter is to interrogate the topic of Mexican undocumented migration to the U.S. through the lens of caring hospitality. I begin with a short presentation of empirical data on immigrant women from Mexico that paves the way for framing hospitality as a feminist issue. Next, a description of the privileged form of hospitality operant today in U.S. political rhetoric surrounding Mexican immigration is offered. I then construct what I describe as caring hospitality and its relations to other forms of hospitality. I conclude with an analysis of how caring hospitality contributes to a robust notion of democracy demanded by the contemporary context.

A Glimpse of Immigrant Mexican Women

The Pew Hispanic Center reports that 4.1 million of the 10.4 million unauthorized adult immigrants in the U.S. are women.[7] Much of the political rhetoric today maps negative or opportunistic motivation onto unauthorized immigrants helping to affirm stereotypes in the minds of the public. Recent social research has given voice to immigrant women thus providing us with a richer understanding of their motivations and experiences. In 2009, New America Media conducted a poll of immigrant women. One question asked was, why did you decide to come to the United States? Of the women from Latin American (almost 2/3 of which were undocumented), 30 percent answered to join other family members, 27 percent responded to make a better life for their children, and 23 percent answered to get a job and make money. Another question addressed perceptions of increased discrimination since arrival to the United States and perceived discrimination against their family. Immigrants from Latin America responded to each question at rates above 80 percent, dwarfing the responses of immigrants from other areas. One other intriguing line of questions in the survey has to do with assertiveness and family leadership. Immigrant women from Latin America reported the highest rate of increased public and private assertiveness from among those polled. Furthermore, they claimed to almost double the rate of position as head of household (to 39 percent), a figure much higher than any other immigrant group.[8] These conclusions are corroborated by a study of the machismo narrative among Mexican workers in the U.S.:

> Over and over, [Mexican male workers] voice their objection to bringing wives and daughters to the United States, because here, as one of them complained, *"las mujeres son muy igualadas"*—women are too "uppity"—and they don't want their own to absorb such alien ways of thinking. One "function" for the folklore of machismo, then, may be linked to this effort to keep feminism at bay, by symbolically confirming men's dominance over women on the one hand, and, on the other, by reinforcing the "evil" nature of women, not so much because of their alleged treachery but because of their real quest for equality. The workers' fear of losing control over traditionally subordinate women torments them, and they circle rhetorically back to this point over and over again.[9]

This report indicates that Mexican women coming to the U.S. often lack support for their own growth and independence in addition to the challenges of thriving in a new country.

The analysis of the writers of the New America Media report is that *immigration is increasingly having a feminine face*, and that women immigrants are thriving despite the obstacles, driven by a desire to improve the lives of their families. What the analysis fails to mention is the disproportionate obstacles faced by women from Latin America and the disproportionate achievements by these women despite the challenges.

Hospitality is a Feminist Issue

Hospitality is a feminist issue for negative and positive reasons. Negatively, hospitality is a feminist issue because it has historically reflected a complex gendered hierarchy. Positively, hospitality is a feminist issue because of the tremendous theoretical work on relationality that feminists have engaged in which has the potential to contribute to our understanding and remaking of host/guest relations.

Gender has played an enormous role in the history of the social construction of the identities of hosts and guests as well as their relationship to one another. The host is traditionally associated with a masculine position, so much so, that Tracy McNulty describes "feminine hospitality" as almost an oxymoron.[10] Even without the title of host, women have historically been responsible for the work of hospitality including preparation for, and tending to guests, as well as the affective work of socializing with guests. Oppressively, sometimes women are objectified through participating in hospitality, becoming the vehicle of hospitality rather than an agent in the host/guest relation. Rosalyn Diprose suggests that hospitality is fundamentally based on patriarchy. In a reading of Derrida's analysis of the biblical story of Lot's offering of his daughters to protect his home from threatening strangers (Gen 19:8), Diprose highlights the patriarchal implications that Derrida criticizes in passing. Derrida points out that "In the name of hospitality, all the men are *sent* a woman, to be precise, a concubine [the host's daughters in this case]."[11] Diprose concludes, "Derrida shows how the condition of a common world is a conditioned and *conditional* hospitality, but also, and more pertinent, that this hospitality is patriarchal."[12] McNulty concurs when she observes that the host's hospitality is often dependent upon "his ability to dispose of the female dependents who make up his personal property."[13] Even more important to this chapter, Diprose finds correlation between national policy on hospitality and the impact on women: "the more that hospitality at the level of the nation becomes conditional under conservative political forces, the more that the time that it takes is given by, or taken from, women."[14] In other words, inhospitable social policies create disproportional work for *women as guests*, in this case the uneven burdens that fall to immigrant women.

Allison Stevens, Washington Bureau Chief for Women's E-news describes a belief among activists in the immigration rights movement that "immigration is a woman's issue even if it isn't always portrayed that way in dominant print and broadcast media."[15] Although many immigrants find the U.S. inhospitable, women face a double bind of risk because sexism increases vulnerability. Lack of available services and fear of deportation result in disproportionate incidents of harassment, assault, and domestic violence among immigrant women.[16] Inhospitable practices combined with sexist beliefs and practices result in greater burdens and work for immigrant women.

Hospitality should be claimed as a feminist issue for positive reasons as well. Feminist theory has made tremendous contributions to the ethical, epistemological, performative, and embodied dimensions of relationality.[17] Because an important aspect of feminist theory has been the rejection of the detached isolated agent, a relational ontology has informed much of feminist thinking. For example, feminist theorists posit that although people are capable of making independent decisions, they are also fundamentally social beings enmeshed in webs of relationships that deeply affect their ethical dispositions and choices. This relational characterization of self is reflected in the notion of "second persons" expounded by Lorraine Code and Annette Baier.[18] The psychology of human development indicates that humans mature in relation to others—independent human development is a fiction. Accordingly, Code claims "Showing how persons *are* second persons has the heuristic value of withholding endorsement of the autonomy, self-sufficiency, and/or self-making that moral philosophers consider integral to an attainment of mature agency."[19] The implication of a relational ontology is that we exist in the tension between an individual identity and a social constitution. For theorists to ignore either individual agency or social identity is to posit an incomplete understanding of the human condition that can only distort social and political theories. Code, and many other feminists, do not want to eliminate the notion of autonomy, but are concerned about the "autonomy-obsession" found in the history of political theory that appears to promote individualism.[20] Theorists including Code and Grace Clement offer various forms of relational conceptions of autonomy that avoid identifying it with self sufficiency. Clement claims "recognizing the extent to which our interests are interdependent with those we care for allows us to find ways to meet the ends of self *and* other, rather than one at the other's expense."[21] Although autonomy is an acknowledgment of the moral sovereignty of the individual, interdependence is a more accurate description of the human condition. Applying this notion to the host/guest relationship implies not taking it out of a wider social context. The host is not merely an isolated agent dispensing with her or his property in a magnanimous manner. The host also exists in a web of interdependent relationships that entail his or her own vulnerability and circumstances for which he or she may be the guest. Furthermore, feminist theory has been extremely concerned with the power dynamics of hierarchy, and the host/guest relationship is seldom conceptualized as between equals. I return to a discussion of feminist theory when I explore integrating care ethics with understandings of hospitality.

The idea that hospitality is a feminist issue is not merely a historical or theoretical one. Gender continues to play an interesting role in the negotiation of hospitality and national identity in regard to the U.S.–Mexican border. Despite contemporary anti-immigration sentiment, the U.S. also has a tradition of providing hospitality to migrants and that hospitality takes a female form. The greatest symbol of this hospitality is the Statue of Liberty. Originally, signifying liberty, the Statue's proximity to Ellis Island and the 1903 addition of the poem, "The New Colossus" by Emma Lazarus solidified the Statue of Liberty as a beacon to immigrants. The poem ends with the epic lines: "Give me your tired, your poor, Your huddled masses yearning to breathe free, The wretched refuse of your teeming shore. Send these, the homeless, tempest-tost to me, I lift my lamp beside the golden door!" The language of "The New Colossus" and the feminine iconography of the Statue of Liberty have inspired countless immigrants regarding the promise of the United States. Of course, the immigrant experience did not always live up to the hospitality ideal. The symbolism is one of an open and caring U.S. that will work with the poor and the oppressed.

Contrast the welcoming feminine symbolism of the Statue of Liberty with the work of Mothers Against Illegal Aliens (MAIA) founded by Michelle Dallacroce in 2006. The logo of MAIA is an American flag with a mother and child stenciled over it. Dallacroce, who has received considerable media attention, spreads the MAIA message that women who cross the border from Mexico are unfit mothers because they are not focused on their maternal duties and that many of them simply wish to give birth to "anchor babies" in order to secure all the advantages of U.S. citizenship. "These women are using their children as pawns to come and stay here illegally," according to Dallacroce, "They should all be detained, sent back and charged with child abuse for putting their children in this situation."[22] The image here is of a woman leading the charge against Mexican immigrants on gender grounds. The Mothers Against Illegal Aliens website contains the following statement:

> WELCOME to our website, which describes our mission, gives you up-to-date information on the growing illegal alien problem and how it effects every aspect of your life and that of the lives of our children. It also provides you links to other websites of patriots who are aiding the United States in eradicating the illegal alien lawbreakers threatening our rule of law, our sovereignty and the future of OUR CHILDREN.
>
> Guide yourself through all the information, and then YOU decide if our children are the forgotten and silent victims when it comes to their education in schools overrun by illegal aliens and to their safety from a border in peril. Ultimately, it is up to you to decide for yourself if you want to get involved, protect your family and country, or if you'd rather watch from the sidelines and let our government do your bidding as it gives away your livelihood, your future and your country to a foreign entity that is dictating U.S. immigration policy.
> —Mission, Mothers Against Illegal Aliens[23]

Notice the intriguing mixture of gender, patriotism, and hospitality in the message of MAIA.[24] The idea that children are threatened is intended to particularly appeal to women who have traditionally been responsible for children. Patriotism is invoked and there is an implication that children as well as the country are under attack. What does this have to do with hospitality? Note the phrase, "Let our government do our bidding as it gives away your livelihood." Even though the message is a bit confusing, there is a sense that the U.S. government is giving something away. The connotation is that hospitality is being abused as the host nation is too generous and the guests are too avaricious. This bitterness is not an unusual outgrowth of hospitality. Because hospitality is a multilayered phenomenon, its positive associations are often shadowed by negative ones. Within this complexity, gender continues to be an important aspect making hospitality a feminist issue.

Hospitality of Privilege

Historically, hospitality has served a variety of purposes. Rituals of hospitality have been employed to determine whether a stranger is potentially dangerous, to structure social patterns of engagement and gift giving, as well as to demonstrate wealth and magnanimity.[25] Seldom do acts of hospitality achieve absolute moral ideals. Jacques Derrida describes the impossible hospitality ideal he terms "unconditional hospitality." Such hospitality is an *aporia* for Derrida, a paradox that defies material application. To be unconditionally hospitable is for the host to give all that they have to the guest but this precludes the host from offering anything further and therefore they can no longer be host. Derrida claims that anything that falls short of this ideal is conditional hospitality. As mere mortals, most humans cannot help but engage in conditional forms of hospitality. Accordingly, hospitality is an offer that extends from a position of privilege.

The host owns something of value—food, shelter, gifts, ideas, experience—that is shared with the guest. The host is therefore in a position of privilege. Of course, privilege is a complex notion that varies by degrees. Owning a sandwich and sharing half with a stranger does not imply a large or oppressive degree of privilege. Other forms of hospitality can entail a largess implicitly or explicitly intended by the host to demonstrate the superior privileges of the host to the guest. For example in analyzing eighteenth century hospitality in American Southern colonies, Cynthia Kierner describes hospitality as intended to reveal "the power and beneficence of these elites whose largesse, in turn, ideally strengthened ties of patronage and dependence between superiors and presumed inferiors."[26] Opulent wedding celebrations, planned media photo opportunities at a large charitable donation, or elaborate dinner parties can be moments of hospitality that have secondary messages regarding how private property determines social hierarchy and position. This hospitality of privilege clouds the relationship between the host and guest, creating distance, resistance and even hostility. Although a metaphor of host and guest evokes images of cordial and positive engagements, very close to the surface of hospitality lurks hostility. The guest is an unknown, a wild card. Having allowed the guest into proximity, the host has been made vulnerable by taking a risk. In her study of hospitality and gender in ancient India, Stephanie W. Jamison finds the experience of hospitality to be one fraught with anxiety.[27] Mireille Rosello describes risk as "one of the keys to all hospitable encounters."[28] The guest may resent the host who can in turn hold the guest in contempt. Derrida describes how closely the shadow of hostility follows hospitality in his neologism, "hostipitality."[29] When hospitality is constructed as the host having power over the guest, that structure is threatened by the possibility that the guest will usurp that power. Conditional hospitality can be offered as an attempt at maintaining control and thwarting revolution.

Perhaps part of the challenge of conceptualizing equitable hospitality in regard to immigration is the implicit application of the host-guest metaphor. Particularly in its privileged form, the connotation of power relations in hospitality, of haves sharing with have-nots, is powerful. Edwina Barvosa suggests that perhaps a "marriage" metaphor might be useful. In one sense, this can be viewed as trading one patriarchal term for another, but Barvosa wishes to apply a contemporary view of marriage among equals which provides stability but also implies fluidity over time: "In most marriages there is room for spouses to have a range of non-marital relationships and to retain loyalties and commitments to other relationships. To some extent, we even judge the health of a married relationship by the hospitableness with which it incorporates pre-existing or new extra-marital relationships."[30] For Barvosa, the experience of Latina/o immigrants in regard to their new country is one of divorce and remarriage with ongoing relationships with their former spouses. Such a metaphor implies interdependence without subservience. As Maria Lugones describes in regard to wanting to transform relationships between white women and women of color, "I am incomplete and unreal without other women. I am profoundly dependent on others without having to be their subordinate, their slave, their servant."[31] Whether or not marriage is the best metaphor to apply to immigration, it is useful to reconsider the underlying metaphors that help frame how we view the issue and the people involved.

Regarding the privilege of property, hospitality has a conceptual cousin in the notion of charity. Hospitality, like charity, can be given with a disposition of openness and earnestness where the well-being of the guest is of the utmost importance. However, charity can also be given to assuage the moral guilt of the giver and reinforce the power positions of those involved. Social change that reduces power/resource differentials and thus the need for charity upsets positions of privilege and the status quo and are thus considered radical. Similarly, challenging the social context, which creates host and guest differentials, are also radical reforms. If one aspect of privileged hospitality is control over property, broadly construed, another aspect is a sense of place. The host not only has something to share with guest, she or he has a place to do it in for which there is some sense of identification. Hosting implies a location of control, whether owned or borrowed, where guests are tended to with the host's resources. Even transient Bedouins employ a particular place of socializing in their homes to engage in acts of hospitality. Charity is often juxtaposed against justice whereby justice is a systemic approach to fairness and charity as a nonmandated moral good. In the case of Mexican immigration, justice becomes the site of negotiation. Immigrants demand human rights and U.S. citizen demand legal rights of protection. Caring hospitality can mediate "better" justice by facilitating better understanding among the claimants.

Taken together, resource and location control in privileged hospitality reinforce boundaries of exclusion (and therefore inclusion). Ironically, the flaunting of possessions and space can send a strong message of who constitutes insiders and outsiders even within a context of giving and hospitality. Privileged hospitality can be applied to the metaphorical mapping of host/guest onto nation state/immigrant relation.[32] Countries have various degrees of resources available to them that sovereignty dictates is theirs to dispose of as they decide through their legitimate leadership structures. Nation states also have a geographic existence for which inhabitants have a strong sense of identification that often manifests itself in patriotism. Accordingly, immigrants are perceived as fortunate guests who should be compliant and grateful to their host nation. As a resource-rich nation, privileged hospitality is particularly apt description of the United States in regard to its Mexican neighbor. The hospitality that the U.S. offers Mexican immigrants not only stems from the standpoint of privilege but it reinforces and maintains that privilege.[33] Legality then becomes a mask to hide behind. By declaring that immigrants are "illegal," many U.S. citizens perceive that they are no longer obligated to care for fellow human beings. Legality is the boundary of privilege that separates the outsiders from insiders. This boundary of legality ignores the notion of "moral luck." Bernard Williams and Thomas Nagel's exploration of whether happenstance is significant in moral deliberation is certainly applicable to the situation of Mexican immigrants.[34] One's birth is something that no moral agent has any control over, and yet the use of geopolitical markers belies the luck of nativity. Nationalistic claims overlook that unearned privilege accrues to native citizens, for example, by being born in the U.S., is by chance. There is a certain hubris in haughty claims to privileges and rights that are largely undeserved. These unearned advantages confer what Peggy McIntosh refers to as "conferred dominance" of one group over another. The insidious nature of this dominance is that it goes largely unacknowledged and can be masked by the implicit hospitality metaphor. There is a widespread perception that the U.S. is the good, albeit rich and powerful, neighbor and that Mexican citizens, particularly when they cross the border without documentation are the perpetrators of wrongdoing. Legal property ownership trumps caring for the oppressed. The reversal of victimization is an often-employed mask for privilege. This reversal is what Allan G. Johnson describes as one of the paradoxes of privilege: "*being* privileged without *feeling* privileged."[35] Accordingly, the rhetoric that opposes open immigration paints a picture of the U.S. suffering. For example, former U.S. representative Tom Tancredo from Colorado claimed: "if we don't control immigration, legal and illegal, we will eventually reach the point where it won't be what kind of a nation we are, balkanized or united, we will actually have to face the fact that we are no longer a nation at all. That is the honest to God eventual outcome of this kind of massive immigration combined with the cult of multiculturalism that permeates our society."[36] The message is that if not controlled, Mexican immigration will overrun and ruin its U.S. host.

A note on the notion of "compatriot privilege" is in order. There is a rich discussion in political philosophy regarding the identity of the nation-state and what are the benefits of membership in the face of modern cosmopolitan and human rights demands of "outsiders." This discussion is very robust and complex making a full consideration beyond the scope of the present project. However given the criticism of privileged hospitality here, the specter of the meaning of citizenship is raised. The trajectory of the discussion surrounding the mutually exclusive categories of host and guest can be applied to compatriot privilege. Rigid dichotomous labels may offer the comfort of linguistic certainty but they may be morally divisive in a destructive sense. I am not suggesting that there should be no compatriot privilege, but that a serviceable definition should be malleable and ambiguous enough to allow for care and inclusivity. Just as caring hospitality attempts to flatten the hierarchy between host and guest, compatriot privilege should not be so great as to contribute to the host being oppressors of the guest.

Two of the common criticisms of Mexican immigration, using up U.S. economic resources and degrading American culture, reveal an underlying host/guest structure. Mexican immigrants are the unruly guests who are taking advantage of U.S. hospitality. By undermining American culture, Mexican immigrants threaten to overturn the host's home. One interesting aspect of these claims is that they appear impervious to contrarian evidence. Indications that the United States economy benefits from the presence of undocumented workers from Mexico are legion, and largely ignored in the public square. Justin Akers Chacon describes, "It has become a rallying cry of the anti-immigrant movement to accuse these workers of subverting the economy. Nothing could be further from the truth."[37] Chacon goes on to cite a variety of recent studies that reinforce the economic benefits of the presence of Mexican immigrants including low-wage labor, increased demand for goods and services, increased federal, state, and local tax payments, increased demand for real estate and increased contributions to Social Security and Medicare.[38] The spurious argument that immigrants drain U.S. resources largely stems from isolated or partial studies that do not consider the whole contribution of the Mexican immigrant worker/consumer. Economists such as Alan Greenspan recognize the value of illegal immigrants to the U.S. economy.[39] Nevertheless, the myth of the Mexican immigrant as the guest who depletes the resources of their American host persists. Such economic analysis is quantifiable and yet somewhat alienating. The Mexican undocumented worker is reduced to their productive and consumptive contribution. A caring form of hospitality is less concerned with a cost/benefit analysis of guests, but seeks mutual growth and understanding.

Caring Hospitality: Knowledge and Identity

Care ethics is a much-misunderstood approach to morality. Part of the confusion is self inflicted, as feminist ethicists have not always been consistent in developing this nascent ethical system. Another part of the confusion surrounding care ethics is simply due to the fundamental shift in framing morality and the relative newness of this approach as compared to traditional moral theories. Today, care scholarship has matured to engage a variety of social and political issues as well as specific applications. Many non-feminist theorists have begun to find care ethics compelling and have incorporated it into their work.[40] Care ethicists share the notion that abstract ethical schemas such as utilitarianism or rule-based ethics do not capture the entirety of morality. Unlike consequence or rule morality, care is a complex mixture of disposition, inquiry, empathy, and action that has implications for adjudicating ethical dilemmas but is not exclusively concerned with decision making. Care ethics describes a *disposition* toward strangers: an openness, combined with a focus on their well-being that entails *inquiry*, which can foster *empathy*, an affective connection that can lead to subsequent *action* on their behalf. Note that caring does not necessitate altruism. For care to be holistic, one must care for themselves as well as for others. In this manner, care does not invoke Derrida's impossible ideal of unconditional hospitality because this kind of selfless caring harms the caregiver and may inhibit future caring. Care posits an affective and empathetic dimension to morality that emphasizes experiences and thus particularism within a relational ontology. It is from particular relationships and particular experiences of care that the imagination can be fueled to extend to distant and unfamiliar others. Fiona Robinson's understands globalizing care to be a critical lens in critiquing uneven relationships such as those found in a hospitality of privilege: "a critical ethics of care begins from a relational ontology; it highlights the extent to which people 'live and perceive the world within social relationships' while, at the same time, recognizing that people use relationships to construct and express both power and knowledge."[41] Because hospitality is fundamentally about a relationship between people, the theoretical work done on caring relationships provides an apt foundation for considering hospitality, and perhaps an ideal of caring hospitality that has implications for knowledge, morality, and identity.

The epistemological dimension of care is often overlooked. Caring actions ideally include a learning component or what might be described as caring inquiry. From its earliest formulations, care ethics has entailed listening and learning about others to form an understanding that goes beyond propositional facts. Nel Noddings employs the evocative term "engrossment": "At bottom, all caring involves engrossment. The engrossment need not be intense nor need it be pervasive in the life of the one-caring, but it must occur."[42] The result of this engrossment is knowledge, but not just any knowledge. The knowledge is affective. It seeks out points of connection even across diversity. It has the power to foster empathy and therefore further actions. In this sense, hospitality can be viewed as caring inquiry. The guest or stranger represents an opportunity to learn but not just a new set of facts; rather, a chance for imaginatively understanding others. Andrew Shyrock describes hospitality as "a rich medium in which to imagine worlds that are more open, and more vulnerable to Others."[43] The openness and vulnerability of caring hospitality creates the potential for tremendous knowledge creation as the host welcomes the guest. According the caring inquiry involves what Marilyn Frye describes as the "loving eye, 'which' knows the independence of the other.... It is the eye of one who knows that to know the seen, one must consult something other than one's own will and interests and fears and imagination. One must look at the thing. One must look, listen and check and question."[44] Conversely, by alienating and objectifying Mexican immigrants, by treating them as stereotypes or economic benefits or deficits, an opportunity for understanding is lost. Caring hospitality entails humility and a profound respect for the one cared for.

A number of feminist theorists have engaged what Maria Lugones first described as "playful 'world' traveling" which is pertinent to a notion of caring hospitality. Playful world traveling describes a holistic approach to understanding others, particularly relatively unknown others, for the purpose of moral action. By holistic, I mean that it entails both imaginative and physical actions, including proximal interactions, to provide robust moral knowledge. The moral demand for this world traveling is particularly placed on people whose social privilege does not require them to know the worlds of others. It is much easier, for example, for those who have material wealth to not know about the lives of those who are struggling around them. Financial resources often have the potential to insulate one from issues of class and race experienced by others as symbolized by the "gated community." Oppressed people do not have this privilege and often must travel to the worlds of those with resources in order to navigate a market-driven society. Marianna Ortega and others have described the moral imperative of the privileged to make the effort to travel to unfamiliar worlds of oppressed others "by learning her language, living in her environment, trying to understand issues from her perspective (as hard as this may be), and imagining what it means to be her in her 'world.'"[45] Caring hospitality can be a vehicle for world traveling that through the knowledge gained reflexively improves acts of hospitality. Caring hospitality can help us understand others and develop a moral response to their situation, but it also helps create our *identity*.

Julia Kristeva points out that when it comes to the self, the perspective of strangers is not trivial. It is the presence of others that allows us to develop identity and allows us to grow. Kristeva suggests an identity paradox: "Strangely, the foreigner lives within us: he is the hidden face of our identity, the space that wrecks our abode, the time in which understanding and affinity founder. By recognizing him within ourselves, we are spared detesting him in himself."[46] Because identity is a relative construct, it is only through confronting others that we develop our identity. The immigrant or stranger provides us with phenomenal experience that becomes the imaginative basis for self identification while simultaneously challenging us to develop moral understanding. The stranger becomes the vehicle for which the moral self emerges. Indeed, it is only through the other that we have morality at all, which is perhaps why Derrida claims that "ethics is so thoroughly coextensive with the experience of hospitality."[47] Kristeva describes this tension: "Living with the other, with the foreigner, confronts us with the possibility or not of *being an other*. It is not simply—humanistically—a matter of our being able to accept the other, but to *being in his place*, and this means to imagine and make oneself other for oneself."[48]

By extension, if a nation can have an identity, it will forge it by confronting immigrant others. Part of that identity is moral self understanding that evolves from these confrontations. The U.S. has a poor history of hospitality with culturally and racially diverse peoples but every interaction is an opportunity for the

U.S to reconsider its self understanding. Daniel Engster reinforces how caring shapes the nation's identity:

> Caring for others on a political level is different from personally caring for a child or friend, but there is no reason why political caring should affect us differently from personal caring. The willful neglect or ignorance of the needs of distant others does not make them go away, but means only that we have shut ourselves off from others and (by extension) from the full recognition of our own humanity. When we turn our backs on others in need, we turn our backs in part on ourselves.[49]

We need others to fire our imagination of what it means to be an other, to build our compassion, and to challenge our notion of moral legitimacy. As Barvosa describes, "Ethnic group identities [are] an asset rather than a challenge to [the whole's] ability to bring disparate people together as a nation."[50] The host needs the guest just as much as the guest needs the host. By extension, the U.S. needs Mexican immigrants, documented and undocumented, not merely as productive members of society but to help define who "we" are and who "we" will become. If the U.S. is to live up to the ideals of the Statue of Liberty and the New Colossus, it will need its Mexican neighbors to help it learn how to care.

Conclusion: Caring Hospitality as A Vehicle to Empathy in a Cosmopolitan World

The short-lived (3 seasons, 18 episodes) television show, *30 Days,* provides an interesting twist on hospitality while demonstrating the potential for caring epistemology to reframe the parameters of the debate. The premise of the reality show created by Morgan Spurlock is a thirty-day immersion of someone in a context foreign or opposed to by the participant (often Spurlock, himself). The guest and the host have periodic opportunities to privately apprise the audience of how they are feeling about the experience. On July 26, 2006, an episode aired regarding immigration that featured the placement of a member of the Minutemen, Frank George, who voluntarily patrols the U.S./Mexican border in search of unauthorized entrants, in a family of undocumented Mexican immigrants living in East Los Angeles.[51] His hosts, the Gonzalez family, Rigoberto, Patty and their five children, live in a five hundred square foot apartment. George is given three stipulations to his participation: he must not carry any personal identification; he must move in and stay with the family for 30 days; and, he must work as a day laborer.

At first George is very strident in his anti-immigration position. He claims that the only rights that illegal Mexican immigrants have are "the right to be deported." As the hour-long show goes on, George develops compassion for the family, particularly after visiting Rigoberto Gonzalez's brother in the squalor of the city where the Gonzalez family used to live in Mexico. By the end of the 30 days, George is offering to sponsor the Gonzalez family should they wish to apply for citizenship. He does not alter his position, nor does he quit the Minutemen (although he does stop patrolling for them). Nevertheless, George has made a human connection and cannot look at the issue in the same way. Of course, the circumstances are a bit contrived and this is a show developed for commercial television, but it reveals the power of proximity and the potential of caring hospitality. The welcoming of George into the Gonzalez family created the opportunity for inquiry and knowledge exchange. For George, illegal immigrants went from an abstract stereotype to people he knew and who had aspirations, values, and feelings that he could identify with. Hospitality provided George with rich knowledge that went beyond facts about the number of immigrants or the resources they might use.

No one can escape the encroaching cosmopolitan world. Population growth and technological advancements have conspired to make encounters with those from other countries and cultures inevitable and more frequent. We can choose to resist multiculturalism against the tide of change, or we can embrace it. Seyla Benhabib describes cosmopolitanism as the "emergence of norms that ought to govern relations among individuals in a global civil society."[52] Caring hospitality, as opposed to hospitality of privilege, can be one of those emergent norms in a cosmopolitan world. Traditional legalistic and formulaic approaches to the needs of world citizens have their place, but cannot entirely replace the very human dimension of caring as witnessed in the story of Frank George. For example, although not a care ethicist, Martha Nussbaum takes issue with John Rawls' social justice framework because it abstractly assumes a starting point of equality rather than friendship or caring. Nussbaum claims, "We ought to think of ourselves as people who want to live with others. A central part of our own good, each and every one of us, is to produce, and live in, a world that is morally decent, a world in which all human beings have what the need to live a life with human dignity."[53] Given Nussbaum's claim, multiculturalism and diversity become modern imperatives rather than discretionary activities. Hospitality can be an entre into meaningful relations that can help mitigate conflicts that arise from misunderstanding. The framework of hospitality can enable people to do the necessary epistemological work to understand the other prior to judgment and action. It is much harder to get to know unfamiliar others than it is to stereotype or judge them. However, knowledge is a prerequisite of care. Virginia Held describes, "a globalization of caring relations would help enable people of different states and cultures to live in peace, to respect each other's rights, to care together for their environments, and to improve the lives of their children."[54]

Mexican immigration to the U.S. is not a problem. People living lives of limited sustenance and where they cannot flourish is a problem. People who hide behind legalism in order not to care for others, is another problem. Caring hospitality on an individual, local, and national level can be a vehicle to better understanding thus facilitating better solutions to real issues with more imaginative responses than building walls and villainizing individuals seeking a better life.

Notes

1. I reluctantly employ the term "illegal" in this context to critique popular discourse on Mexican undocumented visitors. As many commentators have pointed out, invoking "illegality" is an acceptable discourse in a society that favors formal justice over caring. The term "illegal" masks an anti-Mexican bias. See, for example, Justin Akers Chacon, "Constructing the 'Illegal' Mexican Worker," in Justin Akers Chacon and Mike Davis, *No One is Illegal: Fighting Racism and State Violence on the U.S.—Mexican Border*. (Chicago: Haymarket Books, 2006), 195.

2. "Anchor babies" is a derogatory term that impugns that immigrants will give birth on U.S. soil to gain a foothold in the country. HR 1940, "The Birthright Citizenship Act of 2007" attempted to eliminate this path to citizenship but never came to a House vote.

3. Lou Dobbs, "Broken Borders" http://loudobbs.tv.cnn.com/category/broken-borders/ (accessed March 1, 2010).

4. Mireille Rosello, *Postcolonial Hospitality: The Immigrant as Guest* (Stanford: Stanford University Press, 2001), vii.

5. Pat Buchanan, *Where the Right Went Wrong: How Neoconservatives Subverted the Reagan Revolution and Hijacked the Bush Presidency* (New York: St. Martin's Griffin, 2005), 166.

6. Rob Sanchez, "The Morality of Displacing American Workers," *The Social Contract* 17:1 (Spring 2007), 174.

7. Jeffrey S. Passel and D'Vera Cohn, *A Portrait of Unauthorized Immigrants in the United States*, April 14, 2009, http://pewhispanic.org/files/reports/107.pdf

8. *Women Immigrants: Stewards of the 21st Century Family*, New America Media, February 2009 http://media.namx.org/Polls/NAMImigWomenPoll_09.pdf

9. Manuel Peña, "Folklore, Machismo and Every Day Practice: Writing Mexican Worker Culture," *Western Folklore*. 65:1/2 (Winter 2006).

10. Tracy McNulty, *The Hostess: Hospitality, Femininity, and the Expropriation of Identity*, (Minneapolis: University of Minnesota Press, 2007), xxvii.

11. Jacques Derrida, *Of Hospitality: Anne Dufourmantelle Invites Derrida to Respond*, trans. Rachel Bowlby (Stanford: Stanford University Press, 2000), 155.

12. Rosalyn Diprose, "Women's Bodies Between National Hospitality and Domestic Biopolitics" *Paragraph* 32:1 (2009), 71.

13. McNulty, *The Hostess*, xxvii.

14. Diprose, "Women's Bodies Between National Hospitality and Domestic Biopolitics," 70.

15. Allison Stevens, "Women's Groups Differ Over Immigration Strategy," *Women's E-News*, 4/24/06, http://www.womensenews.org/article.cfm/dyn/aid/2715/context/archive

16. Stevens, "Women's Groups Differ Over Immigration Strategy."

17. For a discussion of a distinctive feminist hospitality, see Maurice Hamington, "Toward A Theory of Feminist Hospitality" *National Women's Studies Journal* 22:1 (April, 2010).

18. Annette Baier, *Postures of the Mind: Essays on Mind and Morals* (Minneapolis: University of Minnesota Press, 1985).

19. Lorraine Code, *What Can She Know? Feminist Theory and the Construction of Knowledge* (New York: Cornell University Press, 1991), 85.

20. Code, *What Can She Know?* 73, 78.

21. Grace Clement, *Care, Autonomy, and Justice: Feminism and the Ethic of Care* (Boulder, CO: Westview Press, 1996), 35.

22. Michelle Dallacroce quoted in Teresa Watanabe, "Guidelines to Humanize Immigration Raids" *Los Angeles Times* Nov. 24, 2007. http://theenvelope.latimes.com/la-me-immig24nov24,0,6572648.story (accessed March 1, 2010).

23. Mothers Against Illegal Aliens, http://mothersagainstillegalaliens.org/site/index.php?option=com_frontpage&Itemid=1 (accessed March 1, 2010).

24. For further analysis of the message of Mothers Against Illegal Aliens, see the Anti-Defamation League website: http://www.adl.org/Civil_Rights/anti_immigrant/maia.asp (accessed March 1, 2010).

25. Kevin D. O'Gorman, "Modern Hospitality: Lessons From the Past" *Journal of Hospitality and Tourism Management* 12:2 (August 2005) 141-151.

26. Cynthia A. Kierner, "Hospitality, Sociability, and Gender in the Southern Colonies" *The Journal of Southern History* 62:3 (Aug. 1996) 449-480, 451.

27. Stephanie W. Jamison, *Sacrificed Wife, Sacrificer's Wife: Women, Ritual, and Hospitality in Ancient India* (New York: Oxford University Press, 1996), 6.

28. Rosello, *Postcolonial Hospitality*, 172.

29. Jacques Derrida, *Acts Of Religion*. Trans. Gil Anidjar. (New York: Routledge, 2004), 356-59.

30. Edwina Barvosa, *Wealth of Selves: Multiple Identities, Mestiza Consciousness and the Subject of Politics* (College Station, TX: Texas A&M Press, 2008), 43.

31. Maria Lugones, "Playfulness, 'World'-Travelling, and Loving Perception" *Hypatia* 2:2 (Summer 1987): 7.

32. The host/guest relationship as a metaphor for the nation state/immigrant relationship is deeply structured metaphor or what Mark Johnson and George Lakoff have referred to as an image schema. These metaphoric structures help us navigate our complex world by mapping understandable proximal knowledge onto new and less familiar domains. Because the host/guest is a relationship that we are more familiar with, we map it onto the nation state/immigrant relationship to help us understand it. This mapping can be implicitly operant even when the term "hospitality" is not explicitly employed. George Lakoff, and Mark Johnson. *Philosophy In The Flesh: The Embodied Mind and Its Challenge to Western Thought* (New York: Basic Books, 1999).

33. The geopolitical history of Mexico and the United States makes the present discussion of hospitality particularly ironic. After the U.S. annexed Mexico in 1845, the Mexican-American war ensued. After defeat, Mexico was forced to cede a huge landmass encompassing California, Nevada, Utah and parts of Colorado, Arizona, New Mexico, and Wyoming reducing the size of Mexico by 45 percent. The history of Mexican immigration to the United States is inconsistent with the label of "illegal" varying with social opinion and economic need.

34. Bernard Williams, "Moral Luck." *Moral Luck*. Ed. Daniel Statman. State University of New York Press, Albany, New York, 1993 35-55, and Thomas "Moral Luck." *Moral Luck*. Ed. Daniel Statman, State University of New York Press, Albany, New York, 1993, 57-71.

35. Allan G. Johnson, *Privilege, Power, and Difference* (Mountain Vista, CA: Mayfield Publishing Co., 2001), 36.

36. Tom Tancredo, interviewed for *Right Wing News*, http://www.rightwingnews.com/interviews/tancredo.php (accessed March 1, 2010).

37. Justin Akers Chacon, "Immigrant Workers Continue to Build America," in Justin Akers Chacon and Mike Davis, *No One is Illegal: Fighting Racism and State Violence on the U.S.—Mexican Border*. (Chicago: Haymarket Books, 2006), 161.

38. Chacon, "Immigrant Workers Continue to Build America," 161-70.

39. Nicholas Johnston, "Alan Greenspan Says Illegal Immigration Aids U.S. Economy" Bloomberg.com, April 30, 2009. http://www.bloomberg.com/apps/news?pid=20601103&sid=anIvyAQU6XRk (accessed March 1, 2010).

40. See, for example, Daniel Engster, *The Heart of Justice: Care Ethics and Political Theory* (New York: Oxford University Press, 2007); and, Michael Slote, *The Ethics of Care and Empathy* (New York: Routledge, 2007).

41. Fiona Robinson, *Globalizing Care: Ethics, Feminist Theory and International Relations* (Boulder, CO: Westview Press, 1999), 110.

42. Nel Noddings, *Caring: A Feminine Approach to Ethics and Moral Education* (Berkeley: University of California Press, 1984), 17.

43. Andrew Shyrock, "Hospitality Lessons: Learning the Shared Language of Derrida and the Balga Bedoin" *Paragraph* 32:1 (2009) 32-50, 32.

44. Marilyn Frye, *The Politics of Reality: Essays in Feminist Theory* (Freedom, CA: Crossing Press, 1983), 75.

45. Marianna Ortega, "Being Lovingly, Knowingly Ignorant: White Feminism and Women of Color" *Hypatia* 21:3 (Summer 2006), 70.

46. Julia Kristeva, *Strangers to Ourselves*. Trans Leon S. Roudiez. (New York: Columbia University Press, 1991), 1.

47. Jacques Derrida, *On Cosmopolitanism and Forgiveness*. Trans. Mark Dooley and Michael Hughes. (New York: Routledge, 2001), 17.

48. Kristeva, *Strangers to Ourselves*, 13.

49. Engster, *The Heart of Justice*, 244.

50. Barvosa, *Wealth of Selves*, 53.

51. Morgan Spurlock, "Immigration" *30 Days* [tv show] Season 2, Episode 1, airdate July 26, 2006.

52. Seyla Benhabib, *Another Cosmopolitanism* (New York: Oxford University Press, 2006), 20.

53. Martha Nussbaum, "Beyond the Social Contract: Capabilities and Global Justice" in Gillian Brock and Harry Brighouse, eds., *The Political Philosophy of Cosmopolitanism* (Cambridge: Cambridge University Press, 2005), 210.

54. Virginia Held, *The Ethics of Care: Personal, Political, and Global* (New York: Oxford University Press, 2006), 168.

Part IV: Gender, Hospitality, and Commerce

Chapter 11

The Home/Work Interface In Family Hospitality Businesses: Gendered Dimensions and Constructions

MariaLaura Di Domenico

This chapter is concerned with a context which tends to be ubiquitous in its familiarity and infused with gendered associations and symbolism. It is the context of the home. However, it is not just about any home, but a unique home which is also a business which offers hospitality, such as a small hotel, bed & breakfast or guesthouse. These small-scale hospitality businesses are often run by families who are their permanent space occupants and as such have to negotiate their lived realities not just with other family members but also with their customers. In such a way, the home space becomes further complicated and problematized as it is converted into a small business that is based specifically upon commercial hospitality provision and consumption. Drawing upon empirical evidence from a qualitative study, the experiences and standpoints of hosts as service providers are laid bare in terms of the tensions, ambiguities and constraints that they face and that are imposed on them by this spatial duality. In so doing, this chapter enhances our understanding of gendered host-guest dynamics within the contextual parameters of home-based hospitality businesses. It unpacks the nature of first-hand experiences of a fascinating sphere that operates at the interface between private and public domains, and the worlds of home and work, domestic hospitableness and commercial hospitality.

Traditionally, although not exclusively in this context, the role of host[1] is performed by the woman or mother figure of the household. This role carries with it *a priori* associations in the mind of the commercial guest such as those connected with a feminized status. However, the "real" self is a construction of the enacted self. In the case of the commercial home enterprise such as the bed & breakfast, the host's ideal and desired projections of self are bound up in wider societal constructs with gendered connotations of roles, and the individual guest's interpretations of them. Thus, the staged performance of the host is trapped within broader gendered definitions of their occupational role. This serves to problematize and add to the complexity of dramaturgical constructs[2] within this context, with the hosts as gendered actors not being in complete control of the role they wish to enact or the script they wish to follow. This causes a sense of ambiguity as such "home hosts" have a strong desire to control and orient the host/guest encounter, and which may leave them with a deep-rooted sense of emotional dissonance. This chapter explores all of these issues within a theoretical lens informed by gender and social construction.

Gendered Interactions And Roles At The Home-Work Interface

Gender and the provision of hospitality are deeply engrained within pervasive Western socio-cultural stereotypes and associations. This is due to historical elements and the fact that hospitality is a key defining component of the private home and our interactions and practices therein. The literature on the significance of our associations, uses and the meanings that we invest in the home space is vast and multi-disciplinary.[3] As a highly problematized arena, the domestic space is redolent with gendered norms, meanings, practices and expectations that are regularly engendered and enacted by those residing within it.[4] Typically, the home combines both elements of work and leisure, particularly for its female occupants. There are many "chores" and tasks that must be performed in order to maintain the home, adorn the space according to preferred aesthetics, and present it to the critical eye of its inhabitants and guests.

It is important to be aware of the fact that historically the boundaries that developed between spaces and places for home and work were less clear cut than they are at present. They largely emerged as a result of industrialization which caused a shift away from agrarian forms of income generation and necessitated that places of work be distinct from the home. This had a dramatic effect upon how the home is regarded and, particularly in Western societies, the home became increasingly detached from possibilities of significant income generation.[5] Thus, largely as a result of industrialization and the effects of modernity, this arose due to the shaping of a collective consciousness towards envisaging neat binaries and dialectic distinctions between home and work, and public and private spaces. Notwithstanding paid-for domestic cleaning, activities also typically performed by women, the labor required within the confines of the private home also became increasingly feminized and thus devalued.[6]

Our negotiation of private spaces within our homes, and public spaces beyond the threshold, thus became increasingly gendered. In our collective subconscious, the home implicitly carries with it notions of the feminine, such as sanctity, privacy, safety, nurture and retreat.[7] Indeed, it is almost womb-like in its protective allure. External spaces are seen as more exposed, austere, foreboding, and thus implicitly more masculine or even dangerous or unwelcoming, especially to females who may experience some of these spaces as imbued with the aura of the "gendered other." Consequently, gendered constructions of the house as a feminine, private space have flourished in the modern period. Indeed, it has come to epitomize the patriarchal way of defining and structuring social relations between the sexes and within traditional family life in Western society. In many ways small hotels or bed & breakfasts, run from the private family home, cater to this type of structuring in their more patriarchal orderings, roles and identifications. This particular context can now be unpacked whereby the implications of introducing the logic of remunerated commercial hospitality into the private residence are considered through a gendered lens in terms of the host-guest relationship within this unique home-work setting.

Commercial Home-Based Hospitality Provision: Gendered Permutations Within Host-Guest Dynamics

There are few sites where not only are work and home physically co-located, but where there are also interactive service work encounters between host and guest. Home-based, family-run businesses in the hospitality industry are fascinating in their evocation of complex and intricate, although traditional, domestic and work-based social interactions. Arguably, they may even be unique in this regard. The home does not merely co-exist alongside the interactive service work of commercial hospitality, but it also provides the logical basis, the *raison d'être*, upon which the business is built by the owners and their families, as well as the magnet for customers attracted to such establishments.

For all space occupants it is a negotiation and sharing of space, often involving close interactions between the host/family and guests.[8] The space is a complex hybrid system and an enduring social phenomenon dating back to the earliest days of commercial hospitality provision such as the inns and taverns with rooms and sustenance for the traveler or salesman (use of the gendered term is deliberate as they typically were sales*men*). As they involve private residences, such commercial homes are limited in size and typically have about one to six letting bedrooms, with some larger properties or family estates providing more. It is fascinating that even in countries such as the UK where hotel chains have market dominance, bed & breakfasts/guesthouses are numerically the single most prevalent form of commercial hospitality, and indeed twenty-eight percent bigger than the budget hotels sector.[9] Why is this the case? Why are such establishments enduring in their popularity? It may be partly a question of price and affordability. However, perhaps part of their enduring appeal is that they tap into a psychological need that we have for the familiarity and safety of the home, and part may be based on a need for sociability, and a curiosity which spurs us on to visit the homes of others. These establishments may be contrasted with the identikit and anonymous motels, the so-called *non-places* of modernity[10], designed to a predetermined and standard formula. The bed & breakfast is not purpose-built in this way, but fulfills a variety of functions for both resident family and guests.

It is imperative however to affirm and draw distinctions between these different forms of commercial hospitality, namely those that are performed from an actual private home and those that are detached from it. Although both larger hotels and home-based hospitality enterprises such as the bed & breakfast provide commercial hospitality, the dominance of the respective spatial contexts of either "home" or "business" distinguish each arena. This requires a little extra consideration in terms of how each of these articulations plays out within these different commercial hospitality contexts. The larger hotel can be conceptualized as containing spaces that mimic or copy domestic spaces such as comfortable furniture, décor, fireplaces, and marketing slogans of "home-style" cooked meals, "country" or "hearty" cuisine and surrogate "home away from home" guest experiences.[11] In contrast, the home-based bed & breakfast or guesthouse does not merely mimic the home setting but takes place in a real domestic residence that is actively used and lived in by the proprietor(s) and often their family as commercial hosts. This effectively frames host-guest interactions in terms of the way that hosts articulate boundaries between familial and more commercial space, as well as the ways guests deal with these divisions and overlaps when orienting themselves within what is inescapably the home of someone else.

In such a way, it is perceived to embody a kind of authenticity[12], communicating the ideals of family, neighborliness and bounded local communities.[13] Thus, these home-based businesses contrast with so-called McDonaldized commercial hospitality.[14] Some of these are officially graded by quality assurance standards applied by national tourist boards and marketing organizations with symbols such as "stars" or "rosettes," whilst others remain outside such official modes of judgment and standardization. Nevertheless, all are dynamic performative settings, with "front" and "back" stages.[15]

Gender is a germane and important consideration in accounting for how the multiple space occupants, whether they be guests, hosts, or family members, negotiate their interactions with one another within this complex home-cum-business sphere. Gendered roles, identities and norms are inherently fluid and malleable. As in many walks of life, these are transferred and mirrored in the daily reality of the business. Indeed, due to the nature of the small hotel or guesthouse being one of hospitality provision and consumption, similarities with the private home are numerous. Both involve the common elements of the consumption of food and drink, sleep and rest, bathing and other practical bodily functions, and other creature comforts. Indeed, both contain activities that are preferred to be hidden from collective view but no less present, such as sexual activities.[16] The space is thus infused with body practices which heighten the vulnerabilities of space occupants, the roles that they play and the solidity of boundaries in the host/guest relationship.[17] Indeed, for those familiar with the work of the writer Bill Bryson, one may recall his depiction of his encounter with the officious Dover bed & breakfast proprietor Mrs. Smegma, and his bemusement at her obsession with what he might do on the bed's counterpane. This featured pride of place in the prologue to his classic account of British life, *Notes From a Small Island.* He quotes Mrs. Smegma as saying; "We've had some unfortunate occurrences with stains."[18] Therefore, the familiarity and stereotypes we attribute to the bed & breakfast has become a mainstay of the collective imagination and popular culture. There is a long history of in-home accommodation, for example in the UK it goes back to taverns and inns on popular coaching routes offering rooms upstairs. These have been replaced by the modern-day bed & breakfasts or guesthouses. The prevalence of the bed & breakfast is something particularly linked to the cultures of the British Isles, although you will find them in numerous countries the world over. This is highlighted by the popular, classic 1970s BBC television sitcom "Fawlty Towers" which pokes fun at the high jinks and service encounters with their unfortunate guests of a married couple running a small hotel in the British seaside town of Torquay in the English Riviera. The episodes were infused with gendered stereotypes, with the underlying theme being the frustration of the snobbish, misanthropic but hapless husband, Basil Fawlty, with both the temperament of his sharp-tongued, bossy wife and the intrusion of diverse paying customers.

The main differences between the private home and the home-based hospitality business are the introduction of commercial transactions and the presence of the stranger as customer, often previously unknown, albeit invited, by the resident family. Indeed, the appeal for the customer as "guest" to patronize these establishments rather than some other typically larger, standardized chain or franchise hotel is the appeal of the domestic, "home away from home" experience, and the attraction of experiencing another family setting. However, this perhaps sits in an uneasy parallel with the commercial environment and hospitality enterprise where the "proprietor" and "customer" respectively masquerade as "host" and "guest" in order to emphasize the mutually desirable facets of the private home. The "invasion" of this mode of petty capitalism into the sanctity of the original home space must vie with other aspects of the domestic arena where both practical and intimate family relations and individualized and often more traditionally rooted rituals have endured.

The home-based business reconnects and often entangles these boundaries built up between home and remunerated work place. This is even more so in the case of the home-based guesthouse or bed & breakfast that evokes pre-modern articulations of home and family blurring these divisions. Whilst contesting these divisions, they simultaneously uphold the traditional notions of family and thereby the gendered practices emanating from that social construction. Nevertheless, both female and male hosts who run such hospitality businesses also effectively challenge gendered stereotypes of the home. The female host visibly provides hospitality but only in return for remuneration in terms of her dealings with the paying guest as "customer." This is in stark opposition to expectations of hospitableness within a non-commercial family home and her provision of unremunerated hospitality and care-giving. The male host also challenges our associations of the home and hospitality provision as "women's work" by their use of, and visibility in, the domestic space. Thus, it is interesting to note how this contrasts with our perceptions of gendered norms of hospitality provision by certain clearly defined occupations, such as the chef or waiter, in large hotels or workplaces that are clearly separate from the home. These become legitimized and elevated as sufficiently masculine in nature unlike their counterpart of the male bed & breakfast host. Indeed, the service economy, and in particular the broad and diverse hospitality industry, is heavily gendered.[19] Labor tends to be organized along gender lines.[20] Roles involving cleaning and housekeeping are typically seen as feminized and often demeaned through association with household divisions of labor. These differ from what are perceived to be the more skilled, and masculine, roles of the chef who innovates and creates rather than merely cleans and tidies up after others. In the home, there is an explicit gendering of performance. We are all mindful of the highly gendered labels given to roles such as "housewife," "homemaker" or "breadwinner" that immediately conjure up in the mind's eye gender specific actors.[21]

With this gendered frame of reference in mind, the commercial home-based hospitality business can usefully be critiqued using a dramaturgical perspective.[22] This is an approach that regards social relations as an unfolding drama, drawing heavily on metaphors of performance and theatre in how individuals as social actors interact as if on an imaginary stage or holding up a mirror in an attempt to influence how they are perceived by others. Constraints are imposed on the individual by the service sector occupational roles which they enact and which relate to their performance within a script of *a priori* role definitions and expectations. Home–work and host–guest spatial boundaries are thus actively reinforced by those involved in the performance and service interaction. Such a thesis is particularly prevalent in studies analyzing hospitality as performance and the impression management techniques of the host.[23]

Investigating The Everyday Realities Of The Commercial Home Host

In order to assess the everyday realities and world views of these home "hosts," I spent time speaking to them and visiting their home-based enterprises in two contrasting Scottish cities, tourist-historic Inverness and post-industrial Dundee. Local business listings were combined with the tourist board's databases of guesthouses/ bed & breakfasts in these two locations. In the end, thirty-three hosts, twenty-three women and ten men, were interviewed based upon their willingness to be involved and share their views and also because they fulfilled the necessary criterion of running a home-based hospitality business. All hosts were part of married or cohabiting couples, as typical of the sector, and all were aged between 40 and 69. Fifteen ran the business together with their spouse, and the remaining eighteen ran it more or less predominantly themselves as their spouse held alternative remunerated work outside the home. Out of the latter group, only two were men whose wives held full-time work outside the home.

My conversations with these individuals could often extend to several hours duration and all were carried out in their home-businesses. Tours of the property were also given which laid bare not only "front stage" guest areas but also "back stage" areas of the home used by the host and their family. This provided a vivid insight into their experiences and day-to-day home and work activities which aids our understanding of the gendered realities, roles and constructions of the hosts *per se* and in turn their views on interactions with guests. Many of us know what it is like to be a paying guest in a bed & breakfast or guesthouse, or at least a non-paying guest invited to stay in the homes of friends or family. However, few of us may be able to appreciate the standpoint of these business hosts. Engaging with them helped fill that gap to produce greater insight into the nature of the host-guest relationship from their perspectives within a unique hospitality transaction. Hence, the guest's views are not omitted, but rather approached through the prism of the host's standpoint. It is on this basis that you, the reader, should frame and contextualize the hosts' opinions presented herein.

Boundaries, Roles And Identities: Gendered Ambiguities And Tensions Between Host And Guest

The ability to manage the temporal and spatial overlaps between home and work is a constant challenge for the host of the home-based hospitality enterprise. Both time and space are highly fluid and malleable within this dual domain of home and business and need to be leveraged as key organizing mechanisms for the orchestration of social roles and actions.[24] All hosts who were interviewed spoke about the daily tasks they performed. These were heavily gender-defined, with common depictions of feminine chores being cleaning and making beds, and more masculine ones including maintenance tasks, gardening or cooking, if the male host elected to do. This was often explained through cooking being defined as an enjoyable activity and redefined as in essence being part of a more acceptably "masculine" chef-like role. In the main, notwithstanding the two male hosts who ran the business predominantly themselves, descriptions showed clearly that roles bore close similarity to traditional gender lines of the typical division of labor in the home. Therefore, it became apparent that business norms are heavily influenced by the norms of the home which often encroach and are even deliberately transposed upon the former. The following descriptions illustrate how the "staged performances" of male and female hosts differ by gender role in terms of how they run the business and their interactions with guests.

> We have it worked out pretty well. Ted (reference to host's husband) likes to cook the breakfasts. I think I'm that wee bit more sociable so I serve the breakfast and answer the phone and you know check people in . . . I also do all the cleaning, changing the linen, the bathrooms and all that side of things. Well, he'd be hopeless at cleaning. I'd end up redoing it if he tried (laughs) . . . So we tend to do things that way really. He also deals with anything that needs fixing, you know the odd jobs, taking out the rubbish, that sort of thing (Female host).

> I think the guests like to see a clean and tidy place when they come to stay. Well who wouldn't? It's a reflection of me at the end of the day and how I keep house. I'm a proud person and I wouldn't want anything untoward said about me in that respect. So, I do spend time every morning after serving the breakfast making sure everything is tidy and polished and as it should be. I might rope my husband or my daughter in to give me a hand but they usually find an excuse to get out of it (laughs) . . . No, I probably do more than I should but that's what I'm here for isn't it? I'm the wife and mother and nobody forces me to do this. I've chosen to do it because I want to. Well, I enjoy it most of the time. It gives me a bit of extra pin money and I like meeting people . . . I like the company . . . well, mostly . . . (Female host).

Notwithstanding such gendered role demarcation, both men and women set up spatial or temporal boundaries in order to be able to "shut off" from work, retreat to a space reserved purely for family or leisure, and to psychologically distance themselves from the emotional labor required in their performances with the guest. Indeed, there were references to a deep-rooted sense of emotional dissonance that could emerge if these boundary-maintaining mechanisms were not employed or if the hosts felt that too much of their space or "downtime" was being encroached upon:

> Yes, we have our own private space . . . through there to the left of the kitchen is our own lounge and half of the upstairs is just our own. They're reserved just for us. Well, you've got to have that really. And stick to it. I know one or two of the ladies that do this along the road there and they've said that they've even given up their own room if there were extra guests in. Would you believe it? No, that's a slippery slope . . . You've just got to miss out on the business if you're gonna be turfed out of your own bed. Imagine! No, me and my husband have our own bit and the guests have theirs. It's the only way to remain sane so they don't take total advantage of the place. If you do that then its your own fault really . . . you've no-one to blame but yourself if you then start thinking that you want to pack it in (Female host).

> I have a rule that after about ten o'clock I won't take any bookings. People shouldn't really be calling at that time of night. Or not you'd never have a moment's peace. That's what I do anyway. It's my wee business so I'll run it how I like (Male host).

However, despite the deployment of these boundary maintenance strategies, such attempts were obviously constant challenges for the hosts who had to negotiate this fragile interplay. Thus, the bed & breakfast provides a lively and constantly changing stage that imbues elements of the host's identity and home. This may be desirable for the guests who, whilst demanding tidiness and cleanliness, are patrons of such establishments as they want to experience something authentic, a glimpse into the real home life of someone else, and a home-like experience that serves as a contrast to the more sterile, purpose-built hotel. For this reason, they are seen as being particularly welcoming of the nurturing role of the female host, a physical embodiment of the wife and mother. However, it is clear that the interface with guests may be often left to the female host, and the emotional tightrope of real versus manufactured emotional display[25] with guests clearly varies:

> You have the off day when you just can't be bothered and I think to myself "why am I doing this?" On days like that you just can't be bothered. But you've just got to put a brave face on and smile and be nice to the guests just like every other day. So, you're not allowed to have a bad day . . . no, not doing something like this (Female host).

Host-guest interactions are infused with gendered roles and expectations, reflected by the descriptions given by proprietors of the ways in which this relationship was influenced by *a priori* constructions of gendered roles. For instance, where the bed & breakfast was run jointly by a couple, in the first instance guests tended to approach the female host with any questions or issues. This was particularly the case if queries related to issues such as room cleanliness and the need for additional creature comforts such as toiletry items. Male hosts would only be approached in such a way in the absence of an obvious female resident of the home. Indeed, one proprietor remarked that guests would often approach her teenage daughter with questions concerning the bed & breakfast, whilst her son of a similar age was rarely spoken to by guests.

It was also interesting that the women who ran the bed & breakfast on their own while their spouse held paid employment outside the home attempted to protect their partner as much as possible from any intrusions from customers. This shows that female hosts often reinforce gender-based roles and are also keen to preserve the home space as a zone of rest and leisure, with notions of hospitality consumption to be enjoyed by their working male spouse as well as their guests. Of course, this is historically a very masculine definition of the home,[26] an experience not often shared by the female occupant performing their domestic labor duties. They did this by keeping any requests for help from their husbands/ partners to a minimum and even trying to organize the bookings of the business around his needs:

> When people would come up for the weekend, they would phone up on a Friday night and my husband likes to go out on a Friday night, so I would say to them "what time are you arriving?" and once or twice George has said "oh, I'm fed up with this" . . . and so for a little while I would never take anybody on a Friday night until he got over it again. (Female host)

> I try not to bother him with my side of things. He's busy enough with his work and pretty tired at the end of the day. He's often got to go away for his work so I try to organize it so that I have people in when he's away for his work. It doesn't always work that way but I do my best for his sake . . . He needs a bit of peace and quiet after all and not to be hassled with too much comings and goings around the place (Female host).

On the other hand, the two men who had wives working outside the home did not go to the same lengths to protect their wives from the intrusive nature of the business and/or guests. Indeed, they even expected their wives to share in some domestic duties required by providing commercial hospitality to guests, to be understanding of their need to run the business, and to essentially "put up with" the situation. This would seem to support feminist analyses of the "second shift" which was often imposed on working women in their daily lives when they undertook the bulk of domestic labor/childcare in the home in addition to their "day jobs."[27] It would appear that this "second shift"[28] is no less an expectation when it comes to the bed & breakfast/guesthouse even when it is run "solely" by the male spouse as his exclusive occupation. The approach of these male sole proprietors starkly contrasts with the approach of their female counterparts and again reinforces common gender-based stereotypes both of the home and of this type of micro-hospitality enterprise:

> My wife helps me a lot with the business in the evening when she comes home from work . . . Yes, I must say, she works hard both inside and outside our home. . . . My wife does long shifts at the hospital. She gets annoyed with the business sometimes and complains when she gets in from work that she has no

> peace . . . that she's always working . . . I appreciate how she feels but this is what I do now . . . My wife's a good ten years younger than I am so when I got early retirement I thought well I've got to do something. I've got to do something useful . . . I'm not the sort to laze around doing nothing if you know what I mean? (Male host).

> My wife is a Scots law accountant . . . and an absolutely excellent cook. She took bad to it [opening a guesthouse in the home]. She wasn't keen on it in the beginning but then I thought "well, I've got to do something". So she helps me at the weekend with things like the washing up. (Male host)

It can be seen therefore that gender-based constructions and stereotypes are endemic within this context. These associations are not just evident from descriptions given by both female and male hosts in terms of their interactions with guests, but are also transposed more broadly upon the definitions of their occupational group. These serve to reinforce the significance of gender at a more macro level, thus perpetuating its overlay of meaning onto all actors and wider public perceptions of what it is to be a host of such a business. It is a self-perpetuating cycle that has its inescapable roots in the all-dominant hue of the private home, no matter how cleverly this domain is masked, adorned or separated from the business. Both are co-located and inseparable, and thus mutually reinforcing. Examples of this broader gender depiction of not just themselves/ partners but of their occupational group as a genre are reflected by the following views which demonstrate how men are much more likely to characterize what they do as a "proper" job or occupation and "not just a hobby". This shows a coping strategy or distancing mechanism, away from common female stereotypes of their role, particularly by those men with wives holding alternative paid work. They try to elevate the status of their home-hosting above that of their female counterparts in order to affirm their masculine identities as the highly gendered associations of running a bed & breakfast are for them evidently threatening and demeaning:

> It's not just some kind of hobby for me, it's a business (Male host).

> It's mainly women who do this sort of thing. There are a lot of them who are in it for the social side . . . Well, I like talking to the guests and even sharing a wee dram with them of an evening but at the end of the day I'm not doing this for my health. I'm doing it to make a bit of money. You've got to have that mind set or it's a waste of time really. So, I think I do it differently to a lot of them . . . I've had a long career in the corporate world and to me this is no different. I don't go to all those coffee mornings and what have you and to be frank I don't think they'd want me there anyway. I keep my head down and get the job done (Male host).

These strategies of self-distancing by men in female dominated occupations resemble the findings of other writers.[29] Men may seek to preserve traditional conceptions of masculinity by overtly distancing themselves from female colleagues or feminized working practices. The purpose of these efforts is to elevate the status or perception of their own roles.

Rather than emphasizing the "serious" business side of their occupation, women appeared far more at ease or even modest in describing what they were doing as something "extra," a "hobby" or something "flexible" that they could fit around other demands. They tended to want to emphasize the rewards of autonomy, enjoyment and interest as a key motivation:

> I've been doing this for about the past twenty years. And I continued doing it after first my husband died. It kept me busy and still does. Well, it kept me from being lonely. Even when my husband was poorly I kept it up as it was a distraction . . . yes, a welcome distraction. That is why I continued with it when I remarried as it is what I do and what I am interested in. . . . I like meeting people. I really like it and I can choose who I have to stay and who I don't . . . and if we want to have a break for a week or so then I just shut up shop. I basically can do what I like at the end of the day. It's all up to me (Female host).

Although all proprietors were found to be aware of, and loosely involved, with other bed & breakfast proprietors in their area through mutual beneficial systems of business referrals, few men seemed to participate as actively and eagerly as women in regular social outings or events with other local proprietors. Women showed themselves to be far more engaged in social networks with one another. Therefore, business links with other similarly-minded women running bed & breakfasts and guesthouses were used as a basis for socializing. They appeared to actively enjoy and court not just the reported "companionship" of guests and the interest gained from meeting new people, but also the links and friendships made with other women in the local area running similar home-based hospitality businesses:

> We all work together here actually . . . If I'm busy or if somebody comes to the door and I'm full I'll phone across. We all, you know, we don't turn away anybody . . . we say "well hold on." I'll just check across the road with Sharon or Julia along the road. We all work together. . . . We've all got each others' numbers and if we can't take, you know, we just say "hold on and I can get you somewhere else" because we're all three star kind of thing . . . we're all in the same category. As I say, we're all friends so we all work together (Female host) We're on the phone to each other all the time . . . [to] ask how each others getting on (Female host)

> We normally have nights out kind of thing . . . we go to the next generation sports centre. We're members up there. We try and fit that in two times a week if we can (Female host).

Thus, men tended to emphasize their business acumen and orientation, whereas women spoke at some length about their social concerns although linked to their business acumen and orientation. The latter said that they enjoyed multi-tasking and combining business, social activities, home and family responsibilities together. They saw this as a positive choice which they preferred to the complete separation of home and work. The social relationships stemming from their work-based lives were thus held to be innately important to the value gained from them, as part also of their sense of self identity and group belonging. For instance, a group of about six female hosts living in close geographical proximity to one another even went on short holidays together and had become close friends. They often chose to stay in other bed & breakfasts together when away for such trips in order to compare them with their own businesses and to share in an enjoyable "busman's holiday."

> The four of us [reference to other female B&B owners/friends in the area] were ... speaking about this because we went in the tourist board and I got the tourist brochure and picked some places out of there ... we booked into a three star in Fort William and it was lovely ... They'd just moved in about three years ago and it was all done up (Female host).

Therefore, unlike their male counterparts, the women interviewed in this occupational grouping did not feel the need to elevate the status of what they were doing. On the contrary, they reported feelings of liberation and autonomy in being able to decide upon their own hours, be their own "boss," and enjoy the flexibility of combining family and domestic commitments with remunerated work. Many expressed sentiments such as "I am at home anyway" and "this is what I do anyway so why not get paid for it." Arguably, one could say that this demonstrates entrepreneurial creativity rather than some sort of gendered confinement and meek or passive acceptance of their "role" in the home or society at large. As such, one needs to appreciate the complex dynamics of gendered roles, identities and interactions that belie not just expected traditional gendered norms, but also more ambiguous views and coping mechanisms. These illustrate that these cannot be regarded simply as a heterogeneous group as there are often co-existing dualities of both preference and unease experienced by different hosts faced with managing the many complex gendered, spatial, social and temporal overlaps inherent in this home-work domain on a daily basis.

Conclusions

Using commercial hospitality as the contextual backdrop, this chapter has very much focused on the more traditional small-scale home-based business run by a host and their family such as the bed & breakfast or guesthouse. The bed & breakfast is fixed in location and thus represents in many ways an old mode of technology and more traditional commercial hospitality provision in terms of its longevity and ubiquity as a mainstay of a particularly (some might say peculiarly) British socio-historical heritage with their traditionally female-dominated imagery of the landlady.[30] Nevertheless, it still presents an intriguing shift in our understanding of the respective roles of guest and host within interpersonal interactions playing out within the home due to the introduction to the private sphere of commerce as the logic for interactions between the various space occupants including host and guest. The exchange of money in hospitality provision and consumption has a significant effect in altering the expectations surrounding the host-guest relationship, made more acute when domestic norms, codes and routines become subject to ambiguity in the case of the home business. This is due to the weight attached to the significance of the home space by both host and guest. Indeed, the guest is perceived by the hosts as being attracted to the image of the ideal, traditional home. They are seen to want their expectations of an ideal domesticity, welcoming Scottish hospitality and amenable host to be fulfilled as part of that image. In turn the host, who is wedded to a similar ideal of the traditional home, endeavors to live up to and play out that image for their guest within their home as stage.

Thus, commercial hospitality hosting in the home and its usage for income generation causes ambiguities within what has generally evolved during the industrial era as a site of unpaid domestic labor. This ambiguity is magnified when the host is male as their enactment of socially-accepted norms of traditional masculinity is curtailed by the dominance of the home domain and the expected roles and routines to be found therein.[31] Nevertheless, despite the explicit feminine connotations of bed & breakfast/ guesthouse hosts, they tend to hold a high degree of occupational autonomy and are often homeowners as well as business owners. This differentiates them from individuals working in low-paid roles for commercial hospitality organizations and who hold little occupational autonomy or discretion. Both men and women derive important benefits from their experiences of running these businesses. Men, particularly those running the business whilst their wives hold alternative paid employment outside the home, relish running "proper" businesses from which they derive a sense of independence, autonomy and monetary success. Both men and women appreciate the social interactions of meeting their guests, but women in particular derive most satisfaction from the flexibility afforded to them by being able to generate some extra income whilst combining their multiple roles and responsibilities within the home and family as well as socializing with like-minded individuals. Surely such a fascinating and complex home-work sphere requires greater attention from organizational as well as feminist scholars.

It is also important to address broader social implications and extrapolations from these context-specific insights. There is increasingly a blurring between public and private spaces and places in contemporary society with improvements in technology whereby individuals increasingly have the freedom to work from home or at a distance from traditional places of work, or indeed establish home businesses. The separation between public and private spaces is now increasingly fragmenting, creating more choices and freedoms, but also imposing tensions and ambiguities in terms of spatial and temporal boundary management and separation. The feeling of always being "on call," "at work" or "unable to shut off" despite being at home is thus increasingly an issue for workers, many with fluid working patterns which typify our post-industrial Western world. These workers are increasingly expected to be contactable by colleagues regardless of physical location through the use of increasingly sophisticated and mobile communications technologies. Again, the entrepreneur whose home is simultaneously used a workplace is becoming more common, especially through the use of these new technologies. The development of home businesses with a return to home-based work patterns more typical of pre-industrial times may be more empowering for women than the often alienating, clear-cut separation of work from home and family, more typical of the industrial era.

Thus, this chapter has ventured a look "behind the hearth" of the bed & breakfast as a home sprung and co-located business and family enterprise. I have argued that this neglected arena of boundary-spanning work offers important theoretical, and indeed even political, insights and implications worthy of far greater investigation and critique. To offer my own view, I advocate that the empirical setting of the bed & breakfast, as well as other overlapping home/work domains including other types of home-based businesses and workshops, be explored yet further to unearth the gendered and other insights they would undoubtedly reveal. This will be important for scholars who, like me, are interested in challenging the current overarching dominant focus of workplace research which centers on large organizational bureaucracies. We have much to learn from returning to the home setting, literally and physically, to see what has been left behind, as well as what hues it places upon our working selves. This is key for feminist research, as the separation of domesticity and remunerated employment has tended to further the stereotyping and gendered nature of female roles both within and outside the employment sphere. Politically, such a focus reasserts, and potentially even elevates, the standing and centrality of the home and the variety of work performed therein to the workforce at large and as a hidden [political] economy itself. Ignoring this place of work is to be blind to both socio-historical trends reflecting the ways in which women and other family members have combined work and home, as well as more recent manifestations of flexible working and the enterprising mindset.

1. Traditionally, the man has been referred to as the "host" whereas the woman has generally been referred to as the "hostess." However, for purposes of clarity the word "host" is used throughout as a generic one to include both the male and female role.

2. Erving Goffman, *The Presentation of Self in Everyday Life* (Middlesex, UK: Penguin, 1959).

3. Shelley Mallett, "Understanding Home: A Critical Review of the Literature," *The Sociological Review*, 52, no. 1 (February 2004): 62–89.

4. Witold Rybczynski, *Home: A Short History of an Idea* (London, UK: Heinemann, 1988).

5. Stephen M. Whitehead, *Men and Masculinities* (Cambridge, UK: Polity Press, 2002).

6. Judith Lorber, *Paradoxes of Gender* (New Haven, CT: Yale University Press, 1994).

7. MariaLaura Di Domenico, "'I'm Not Just a Housewife': Gendered Roles and Identities in the Home-Based Hospitality Enterprise", *Gender, Work and Organization*, 15, no. 4 (July 2008): 313-32.

8. Paul Lynch, MariaLaura Di Domenico and Majella Sweeney, "Resident Hosts and Mobile Strangers: Temporary Exchanges Within the Topography of the Commercial Home," in *Mobilizing Hospitality: The Ethics of Social Relations in a Mobile World*, ed. Jennie Germann Molz and Sarah Gibson (London, UK: Ashgate, 2007), 121-43.

9. Bed and Breakfast Association 2009, http://www.bandbassociation.org/ (accessed April 16, 2009).

10. Marc Auge, *Non-Places* (London, UK: Verso, 1995).

11. Yvonne Guerrier and Amel S. Adib, "'No, We Don't Provide That Service': The Harassment of Hotel Employees by Customers," *Work, Employment & Society*, 14, no. 4 (December 2000): 689-705.

12. Dean MacCannell, *The Tourist: A New Theory of the Leisure Class* (Berkeley, CA: University of California Press, 1999).

13. John Urry, *The Tourist Gaze* (London, UK: Sage, 2000), 48.

14. George Ritzer, *The McDonaldization Thesis* (Thousand Oaks, CA: Sage, 1998).

15. Goffman, *Presentation of Self*.

16. MariaLaura Di Domenico and Peter Fleming, "'It's a Guesthouse Not a Brothel': Policing Sex in the Home-Workplace," *Human Relations*, 62, no. 2 (February 2009): 245-69.

17. Jacques Donzelot, *The Policing of Families* (Baltimore, MD: Johns Hopkins University Press, 1997).

18. Bill Bryson, *Notes From a Small Island* (London, UK: Random House, 1996), 16.

19. Louise Howe, *Pink Collar Workers: Inside the World of Women's Work* (New York, NY: Avon, 1977).

20. See for example Rosemary Lucas, *Managing Employee Relations in the Hotel and Catering Industry* (London, UK: Cassell, 1995) or Roy Wood, *Working in Hotels and Catering* (London, UK: Routledge, 1992).

21. Ann Oakley, *The Sociology of Housework* (Oxford, UK: Blackwell, 1974).

22. Goffman, *Presentation of Self*.

23. See for example the following work which gives an excellent critique of impression management and so-called "emotional labor" prevalent in hospitality and broader service sector roles. Arlie Hochschild, *The Managed Heart* (Berkeley, CA: University of California Press, 1983).

24. Anthony Giddens, *Central Problems in Social Theory: Action, Structure, and Contradiction in Social Analysis* (London, UK: Palgrave Macmillan, 1979).

25. Hochschild, *The Managed Heart*.

26. Rybczynski, *Home*.

27. Oakley, *Sociology of Housework*.

28. Arlie Hochschild, *The Second Shift: Working Parents and the Revolution at Home* (London, UK: Piatkus, 1990).

29. See for example Mats Alvesson, "Gender Relations and Identity at Work: A Case Study of Masculinities and Femininities in an Advertising Agency," *Human Relations*, 51, no. 8 (August 1998): 969-1005. Also see Ruth Simpson, "Masculinity at Work: The Experiences of Men in Female-Dominated Occupations," *Work, Employment & Society*, 18, no. 2 (June 2004): 349-68.

30. John Walton, *The Blackpool Landlady* (Manchester, UK: Manchester University Press, 1978).

31. Peter Stringer, "Hosts and Guests: The Bed-and-Breakfast Phenomenon," *Annals of Tourism Research*, 8, no. 3 (1981): 357-76.

Chapter 12
Hospitality in the Doctor's Office[1]
Patricia Boling

This chapter examines the question of hospitality in the oncologist's office from the point of view of cancer patients, oncology care providers, and public recognition for care and those who do the work of providing it, as reflected in health care policies. Joan Tronto identifies four analytically distinct phases of the practice of care: recognizing that care is needed; assuming responsibility for an identified need and figuring out how to respond to it; doing the work of providing care, and responding to the care received.[2] I draw on these distinct notions of care to distinguish between what care-givers and care-receivers think are the ideals of good care are in the context of long term cancer care, and to consider what impact cancer care might have on public and political support for policies that insure appropriate medical care for all.

There are several reasons to consider what hospitality means in the context of long-term cancer care. First, treating cancer patients hospitably matters because cancer is a serious, often life threatening illness, and cancer patients face emotional challenges wrapping their heads around the enormity of the disease; they need sensitive, emotionally supportive care. Furthermore, grasping the particular circumstances, identities, needs, problems and strengths a patient brings to the treatment process may improve levels of satisfaction and treatment outcomes. Second, medical and radiation oncology often involve a long-term course of treatment during which patients and staff members get to know one another and develop a sense of connection and attachment, one in which hospitality seems normal and called for. Third, there are competitive pressures in medical care that militate toward offering hospitable care. Cancer patients frequently seek second opinions and check out more than one care provider in the course of deciding on their physicians and clinics, and how they are treated by doctors and other staff members can affect their decision about where to pursue treatment. A patient who feels regarded as a full person, respected, and treated with empathy and care is more likely to feel satisfied with her treatment than one who does not. At the same time, health care reform, bottom-line pressures, and the need to adopt cost containment measures could lead care providers to spend less time patients and put a squeeze on ameliorative care, hospitality and other non-treatment healing elements. Knowing why hospitality is important might bolster policy arguments for valuing and funding the "non-treatment" side of oncology.

As a way to start thinking about hospitality and patient care, let us consider the etymology of "hospitality"-related words. "Hospitality" is connected to a variety of other words: hospitable, its opposite, inhospitable; hospital, hospice. The *Oxford English Dictionary* tells us that hospitality and hospitable both come from Latin roots by way of French, and that their meaning originally had to do with extending a generous welcome to strangers. Hospital and hospice share the same root as hospitality; both used to carry meanings related to providing a place of rest and entertainment for pilgrims, travelers or strangers, and more recently, institutions for housing poor people or students. Now of course hospitals are places where sick or injured people receive medical care, and hospices are places where people receive end-of-life palliative care.

The notion that hospitality is something extended to pilgrims or strangers travelling in a strange land is resonant; one oncology nurse I spoke with characterized people recently diagnosed with cancer as having embarked on a trip they never planned to take, plunked down in a country they never planned to visit, and having to learn a new vocabulary for dealing with cancer. Other oncology practitioners talk about cancer as a journey, and for many cancer patients, the journey includes visits to or stays in hospitals or hospices. Finding oneself suddenly a cancer patient is an upsetting, life-changing experience. How bad is it? How far advanced? What are my chances? What does treatment involve, and how will it make me feel? Will I be able to go on with my life, my work, my plans? More fundamentally, will I die, or perhaps, how soon? Cancer is fearsome: treatable but not curable, casting a cloud over one's entitlement to live to a ripe old age.

Given the magnitude of this metaphoric journey into the land of mortal illness and major medical treatment, "hospitality" might be defined in terms of the characteristic goals or aspirations of those who provide treatment and care to cancer patients. How consciously do care providers think about welcoming patients into the office, making them feel well-cared for, and meeting their emotional or spiritual needs, and how much do such concerns matter compared to issues of medical expertise? What sorts of needs and expectations do patients bring to treatment, and how well are they met? In the course of my research, it became apparent that patients and different medical personnel—receptionists, nurses, techs, and doctors—define and value hospitality differently, and I describe how different participants in the care process see themselves living up to ideals of care or hospitality. Clearly there are gendered expectations about who should be providing hospitality, how they provide it, and patients' senses of entitlement to warm, hospitable care. I explain where these gendered expectations come from, connect them to structures of power and subordination and to feeling entitled to care rather than dependent on the generosity and good will of care givers.[3] I conclude by suggesting how this study of hospitality in long-term oncology outpatient care might contribute to broader notions of hospitality and care and debates about universal health care.

This chapter is based on research I conducted with cancer care providers and cancer patients. Because I was only able to speak with small numbers of providers and patients, my findings are preliminary and suggestive. I did two focus group discussions with nurses, receptionists, schedulers, and technicians from a medical oncology practice in a mid-sized Midwestern town, and conducted one-on-one interviews with a set of cancer survivors, all of whom had been through extended outpatient treatment in oncology offices or facilities for radiation therapy or chemotherapy or both, some in big cities and others in medium-sized Midwestern towns. Everyone in this group of patients was cancer-free at the time of the interview, and most of them believed that they had a good chance of remaining so. The patients were diverse in terms of the kinds of cancers for which they were treated, gender, and age, but they did not represent much diversity with respect to access to health insurance, class, race or education (the sample was entirely white, middle class, and well-educated). I decided to work on this topic in part because of my own diagnosis and treatment for breast cancer in 2005-2006, a fact I made all my interlocutors aware of during the recruitment phase of the project in order to establish credibility and rapport with them.

Patients

What does hospitality mean or entail to a patient in treatment by an oncologist? One walks in the door, signs in at the receptionist's desk, takes a seat and waits to be called for an appointment. Magazines and newspapers may be lying around, a jigsaw puzzle under construction. Coffee, tea and water are probably available. Interesting art may adorn the walls (though more often than not it resembles "hotel art"). Patients tend to be older, and some of them look haggard, others matter-of-fact and businesslike. Some are waiting with a relative or friend, though most are by themselves. They generally don't talk much with one another, unless they've gotten to know other patients who have appointments on the same days and times.

While the public side of an oncology clinic usually strives for a bit of cheer and warmth, the contrast between the front and back "offices" can be stark. Some patients commented on the physical set up of clinics, which are often intimidating and even scary looking when one gets past the waiting room and is ushered into a suite of leather recliners with business-like IV drips set up side by side, or a chilly room dominated by a steel table, various personalized support devices and masks to insure that the proper body part receives exactly calibrated doses of radiation, and a hulking radiation machine that needs to be screened from weather and from possibly emitting radioactive beams or particles.

More than the physical space, patients mentioned that they were pleased that staff members greeted them, usually by name, with a pleasant exchange. They expected to be recognized, and most patients over the course of treatment got to know most of the nurses and technicians too. People were addressed differently, depending on the clinic; many Midwestern clinics use first names with all patients, though one male patient said he was always addressed as "Mr. X." In contrast to this common Midwestern practice, one female patient said she was called "Ms. Y" at the big east coast university teaching hospital where she was treated. Patients did not express uniform reactions to forms of address that were used; so long as there was recognition, respect and warmth, they seemed to find more and less formal approaches OK. There was however a pattern of cultural "fit" with patients who are native Midwesterners feeling like the clinics/ practices they went to suited them well: the forms of address and friendliness commonly employed "worked" well for them, and they reported readily feeling at ease. Others who diverged from the mainstream—intellectual women, a Jewish woman in an overwhelmingly Christian Midwestern town—noted a bit more tension with their physicians and their doctors' support staff. One patient noted that her surgeon's nurse was curt and rude on the phone when she indicated that she was seeking a second opinion regarding a damaged port. She also mentioned that her doctor was more respectful and nicer to her when her husband was present, experiences which prompted her to switch to a clinic in Evanston (near Chicago) in the middle of an extended course of chemotherapy. Another woman noted that she felt some cultural distance from the nurses who cared for her due to differences in education, class and race, though she felt at ease with her doctors.

All the patients mentioned how important they found their doctors' and nurses' willingness to answer their questions, spend time on explanations, and respond to their concerns with careful explanations. Breast cancer patients noticed what physicians said about the possibilities for preserving or restoring breast tissue during or after cancer surgery; they wanted their doctors to be forthright about such possibilities, and clear and unambiguous about the surgery they recommended. Patients asked many detailed questions about the efficacy of different approaches to treatment and the side effects of the treatments. They noticed and commented on their doctors' ambiguity or unwillingness to answer their concerns fully, something which undercut their confidence and in some cases led them to choose other doctors. They expected their physicians to be professional; in one case, a surgeon's sexualized comments about her breast shape and size decided one patient against having him treat her. Several patients mentioned that they valued their doctors' and nurses' willingness and ability to respond to their spouses. Taking their partners' questions and concerns seriously and addressing them well was important for helping both the partners and the patients feel reassured and more at ease.

All the patients I spoke with indicated it was important to feel that they were being taken seriously by their doctors and nurses, that their concerns were not dismissed, and that their worries about choosing the most efficacious approach to eliminating cancer were addressed professionally and specifically. Although there were differences among patients whose treatment was more straightforward and whose cancers were less imminently less life-threatening, and those who had more complicated or serious prognoses, in every case, high quality medical care trumped issues related to hospitality or "bedside manner": patients did not choose an oncologist because they like the homey living room feeling of the waiting room or the "warm fuzzies" they got from the receptionist or nursing staff, but because they thought they would get the best possible care at his or her office. At the same time, most patients also indicated that personal recognition and emotional warmth were an important part of the ongoing, daily treatment of cancer in the oncologist's office.

Care Providers

I conducted two focus groups with staff members (oncology nurses, staffers responsible for scheduling appointments, billing, and the nurse-practitioner who was the right-hand of the doctor) at a medical oncology office in a medium-size Midwestern town with a diverse population. I also conducted separate one-on-one interviews with the nurse practitioner and physician whose practice this was in order to see what else they could tell me about hospitality issues and to gauge their roles in setting the tone for the practice. These conversations addressed a variety of topics: staff members' aspirations with respect to giving excellent care; the pattern of typical changes that patients go through over the course of treatment; whether the staff members either separately or as a group self-consciously address or think about hospitality issues vis à vis patients; what expressions of appreciation from patients were particularly memorable; what would make their day-to-day jobs easier and more satisfying, and how they respond to the needs of partners, family members and friends who accompany the patient.

The focus group discussions made several things clear: first, practitioners think quite self-consciously, as individuals and as a group, about the care needs of their patients. They realize that patients come from different social and personal backgrounds, and that they bring all kinds of issues and needs into cancer care; they noted that people might be hooked up side-by-side to chemo drips, one of whom can't read and the other a college professor, or one who is shy and anti-social, the other a "talker." Staff members discuss patients regularly, and are made aware of special needs particular patients might have. Staff are assigned to work with patients with no particular effort to "match" them to patients who are similar in style or background—if anything, they are assigned to work with patients who are different from themselves.

Many staff members articulated an ideal of making patients feel that they are loved and cared about; they mentioned empathy, honesty, compassion, physical reassurance (touch, hugs), being attentive, not being distracted; being able to individualize care and adapt to the needs of particular patients, and giving encouragement. They also spoke of working at a high level of skill and competence, and communicating to patients that the staff is giving them the medical care that they need with absolute dependability. As one nurse put it, "my goal is to try to reassure patients when I bring them back for chemo by setting a tone of competence and taking good care of them, conveying that things are being done right--not in the touchy-feely sense of taking a personal interest in them, what they do for a job, their family, and so on, but in a professional, 'we are taking good care of you' sense."

The nursing and office staff spoke of needing to be honest with patients, sometimes brutally honest, and of telling them what they must know about their condition and treatment, but tempering this honesty by paying attention to how they're reacting, watching their patients' eyes. One nurse put it this way: "They feel overwhelmed: it's hard for them to understand and believe that this is happening to them. They don't yet have the tools, words, the lingo for dealing with cancer—it's like a country they never planned to visit, an environment they never planned to be in." Some come to cancer care with a myriad of personal or medical problems that have nothing to do with their cancer; they may not have family members to take care of them, they may be dealing with domestic violence at home, or have been laid off from work, they may not have adequate health insurance, and they have to deal with all this on top of a scary or dire diagnosis and going through treatment.

Staff members endeavor to treat all with kindness and compassion, and to be as available for the shy and quiet as much as for the gregarious and sociable patients who demand a lot of verbal attention. The staff made note of many expressions of gratitude and appreciation from patients and patients' families, ranging from invitations to weddings, to bringing in home-made goodies and Christmas gifts, to bouquets and funny cards, to special gifts and remembrances. Occasionally staffers go out of their way to meet the needs of patients who don't have family or loved ones in their lives, sometimes taking Christmas gifts or food to their homes, or buying them new clothes. Less cheerily, medical personnel are obliged to tell social workers when patients are having problems with which they need help, e.g., not receiving proper nutrition or adequate care at home, even when it makes patients angry or resentful to have their needs reported in this way.

Not all patients are equally easy to deal with, and staffers admitted that there were some patients they would just as soon avoid. But staff members noted that sharpness, unpleasantness or rudeness from patients is not about them, so much as the fraught character of the diagnoses and treatments patients are dealing with. Several spoke of the fact that no one chose to get sick with cancer. One staffer referred to letting unpleasant encounters "roll off my back like water off a duck"; another noted that "not much bothers me." When I asked them about what patients could do to make their workaday experiences happier and more fulfilling, one responded that "we don't expect anything from the patients." I explained that I was interested in trying to articulate an ideal of adult maturity, the capacity to receive care with grace, gratitude and recognition—but even then, the participants in that focus group didn't have much to say on this score.

While I heard little in the way of anecdotes or themes related to feeling annoyed with patients' behavior or rudeness, one nurse commented that patients tend to approach the all-female staff of this particular oncology practice with a sense of treating nurses and staff members a bit like hired help. Generationally, some older people might view women in the helping professions as quasi-servants with whom one can be imperious or demanding; one nurse illustrated this by telling a story of walking across the front waiting room and having one of her patients call at her across the room, "could you bring me a Coke?" A few of the back-room nurses talked about a younger male patient who was overly friendly, and who ogled and touched them in ways they found inappropriate and creepy—but this man was exceptional, and most of the staff said for the most part that ordinary encounters with patients did not ruffle their feathers.

Discussion

I encountered strikingly different discourses about care and hospitality in my patient interviews and caregiver focus groups. From the patients' point of view, at least for this sample of patients who after their initial treatment were cancer-free and looking at good prognoses, their experience with the oncologist's office is about the *beginning* of cancer, an experience that for most people elicited fear, anxiety, hope, questions about the pros and cons of different care options, efforts to "learn the lingo" of cancer and cancer care. Most of the patients talked about their experiences in a self-preoccupied way: they were the center of the drama, the focus of care and sympathy from doctors, nurses and others. They focused on how well their needs were met, and especially on the ability and willingness of care providers to recognize them as people and respond to their questions. Few of my interlocutors had much interest in the spiritual or emotional dimensions of care, a finding consistent with those of other researchers who study cancer patients with a good chance of full recovery.[4] For emotional support, they turned to family and intimates. When asked, few of the patients thought they had changed much over the course of several months of treatment, nor did they say much about connecting with or expressing appreciation to caregivers, many of whom are modestly paid to do hard, emotionally draining work. A few patients commented on lack of rapport or even occasional conflict with nurses and staff members, while staff members reported that they let curtness or rudeness on the patients' side slide off their backs, and chalked up such behavior to the patients' worries about their illness. An exception was an older, semi-retired man who developed warm relationships with the staff who cared for him. He was always ready with a joke or light banter, and often brought treats into the clinic to share with staffers.

In contrast, oncology care providers talked mostly about patients with difficult, advanced or recurrent cancers: these were the patients with whom they worked most intensely, watched struggling with metastatic disease, and to whom they developed attachments. From their point of view, care for cancer patients who are dying is a central dimension of care giving. The nurse practitioner gave me things to read about psychological care and nursing "presence," "a way of being with another person in a setting where the nurse is an instrument for the patient to experience physical and spiritual healing and to help understand what gives his/her life meaning and purpose."[5] From the caregivers' point of view, oncology care is respectful, sympathetic care for people who are seriously ill, many of them struggling with the end of life.

The two sets of perspectives on hospitality may partly reflect the skewed sample of patients with whom I spoke. Because of the snow ball recruitment process I used and the small sample, I ended up talking to a homogeneous sample of well educated, insured, employed, youngish patients with good prospects for long term remission. It was not a very typical group because, as cancer patients go, they were relatively privileged, and this made certain issues hard to explore, such as the impact of race, age, class, lack of education or the severity of their disease. All of them had employment-based private health insurance or Medicare with good supplementary insurance coverage, and all had early-stage cancers that were treated initially with good success. They were lucky on two scores, by virtue of having good resources (friends, family, ready access to information, good insurance coverage), and by virtue of having good prospects for recovery and long-term remission. They could in fact expect to be in long-term care.

Interestingly, this group of patients fits the pattern of people who purchase care "services," a word that Joan Tronto associates with "more powerful, or active, actors [who] command the care work which is provided by care workers," in contrast to when people talk about "care," which usually signals that

> the more powerful, active, actors provide the care work for recipients. . . . Thus, service is a way to receive care without surrendering one's sense of command or autonomy. . . The language of service preserves the illusion of independence and obscures dependence. It permits those who are relatively autonomous and able to act with discretion about how to fulfill their caring needs to rationalize the way in which they depend on others. It permits the myth of market choice to replace the reality of deep interdependency, and it obscures the social and political dimension of our collective need for care. Further, it allows people to continue to avoid recognizing their responsibility for such collective care through a kind of privileged irresponsibility.[6]

My sample group of patients tended to treat cancer care as simply a form of medical care like any other, something that they felt entitled to as part of their employment provided compensation and fringe benefits, and treated in the spirit of well-educated and savvy consumers. At a personal level, of course they understood their need for appropriate, hospitable care for cancer, but the need of our society or state to recognize need, care and dependence as universal experiences did not figure in our interviews.

Who feels obliged to be hospitable, who does not, and why? It seems clear that expectations about care and hospitality are gendered, and that care givers feel responsible to be hospitable to patients, but not vice-versa. Both care providers and patients seem to have internalized an understanding of care, generosity, sympathy, etc. as feminized, in the sense that women are thought to be better at expressing care and concern than men, and in the sense that these virtues are expected of women more than men, especially women in subordinate, hands-on jobs. Female staff frequently mentioned ideals of care that fit with stereotypically feminine notions of warmth, generosity, openness, and empathy. Care givers expected empathy and warmth to be a one-way street in working with their cancer patients; when I asked the focus groups what patients could do to make their jobs happier, there was almost no response. One said "we don't expect anything from the patients."

A couple examples illustrate these gendered expectations about who should provide care, and who is exempt from virtues related to sympathy, patience, good humor, etc. Consider the patient who was angry that the surgeon's nurse was rude to her on the phone; the female nurse was more the focus of the patient's ire than the male surgeon, even though he did not even speak with her about her concerns. Recall the nurse who commented that some patients regard female skilled care providers as akin to hired help or servants. Finally, one of the patients I interviewed who was treated at a clinic where the physician and physician's assistants were male, and rest of the staff was female, commented that she thought the decision to have a mostly female staff might have been an intentional strategy to compensate for the doctor's chilliness.

Patients and care givers alike seemed to take for granted that female care givers should accept patients' bad moods, terseness, being withdrawn or crabby, all the while remaining warm and friendly, enacting and mirroring a gendered set of norms that the staff accepted about care givers being warm and comforting, noticing the needs of the patient without expecting any reciprocity. England et al. note that care work is often viewed as women's work or work done by mothers, and argue that because care is symbolically associated with women and mothering, this affects people's sense of how much the job is worth. "Skills associated with mothering are more likely to be seen as 'natural' and thus, either to be unnoticed or be seen as not deserving of remuneration."[7] If care work is associated with women and mothers, it may help explain the tendency to take care for granted that I observed among patients I interviewed. Patients are entitled to care and hospitality, and it is the job of staff to provide this, tailored appropriately to each patient's needs and circumstances.[8]

This group of patients had little to say about how they treated their care providers, nor was being gracious and generous in terms of noticing or expressing appreciation to care givers something they seem to have thought a lot about. Two things might explain this: first, this group of patients was in the early stages of cancer, and they mostly focused on the treatment-related aspects of care, on eradicating the cancer. The "warm fuzzies" were peripheral considerations for younger, healthier patients who were more concerned with medical or scientific considerations. Secondly, these patients were generally treated with sympathy and concern by friends, acquaintances, and care providers. They *expected* to be treated with warmth and kindness by techs and nurses because that was the kind of behavior they saw exhibited. Daily unstinting generosity and good cheer set the bar for the norms of what they expected. Along with caregivers, patients are participants in a culture where care giving and care of the body's needs are traditionally women's work, and not highly respected.[9]

It is interesting to notice the difference between the needs of relatively well, early-stage patients with good resources (insurance, supportive family and friends), vs. those of seriously ill, perhaps terminal, patients, as it helps account for the different approaches to hospitality of the patient and practitioner samples interviewed here. But both groups saw warmth and care as virtues care givers should show in caring for patients, and neither expected reciprocal consideration from patients toward their caregivers. Beyond this, perhaps this study can illuminate notions of care and hospitality at the level of broader policies and public recognition of the need to care.

Public Recognition for Care

Thus far my discussion has focused on similarities and differences in expectations of hospitality on the part of oncology patients and care providers. The patients with whom I spoke were focused on getting the best possible care for their illnesses, recovering, and going on with their lives; they didn't think deeply about how they treated their care givers, or their role as care receivers, but tended to take for granted that they would be treated in a compassionate, kind, friendly way while receiving radiation or chemotherapy treatments. The care givers had ideals of care in their heads that reflected the intense relationships that develop when they are treating seriously ill patients of being honest, compassionate, thorough and competent. They expected patients to be ill and crabby, and let their grumpiness or unpleasantness slide off their backs. They did not expect or feel entitled to gracious recognition and thanks for their work, though this was certainly appreciated. Both sets (patients and care givers) took for granted the gendered character of hands-on care. Patients and care givers do not have a reciprocal or equal relationship: there was little consideration on the part of the patients with whom I spoke of their dependence upon the care of those who cared for them. Cancer care was more like the simple purchase of care services, like other kinds of medical care except more long-lasting.

How might these insights about hospitality in the world of oncological care be of use for thinking about broader issues related to the systemic approach we take to medical care in the United States? Can they help us think about the on-going debate over health care reform and the difficulties many people have recognizing relationships of care and dependence that Tronto short hands as "privileged irresponsibility"?

Recall that Tronto divides care into four separate practices, 1) *caring about others,* the initial recognition that care is necessary; 2) *taking care* by "assuming some responsibility for the identified need and determining how to respond to it," 3) *care-giving,* the direct physical work of meeting another's needs for care, and 4) *care-receiving*.[10] I have focused on the care giving and care receiving aspects of care, but the other senses of care that Tronto articulates are also relevant to the world of oncology. The first sense of care, the recognition that care is necessary, is the political insight that *all* cancer sufferers are in need of immediate and appropriate care, and that all people (not just those fortunate enough to have jobs that provide health insurance) need regular medical care and screening tests that might detect cancer early. "Taking care" in Tronto's second sense is related to the practical, messy, and also quite political job of ascertaining and passing policies that will assume responsibility for unmet needs and how best to meet them.

With respect to health care, these two aspects of care are enormous problems in the United States, where access to health care is based on employment-based private insurance policies or Medicare coverage for the elderly. "Hospitality" for those who have no health insurance is a huge problem, and one not fully addressed by our public safety net programs like Medicaid or state-level health coverage for the medically indigent. The difficulty of accessing such programs, the limited funds to support them, and the disincentives that people without medical coverage have to seek out ordinary check-ups or screening tests mean there is a greater likelihood that illnesses, including cancer, will go undiagnosed and untreated, and that the disease will be more advanced and serious when it is detected.[11] With jobless rates in early 2010 hovering around 10 percent and large numbers of people who want to work full-time forced to take part time jobs, access to employment-sponsored insurance (ESI) is more than ever an earmark of those lucky and privileged enough to land and keep good jobs.

Considering the provider side of how medical care is structured in the United States, I tried to determine whether oncology is unusual with respect to the degree to which care is feminized. With respect to doctors, oncology as a specialty is not particularly a haven for women. Slightly less than a third of physicians who specialize in internal medicine (the field for which oncology is a subspecialty) are female,[12] and data on members of the American Society of Clinical Oncology indicate that roughly 70 percent of its members are male, 30 percent are female,[13] in line with the overall percentage of female doctors, but lower than the percentages of women who specialize in family medicine and OB/Gyn. Physicians aside, the overwhelming majority of care providers in the cancer-care industry are women,[14] and pressures on cost containment and rising demand are such that reliance on relatively low paid nurses, physicians' assistants, and technicians is increasing.[15] Oncology is an enormous service sector which employs a range of workers with differing degrees of training, education, and pay.[16] Although clinic or office-based treatment by technicians is more common in oncology than many areas of medical care, the move to rely more on physicians' assistants, nurses, nurses' assistants, and relatively low-paid techs and orderlies is a key cost-cutting measure throughout American medicine.

Examining the power dimensions of how medical care in the U.S. is organized, one might see doctors, well-trained nurses (such as the 65 percent of Oncology Nursing Society members who make upwards of $48,000 a year), and middle or upper class people who receive health insurance through their work as the "haves," and less skilled, lower-paid workers and uninsured people as the "have nots."[17] Notions of hospitality and care are overlaid on top of these fundamental divisions of privilege and power. Thus the low-paid tech who takes blood samples all day long is expected to treat the patients she encounters pleasantly and kindly, and to overlook their bad moods and irritableness. Expecting hospitality from others often goes along with treating them as subordinates whose *job* it is to be warm and comforting. Patients who have no insurance to pay for their medical care either pay out of pocket, risking enormous personal debt, or must wait to be seen until they have dealt with the none-too-hospitable public bureaucracy that ascertains eligibility for programs like Medicaid.

The political debate dominating the news as I write in January 2010 over extending affordable health insurance to all and eliminating the practice of private insurance companies of refusing coverage to those with pre-existing conditions (or charging exorbitantly to cover them) underscores the difficulty of deciding to take public responsibility for providing care for the millions of people who get inadequate health care in a system based on private provision of health insurance. The problem is politically intractable because the most powerful citizens in our society—those who are best informed, well organized, who have financial resources and effective interest group representation—have a vested interest in maintaining the status quo, under which they receive high quality care, while a minority has no or inadequate health care. A key stumbling block is that those who currently have benefits will get the same level of care, but pay more, or get less care (due to cost containment or rationing) but pay the same—and neither alternative seems acceptable to the "haves" under the current system, even if such changes are necessary for millions of people who are presently uninsured to have access to similar levels of health care. Unless those who have little to gain in overhauling how we provide medical care can be persuaded to regard care and hospitality as public goods which any decent society should guarantee to all its citizens, altruism will most likely lose out to market-based care and health provision.

This chapter has shown that privileged cancer patients with good prognoses see hospitable care as the norm, simply part of the situation they are in. The feminization of care reinforces the notion that patients can take hospitality for granted. After all, the sick and afflicted are expected to be cranky and self-absorbed, their failure to be other-directed or generous with recognition and thanks is overlooked, seen as part and parcel of taking for granted those who do maternal or women's work, such as caring for the ill, dealing with bodily fluids, and providing encouragement and support. But being the recipients of care, not just of prescribed medical treatment, but of warmth, kindness, sympathy and recognition, might have transformative potential if it helps cancer patients and those close to them realize that hospitality is an important public value that that should inform our health care policies. Connecting the personal importance of receiving care to the political might enable cancer patients to value the work that cancer and other medical care providers do, not just by expressing their personal appreciation, but by fighting for policies that recognize the value of hospitality in the doctor's office by rewarding the humble care givers along with those who have professional degrees, resisting cost-cutting measures that cut corners on the affective elements of cancer care, and fighting for universal access to health care.

Notes

1. I am beholden to a number of cancer patients and oncology physicians and staff members for their help with this project; this chapter is based on discussions with patients and caregivers in the context of on-going care for cancer in medical and radiation oncology offices.

2. Joan C. Tronto, *Moral Boundaries* (New York: Routledge,1993), 106-8.

3. Joan C. Tronto, "Vicious Circles of Privatized Caring," in *Socializing Care* ed. Maurice Hamington and Dorothy C. Miller (Lanham, MD: Rowman & Littlefield, 2006), 3-21.

4. Elizabeth Johnston Taylor. "Prevalence and Associated Factors of Spiritual Needs Among Patients With Cancer and Family Caregivers," *Oncology Nursing Forum* 33, no. 4 (2006): 729-35.

5. Jill H. Anderson, "Nursing Presence in a Community Heart Failure Program," *The Nurse Practitioner* 32, no. 10 (2007): 14-21, 15.

6. Tronto, "Vicious Circles," 16-7.

7. Paula England, Michelle Budig, and Nancy Folbre, "Wages of Virtue: The Relative Pay of Care Work," *Social Problems* 49, no. 4 (2002): 455-73, 457-8.

8. Do men and women expect different kinds of treatment from their oncology staff members, and do oncology staffers expect male and female patients to have different needs or capacities for expressing recognition or appreciation? These are interesting questions, but not ones I can answer, given the limited interviewing I did.

9. Tronto, *Moral Boundaries*; Eva Feder Kittay, *Love's Labor: Essays on Women, Equality, and Dependency* (New York: Routledge, 1999; England et al., "Wages of Virtue."

10. Tronto, *Moral Boundaries*, 106-8.

11. Swartz, Katherine, "Uninsured in America: New Realities, New Risks," in *Health at Risk: America's Ailing Health System—and How to Heal It*," ed. Jacob S. Hacker (New York: Columbia University Press, 2008), 34-5.

12. American Medical Association, "Table 15: Percent Distribution of Female Physicians by Age," *Physician Characteristics and Distribution in the US*, 2008 edition, http://www.ama-assn.org/ama/pub/about-ama/our-people/member-groups-sections/women-physicians-congress/statistics-history/table-15-percent-distribution-female-physicians.shtml (accessed June 28, 2009).

13. Richard Pena, Member Services representative for ASCO, personal correspondence, July 6, 2009.

14. More than 96 percent of the members of the Oncology Nursing Society are female, with membership shifting gradually toward more men (percentages calculated by author). Among new members, 4.0 percent are male; among those who have been members for ten years, 2.2 percent are male, and among those who have been members for fifteen years, 1.6 percent are male. The ONS is one of the major professional organizations for oncology nurses and other professionals; it charges about $100 a year for membership fees and has over 35,000 members. Thus it does not cover all oncology-industry workers, only those with professional aspirations. (Oncology Nursing Society (ONS), home page information on members, 2009. http://www.ons.org (accessed June 30, 2009).

15. American Society of Clinical Oncology (ASCO), Press release, "With an Oncologist Shortage Looming, Leading Cancer Groups Study New Solutions: New ASCO Workforce Study, Funded by Susan G. Komen for the Cure® Will Examine the Role of Non-Physician Practitioners in Treating Cancer Patients," http://www.asco.org/portal/site/ascov2 (accessed June 30, 2009). Of the eleven oncology staff members I interviewed, eight had a high school degree (perhaps with some college or professional training), and three had bachelor's or more advanced degrees. These staffers covered a range of positions, e.g., receptionist, billing clerk, appointment clerk; many were not involved in direct patient care.

16. According to the 2004 Oncology Nursing Society (ONS) member survey, "Most frequently, the respondents' primary positions were described as direct patient care providers (47 percent) or nurse managers (26 percent). Current salary ranged from $15.01 to more than $30 an hour, with 29 percent reporting more than $30 an hour and 36 percent reporting $24.01-$30 an hour" (Anne M. Ireland, Judith A. DePalma, Linda Arneson, Laurel Stark, and Judy Williamson, "The Oncology Nursing Society Ambulatory Office Nurse Survey," *Oncology Nursing Forum* 31, no. 6 (November 2004). Based on working full time for 50 weeks a year, this works out to 65 percent of the ONS members surveyed earning more than $48,000 a year, and 35 percent earning less than that. But ONS members represent a relatively professionalized cohort of oncology industry employees.

17. Swartz, "Uninsured in America," provides data that link lack of employer sponsored insurance to people who are younger, those with less education, and those who earn less.

Chapter 13

Providing Hospitality In Mid-Nineteenth-Century West Virginia Cities

Barbara J. Howe

"WANTED. By applying immediately at the Franklin Hotel, a GOOD FEMALE COOK can find steady employment."[1] "BLACK BEAR BURRITOS now accepting resumes for full time prep cook. . . . Apply within 132 Pleasant St."[2] Those two ads appeared 144 years apart, the first in May 1865 in Wheeling, West Virginia, and the second in June 2009 in Morgantown, West Virginia. The first could specify the employer wanted a woman. By 2009, that was illegal, but women do work at Black Bear, and a woman is co-owner. The two ads, so similar in language, show the essentially unchanged roles of those providing hospitality over that span of time. Indeed, one might argue that this sector of the economy has changed less than any other in terms of job descriptions, for it is still based on providing food, drink, and lodging, as regulated by state and local governments. Some of the major changes in providing hospitality, such as laws regulating wages, board of health regulations, and fire marshals insuring public safety, and, occasionally, workers organizing in unions, do not override the basic "products."

Cities have always been magnets for those seeking work, and this essay focuses on women's roles in providing hospitality in three communities—Wheeling, Parkersburg, and Martinsburg—in that part of Virginia that became the new state of West Virginia in 1863. As transportation centers and county seats, they were centers of hospitality for travelers and those doing business at each county courthouse. Beyond that, though, their diverse economies, demographics, and geographic settings provide multiple perspectives, focusing primarily on women's roles.

European Americans founded Wheeling in 1769. The city's location on the Ohio River, the National Road (which roughly parallels Interstate 70 today) after 1818, and the Baltimore & Ohio Railroad after 1852 made it a major transportation center for those heading west and provided the most opportunities for women to provide hospitality. The city grew from 5,221 residents in 1830 to 19,280 in 1870, making it the largest city in Virginia west of the Appalachian Mountains and the most heavily industrialized city in western Virginia, with glass factories, breweries, iron foundries, cotton and woolen mills, and merchant tailor firms. It was the most ethnically diverse city in Virginia, with a large population of Germans and Irish but very few African Americans before the Civil War because free African Americans needed legal permission to stay in Virginia, and freedom was across the river in Ohio or nearby in Pennsylvania. The county seat of Ohio County, Wheeling was the capital of the Restored Government of Virginia during the Civil War and the first capital of West Virginia.[3]

Parkersburg, the county seat of Wood County, is on the Ohio River at the mouth of the Little Kanawha River, so it became an early important shipping center along both rivers, as well as the terminus of the Staunton (Virginia)-to-Parkersburg Turnpike. The first settlement took place in 1773. In 1857, a branch of the Baltimore & Ohio Railroad reached the city, and Parkersburg was eventually linked to rail lines running to Cincinnati and from Wheeling to Charleston along the Kanawha River. By 1860, Parkersburg had 2,493 residents; with 5,546 residents in 1870, it was the second largest city in the state, thanks to the discovery of oil in nearby Wirt County.[4]

Martinsburg, the county seat of Berkeley County, was incorporated as a village in 1779 and as a city in 1860. The Baltimore & Ohio Railroad reached Martinsburg in 1842, and the city's economy revolved around the railroad and its role as the regional marketing center for the surrounding agricultural lands. The city suffered heavily during the Civil War, changing hands between Union and Confederate forces ten times. In 1860, Martinsburg had a population of 3,364, making it the second largest city in what would become West Virginia, and it was the only city in this study with a significant number of enslaved people. By 1870, it had a population of 4,863. This city reflected the southern, pro-slavery orientation of the rest of eastern Virginia, and its inclusion here allows the opportunity to look at how slavery affected women's roles in providing hospitality before the war.[5]

With examples from these cities, this essay provides a case study in documenting women's roles in the commercial enterprise of providing hospitality in the past, with some speculation on gender relationships. While this anthology focuses on feminism and hospitality, it is not possible to ascribe feminist motives to the women who worked in these businesses 150 years ago for they lived before the word "feminism" came into usage at the end of the nineteenth century. Also, without personal papers like diaries, memoirs, and letters, we can only speculate about WHY they provided hospitality and how they saw their relationships with their spouses or other family members and with the men and women who were their customers, co-workers, employers, and, in the case of enslaved women, owners. For example, these relationships must have varied, in part, based on the length of time the hosts and employees knew the guests. Today, hotels are for transient guests, but, then, hotels were also more permanent residences for individuals and families in lieu of apartment houses, so it is certainly conceivable that some host-guest relationships were collegial or friendly instead of strictly business relationships.

We should care about the women who operated and worked in taverns, coffee houses, boarding houses, and hotels because they provided vital services to the city's residents and visitors and because some of the issues they faced are still with us today. Balancing work and family must have been as important for working women then as it is now, and some of these women addressed that by having their children or other family members living with them in the hotels or boarding houses where they worked. In the days before corporate ownership of hotels, the owner/manager also usually lived in the hotel with his/her family. While we do not know what role a wife may have played in the daily operation of the hotel, surely she benefitted from the services of the hotel's cooks and chambermaids. Women who were hotel owners and boarding house keepers regularly interacted with more men than women as guests, and, as the illustrations below show, the customer was not always right. There is only fragmentary evidence of employer-employee interactions, with no evidence of whether there were gender differences in such treatment. There were also definite gendered dimensions to space in these establishments. Women guests in large hotels used the "ladies' parlors," perhaps with the wife of the hotel keeper there as hostess, and men used the "gentlemen's parlors" and smoking rooms, again perhaps with the male hotel keeper as host. Women employees were usually relegated to the "hidden" parts of the establishment, i.e., as hotel washwomen and kitchens, or had access to guests' rooms only to clean them, while male employees provided more direct personal services as dining room waiters, hostlers, porters, and bar tenders. Hotels needed hostlers to care for the horses of their guests or of the coach lines that brought guests to the hotel.

Reconstructing women's roles in these cities must be done through surviving public records, recognizing that census enumerators were often inconsistent in their terminology, which means it is sometimes difficult to compare data between jurisdictions. Also, the census privileged information about males as it did not identify all household residents before 1850 and did not give occupations for females over fifteen before 1860. These records give few glimpses into women's personalities, as the stories we might most want to know would not have been deemed worth recording, even if those women were literate. However, occasionally, we can get glimpses through newspaper accounts of their interactions with men, especially if violence was involved in any way. While some of the stories below will read like accounts from a tabloid gossip columnist, the *Wheeling Intelligencer* was the most influential newspaper of its day in western Virginia, and its use of stereotyped language toward minorities was common.

As examples of these newspaper vignettes from Wheeling illustrate, hosts and employees could be victims of violence or face occupational hazards. Two Irish women, Biddy Baggs and Ellen Salvatin, were servants at Beymer House in the fall of 1858, when two men grabbed them near the Second Ward Market House and tried to drag them into the stables. The women "employed their 'sweet Irish brogue' in making a terrific cry for help," and the hotel proprietor chased the men away.[6] In April 1863, a man broke into the room of a servant girl at the Swan House and stole $10 from her trunk, a substantial sum of money.[7] John Johnson, an African American waiter at the Sprigg House was guilty of the "unpardonable offence" that was "committed sometimes by white men, namely, striking a woman." In this 1866 case, the woman was a hotel pastry cook. Johnson told the unnamed woman of "his contempt of such pies, &c.," and she was "immensely indignant that a 'nagur'" should dare criticize her. Her reply "rouse[d] the hot African blood" of Johnson, leading to the strike.[8] This was the only incident the author has discovered where racial differences impacted relationships between whites and free people of color, but it is unlikely it was the only one. Frank West was already drunk when he "wanted to be more inebriated." The saloon keeper refused to serve him, so West "made an onslaught on the saloon keeper," and, in the process, hit "Mrs. Saloon keeper." The police arrested West.[9] Mrs. James Turton kept a tavern with her husband. When he "accused her of being too familiar with other men during his absence," she falsely denied the accusation. That led to such a "racket" that two police officers came into the house and arrested them both.[10] Mrs. McNess had to seek help from Sergeant McDonald when James Copeland, her nephew and boarder, chased her and her daughter out of her boarding house when he was drunk. McDonald arrested Copeland, who paid his fine and returned to the boarding house to renew his drunken ranting. McNess called the police again, and two officers carted him off to jail.[11] Mary Muffiny, a chambermaid at the McLure Hotel, made the news when she slipped and fell down through an open space thirty-five feet from the third floor to the first floor. A "gentleman," presumably a guest, caught her "and turned her around so she fell on her side." Fortunately, she broke no bones.[12]

Some of the Wheeling women were not afraid to resort to verbal or physical violence, although that is obviously an anathema to the notion of "hospitality." They definitely did not act is if the "cult of true womanhood," with its precepts of piety, purity, domesticity, and submissiveness to men, that was so prominent at the time applied to them. When a drunken unnamed Irishman tried to rape his landlady in her bedroom, "she defended her castle and her honor with a broom and a pair of tongs."[13] A "young woman employed in some subordinate capacity" at the Monroe House attacked a male resident, whom she thought had been pursuing her with his "pretty talk." When she noticed that he no longer seemed interested in her and "had betrayed her confidence," she grabbed a pistol and was about to shoot him when he ran up the stairs, locked himself in his room, "and bawled lustily for assistance." Others came to his rescue and sent the woman away in a coach.[14] Cecelia Cashmar, who owned a whiskey shop, was arrested in 1857 after trying to hit Mrs. Meyer with a hatchet. Her shop was known for being disorderly with many "boisterous difficulties" going on. She paid a $3 fine.[15] When she was then arrested for selling liquor without a license, the city sergeant suggested that a German husband might solve her problems because she claimed that, as a widow, she had to work to eat. Cashmar told him "she would marry a 'country born, a baboon, or a Turk, but never a Dutchman.'"[16] When two young men at Mr. Cline's beer saloon decided they did not like their drink and threw it out, Mrs. Cline "interpreted this act as indicative of a reckless indication to kick up a row." She made it a point "never to disappoint her patrons," so she picked up a poker and started beating them. Fortunately, neither of the men was badly hurt.[17] Mrs. Rohan ordered a drunken Robert McBride out from behind the counter of her eating stand at the fairground. When he did not leave on his own, she "ejected him summarily." McBride returned, pulled out a knife, and "said he would slaughter Mrs. R. like a sheep." She had him arrested.[18] Mrs. Denie got so mad at a male tenant that she had him arrested. The unnamed tenant had earlier had a "falling out" with her and her husband when the tenant intimidated that, if Mr. Denie were not so old, he would "beat him within a very short distance of his life." The tenant must have left the Denies' home, but Mrs. Denie "assumed the championship of the house and abused the tenant whenever she met him—in the market, on the street, and in his house, until she became a positive bore, when he had her arrested and fined." In turn, Mrs. Denie had the tenant arrested for the earlier argument with her husband. The alderman hearing the case dismissed it and charged the costs to Mrs. Denie.[19] Mrs. Mountain and her female boarder, both Irish women, fought over "some unknown cause." The boarder defended her rights "and a combat uproarious, both 'going in' glorious" resulted. "Eyes, faces and noses, arms, bodies and toeses [sic], with scratches and bruises abound, till in embrace so loving, by pushing and shoving, both heavily fell to the ground." Neighbors finally pulled the two apart.[20]

Wheeling employees could also commit crimes against their employers or guests. In 1862, a "girl named Reynolds, employed as a domestic at the Union House," stole some coffee and tea from the hotel and was boarding a boat on the Ohio River when she was caught. The male police officer successfully searched her skirts and found the items. He let her leave without further ado, though, "in consideration of her piteous appeals."[21] At least one guest found his own way to redress his grievances against employees. The man lived at a boarding house and had the last laugh when the female servants pressured him "to supply them with bears [sic] grease, eau de cologne &c., at a rather heavy expense." Even after labeling the bottles with a "raw head and bloody bones" to indicate the contents were poisonous, the girls knew he was tricking them and kept taking the contents. In desperation, he filled a bottle with "a thick, tenacious, sticky fluid, very destructive when applied to the hair." That proved to be an effective deterrent, as the chambermaids were soon sporting white handkerchiefs around their heads.[22] Ellen Brady, a pastry cook at the McLure House, took the train to Fairmont in January 1863, allegedly carrying "rebel mail." When she reached Fairmont, some women searched her, on orders from officials in Wheeling. Brady soon returned to Wheeling and took the oath of allegiance to the Union. While the newspaper reported that "no particular attention is attached to the woman herself or her actions," she had "been frequently found in suspicious conversations with prominent rebels, who appear to be making a tool of her." Brady was listed in the 1860 census as a twenty-three-year-old born in Ireland and working as a domestic at the McLure House. Perhaps, she had had those conversations with people she met through her work at the hotel, for how else would a cook meet "prominent rebels"?[23]

Aside from the scattered accounts above, the women who owned ordinaries ("an inn, public house, tavern, etc., where meals are provided at a fixed price"), houses of private entertainment (providing food and lodging but no alcoholic beverages), coffee houses, saloons, hotels, and boarding houses left better records of their lives because they had to receive licenses from the county court (now the county commission), often on the recommendation of the city council.[24] This meant that any woman seeking to be in those businesses had to prove that she met the requirements for these licenses to the men who were members of the city council and county court. Men also enforced the laws at the state and local levels that regulated these establishments and collected the required taxes.

In May 1836, the City of Wheeling passed an ordinance related to granting licenses to keepers of ordinaries, inns, taverns, and houses of public and private entertainment. Those getting licenses had to be of "good order, sobriety & honesty, and [prove] their ability to provide & keep good & sufficient houses, lodging and entertainment for travellers [sic], their servants & horses." They could not be "addicted to drunkenness or gaming."[25] If they violated the law while providing hospitality, the women dealt with the legal system. Ellen Sullivan, for instance, appeared before the aldermen who ran the Wheeling municipal court on several occasions after the Civil War for selling liquor on Sunday in violation of the city ordinance.[26]

A married woman business owner could obtain a license in her own name, although she had no property rights of her own under common law. Under the legal system of equity, she could acquire a "separate estate," meaning "she could own property and exempt it from her husband's control, in some cases exercising the same rights as a man." The main drawback to equity was the implication that the husband was incompetent.[27] This law also meant that widows, like Christenah Beymer (discussed below), or single women had to assume the risks of operating their own businesses but could also reap the profits of providing hospitality to support themselves and any dependents in ways that married women could not unless they could prove their husbands to be incompetent—which could have led to interesting gender relations within the household! Addressing the lack of such property rights for married women was a primary cause for woman's rights advocates in the mid-nineteenth-century, far more important and immediate than the right to vote. There was no such woman's rights movement in antebellum Virginia, though, and there would be no change in the law until 1868.

Married women or widows who managed hotels and boarding houses could care for their families and boarders under one roof, perhaps having their children help with the chores. Running a small hotel or boarding house also required many of the same skills as managing a successful home, i.e., cooking, cleaning, and doing laundry for residents or supervising employees who did this work. Those employees we can identify lived in the hotels and boarding houses in exchange for room, board, wages, and some more companionship than being the sole live-in servant for a family, an isolating position that could demand round-the-clock service. One can imagine that this arrangement might have been especially appealing to single women because it allowed them to live apart from their families with more independence than they would have had if working for a family. Women who were the live-in domestic servants at places like August Rolf's coffee house, though, might have had almost constant responsibilities, caring for the owner's household and/or working in the coffee house.[28]

In the 1830s, in Wheeling, married women (presumably widows) who owned boarding houses specified that they were looking for gentlemen as boarders, and it is unlikely that respectable women would have been moving to the city alone to live with strangers.[29] Boarding houses provided a vital service to urban transients well into the twentieth century because single people moving to a city to find employment did not live on their own in apartments as they do now. Boarding meant getting your room and board (meals), plus possible laundry services, for one price, perhaps even from someone from your home country if you were an immigrant. That could help ease the adjustment to living in a new location, which could be seen as another form of hospitality.

In fact, in one case in Wheeling in 1866, one might argue that the boarding house provided a much too easy way to ease that adjustment. A "gentleman boarder," who had a wife and children and "standing and influence in the community," was doing business in the city, *sans* family, and introduced a woman to the landlady at his boarding house. The beautiful woman attracted the attention of young men at the boarding house but "conducted herself with the utmost propriety," associating "with the most respectable ladies, and not a breath of suspicion rested upon her." However, one day, when the "*femme de chambre*" who worked at the boarding house went to the gentleman's room to make his bed, she discovered that the bed and pillows were "inviolate." Inhaling "the odor of a diminutive rodent," the *femme de chamber* knew the man had come in the night before, found the evidence of his whereabouts when she went to the woman's room, and went to tell her landlady, who was indignant. That night, the landlady peeped through the keyhole of the woman's room, saw the two together, and rapped on the door. The woman opened the door, and "the landlady boiled over. She enunciated her opinions with the utmost swiftness and distinctness. She plainly stated what course the lady and gentleman must pursue." Caught, the man knew "he was ruined" and left the scene "with a heavy heart." The next morning, the lady, with her face covered by a veil, left Wheeling by train.[30]

Women who operated these businesses faced risks other than the threat to their reputations implied in the story above and were not afraid to demand redress of their grievances. If necessary, they would seek the assistance of law enforcement officers to demand justice or might undertake to resolve the problem with a troublesome tenant themselves. Mary Ann Richardson, for instance, posted a notice in the *Wheeling Gazette* in 1830, announcing that William Lackey, a carpenter, had absconded from her boarding house, owing her for his board and money she had lent him. He was not the first, as "several others have acted in a like ungenerous and unjust part towards me—and I am determined hereafter to publish the names of all who are thus mean enough to cheat a widow."[31] Almost forty years later, when an unnamed woman discovered a boarder was going to abscond without paying his bill, she went to a justice of the peace for help. Fearing the man would leave before she could get the proper legal paperwork to force him to pay, she asked another boarder to enter the scofflaw's room and remove all his clothing while he slept. In the morning, the landlady told him he could have his clothing when he paid his bill. He paid up, she pulled his clothing out from her hiding place behind the woodpile, and he "left immediately, with a more lively apprehension, no doubt, of a lady's acuteness in devising modes of accomplishing her object."[32]

Nor were the women afraid to go to the men who worked at the *Wheeling Intelligencer* and demand that the paper correct mistakes in stories about them. For example, Mrs. Keline complained in 1860 that the paper reported that she was fined for selling liquor. In fact, she had only been fined for selling "ale, beer, &c." without a license. Not disputing the fine, Keline wanted "her character vindicated before the world, as a dealer only in light drinks."[33] Mrs. Martin also complained that the paper had said she was selling liquor without a license in 1862. She wanted the public to know that she had a license and would not sell "contraband beverages" without it.[34]

Combining a variety of historical records can help us document the story of one woman who played a prominent role in the business of providing hospitality in Wheeling. Christenah (also sometimes known as Christiana or Christianna) Beymer operated an ordinary or house of private entertainment at the corner of Main and Ninth streets, a prime location near the Ohio River where the National Road joined the river. She was the widow of Capt. Frederic Beymer, who had had a tavern and kept boarders in Wheeling as early as 1802.[35] Christiana first appeared in the Ohio County court records in 1813 and first had a license in her own name in 1819, a year after her husband last appeared there.[36] The next year, the census taker identified twenty-one people in her household, including four enslaved males and two free African American males, but the census would not identify women's occupations for another thirty years.[37] In the 1830 census, Beymer was the head of a household of twenty-two people, including nine white men between the ages of twenty and thirty, one woman between the ages of sixty and seventy (undoubtedly Beymer), and six enslaved people, including two boys under the age of ten, two males between the ages of ten and twenty-three, one female between twenty-four and thirty-five, and one female over fifty-five.[38] There is no way to know if or how these enslaved individuals may have been related to each other or, again, what their specific jobs may have been. On May 8, 1832, Beymer received a license to operate an ordinary at her home from the Ohio County Court after producing a sheriff's receipt for the required tax and entered into a bond with proper security, as well as certifying that she was a person "of honesty, probity & good demeanor."[39] Again, all the officials she would have encountered in the business of providing hospitality would have been men, but, here, as an established businesswoman and widow of a respected businessman, she likely would have encountered these men on a reasonably equal basis.

Beymer got her first license to operate an ordinary from the City of Wheeling in 1836.[40] The 1839 city directory identified her as an "innkeeperess" who operated a hotel.[41] Christenah Beymer was the head of her twenty-six-person household in 1840. She was almost certainly the woman between seventy and eighty, and there was another white female between the ages of ten and fifteen. She clearly operated in a male-dominated arena, even though she was in charge. There were fourteen men in the household, most of whom were between the ages of twenty and thirty, so these were probably boarders; eight of the fourteen were employed in commerce. Among the twenty-six were seven enslaved persons: two males between the ages of twenty-four and thirty-six, three females between the ages of ten and twenty-four, and two females between the ages of twenty-four and thirty-six.[42] This likely made her one of the largest owners of enslaved people in the city, the majority of whom have remained nameless.

On December 31, 1845, Beymer received permission from the Wheeling city council to transfer her license to keep an ordinary to Samuel Beymer, the son with whom she ran the business.[43] She was apparently out of the business completely by 1850, as the census then just identified her as an eighty-one-year-old woman, born in Pennsylvania, who owned real estate worth $5,000, a handsome sum at the time, and who shared her household with two African American men, one of who was named Hyram Beymer.[44] We do not know if that was his choice to use that last name, but we do know the two men would not have been enslaved if they were listed in her household by name and that they would have needed permission to stay in the state if they were free. Neither she nor her son was listed as an owner in the census's slave schedule that year. However, in March 1854, she freed two of her women slaves, Caroline and Frances.[45] Beymer lived a long life and apparently prospered in her business, as, in the 1860 census, she was eighty-six years old, with $8,000 in real estate and $500 in personal property.[46] Census enumerators relied on what people told them as they went door-to-door, as they do now when people mail in their information, so they would not have known that Beymer aged only five years in a decade! Mrs. M.J. Rohan took over ownership of Beymer House in the summer of 1860.[47]

The only other Wheeling reference to enslaved women providing hospitality was in 1858. At that time, a mulatto enslaved girl had done housework by hire for a Wheeling tavern keeper for twenty years and had two children by him. Overburdened by debts, the man sent the unnamed woman and their two children off on a trip by boat to Cincinnati, selling them to the person who was to "take care" of them on the trip. Instead of landing in Cincinnati, where she would be free, she was taken off the boat across the river in Kentucky, a slave state.[48] There is no further record of her, the children, or the man who cared so little about them that he was willing to send them away.

At least eleven Wheeling women operated boarding houses by 1860. Ten of these were heads of households, putting them in positions of authority, at least within their own homes. The youngest household head was just twenty-two, but eight of the others ranged in age from forty to fifty-nine. One of the eleven was born in England, three in Ireland, and the others in the United States.[49] These were just the women whom census takers identified as keeping boarders. While many other women may have kept boarders, the census did not then specify the relationships among all members of the household. Therefore, we one can only speculate whether those whose last names differed from the household head's were boarders, either strangers or relatives sharing the family's home. These varying scenarios would have resulted in different gender relationships between the woman household head and other male residents, but it would be pure speculation to try to unravel them.

Immigrants and free people of color who lived at the hotels provided hospitality in Wheeling in 1860. The McLure House, the city's premier hotel, then employed fourteen Irish immigrant women as domestics and a Virginia-born housekeeper. The employees the thirty-two resident guests and manager would have seen most often were the ten male waiters, including seven African Americans or mulattos, and two male porters (one African American and one mulatto). Therefore, any gender relationships among the staff would have had the extra factor of inter-racial relationships between immigrant women and free men of color.[50] Seven smaller hotels apparently relied on female family members as staff or employed from one to four women each, including three Irish and seven Germans, but the only identifiable male employees were three hostlers, one cook, and two waiters.[51]

We can surmise something about the work environment in a large hotel from an 1853 description of the McLure that mentioned wash rooms (laundry rooms) with vats connected to water and steam pipes so that the clothes "may literally be said to be washed by steam" and ironing rooms with a West & Duncan Patent Mangle in the basement, plus a drying room with steam-heated pipes so that clothes from the ironing room could be hung on them. In the kitchen, everything was cooked by steam, including eggs "cooked by pouring in steam upon them," but there was also a "roasting apparatus," "cake furnace," "baking furnace," a "huge tea kettle," and a "large plate warmer." The dining room could seat 225, and there were 150 sleeping rooms that could house some 300 people. With the men working elsewhere, the women would have been the ones working around the hot steam, preparing the food, washing the clothes, and cleaning the rooms.[52] The servants were "in the highest degree attentive and obliging," but those guests saw most often were the men.[53]

In Parkersburg, Irish and free people of color also provided hospitality in 1860. Two Irish women worked for Thomas S. Conley, proprietor of the Swann House hotel, as "house servants," while men were the "stuard" (steward) and "assistant steward." There were only two residents at this hotel, in addition to the family, so this establishment served a transient population. Charles and Rebecca Murray, a house servant and washwoman, respectively, may also have been on the staff, although they lived next door with their two young daughters. They were a family of free African Americans.[54] The two Irish women who were "house servants" for William A. Tefft, proprietor of the United States Hotel in Parkersburg, worked with the men who were the porter, "stuard" (steward), and hostler to care for the twelve resident guests and members of Tefft's family.[55] The two women who owned hospitality-related businesses that year were also both Irish. Sixty-year-old Mary A. Coneys ran a boarding house, although no one except two younger women who were family members lived there. Given Coneys's later reputation, this may not have been a legitimate business. Finally, seventy-six-year-old Johannah Burns ran a bar room.[56]

Meanwhile, in Martinsburg, slavery played an important role in the hospitality business by 1860. Mary Oden, one of two women operating boarding houses then, was forty-five years old and may have been a widow, as her household included four young adults with the same last name in addition to her four boarders.[57] She owned two female slaves, a forty-nine-year-old black woman identified as a fugitive from the state in 1860 and a seven-year-old black girl.[58] Henry Staub, George Ramer, and William Reamer were hotel keepers who owned a total of eighteen enslaved people (ten females and eight males); one of Reamer's women and one of Ramer's men were fugitives from the state. None identified any employees living at their hotels, as happened in Wheeling and Parkersburg, so we can only conclude that the unnamed enslaved people provided all the services for guests and the owners' families.[59] We cannot know much about their working conditions, but the City of Martinsburg regulated slavery in 1860 by saying that anyone found laboring or employing his apprentice, servant, or slave in labor or other business, "except in household or other work of necessity, or charity &c" shall forfeit and pay a fine of not less than $5 nor more than $20 for each offense. Every day this happened was a separate offense, and any informer would receive half of the forfeiture or fine.[60] Presumably, hotel work was considered household work. Three other men who were hotel keepers in the census had no resident employees, and none can be identified as owners in the census's slave schedule.[61] Perhaps they hired slaves who lived with their owners but worked at the hotels. The only other hotel owner, Jno. Kennedy, employed an Irish chambermaid to work with a male waiter to care for his seven residents and his family.[62]

During the Civil War, businesses providing hospitality found new challenges and new opportunities. Union soldiers were stationed in Wheeling and Parkersburg throughout the war, as both cities were major staging areas for troops headed east, while Martinsburg was a battleground. And, in Wheeling, women who ran boarding houses found new boarders among delegates in town for the various conventions that lead to the creation of the new State of West Virginia and then for sessions of the West Virginia legislature.[63] There is less information about Martinsburg during the war because the city was so devastated that few records survived. It would be interesting to know if any of these women who opened new businesses or moved into hotels with their children during and after the war lost their husbands during the war, but there is no evidence of that to date.

The war also complicated gender relationships between women who ran saloons and soldiers who wanted to be their guests. On October 15, 1861, at the request of military officials, the Wheeling City Council passed an ordinance similar to one that Congress had passed for Washington, D.C., prohibiting the sale of liquor to soldiers. Anyone "convicted of selling, giving, or administering liquor, knowingly, to officers or soldiers, or those wearing the uniform of soldiers," was subject to a fine of $10 to $20. If the person could not pay, the offender was to work out the fine on a chain gang.[64] When a circuit court judge dismissed the charges against saloon keepers who appealed their fines, the provost marshal in charge of martial law in Wheeling took over enforcement in 1862.[65] A soldier who came to Mrs. Collins's tavern in May 1863 "abused her outrageously" when she refused to serve him whiskey. She called the police, who took the soldier to jail.[66] Anne McCluskey did, in fact, sell "intoxicating drinks" to soldiers and was fined $20 and court costs in June 1865. When she broke the law by selling such drinks on Sunday, she was fined an additional $10 and costs.[67]

In Parkersburg, Mary A. Coneys was very well known to the Wood County Court during the war years. In November 1861, the grand jury indicted Coneys for unlawful retailing of ardent spirits.[68] The following June, the Commonwealth of Virginia indicted her again for unlawful retailing of ardent spirits. She pleaded "not guilty," but the jury did find her guilty and fined her $60, plus costs.[69] In December 1863, the State of West Virginia indicted her for two more counts of unlawful retailing, which were eventually dismissed in April 1864.[70] At other times, beginning in October 1863, Coneys was also charged with petit larceny, with co-defendant Frances McCombs, but these charges were finally dismissed in June 1865.

Even those women who tried to run honest businesses during the war faced challenges. Mrs. Rohan ran a boarding house in Wheeling in 1862 and, when one of her boarders, Charles Tyan, came down with the measles, she "gave him every attention, furnishing him with all the little comforts and delicacies which sick people so much need and desire." Tyan recovered, went back to work as a cordwainer (shoemaker), and continued to stay at Mrs. Rohan's. One day, though, "the ungrateful rascal stealthily carried out of the house all his clothing and other valuables, and left for parts unknown, without paying his board." The *Wheeling Intelligencer*, in reporting the story, found Tyan's "ingratitude" even "more shameful and apparent" because he was "known to have had plenty of money."[71] It is unlikely she ever got her money, as it would have been very difficult to track him down.

There was also trouble in Mrs. Ellen Robinson's boarding house. Robinson, a widow, was the only woman of color identified as running a boarding house. One evening in 1863, her two male boarders and their two male friends were drunk after dinner and "tumbled into Mrs. Robinson's beds, like a lot of horses, with their shoes on." Seeing them like this, Robinson angrily told them "that that sort of lolling around did not suit her." The boarders paid their bills and stalked out of the house, with one insulting her by "touching her character for chastity." Robinson did not allow "*any* nigger to talk to her in that manner," and later remembered that she was surprised she did not shoot him on the spot. Instead, she pushed them out of the house with a poker and, the next day, went to the police to have the insulter arrested. He was fined $5.50.[72]

With the war over, local governments expanded their control of hospitality businesses. For example, in October 1865, the Martinsburg City Council passed an ordinance on licenses, requiring that only city residents could keep a hotel or tavern; sell drinks or refreshments at a public theater; sell, offer, or expose for sale at retail spirituous liquors, wine, porter, ale or beer "or any drink of like nature," meaning selling in quantities of less than five gallons; or "keep for public use or resort" a bowling alley or saloon, billiard table, "or table of like kind" within the corporate limits. Violators risked forfeiting their license or paying a fine of $10 to $100. One did not need a license to keep a boarding house or boarding school if boarders stayed longer than three days. Nor did one need a license to sell porter, ale, or beer or any drink of like nature if one already had a license to sell spirituous liquors.[73] The mayor and clerk issued all licenses after the council authorized them to do so. If the license was for a hotel or tavern, bowling alley or saloon, billiard table "or table of like kind," or to sell liquors, drinks, or other refreshments, the license had to designate the building where it would be kept or sold. All applicants for licenses to keep hotels or taverns or sell at retail spirituous liquors, etc. had to "make satisfactory proof" to the council that they were "of good moral character and demeanor & not of intemperate habits," and, in the aftermath of the war, take an oath to support the constitutions of the United States and of the State of West Virginia, a provision which remained in effect until June 1869. Those seeking licenses to sell spirituous liquors or keep bowling alleys, saloons, or billiard tables had to execute a bond of not less than $500 nor more than $1000, with security approved by council, with the condition that the licensee not permit anyone to become intoxicated on the premises and not to sell any intoxicating drink to anyone who was intoxicated or anyone known to have a habit of becoming intoxicated, to anyone under twenty-one, or to anyone on Sunday or election day, or to anyone after 9:00 p.m. For any breach of these conditions of the bond, the City of Martinsburg could recover $10 for the city for each breach until the penalty was exhausted before the mayor or justice of the peace or circuit court took its share of the fine, and the license and bond would be subject to revocation for each breach. Any license could be revoked on the written petition of any inhabitant of Martinsburg. State law set the rate of the annual tax license holders had to pay to the city.[74] It is hard to get data to put these bond and fine amounts in perspective, but we can turn to the 1870 census of manufactures for Berkeley County to see that Henry Kratz, a tailor, paid his employees an average of $6.89 a week.[75] Clearly, women had to have some financial means to afford these licenses, or they had to have the financial backing of people who could post bonds for them.

We know three Martinsburg women had these licenses, two of whom also owned hotels. The City of Martinsburg granted Mrs. Mary Staub a license to sell spirituous liquors on June 19, 1865.[76] She presented her petition as a hotel keeper and retail dealer in liquor on June 20, 1865, and the county Board of Supervisors granted her license.[77] Staub was the wife of Henry Staub, the hotel keeper, in 1860, so she would have had the opportunity to learn the hospitality business by working with her husband.[78] Mrs. Ann V. Little petitioned for a license to sell at retail spirituous and malt liquors in her hotel at the railroad in August 1867, but there is no reference the license was actually granted to her.[79] Then, in February 1870, she again applied for a license with acceptable security for her bond, asking to take over the license of Josiah Ettin, who, in turn, had taken over the license of Josiah Little issued in August 1868. This license was granted.[80] She renewed this license in May 1870 to keep a hotel and sell at retail spirituous liquors.[81] She lived at the hotel with her six children, a male bar keeper, the native-born woman who was the domestic servant, and three members of that woman's family. The only other residents were a couple, so this was likely a small hotel for transients.[82] In 1869, Baden-born Mrs. Julia C. Westphal purchased the Valley House hotel.[83] On April 1, 1869, Mrs. Catharine Westphal applied for and received her first license to sell spirituous liquors at retail at the Valley House, with Lewis Schew serving as the security for her bond.[84] The City apparently contracted with Mrs. Westphal [no first name] to keep a "destitute woman," since they paid her $2 for this service in October 1869.[85] This would have been another form of providing hospitality, albeit at public expense, and perhaps could be compared to the way an organization like the American Red Cross today pays for disaster victims to stay in hotels. In 1870, Julia Westphal was thirty-five years old and shared her household with two children. She employed an African American man as a hostler and an Irish woman as a domestic servant. The male bar keeper may also have been an employee. This was apparently a small hotel for transients, as there was only one other resident and so few employees. She owned $8,000 worth of real property and $350 worth of personal property.[86]

There is no evidence that any of the married women in this study were conducting businesses that they owned in their own names while their husbands were living. However, they were the last to be so restricted. In 1868, West Virginia passed its first Married Women's Property Act, which "provided that property conveyed to a married woman be 'her sole and separate property.'" However, she could only convey her real estate with her husband's approval. She could be responsible for her debts before her marriage, sue and be sued in some cases, and, if living apart from her husband, could "'in her own name, carry on any trade or business,' and keep her earnings."[87] Before this act, the R.G. Dun and Co., which provided credit reports much like Equifax does today, had to record whether women business owners were married and, if so, if their husbands were creditworthy. The woman's rights movement at the time was still fighting hard for married women's property rights, so this was a very important act. One might even argue that the next step in married women's legal rights did not come until over a century later, in 1974, when Congress passed the Equal Credit Opportunity Act, giving married women the ability to get credit in their own names and to have their incomes counted when their husbands wanted credit.

This study ends in 1870. At that time, immigrants continued to be important in the hospitality labor force. In Parkersburg, five women, all Virginia-born white women, ran boarding houses. The women ranged in age from forty to fifty-four, three were neighbors, and four were household heads, so they were probably widows. The three who had live-in employees hired six women (three native-born whites, one Irish, one German, and one African American). Most of the six men in Amanda Sleigh's household who were the likely boarders were only a few years older than seventeen-year-old Bettie, who was probably her daughter, but we can only speculate about whether Amanda saw them as sons or a potential partner for Bettie or whether Bettie saw them as big brothers, potential husbands, or simply men whose room and board payments supported her family while she helped cook and clean for them, as there were no live-in employees. We might ask the same questions about the household of Susan Langfitt, who had a twenty-two-year-old daughter and employed two women as domestics to serve eight boarders (seven men and one woman).[88] Eleven women domestics (three African Americans, one German, two Irish, one Swiss, four native-born whites) and one native-born white washwoman worked at eight smaller hotels.[89]

With the end of slavery, census enumerators in 1870 identified all people of color by name and occupation in Martinsburg. Unfortunately, there is no way to know if any of them had been working at hotels while enslaved and stayed in these same positions after emancipation because Staub, Ramer, and Reamer were not hotel keepers in 1870. James Boyd employed four men (one white clerk, one African American and one mulatto dining room servant, and one African American hostler) and three women. The clerk and housekeeper, both native-born whites, may have been married. The two mulatto women, a chambermaid and cook, had young children listed with them.[90] Henry Wilen's hotel had two men as dining room servants and one as hostler, while the three women were the washwoman, cook, and chambermaid. All were African American or mulatto, and two-year-old George was probably the son of Ellen Wood, the cook.[91] Henry Paull's "R.R. Boarding House" would have served a very transient population of Baltimore and Ohio Railroad employees. He had only two employees, a cook and domestic servant who may have been mother and daughter. Emma Wilson, the cook, was African American, and Mary, the fourteen-year-old domestic servant, a mulatto. Since Mary was born before the Civil War, was she born into slavery and, if so, was her white father her former master or a member of the master's family?[92] William Rutledge's hotel also predominately served railroad workers, with three women employees (an African American cook, a native-born white chambermaid, and a native-born white domestic) to care for the fourteen resident guests and the Rutledge family.[93]

The women providing hospitality in Wheeling at boarding houses and smaller hotels in 1870 reflected the ethnic diversity of that city, although six of the seven boarding house keepers were native-born, and the seventh was Irish. Sarah Sims, the only woman running a boarding house who was not the head of her household, was in business with Martha Sims, who may have been her twin sister. The Simses employed four Irish and three native-born women as domestics to care for their thirty-one boarders; the household also included a girl who may have been a sister of one of the domestics. The other houses were much smaller, employing a total of five native-born women as domestics; one had two young children living with her.[94] Twenty-seven women (twelve Germans, one Dutch, two Irish, two French, eight native-born white, and two mulatto) were identified as domestics or simply "works hotel" in seven small hotels, where, in four cases, they worked with sixteen men (one German, two Dutch, six native born whites, and six mulattos) with occupations of domestic servant, bar keeper, and hostler, in addition to doing unspecified work.[95]

Compared to the relative informality one might imagine in those boarding house and small hotel settings, gender relationships, and possibly racial relationships, were likely more complicated in larger hotels, such as Wheeling's Grant House and McLure House or Parkersburg's Swann Hotel and Stahlmann's United States Hotel. Contacts between guests and employees and between hotel owners/managers and employees may have been more impersonal in 1870, but the larger number of both male and female employees could have created a sense of community among employees within the specialized work spaces of these hotels. For example, in Wheeling, Samuel Lewis, probably with the help of Susan (his wife?), ran the Grant House. He employed thirty people, eighteen women and twelve men, twenty-one of whom were white, one mulatto, and eight black; they lived at the hotel and worked as waiters, cooks, hotel clerks, a porter, and in otherwise unidentified positions as "works at hotel." Here, six of the women were waiters, a job that was more common for men, and three men were cooks, a job that had been more common for women. Seventeen of the white workers and all of the African American and mulatto workers were native born, although seven of them were the children of immigrants; the immigrants were from Ireland (one), Germany (one), and Holland (two). One of the male clerks had two family members with him, probably his wife and child, and there may have been two pairs of sisters or cousins among the women employees. The Lewises had no identifiable children in the household, but there were sixty-four resident guests.[96] Two resident couples, each with a young child, managed the McLure House. The clientele seems to have been more transient, as there were only forty-seven residents listed in the 1870 census. The forty-three employees who lived at the hotel included twenty-two women and twenty-one men. It is harder to identify their jobs because all but four female domestics and one male clerk were simply identified as "employees." Among the forty-three were four mulatto males, five black males, twelve white males (two Dutch and three Irish), one black female, and twenty-one white females (fourteen Irish, one German, and one Dutch); eight of the native-born employees had foreign-born parents.[97] At the Swann Hotel, Benjamin and Mary Gilbert managed an establishment with just thirteen residents but, probably, with a large transient population, because they employed ten white female domestic servants (five Irish and five native-born with foreign-born parents), one African American woman ironer, and ten men (two native-born whites and eight African Americans or mulattos), as clerks, porters, and waiters.[98] The United States Hotel employed five white women (four Irish and one native born) as chambermaids, cooks, and a wash-woman, while four white men (three native born and one German) were the waiters and hostler. In both cases, then, men were the employees guests saw most frequently, while women worked behind the scenes.[99]

Finally, a new form of hospitality arose in the post-war years with the free-standing restaurant. In Parkersburg, in 1870, Hildegard Anubrush, born in Bavaria and then thirty-eight years old, was a cook in Andrew Als's restaurant, where she worked with Louisa Reizinger, a twenty-two-year-old pantry worker from Bavaria, and Mary Lewis, a thirty-five-year-old from Ohio and a dining room waiter who was probably related to Willie Lewis, an older male dining room waiter; all lived at the restaurant with one male boarder and members of the Als family.[100]

Thus, by 1870, women in West Virginia's cities working in the new state's hospitality industry had pioneered in commercial enterprises that would employ women throughout the state (and country) in the twenty-first century in jobs that were not really very different than those of their nineteenth-century sisters. Today, women are owners, managers, receptionists, and housekeepers in lodgings as varied as bed and breakfast establishments and the exclusive Greenbrier Resort; and as owners, managers, and servers in restaurants and bars. Newspapers and court records will continue to be available to document their work, but, because the federal census no longer collects data on individuals' occupations, it will be impossible for historians in the future to know as much about individual workers in 2010 as we know about their ancestors.

Hospitality-related businesses are especially important today in West Virginia because the state is "within driving distance of more than fifty percent of the U.S. population" and has "attractions that fit any budget and interest."[101] From 1990 to 2005, for example, the state's leisure and hospitality industry; arts, entertainment, and recreation industry; and accommodation and food services industry grew at a higher percentage in terms of gross domestic product than did other selected industries.[102] In addition, Allbusiness.com identified a total of 577 drinking places, restaurant and food service businesses, and lodging businesses in Wheeling, Martinsburg, and Parkersburg as part of the "Travel, Hospitality & Tourism" industry in West Virginia in May 2009; these had estimated annual sales of $1,036,453,994, and employed an estimated 22,796 people.[103]

But one very important part of the hospitality business has not changed—the pay for those at the lower end of the wage scale in the hospitality industry. In 1850, a domestic in Virginia, almost certainly a woman, earned a little over twice in one week what a day laborer, almost certainly a male, earned in a day. The jobs in this industry today, many of which are similar to those women held at that time, still include those that were among the twenty lowest paid occupations for year-round full-time workers in 1999, the latest figures available.[104] Certainly, cleaning hotel rooms is easier now than it was before there was electricity to power vacuum cleaners or laundry equipment, but the heart of the hospitality industry has always been meeting the needs of guests, whether those guests are at boarding houses, bed and breakfasts, hotels and motels, fast-food places or ethnic restaurants. Today, employees may be unionized and are likely to work in an establishment that is a franchise for a national or international chain restaurant or hotel. If that is the case, they are likely following procedures that those franchises mandate and may be subject to personnel policies, health department policies, and state, local, and federal laws that would seem like a foreign language to their nineteenth-century predecessors. And, while men and a few women may be chefs in upscale restaurants or while couples (married or same sex) may own and operate bed and breakfast establishments, this author has never seen a man cleaning a hotel room. Immigrant women did this job in mid-nineteenth-century cities, and immigrant women still do this job—they just come from a different country now and no longer live in the hotel. As enslaved women were nameless in the past, so, too, are hospitality employees often nameless to us as guests today, especially if they are low-income minorities or unskilled recent immigrants. Nor do we often record their stories today unless in a volume like Barbara Ehrenreich's *Nickle and Dimed: On (Not) Getting By in America* (New York: Metropolitan Books, 2001) or Barbara Ehrenreich and Arlie Russell Hochschild's *Global Woman: Nannies, Maids, and Sex Workers in the New Economy* (New York: Metropolitan Books, 2003).

So, if that 1865 cook could meet the successful applicant for the 2009 position, what might be her first question? I would guess it would be "How do you make a burrito?" And the next questions might be "What are these policies about sexual harassment? Do they really give you recourse if you have problems on the job? And, if this thing you call 'feminism' instead of 'woman's rights,' is so wonderful, why are these jobs still so poorly paid? Didn't you learn *anything* from our experiences?"

Notes

1. "Wanted," *Wheeling Intelligencer*, May 26, 1865, 2:4.
2. Untitled, *Morgantown Dominion Post*, June 14, 2009, 3(G).
3. The 1830 population figure is from J.B. Bowen, *The Wheeling Directory and Advertiser* (Wheeling, Va.: John M. M'Creary, 1839), n.p. (page facing d2); this 5,221 figure is in a section identified "*From the Wheeling Gazette.*" The remaining population figures and sources are: 7,885 in 1840 (Campbell Gibson, "Population of the 100 Largest Cities and Other Urban Places in the United States: 1790 to 1990," U.S. Census Bureau Population Division Working Paper No. 27, June 1998, Table 7. Population of the 100 Largest Urban Places: 1840); 11,435 in 1850 (11,179 whites, 212 free African Americans, and forty-four enslaved people), 14,083 in 1860 (99.2 percent white and .7 percent African Americans), and 19,280 in 1870 (ninty-eight percent white, two percent African American, 28.2 percent foreign-born) (Francis A. Walker, *Ninth Census*. Vol. 1.: *The Statistics of the Population of the United States* [Washington: Government Printing Office, 1872], 286. The census did not collect data on birthplace before 1850 and did not report data on foreign-born residents below the county level before 1870. The population of enslaved people was too small in 1860 to be separated from that of Ohio County, which had 100 enslaved people. A general history of Wheeling and Ohio County during the years covered by this essay can be found in J.H. Newton, ed., *History of the Pan-Handle; Being Historical Collections of the Counties of Ohio, Brooke, Marshall and Hancock, West Virginia* (Wheeling, W.Va.: J.A. Caldwell, 1879). An overview of women's employment in Wheeling during this period can be found in Barbara J. Howe, "Patient Laborers: Women at Work in the Formal Economy of West(ern) Virginia," in *Neither Lady, Nor Slave: Working Women of the Old South*, ed. by Michele Gillespie and Susanna Delfino. Chapel Hill, N.C: The University of North Carolina Press, 2002, 121-51; and Barbara J. Howe, "Urban Wage-Earning Women in a Rural State," in *Beyond Hill and Hollow: Original Readings in Appalachian Women's Studies*, ed. by Elizabeth Engelhardt (Athens: Ohio University Press, 2005), 101-23.
4. In 1860, the population was 97.6 percent of whom were whites and 2.4 percent free African Americans. The population of enslaved people was not separated from that of Wood County, which had 176 enslaved people. In 1870, the population was 91.9 percent white and 8.1 percent African-American; 14.4 percent were foreign-born. Census information is from Francis A. Walker, *Ninth Census*. Vol. 1.: *The Statistics of the Population of the United States* (Washington: Government Printing Office, 1872), 286. Other information on Parkersburg is from *Industrial Parkersburg* (Detroit: Richard R. Barnes & Co., [1907?]), 6; J.E. Wharton, *A Sketch of the City of Parkersburg, West Va., Its Mercantile, Manufacturing, and General Resources, January 1865* (Parkersburg, W.Va.: Blair & Deshler, 1865), 3, 5; and Eugene D. Thoenen, *History of the Oil and Gas Industry in West Virginia* (Charleston, W.Va.: Education Foundation, 1964), 154.
5. Information on the history of Martinsburg is from William T. Doherty, *Berkeley County, U.S.A..: A Bicentennial History of a Virginia and West Virginia County, 1772-1972* (Parsons, W.Va.: McClain Printing Co., 1972) and F. Vernon Aler, *Aler's History of Martinsburg and Berkeley County, West Virginia* (Hagerstown, Md.: The Mail Publishing Co., 1888). In 1860, the population of Martinsburg was 89.6 percent white, 3.3 percent free African Americans, and 7.1 percent enslaved people. In 1870, the population was 90.2 percent white, 9.8 percent African American, and 9.8 percent foreign-born. Census figures are from Francis A. Walker, *Ninth Census*. Vol. 1.: *The Statistics of the Population of the United States* (Washington: Government Printing Office, 1872), 286.

6. "Molesting Females on the Street," *Wheeling Intelligencer*, November 1, 1858, 3.
7. "A Successful Robbery," *Wheeling Intelligencer*, April 24, 1863, 3.
8. "Put in the Lock-Up," *Wheeling Intelligencer*, December 20, 1866, 4; and "About Pies and Cakes," *Wheeling Intelligencer*, December 31, 1866, 4.
9. "Police Court," *Wheeling Intelligencer*, December 12, 1867, 4.
10. "A Pretty Pair," *Wheeling Intelligencer*, November 27, 1861, 3.
11. "Desperate Rowdy," *Wheeling Intelligencer*, April 28, 1858, 3.
12. "A Miraculous Escape," *Wheeling Intelliencer*, February 13, 1864, 3.
13. Untitled, *Wheeling Intelligencer*, December 23, 1858, 3.
14. "An Exciting Scence," *Wheeling Intelligencer*, August 5, 1857, 3.
15. "Assault," *Wheeling Intelligencer*, August 22, 1857, 3.
16. "Selling Liquor Without License," *Wheeling Intelligencer*, August 24, 1857, 3.
17. "A Row," *Wheeling Intelligencer*, March 10, 1859, 3.
18. "Drawing a Knife," *Wheeling Intelligencer*, September 18, 1858, 3.
19. "A Spiteful Old Lady," *Wheeling Intelligencer*, April 19, 1858, 3.
20. "Another Muss," *Wheeling Intelligencer*, July 31, 1858, 3.
21. "A Modest Policeman," *Wheeling Intelligencer*, March 15, 1862, 3.
22. "A Good One," *Wheeling Intelligencer*, September 23, 1857, 3.
23. "Arrest of a Rebel Termagent," *Wheeling Intelligencer*, January 12, 1863, 3; and U.S. Bureau of the Census, Census of Population, Ohio County, Wheeling, 1860, 3-1740-1814.
24. The definition of "ordinary" is from the on-line *Oxford English Dictionary*, accessed June 26, 2009.
25. City of Wheeling, Minute Book, 1833-1840, May 19, 1836, 8.
26. See, for instance, "Police Court," *Wheeling Intelligencer*, September 22, 1865, 4; January 27, 1866, 4; and May 23, 1867, 4.
27. Suzanne Lebsock, *"A Share of Honour:" Virginia Women 1600-1945* (Richmond: Virginia Women's Cultural History Project, 1984), 81, 83; and Suzanne Lebsock, *The Free Women of Petersburg: Status and Culture in a Southern Town, 1784-1860* (New York: W.W. Norton & Co., 1984), 54-57.
28. U.S. Bureau of the Census, Census of Population, Ohio County, Wheeling, 1860, 4-1954-2035.
29. For sample ads, see "Boarding," *Wheeling Tri-Weekly Times*, February 1, 1834; and Untitled, *Western Virginia Times*, May 7, 1839.
30. "She Was More Than Fancy Painted Her," *Wheeling Intelligencer*, October 1, 1866, 4.
31. "Notice!," *Wheeling Gazette*, July 10, 1830.
32. "A New Way To Collect A Boarding Bill," *Wheeling Intelligencer*, December 7, 1869, 4.
33. Untitled, *Wheeling Intelligencer*, January 13, 1860, 3.
34. Untitled, *Wheeling Intelligencer*, September 26, 1862, 3.
35. Thomas B. Searight, *The Old Pike: A History of the National Road, with Incidents, Accidents, and Anecdotes Thereon* (Uniontown, Pa.: Thomas B. Searight, 1894), 296.
36. Kenneth Fischer Craft, Jr., *Ohio County (WV) Index, Vol. 7C, Cumulative 'Personal Time Line' Index to Volumes 1-7, Pages 1-1876, Index to County Court Order Books, 1777-1881* (Bowie, Md.: Heritage Books, Inc., 2001), xxxvii-xxxviii.
37. U.S. Bureau of the Census, Census of Population, Ohio County, District Allotted to Satethiel Curtis, 1820, 12.
38. U.S. Bureau of the Census, Census of Population, Ohio County, Western District, 1830, 259.

39. Ohio County Order Books, Book 25, May 8, 1832, 100; and U.S. Bureau of the Census, Census of Population, Ohio County, Western District, May 7, 1832, 96.
40. City of Wheeling, Minute Book, 1833-1840, May 19, 1836, 8.
41. J.B. Bowen, *The Wheeling Directory and Advertiser* (Wheeling, Va.: John M. M'Creary, 1839), 21.
42. U.S. Bureau of the Census, Census of Population, Ohio County, Wheeling, 1840, Ward 2, enumeration schedule, 39, line 20.
43. City of Wheeling, Minute Book, 1840-1849, December 31, 1845, 303; and Searight, *The Old Pike*, 296.
44. U.S. Bureau of the Census, Census of Population, Ohio County, Wheeling, 1850, 2-1493-1551.
45. Ohio County Court Records, Book 33, April 3, 1854.
46. U.S. Bureau of the Census, Census of Population, Ohio County, Wheeling, 1860, 2-1354-1407.
47. "Reopened," *Wheeling Intelligencer*, June 21, 1860, 3.
48. "Alledged Kidnapping in this City," *Wheeling Intelligencer*, December 10, 1858, 3.
49. U.S. Bureau of the Census, Census of Population, Ohio County, Wheeling, 1860. The boarding house keepers were Jane Shaws (4-306-2052-2138), Mary Kierns (4-341-2311-2417). Margaret Culp (S-505-3486-3606), Lucy Briggs (5-391-2694-2812), Ouha Balzel (3-259-1737-1811), Elizabeth Little (4-315-2118-2208, Rebecca Witten (2-226-1517-1578), Mary A. Hoge (3-284-1918-1999), Rachel Norris (5-412-2840-2958), and Elizabeth Wells (5-452-3112-3232).
50. U.S. Bureau of the Census, Census of Population, Ohio County, Wheeling, 1860, 3-260-1740-1814.
51. U.S. Bureau of the Census, Census of Population, Ohio County, Wheeling, 1860. These other hotels were: Isaac Packer's Union House-four women (one Irish, one German, two native born) and one hostler (4-1973-2055); John Rider-one female, no men, (5-2464-2682); and Jacob Kurtz- two German women and one hostler (5-2826-2944); George Dusch-one hostler and female family members (2-1395-1450); John M. Ball's New Home-one female (2-1398-1453); Thomas Brues's Monroe House-four German women and no men (2-1504-1505); and Jason Stockbridge's Sprigg House-two Irish women domestics, one washwoman, one African American male cook, two white waiters (3-1583-1648).
52. "The M'Lure House," *Wheeling Intelligencer*, February 9, 1853, 3.
53. "The McClure House, Wheeling," *Wheeling Intelligencer*, July 13, 1854, 3.
54. "United States Hotel," *Parkersburg Gazette*, March 24, 1860, 2; and U.S. Bureau of the Census, Census of Population, Wood County, Parkersburg, 1860, 1328-1333 (Conley) and 1329-1334 (Murray).
55. "Swann House," *Parkersburg Gazette*, March 24, 1860, 1; and U.S. Bureau of the Census, Census of Population, Wood County, Parkersburg, 1860, 1303-1308.
56. U.S. Bureau of the Census, Census of Population Wood County, Parkersburg, 1860, 161-1235-1237 (Coneys) and 125-956-956 (Burns).
57. U.S. Bureau of the Census, Census of Population, Berkeley County, Martinsburg, 1860, 1108-1130.
58. U.S. Bureau of the Census, Berkeley County, Schedule 2 (Slave Inhabitants), Martinsburg, 1860, 15.
59. U.S. Bureau of the Census, Berkeley County, Schedule 2 (Slave Inhabitants), Martinsburg, 1860, 15 (Staub and Ramer), 16 (Reamer); and U.S. Bureau of the Census, Berkeley County, Martinsburg, 1092-1112 (Staub), 1104-1126 (Ramer), and 1325-1368 (Reamer).

60. City of Martinsburg, Minute Book No. 3, August 17, 1860, 88-89.
61. U.S. Bureau of the Census, Berkeley County, Schedule 2 (Slave Inhabitants), Martinsburg, 1860; and U.S. Bureau of the Census, Census of Population, Berkeley County, Martinsburg, 1168-1176 (Jno. McAbee), 1152-1178 (Benj. Carpenter), and 1261-1178 (John Billmine).
62. U.S. Bureau of the Census, Census of Population, Berkeley County, Martinsburg, 1191-1223.
63. See, for instance, "Boarding," *Wheeling Intelligencer*, December 2, 1862, 3.
64. "City Council—The Liquor Sellers and the Soldiers," *Wheeling Intelligencer*, October 16, 1861, 3.
65. "Selling Liquor to Soldiers," *Wheeling Intelligencer*, September 4, 1862, 3.
66. "Insulting a Woman," *Wheeling Intelligencer*, May 13, 1863, 3.
67. "Police," *Wheeling Intelligencer*, June 20, 1865, 3.
68. Wood County Circuit Court, Law Order Book 5, 1858-1864, November 6, 1861, 306.
69. Wood County Circuit Court, Law Order Book 5, 1858-1864, June 13, 1862, 336.
70. Wood County Circuit Court, Law Order Book 5, 1858-1864, December 16, 1863, 489; and Ibid., April 15, 1864, 529.
71. "An Ungrateful Cordwainer," *Wheeling Intelligencer*, April 2, 1862.
72. "Difficulty Among the Colored Population, *Wheeling Intelligencer*, March 19, 1863, 3.
73. City of Martinsburg, Minute Book No. 3, October 2, 1865, 113.
74. City of Martinsburg, Minute Book No. 3, 114; and City of Martinsburg, Minute Book No. 3, June 10, 1869, 228.
75. Kratz was the only employer listed in Martinsburg who employed women, and he had four women and eight men who earned a total of $4300 for the year. The figure of $6.89 per week assumes the twelve were paid the same, although that is not likely to have been the case (U.S. Bureau of the Census, Schedule 4. Products of Industry, 1870, Berkeley County, 2.
76. City of Martinsburg, Minute Book No. 3, June 19, 1866, 129.
77. Berkeley County, County Court Order Book V, June 20, 1865, 17.
78. U.S. Bureau of the Census, Census of Population, Berkeley County, Martinsburg, 1860, 1090-1114.
79. Berkeley County, County Court Minute Book V, August 12, 1867, 165.
80. Berkeley County, County Court Minute Book V, August 10, 1868, 218 (license to Little); April 12, 1869, 271 (license to Ettin—Little is dead); February 14, 1870, 316 (license to Ann Little).
81. Berkeley County, County Court Minute Book V, May 9, 1870, 338.
82. U.S. Bureau of the Census, Census of Population, Berkeley County, Martinsburg, 1870, 755-830.
83. Berkeley County Deed Records, vol. 65, 379.
84. City of Martinsburg, Minute Book No. 3, April 1, 1869, 212.
85. City of Martinsburg, Minute Book No. 3, October 21, 1869, 244.
86. U.S. Bureau of the Census, Census of Population, Berkeley County, Martinsburg, 1870, 281-311.
87. Donna J. Spindel, "Women's Legal Rights in West Virginia, 1863-1984," *West Virginia History* 51 (1992): 30-31.

88. U.S. Bureau of the Census, Census of Population, Wood County, Parkersburg, 1870. The census did not consistently differentiate between those born before 1863 in what became West Virginia and those born in what remained Virginia. The five were Priscilla Foley (4-129-124), Mary Harriss (4-120-115), Susan Langfitt (1-055-048), Amanda Sleigh (1-053-046), and Cora Stringer (1-056-049).

89. U.S. Bureau of the Census, Census of Population, Wood County, Parkersburg, 1870. These employees were domestics with one African American at Charles Buehler's hotel (1-003-003), one German at Ernest Tillner's hotel (1-115-101), three native-born at George Roland's hotel (6-051-051), one African American at Preston Pew's hotel (6-081-080), one African American and one Irish at Neil McCombs's hotel (6-124-122), one Irish and one native-born white at Jesse Pernell's hotel (6-125-123), and one Swiss at Adam Hettick's hotel (6-162-159). The washwoman was at Michael Egan's hotel (1-134-119).

90. U.S. Bureau of the Census, Census of Population, Berkeley County, Martinsburg, 1870, 335-366.

91. U.S. Bureau of the Census, Census of Population, Berkeley County, Martinsburg, 1870, 001-001.

92. U.S. Bureau of the Census, Census of Population, Berkeley County, Martinsburg, 1870, 250-275.

93. U.S. Bureau of the Census, Census of Population, Berkeley County, Martinsburg, 1870, 270-296.

94. U.S. Bureau of the Census, Census of Population, Ohio County, Wheeling, 1870. The 7 were Elizabeth Bane-1 with 2 young children (6-018-018), Mary Deaken-1 domestic (S-161-154), Ann Dorsey-2 domestics (3-056-056), Elizabeth Dow-1 domestic (4-387-381), Catharine Holland- no domestics (5-189-189), and Martha and Sarah Simms (3-520-515).

95. Specific listings are as follows for the domestics at other hotels: U.S. Bureau of the Census, Census of Population, Ohio County, Wheeling, 1870: Kiem House-three native born, two German, and one Dutch domestics; one Dutch male domestic (3-533-528), Henry Deusch's hotel-two French domestics both named Deusch so presumably his relatives; one Dutch hostler (2-231-230), Henry Crissman's hotel-two native born and one Irish domestics; no men, 2-221-220), Louis Bumgardner-two German domestics; one Swiss hostler (2-225-224), John McGarrel's hotel-one native born domestic; no men (2-219-218), Lewis Singman-one Irish, one German, one native born women domestics; one German bar keeper (3-248-247), and Henry Stamm-one native born woman domestic, five German women "works hotel," including possible pair of sisters; no men (3-250-249); John Daily—two mulatto women, two white women, six mulatto men, six native-born white men "works hotel" (3-034-034).

96. U.S. Bureau of the Census, Census of Population, Ohio County, Wheeling, 1870, 2-255-254.

97. U.S. Bureau of the Census, Census of Population, Ohio County, Wheeling, 1870, 3-261-260.

98. U.S. Bureau of the Census, Census of Population, Wood County, Parkersburg, 1870, 1-080-071.

99. U.S. Bureau of the Census, Census of Population, Wood County, Parkersburg, 1870, 1-180-163.

100. U.S. Bureau of the Census, Census of Population, Wood County, Parkersburg, 1870, 1-050-057.

101. "West Virginia Division of Tourism Offers Travel Ideas to Experience the Best of Spring," March 13, 2009, press release from West Virginia Division of Tourism, http://callwvanews.com/story_ideas.html (accessed May 29, 2009).

102. Tom S. Witt and J. Sebastian Leguizamon, "Tourism and the West Virginia Economy," Report to the West Virginia Division of Tourism and the West Virginia Chamber of Commerce, February 2007, Chart 1, n.p. The respective percentages were approximately 3.5, 6.4, and 2.7. The other industries were mining, durable manufacturing, construction, finance and insurance, educational services, and government.

103. The following data was accessed on May 31, 2009, from www.allbusiness.com/company index/West Virginia, and is organized by number of companies, estimated annual sales, and estimated number of employees:

Drinking Places: Wheeling, 34-$95,416,000-1,282; Martinsburg: 29-$3,811,000-112; Parkersburg: 27-$10,242,000-385. Totals for three cities: 90-$109,469,000-1,779.

Restaurants & Food Service: Wheeling: 150-$460,130,995-4,668; Martinsburg: 135-$21,586,000-868; Parkersburg: 150-$54,437,000 -1,863. Totals for three cities: 435-$536,153,995-7,399.

Lodging: Wheeling: 11-$147,958,999-2,790. Martinsburg: 20-$14,870,000-416; Parkersburg: 21-$9.997,000-316. Totals for three cities.: 52-$162,828,999-3,522.

104. The 1850 census recorded that domestics in Virginia earned 96 cents per week with board, while a day laborer with board earned forty-seven cents a day (J.D.B. DeBow, *Statistical View of the United States* (Washington: A.O.P. Nicholson, 1854), 164. Unfortunately, the census collected very little other wage data in the mid-nineteenth century for positions outside of manufacturing establishments. Unfortunately, it is not possible to get current gender-specific statistics comparable to those available in the nineteenth-century censuses of population, but the wage data that is available today shows gender differences. Among the twenty occupations with the lowest median earnings, in 1999, that were related to the hospitality industry were, for men, in order of lowest paid to highest paid: dishwashers ($14,000); dining room and cafeteria attendants and bartender helpers; counter attendants cafeteria, food concession, and coffee; food preparation workers; combined food preparation and serving workers, including fast food; maids and housekeeping cleaners; waiters and waitresses; hosts and hostesses, restaurant, lounge, and coffee shop; hotel, motel, and resort desk ($20,000), with the median income for all year-round full-time men workers being $38,000. For women, among the twenty occupations with the lowest median earnings the same year were dishwashers ($12,000); counter attendants, cafeteria, food concession, and coffee shop; combined food preparation and serving workers, fast food; cooks; dining room and cafeteria attendants and bartender helpers; food preparation workers; host and hostesses, restaurant, lounge, and coffee shop; maids and housekeeping cleaners; waiters and waitresses; bartenders; hotel, motel, and resort desk clerks ($16,000), with the median income for all year-round full-time women workers being $28,000 (U.S. Department of Commerce, Economics and Statistics Administration, U.S. Census Bureau, "Evidence From Census 2000 About Earnings by Detailed Occupation for Men and Women." Census 2000 Special Reports, CENSR-15, May 2004, 13).

Part V: Feminism and Hospitality in Film and Literature

Chapter 14
Reading Levinas in *The Apartment*
Jacqueline M. Davies

And the other whose presence is discreetly an absence, with which is accomplished the primary hospitable welcome which describes the field of intimacy, is the Woman.[1]

An Opening

Hospitality is a key metaphor in the work of the Jewish, Lithuanian born, naturalized French philosopher, Emmanuel Levinas.[2] Like most of his rhetorical figures, it is heavily gendered, which is a matter of scholarly interest and political concern for his feminist readers.[3] Such concerns are all the more pressing given the self-sacrificial dimension of his ethics.[4] Could the identification of home as archetypically feminine really be something liberating for women, or men? Or, does Levinas's phenomenology of welcome risk reinforcing women's social confinement to what is often a site of exploitation and violence? To answer these questions deeper exploration of the meaning of welcome and hospitality in Levinas's philosophy is necessary. A possible exploratory approach might include thought experiments attending to and playing with the gender of welcome and hospitality in imaginary contexts. Insofar as cinematic fiction can be treated as a genre of thought experiment, this is the approach I take by reading Levinas in Billy Wilder's film *The Apartment*.

In *Totality and Infinity*, Levinas describes the ethical significance of home not as a place of origin or real property, but as a site of welcome; it is "welcome in itself," and this welcome is itself "feminine being."[5] This holds, he maintains, even in the "empirical absence of the human being of the 'feminine sex.'"[6] What could this mean? Could such femininity manifest itself even in the home of a single heterosexual man?[7] These are questions which we can take to a Levinasian reading of *The Apartment*. While engaged in this reading we will encounter illustrations of Levinasian welcome, hospitality and femininity that make these concepts more accessible than they are in the primary texts. This enables a better grasp of these difficult concepts, as well those of "the neighbour," "substitution," and "the face," which in turn makes them more readily available for critical examination. Reading Levinas in *The Apartment* also reveals the depth of ethical comment expressed in a Hollywood film that as a piece of light entertainment swept the 1961 academy awards for its Polish born, Jewish American director.

The Apartment stars Jack Lemmon (as C.C. Baxter) fresh from his cross-dressing role in Wilder's *Some Like It Hot*. A young Shirley MacLaine plays Miss Kubelik, the "elevator girl." Both of these figures are gendered by Wilder in ways that resonate with the Levinasian "feminine," as well as with women's place in a man's world as a site of exploitation, particularly sexualized exploitation. Let's begin with Miss Kubelik. Always moving though never really getting anywhere, she spends her days confined within the cramped and often crowded space of the elevator. Nonetheless, within this space she is remarkable as a figure of hospitality. She brightly welcomes all of her temporary guests, by name, on their way up and down the towering office block in which they work. Described as a nice respectable girl by Baxter, her would-be suitor, Miss Kubelik has to defend herself from a constant barrage of sexual innuendo and the wandering hands of the men who enter her small domain (with the notable exception of Baxter, our everyman hero). Curiously, Baxter suffers a similar pattern of abuse. His life is made miserable on account of the handy attractions embodied by his little Manhattan apartment, seen from the point of view of his wolfish office superiors. For C.C. Baxter as for Miss Kubelik, success in this man's world turns out to depend on alignment with the man at the top and the displacement of others who through their relations with the boss might gain access to the executive men's room or the house in the suburbs. In Wilder's film liberation from this form of gendered victimization and exploitation is a precondition of ethical maturity for both its male and female leads.

In a world of statistics and human meal tickets the man who is known by his initials, or by the superficially familiar nickname "buddy boy," must resist exploitation and transform himself into a mensch. In the course of this transformation he transforms his apartment from a swinging bachelor pad where he himself has no fun at all, into a refuge for another person. He is finally empowered to do this not by an impulse to defend his property rights or sense of self-respect or even a right to the pursuit of his own happiness. Rather, he achieves this transformation, in a Levinasian spirit, through his caring response to a vulnerability that he does not invite into his life but whom he discovers already occupying his space. This encounter occurs when he finds the near lifeless body of Miss Kubelik, who was left in his apartment by her heartless lover, none other than the boss man himself, Mr. Sheldrake.

The fact that Baxter discovers rather than invites the Other into his home resonates with the passivity of the ethical encounter as it is described by Levinas. What follows this pivotal encounter in the film can also be read as an allusion to Levinas's concept of "substitution" in the ethical encounter with the face of the Other. Baxter experiences slaps to the face of the barely conscious, drug overdosed, Miss Kubelik as slaps to his own face. As she is brought literally to her senses he is brought to his ethical senses. Once ethically awakened he offers all he has before it is asked. In providing refuge, Baxter, like his apartment, becomes a site of welcome; the host becomes an embodiment of hospitality. In Levinasian terms, Baxter comes to embody "feminine being." Ethics according to Levinas is not about constructing or acquiring or choosing from amongst some principles you already possess and then apply to some problem. Rather it is engendered in an encounter that you do not control, in an exposure to the vulnerability that is revealed when you discover yourself faced by an Other, by the discovery that one is not alone but lives next to another, the neighbour.

The Other is the term that Levinas used in *Totality and Infinity*, and in some of his earlier works, to indicate the figure with whom ethical encounter is experienced. In his subsequent work, *Otherwise than Being*, Levinas moves away from talk of the Other in favour of "the neighbour" (*le prochain*). This shift in Levinasian language is worth noting given the role played by the neighbours who encounter Baxter in the building within which his apartment is housed. The figure of the neighbour is crucial to Baxter's development in various ways. Neighbour. Taking note of this we see that it would not be wholly correct to say that Baxter accomplishes hospitality, and welcome, that is "feminine being" without the aid of an "empirical female." During the first days of Miss Kubelik's sojourn in the apartment, Baxter relies on the skills and tools of the Jewish mother next door as well as those of her neighbourly husband, Doctor Dreyfuss. Mrs. Dreyfuss's chicken soup is part of a feminine language of care with a specifically Yiddish accent. And, like the tools of her husband's trade, it is part of the treasures carried in the baggage of the eternally wandering Jew. For Wilder, as for Levinas, welcome comes from those who are displaced rather than from those who are comfortably in full possession of home and homeland. If the Dreyfusses in Wilder's picture function as a unit represntative of Jewish *heymishkeyt* rather than femininity, we can perhaps imagine Baxter's achievement of the feminine welcome as one which though dependent on the neighbour is not dependent on the presence of an empirical female as such. In any case the Jewishness of these figures is important since Levinas suggests, as perhaps does Wilder, that welcome is conditioned by dispossession itself. For Levinas, ethical encounter dispossesses and displaces one from one's comfortable (or for Baxter, uncomfortable) private sphere and leaves movement towards the neighbour the only possible ethical point of reorientation. Levinas and Wilder knew only too well the vulnerability to exploitation and violence familiar to the Jewish "Other."[8] Their work also suggests an awareness of the extent to which this is also feminine experience. But both recognize this vulnerability as more than a feature of victimization. Vulnerability to suffering is a recurring risk for those who would be good, nonetheless, to be good is not simply to suffer. To be a *mensch,* a person must learn how to stop being taken and to offer to take in the vulnerable. Such hospitality, as Levinas wrote and Wilder shows us on screen is something one learns from the neighbour.

Gendered Façades: Bosomy Bay Windows, Phallic Office Towers And Hard Park Benches.

Wilder's film subtly thematizes gender from its opening to its ending in ways that could easily be overlooked without close attention to the nuances of architecture, art direction and music which otherwise simply slip into the background.[9] Racialization is thematized at a level that is so much further underground that audiences can even more easily miss it. Let's start, then, with the more obviously noticeable, gendered frame of the film.

A starker contrast between feminine and masculine worlds could hardly be found than that revealed through the film's first few shots. Wilder opens with a steady image of the eponymous figure of the film—the apartment itself. A warm glow emanates from one of the two curving bay windows of a solidly built brownstone—a formerly generous single family home that has been divided up into small apartments. As spectator one finds oneself in a softly lit evening scene, eye-level with the upper windows of a cozily desirable address which Wilder soon introduces as one to which it is in fact hard to come home. Over this image roll the opening credits, printed text naming those who make up the film's creative matrix.[10] The lush symphonic score opening the film is suggestive of its subtext, the serious matters that underlie the movie's more comic and commercially appealing surface meanings.

The film abruptly shifts to the commercial world when the credits end. Seen from a bright, day-lit aerial perspective, the camera presents the skyscrapers of Manhattan's business district. A Freudian could hardly dream of a more phallic prospect. The soundtrack that marches us into this new scene is also bright and bracing. Its brisk, get down to business rhythm is further emphasized by the voice-over of the male lead. He introduces the site and his place in it using the strictly statistical terms in which individuals and relationships are accounted for at Consolidated Life. Consolidated Life is the insurance company whose official business and private transactions define the lives of the film's main characters.

The external curves and narrow staircases that wend their way into the private space of the apartment are repeatedly contrasted with the precisely parallel lines of public spaces. The distance covered by these lines is vast but finite. Indeed they are often precisely, quantifiably defined. Sometimes the lines are static and vertical, as in the impressively towering office buildings which we first see side by side in long shot. Later we get a closer shot from the ground as we focus in on the particular building into which workers stream. Before we move into the building with the men and women in suits and black pumps, the camera sweeps vertically up the face of the office. Baxter's voice continues to rattle off facts and figures as the visual scene shifts to the interior, which, we are told, is the nineteenth floor of the building. At work, time as well as space is tightly organized. Hours are staggered, by floor, in order that the sixteen elevators which service the building can accommodate the movement of its 31,259 employees without a traffic jam. In this building we are confronted by a comic version of the workplace world of Fritz Lang's *Metropolis* (1927) and Charles Chaplin's *Modern Times* (1936), transposed from literal industrial machinery to the figurative as well as literal machinery of commercial accounting. We see the horizontal lines of row after row of clerical workers, male and female, all at their desks working in synch with the staccato rhythms of their calculating machines. The space of the office is vast, the lines of desks seem to go on forever into a vanishing horizon. We know, however, that the vanishing point is fixed because the voice over so precisely numbers the cogs in this commercial wheel. Thus, we meet our hero precisely at desk number eight hundred and sixty one. Later that night we will see him again placed squarely in an image of the apparently endless but definitely numbered vertical lines that frame public spaces: the line of park benches where our hero tries to take refuge when he cannot find it at home.

Trade In (Stereo)Types

Space is definitively gendered in *The Apartment*, and the apartment itself, like the man, the single heterosexual man, whose bachelor pad it is, is gendered feminine. But what kind of femininity is this? Is it the kind of femininity which can offer the hospitality in which Levinasian ethics is situated? Let us consider the Talmudic quote with which Levinas opens his essay "Judaism and the Feminine," along with his comment on it.

> "The house is a woman," the Talmud tells us. Beyond the psychological and sociological obviousness of such an affirmation, the rabbinic tradition experiences this affirmation as a primordial truth. The last chapter of Proverbs, in which woman, without regard for "beauty and grace," appears as the genius of the hearth and, precisely as such, makes the public life of man possible, can, if necessary, be read as a moral paradigm. But in Judaism the moral always has the weight of an ontological basis: the feminine figures among the categories of Being. (31-32)

Private feminine being makes masculine public life possible according to Levinas. Though the male lead in *The Apartment* has a place in the life of the public sphere—in the territory marked as masculine, namely at the office—his position there is a feminized one. In this commercial public world the feminine is a site of (private) exploitation. To rise to the top of this competitive business one must participate—one way or another—in the relations of exploitation. The shift between feminine and masculine here is a shift from offering oneself up for use on the one hand—literally or metaphorically sleeping one's way to the top— or, on the other hand, participating in the exploitation of others—directly or indirectly screwing them.

C.C. Baxter is an everyman figure. Though he shares his given name with the audience ("C. For Calvin, C. for Clifford. However, most people call me Bud.") he locates his identity in numbers and other symbolic figures. His initials, the familiar abbreviation for carbon copy, express his status in the workplace as an expendable, replicable, replaceable, example of a type. No sooner are we introduced to him typing away at his calculating machine, as a piece of a larger apparatus of calculation, than we learn that his exploited condition extends beyond his position at work into the use of his personal space—his apartment. We soon learn that C.C. Baxter has become a target for sexual harassment. He has not, strictly speaking, been pressured into providing sexual favors. He is, however, pressured into enabling others to engage in more traditional forms of morally suspect sexual traffic. Baxter's apartment is prized by his (male) superiors on the job as a convenient spot for extra-marital hanky-panky with the office girls, telephone and elevator operators, or the women of easy virtue who populate public bars.

Though most people may call him Bud, or buddy boy, other references to the film's protagonist underline his degraded feminine positioning in a man's world. Sylvia, one of the women from the office taken to the apartment by a manager, Mr. Kirkeby, asks "Whose apartment is this anyway?" Kirkeby answers, "What's the difference? Some schnook that works in the office." Another manager, a Mr. Dobisch, uses similarly careless but more pointedly gendered language to express this attitude. When he calls Baxter late at night to arrange a place to take a woman with whom he thinks he "got lucky," the woman interjects, "I'm getting lonely. Who are you talking to anyway?" "My mother," Dobisch answers. When Dobisch's date worries out loud whether it is really ok to be "barging in on your mother in the middle of the night," he replies, "Don't worry about the old lady. One squawk from her and she's out of a job."

Baxter's life is turned upside down, and even his health endangered, by the unceasing demands of the guys in management who use his space at all hours of the day and night. We see Baxter struggling to juggle bookings, to clean up the mess left by those who pass through, trying to keep up with orders to stock the apartment with drinks and appetizers and decorations according to seasonal tastes, passing whims, sudden urges and opportunities. We see just how little respect Baxter's exploiters have for his integrity or his most basic bodily needs when he is pressured to leave his bed to spend the night on the benches of a public park in order that one of the guys can take advantage of a his once in a lifetime chance with a Marilyn Monroe look-alike.[11]

Baxter's fate is paralleled by that of the film's female lead, Miss Fran Kubelik. Played by a very young Shirley MacLaine, Miss Kubelik is one of the brigade of young women in uniform who operate the machinery that efficiently, every day, transports the 31,259 workers up and down the skyscraper like clockwork.[12] The movement of the elevator girls' passengers symbolizes the level of success to which would-be executives aspire (and the heights from which they can fall) as well as their daily return to the ground floor for the commute back home to wives and families located at a safe distance from the business of this "man's world." But not everyone has such a refuge to come home to. C.C. Baxter's apartment is unfortunately located within easy reach of management. And Miss Kubelik has no home of her own either. She has a bed under her married sister's roof and the watchful eye of her brother-in-law.

At work Fran seems to exert a measure of control over the space she has been assigned. Though this small and highly trafficked area is subject to frequent attempts to cross the line, by the same oversexed managers who make Baxter's life a misery, Miss Kubelik holds her own. She meets these incursions with sharply witty ripostes and comically mimed threats. She also personalizes the space she inhabits, welcoming her temporary guests by name, and even offering to one the carnation she wears as a personal touch on her uniform. Best of all, she makes conversation with passengers in a way which subverts the logic of Consolidated Life. When, in Miss Kubelik's elevator, Baxter warns against getting too close on account of his cold, she replies, "Oh, I never catch colds." Surprised, Baxter responds, "Really? I was looking at some figures from the Sickness and Accident Claims Division—do you know that the average New Yorker between the ages of twenty and fifty has two and a half colds a year?" "That makes me feel just terrible," says Miss Kubelik. "Why?" says Baxter. She explains, "Well, to make the figures come out even—since I have no colds a year — some poor slob must have five colds a year."

Neither her robust good health nor the control Miss Kubelik enjoys in the elevator protects her from exploitation by the man at the top, or at least the man in charge of who gets to go places at Consolidated Life. We soon learn that she is the mistress of Mr. J.D. (Jeff) Sheldrake, Director of Personnel. In the course of the film we learn, as Fran in the end also does, that she is not his beloved, or even the other woman in his life, but merely one in a series of other women. She, like C.C. is as replaceable and expendable as all the other cogs in the machinery of the corporate world. This revelation occurs for Fran in Baxter's apartment, which Sheldrake has booked for his Christmas rendezvous with her. When Fran confronts him there with what she has learned about the others who came before her, she learns precisely how cheaply the man she loves calculates her worth. In response to her meaningfully chosen Christmas gift of an L.P. recorded by the piano player from the restaurant where they meet, he offers her a hundred dollar bill and the suggestion to "go out and buy yourself something."

To see the face of the Other, in Levinasian terms, is to know one is accountable to the Other. Though Sheldrake is prepared to pay for what he wants he is accountable to nothing outside of the private market and its relations of exchange where goods and favours are traded, and everything can be cashed out in common currency. Sheldrake does not see Fran's face. When he heads off to his family Christmas in the suburbs, he leaves her broken in Baxter's apartment. When he asks if she is leaving with him, she answers bravely, "You run along— I want to fix my face." She waits behind meaning to pull her self together before she must go out to make her own way alone. As she starts to put on some lipstick, it is not her own face that she sees in the bathroom mirror but rather the reflection of a bottle of sleeping pills in Baxter's medicine cabinet. Unseen in the face to face encounter with her lover, Fran is broken. She can not see her own face, she cannot fix it alone.

The visual motif of the mirror which figures so prominently in this key scene recalls an earlier moment of insight in the film. When she runs into one of Mr. Sheldrake's jilted former lovers at the office Christmas party, Fran learns how she is really seen, as just the latest in a long line of women seduced by the boss. Though still in shock from this revelation she attends to Baxter's need to be seen by her at the party. He asks if she likes the new hat he bought to celebrate the promotion he got for making his apartment available to Sheldrake. When she offers him her compact mirror to see how he looks, he sees more than he expected. He recognizes it as the one he found earlier at his apartment and returned to Sheldrake after one of his visits. The mirror is used to reveal even more in this scene. Surprised by the look on Baxter's face as he realizes the significance of the mirror, Fran asks what's wrong. He stammers, "The mirror— it's broken." "I know," she says. "I like it this way—makes me look the way I feel." Later, as we see Fran standing in front of the bathroom mirror in Baxter's apartment she clearly feels much worse. Finding herself unseen having exposed her hurt and vulnerability to her lover, she moves beyond pain towards the promise of permanent loss of feeling. The scene closes with Fran filling a glass of water after having taken another long deliberate look at the pill bottle. She has discovered her place as a playing piece in the zero-sum game whose ultimate prizes are the keys to the executive men's room or the key to an executive's suburban heart(h). This game is one that makes people sick, but where Baxter suffers exhaustion and colds, Fran's unseen heartbreak is potentially fatal.

Preoccupation And Prepossessing Vulnerability

The feminized position occupied by C.C. Baxter and Fran Kubelik in the phallic structure of the office tower is one of more or less hapless victimization and exploitation. If this is the kind of femininity that Levinas identifies with hospitality and ultimately ethics, we have a problem. If so, then Levinasian ethics is something from which we, particularly we women, should seek shelter. However, I think this is not the case. I think there is an alternative meaning for the feminine in Levinas and moreover, this alternative meaning of the feminine is mirrored in Wilder's imagination of *The Apartment*.

While Wilder reveals the feminized exploitation and victimization of his male and female leads they are more than simply tokens circulated in the sexualized traffic of the business world.[13] In their relation to each other Miss Kubelik and Mr Baxter manifest two other dimensions of the Levinasian feminine. These faces of the feminine are revealed to us in the moment of our hero's return to his apartment, when he finds it occupied—preoccupied—by a vulnerable Other. That vulnerable Other is none other than Miss Kubelik herself, who until he realized her status as the boss's mistress, was the object of his fantasies of the "nice respectable girl."

Here we need another word or two about Levinasian terminology, specifically "the Other."[14] This expression is key to understanding the insight at the heart of Levinas's phenomenology of ethics. The Other is the source of the ethical command; the force who generates the ought. The human Other is not a special category of person or other kind of being; the human Other is not a category at all. The mere presence of an Other, any other,[15] is a confrontation which puts one fundamentally into question. This fundamental question is "What ought I to do?"[16] Levinas locates the authority to raise this fundamental question not in an elevated third party, whether divine, legal, cultural, or in the scientifically or religiously defined nature of the universe, or human nature. Rather, it is located in the face which addresses one in the second person. It is located there every time one is so addressed; and, it is located, there, even, as we shall see in the case of Mr. Baxter and Miss Kubelik, when it is expressed without being said in so many words. Finally, the Levinasian Other is not the other in the sense in which one might use this term to speak about different *types* of people. The alterity of the Other is the more radical difference with which one is faced when confronted by the simple fact that one is not alone in the universe, the fact that one could be held accountable, something that would be impossible if there were no one to account to.

To return to the scene of the ethical in *The Apartment*, let's return to our hero's preoccupation. The way in which Miss Kubelik occupies his home and preoccupies his attention is different from the ways in which his home has been used and his services abused by the office managers. It is true that C.C. had been infatuated with Miss Kubelik and so her appearance in his apartment, in fact in his bed, might be seen as a windfall. This potential benefit to Baxter might constitute a significant difference, but it is not the difference that is significant from a Levinasian perspective. From this perspective the important point to notice is that those short term informal "rentals" by the managers, though exploitive, were voluntary and, consensual.[17] In contrast Baxter's discovery of Miss Kubelik simultaneously constitutes a discovery of himself in an involuntary relationship with her. He has not invited her into his home out of fear of losing something or out of a desire not to pass up some opportunity. He is not motivated by any hope of gaining anything from her. Rather he *discovers* her *already* there. He has no room to decide whether or not to invite her in; rather, he must decide what to do now that he is faced with the fact of her preoccupying presence. This is an essential feature of the encounter which, according to Levinas's phenomenology, characterizes the ethical. One does not choose to face the Other; one comes to consciousness that one is already faced by the Other. One discovers one's autonomy, one's right to oneself and all that one possesses (emblematically one's home) already violated. One is "taken hostage" by the Other, who "interrupts" and put's one's very right to be into question.[18]

To be faced by the Other depends on a passivity which Levinas characterizes as maternal.[19] In his apartment, when he discovers Fran Kubelik unconscious on his bed with a bottle of sleeping pills in her near lifeless hand, Calvin Clifford Baxter is faced by the Other in exactly that way. In Wilder's film the maternal site of the feminine is inhabited most notably by an unattached heterosexual male character. Thus C.C. Baxter represents at least one conceivable example in support of Levinas's protestation that his reference to the feminine in habitation does not depend on the presence of an empirical female.[20]

Fran Kubelik's role in the ethical scene is also, in Levinasian terms, a feminine one. Her role in this scene reveals the other feminine face of the ethical, the flip side of the feminine position occupied by C.C. Baxter. Where Baxter is involuntarily, helplessly confronted by the Other, Fran is the vulnerable, helpless feminine Other herself. To describe the Other as feminine is no more to suggest that Levinas believes this role is only and always occupied by girls and women than to suppose that the feminine in habitation depends on the presence of a girl or woman. One encounters the Other when one faces a boy or a man just as in the face-to-face with a girl or a woman. Nonetheless, the Other is definitely a feminine figure in Levinas's writing. In discussing one's responsibility to the Other he frequently cites the biblical injunction to aid the "widow, the orphan, and the stranger."[21] Though orphans and strangers of course can be male, what they share with the widow is their marginal legal status in the biblical context in which this injunction arises. In that context they cannot speak for themselves. They have human needs, which biblical laws command be met (though their human needs are not necessarily any greater than those of a community member who has full legal standing) because they have no-one to speak for them. In a patriarchal society in which the interests of family members are represented by the male head of the household, the widow and the orphan, like the foreigner or resident alien who is identifiable through his lack of or reduced civil status, is legally not an agent but at best a legal, or moral, patient. Within this context this voiceless passive status marks the Other as a feminine figure.

When one is faced by the Other one is faced not by a type of being characterized by her rights. When one is faced by the Other one is faced by her/his nakedness, unadorned by the customary garments of legal status or cultural masks, and unsheltered by civil or moral rights. When C.C. Baxter is confronted by the Other who preoccupies him, she is literally incapable of speaking for herself; she lies unconscious on his bed. To identify this Otherness as feminine may be misunderstood to mean that women (or other socially marginalized people) are constitutionally or politically unable to speak for themselves. This, of course, is not the case (at least not always) in societies in which women are recognized as people who can speak and have a right to speak for themselves. It is not even the case in the fictional world created by Wilder.[22] Miss Kubelik does express herself on the job, even playfully, "Watch the door, please. Blasting off." She makes friendly conversation with her elevator passengers, and does not hesitate to put wise guys in their place when they cross the line: "Watch your hand, Mr. Kirkeby!" She says after he has slapped her behind with his newspaper. "One of these days I'm going to shut those doors on you and." Instead of speaking the rest of the thought she withdraws her hand into the sleeve of her uniform, and waves the "amputated" limb at him. She also expresses her feelings to the man who breaks her heart even though he has no interest in listening to her. And, eventually, she tells her story to her host in the apartment as he helps get her back on her feet after her overdose. But when Fran speaks on these occasions she wears the uniform and masks of her public and private roles. She is the "elevator girl," "mistress," "nice respectable girl," "good patient," and even playful "dinner partner" when Baxter serves her up a special treat as her health recovers under his care.

A woman (or man) can play all of these roles; they are all speaking parts. The feminine Other, however, is the feminine that exists before the exchange of words, outside of the framework defined by a phallic logic. To call this dimension of language phallic is not to suggest that it is only accessible to men or that it is sustained by a male conspiracy. Rather it is to signal its history, in western culture, as the incarnation of the law of the father.[23] Wilder's film subtly suggests that this framework is not only phallic but also WASP-ish. It is only in the more softly lit and shadowy neighbourhood that Jewish voices are audible as such. Black and Asian figures speechlessly occupy even more obscure positions in the film. One example of this is the pianist who performs the background music for Sheldrake's romancing of Fran (and others) at the Chinese restaurant. His full name appears on the cover of the L.P. album Fran gives Sheldrake at the apartment: "RICKSHAW BOY - Jimmy Lee Kiang with Orchestra." In another very telling scene, the only words spoken by a Black "bootblack" to whom Sheldrake tosses a coin when he gets up from kneeling at his work, is "much obliged." Another black actor appears in a silent role as the bewildered handyman upon whose head Baxter places the bowler hat that had symbolized his executive aspirations, after the scene in which he took a stand and turned in his key to the executive men's room. Even more obscure, but worth remarking on in this context, are the whooping Hollywood representations of North American Indians, chased across the land by cowboys in the movies that noisily dash Baxter's hopes of enjoying his T.V. dinner in the company of Greta Garbo and co. in *Grand Hotel*, which is persistently interrupted by "a word from our sponsor."

While there is plenty going on in the background of Wilder's film, the viewer's attention is directed primarily to the male and female leads, both of whom occupy feminine positions at two distinct levels. They occupy parallel feminine roles in the public man's world, the business world, where at various stages they are each participants in, resisters of, and victims of exploitation. They also occupy complementary feminine roles in the ethical encounter: Baxter, is the preoccupied hostage to the Other, and Miss Kubelik is the Other, whose prepossessing vulnerability and silent cry for help preoccupy Baxter and take him hostage.

The price to be paid for this hostage taking is the fall into being human—the painful birth of ethical conscience, the cost of becoming "a mensch." This pain begins when Baxter calls his neighbour, Dr, Dreyfuss, for help. To protect Miss Kubelik's reputation and dignity Baxter lets his neighbours think he is to blame rather than sharing the sordid details of Fran's predicament. He takes on her burden as his own. This shift of conscience, manifested in consciousness and action, illustrates what Levinas calls "substitution." It is dramatically expressed when we see Baxter visibly feeling Miss Kubelik's pain. Dr. Dreyfuss slaps Fran repeatedly in the face, literally to wake her up, to bring her to her senses, asking her to recollect who she is, where she is, with whom she is. Each time we hear the doctor's hand hit Fran's face the camera cuts to the pain on Baxter's face. Before she is conscious enough to feel her own pain, he feels it for her.

Hospitality And Homelessness On The Way To Becoming A Mensch

Baxter's concern for Miss Kubelik does not end with his sympathetic pains. He takes caring action, drawing on the resources provided by his neighbour, the embodiment of the yiddishe mama. Mrs. Dreyfuss takes over with the bedridden Fran where her husband Dr. Dreyfuss left off, delivering chicken soup and advice for the lovelorn. Levinas too was emphatic that care is more than an attitude. It has material meaning and depends on material means. He noted the contrast of this perspective with that of Heidegger in his famous remark, "Dasein in Heidegger is never hungry."[24] The technology of care, the food, equipment and know-how with which to make it are introduced into Baxter's home by Mrs. Dreyfuss who has inherited it as the legacy of a rich tradition of learning how to be human. Our hero, however, is a quick study and he soon learns how to look after his unexpected guest on his own. He communicates with Mr Sheldrake on Miss Kubelik's behalf, invents messages of concern to pass on to her, distracts her with simple card games and listens to her troubles until she is able to rest. When she recovers more strength he improvises in the kitchen, using a tennis racket as a spaghetti strainer, to make her a special candlelight and tablecloth dinner at home.

Unfortunately for Baxter, the dinner is interrupted by Fran's brother-in-law who has been directed to the apartment by jealous management guys. The brother-in-law gets entirely the wrong idea, Baxter gets a black eye, and Fran gets whisked away to the custody of her sister. Untroubled by his black eye and full of the idea that Mr. Sheldrake is no longer interested in Fran, he marches merrily into the boss's office the next day to tell him that their worries are over as he wants to marry Fran and take her off the boss's hands. Things do not go as smoothly as Baxter had imagined, however. While Fran was recuperating at home with Baxter, Mr. Sheldrake was kicked out of his family home by Mrs. Sheldrake who learned about her husband's philandering from Miss Olsen, Sheldrake's secretary (one of his jilted lovers). Unperturbed Sheldrake sees this as a chance to enjoy the bachelor life and moves in to his men's club in town. But since the men's club is "strictly stag" he needs the key to Baxter's apartment again; having made up with Fran, he needs somewhere private to take her.

This key scene is a turning point for Baxter. We see a man clearly distressed by what is being asked of him. It is distressing also for the audience to see him, after some hesitation, give the boss the key. Shortly after, however, the tension is broken and our faith in our hero restored. Sheldrake walks in to the executive assistant's office to tell Baxter that he had mistakenly handed over the wrong key; this is not the key to the apartment, but the key to the executive men's room. When Baxter assures him that this is no mistake, Sheldrake threatens him with losing his job, "Baxter, I picked you for my team because I thought you were a bright young man. You realize what you're doing? Not to me—but to yourself. Normally it takes years to work your way up to the twenty-seventh floor—but it takes only thirty seconds to be out on the street again. You dig?" "I dig," says Baxter, clearly having expected this outcome. "Just following doctor's orders," he explains, putting on his coat and hat. "I've decided to become a mensch. You know what that means? A human being."

This order, the fundamental ethical order, was given to Baxter by his neighbour Doctor Dreyfuss as they worked together to revive the half-conscious Fran. At that point Dreyfuss was under the mistaken impression that Fran had taken the overdose because of Baxter, the bachelor who Dr. and Mrs. Dreyfuss believed was partying in his apartment with different women every night, sometimes with several women in a night. They knew nothing about how the apartment was being used by other men. "I don't know what you did to that girl in there," says Dreyfuss to Baxter about Fran, ". . . and don't tell me—but it was bound to happen, the way you carry on. Live now, pay later. Diner's Club!" He continues, "Why don't you grow up, Baxter? Be a mensch! You know what that means?" "I'm not sure," says Baxter. "A mensch," comes the emphatic reply, "a human being!"

The expression "be a mensch" is a Yiddish one. The German expression from which it originates literally does mean be a human being. In Yiddish usage it means be a *good* human being, be a decent, caring, ethical human being. The film's narrative, in the end, is essentially a story of how to become a mensch in this sense. Strikingly the climax of this story follows a figurative fall. Baxter suffers a fall from, if not the pinnacle of the corporate ladder, at least from a decent job (on the twenty seventh floor) with prospects of upward mobility. He ends up jobless, facing homelessness, and thinking he has lost the girl of his dreams. Baxter has literally exchanged the key to the men's room and all that it represents for the opportunity to become a mensch. Miss Kubelik also, in the end, slips away from the promise that she may some day receive the keys to the heart and hearth of the successful business man to whom she offered her heart. She decides instead to take her chances playing the cards she will be dealt, over cardboard moving boxes if necessary, with Baxter. They fall, like biblical man and woman, into the knowledge of mortal human vulnerability. This for Levinas is precisely the realm of ethics.

Having heard about Baxter's refusal to participate in Sheldrake's schemes from the indignant Sheldrake himself, Fran runs over to the apartment to see if Baxter is alright. They have both become mature human beings, no longer willing participants in their own exploitation. They reach this stage not by learning better to defend their own territory, or even by getting their own back at their exploiters (as Miss Olsen does with Sheldrake) but through the willingness to selflessly risk loss for the sake of another's well-being. It is at the point of displacement, taking the risk of homelessness, that Mr. Baxter and Miss Kubelik are able to follow the ethical order to be a mensch.

The coincidence of the view from *The Apartment* with a Levinasian perspective is remarkable. "No human or interhuman relationship can be enacted outside of economy; no face can be approached with empty hands and closed home," wrote Levinas in *Totality and Infinity*.[25] But to offer hospitality one must have achieved self-possession, be the master of one's own home: "the body as naked body is not the first possession; it is still outside of having and not having ... The body is my possession according as my being maintains itself in a home at the limit of interiority and exteriority."[26] Yet having a home is bound up with hospitality. "The possibility for the home to open to the Other is as essential to the essence of the home as closed doors and windows."[27] Nonetheless, there is a crucial difference between opening one's home to the stranger and selling it in exchange for profit, or the hope of profit. This insight can help us explain C.C. Baxter's anonymous status in the world in which he tried to make his way. Levinas explains: "Property alone institutes permanence in the pure quality of enjoyment, but this permanence disappears forthwith in the phenomenality reflected in money. As property, merchandise, bought and sold, a thing is revealed in the market as susceptible of belonging, being exchanged, and accordingly as convertible into money, susceptible of dispersing in the anonymity of money."[28]

In a spirit that is consistent with the insights revealed by Levinas's phenomenology of ethics, in *The Apartment* we see the anonymity and relations of exploitation that threaten anyone who is not master (or mistress) in her or his own home. This non-masterful position is coded as feminine. The film also reveals the displacement that generosity can generate, the homelessness that one must risk in order to achieve the capacity for welcome whose achievement marks a mensch. This is the feminine which Levinas calls maternal and out of which human ethical conscience is born. *The Apartment* is laden with references to displacement—an experience all too familiar in both Levinas and Wilder's lives. Both Fran and Baxter are new arrivals to the city. They are like refugees in their own lives. While recovering in the apartment from her most recent heartbreak, Fran tells the story of the unsuccessful search for love that led to her latest move: "So I came to New York and moved in with my sister and her husband," she says. "He drives a cab. They sent me to secretarial school, and I applied for a job with Consolidated—but I flunked the typing test." "Too slow?" asks Baxter. "Oh. I can type up a storm," she replies, "but I can't spell. So they gave me a pair of white gloves and stuck me in an elevator—that's how I met Jeff." Later, Baxter shares the story of the journey that led him to where he is now. It also involves a history of a potentially home-wrecking star-crossed love. "She was the wife of my best friend—and I was mad for her. But I knew it was hopeless." Baxter continues with a comic re-telling of the story of his incompetent efforts "to end it all," that preceded his move to the big city.

Baxter's apartment in the city is furnished with signs of impermanence including the posters on the wall. One of these is a copy of a painting by Marc Chagall, a painter who himself lived most of his life effectively in exile. His work is populated with nostalgic dream-like references to the lost *shtetls* of East European Jewry. The neighborhood that Wilder and his creative team constructed for a character running away from an unhappy past contains comparable references to a community nostalgically remembered by the displaced. Baxter's neighbours, the Dreyfusses, carry a name evocative of one of the shocking moments in Enlightenment European Jewish history.[29] On top of this, the language of this lost European community, the *mama loshn*, is also part of the neighbourhood in which Baxter has sought refuge, indeed it is an integral part of the environment.[30] The first words we hear from the landlady, Mrs. Lieberman, a comment on the weather, is laced with Yiddish: "Some weather we're having," she says. "Must be from all the *meshugass* at Cape Canaveral."

The film subtly offers an opportunity to recollect and reflect on loss, but most importantly it emphasizes the ethical meaning of how we move on when we must move on if we are to hope to become human. In the closing scene Mr. Baxter and Miss Kubelik, with her coat still on, sit in the apartment among the packing crates and rolled up posters. We do not know where they are headed next, but we know that they have come home to the condition of exile that Levinas understood as the basis for hospitality.[31]

So, before we once more take up our own journeys, and to end, for the time being, our sojourn with Levinas in *The Apartment*, I'd like to offer, for the road, a couple of concluding remarks, borrowed from Levinas commentator Desmond Manderson:

Dwelling is a complacency that never allows us to grow or learn. If it allows others into our lives and our thoughts only on our own terms, then it does not really allow others at all. The solution is to eschew forever a world of psychological or intellectual comfort in favour of "the exteriority of absolute exile." "As in a desert one can find no place to reside. From the depths of sedentary existence a nomadic memory arises." Levinas wishes us to remain always unsettled and restless, "driven from the outside," being "in exile in itself." To be at home, to possess our thoughts and our experiences as we would possess a comfortable armchair, is the prelude to solitude and to a violence in which we protect "our" possessions through the totalities of appropriation, assimilation or conquest . . . Levinas defends a life spent wandering in the desert. We can be open to others and allow their pluralism to affect *us* only if we resist all the accumulation of intellectual furniture. Internal exile alone makes both communication and responsibility continually possible. More, it allows us to be influenced by those around us without possession or control.[32]

Notes

1. Emmanuel Levinas, *Totality and Infinity: An Essay on Exteriority*, trans. Alphonso Lingis (Pittsburgh: Duquesne University Press, 1969), 155.
2. See Derrida's "Violence and Metaphysics" and "A Word of Welcome" for two especially important discussions of this theme in Levinas.
3. See Katz and Guenther for two especially valuable recent contributions to feminist Levinas scholarship.
4. See Davies 2009 for a feminist response to feminist critiques of maternal self-sacrifice in Levinas.
5. Levinas, *Totality and Infinity*, 157.
6. Levinas, *Totality and Infinity*, 158.
7. I specify the hypothetical single man's heterosexuality not because I equate male homosexuality with femininity, but to evade the suggestion that any man who is in some sense identified with the feminine must be homosexual following the stereotypical association of effeminacy with male homosexuality.
8. Strictly speaking, in Levinas's phenomenology of ethics, the Other is not a *type* of person. Otherness in Levinas's work is not a synonym for marginalized or despised difference. At the same time Levinas frequently appeals to the cultural meanings of Jewishness and femininity and Jewishness in western history to allude to certain dimensions of the Other who does call one to account. A fuller discussion of the meaning of the Other in Levinas is provided below in the subsection titled, "Preoccupation and prepossessing vulnerability."
9. The film's award winning art direction was provided by Alexander Trauner.
10. In addition to Wilder as director and I.A.L. Diamond who co-authored the screenplay with Wilder, and Trauner as the art director, and a talented cast of actors, the film-making team included Joseph LaShelle (photography), Daniel Mandell (editing), Fred Lau (sound), and the music of Adolph Deutsch.

11. This woman is just the clearest, but only one example of a number of women in the film presented as carbon copies of a certain type of the feminine. It is worth noting that *The Apartment* was the film Wilder made right after completing the filming of *Some Like It Hot* with the actual Marilyn Monroe. At the time, and long after, this type was iconic.

12. While both women and men sit at the accounting desks, and women serve as secretarial gatekeepers to management, in addition to the job of elevator girl it is worth noting that the only other all female job category in this office building, namely the telephone operator, involves the circulation of information. Women in these jobs facilitate the traffic in tokens of meaning (words and workers) which in this film are represented as debased and of little intrinsic worth. Consider, for example, how the lingo of this office in which x and y become x-wise and y-wise undermines any real impulses to communicate meaningfully.

13. For a fuller exploration of the relationship between the exchange of tokens of speech and the literally sexed traffic in women in patriarchal kinship systems, see Rubin (1975). For an application of this analysis illustrating the distinction between trade in actual women and trade in multiply copied images of them, see Davies (1988).

14. The standard orthographic conventions to express the distinction between other and Other is explained by Levinas translator Alphonso Lingis: "With the author's permission we are translating '*autrui*' (the personal Other, the you) by 'Other,' and '*autre*' by 'other.' In doing so we regrettably sacrifice the possibility of reproducing the author's use of both capital or small letters with both these terms in the French text." (Levinas, *Totality and Infinity*, 24–25.) I follow Lingis's practice except when quoting other translators or commentators who do not.

15. It is tempting to write "any *other* human" here, which is a reasonable interpretation of what is intended. However, that may be taken as a misleading reference to the controversies surrounding the question of Levinas's attitude to animals, which in turn may misleadingly imply that the Other is a term signifying the elevated ontological status of human beings as a species. This would be misleading because Levinas was emphatic that the face if the Other is not a *phenomenon* and the Other is not an ontological category.

16. A more radical version of the fundamental question is formulated in the title of Jill Robbins's collection of interviews with Levinas: *Is It Righteous to Be?*

17. Depending on the nature of the structures within which transactions are made and the specific histories of sexism, racism, class conflict, anti-antisemitism, colonialism and so forth which have informed them, radical exploitation is consistent with consensual relationships and voluntary agreements and contracts, as Marxist, feminist and other critical analyses have demonstrated. See, for example, Catherine MacKinnon's groundbreaking exploration of the inadequacy of the concept of consent or its absence for capturing the difference between rape and ethical sexual relationships. "Feminism, Marxism, Method and the State."

18. See especially the chapter on "substitution" in Levinas's *Otherwise than Being*, for fuller discussion of the metaphor of being "taken hostage." For more on interruption see Pinchevski, for example.

19. See especially Guenther, and also Taylor.

20. Levinas writes, "The feminine has been encountered in this analysis as one of the cardinal points of the horizon in which the inner life takes place—and the empirical absence of the human being of 'feminine sex' in a dwelling nowise affects the dimension of femininity which remains open there, as the very welcome of the dwelling." *Totality and Infinity*, 158.

21. See, for example, Levinas, *Totality and Infinity* p.77, 245. Relevant biblical sources include Exodus 22:20-23. and Jeremiah 22:3.

22. This comment needs qualification with respect to the small number of racialized figures (Black, Chinese, and North American Indian) who appear in the film. These people do not speak in the film. Their voicelessness is perhaps a silent comment (intentional or not) on racist laws and a culture built on colonialism and which at the time of filming still tolerated lynching and all manner of racist violence. It may also reflect Wilder's personal knowledge, as a European born Jew, of just how easily people can be stripped of their civil and human rights, and what it means for the voices of those who suffer these indignities to go unheard or be utterly silenced. Born in 1906, the same year as Levinas, Wilder, emigrated from Berlin first to Paris and then to the States. He arrived in Hollywood in 1933. His mother, grandmother and stepfather died in Auschwitz.

23. This idea is more fully developed by those twentieth century French philosophers who refer to it with the term phallogocentrism. This neologism plays a particularly important role in the works of Jacques Derrida, Hélène Cixous, Julia Kristeva and Luce Irigaray.

24. Levinas, *Totality and Infinity*, 134. *Dasein* is Heidegger's central philosophical term and the cornerstone of his magnum opus *Being and Time*. Literally it means something like existence, specifically human existence or way of being.

25. Levinas, *Totality and Infinity*, 172.

26. Levinas, *Totality and Infinity*, 162.

27. Levinas, *Totality and Infinity*, 173.

28. Levinas, *Totality and Infinity*, 162.

29. See, for example, *The Dreyfus Affair: J'accuse and other writings*, by Emile Zola's. The impact of the Dreyfus affair also figures prominently in Marcel Proust's *A la recherche du temps perdu*.

30. While Hebrew, the holy language of the sacred texts—Torah and Talmud—is a language traditionally spoken among men, Yiddish is the mother tongue (the *mama loshn*) of European Ashkenazi Jewry, the community decimated by the Shoah less than two decades before *The Apartment* was filmed. For further reflection on gendered dimensions of language and Jewish memory, see Klepfisz.

31. See Wyschogrod for more on the role of exile in Levinas's thought.

32. Desmond Manderson, *Proximity, Levinas and the Soul of Law*, (Montreal: McGill-Queen's University Press, 2007), 71.

Chapter 15

Reading Feminist Hospitality In Plato's *Timaeus*: Possibilities For Education

Stephanie Burdick-Shepherd

It is as a female, feminist professor I welcome my students. Thus, I invite them into my classroom so that we may discuss the philosophical texts at hand while also acknowledge in my invitation that there are gender, race, and class differences between us, their selves, the texts, and each other. But what, often, does my invitation look like? I am caring, warm, and approachable. I tell them, this is my class on such and such a topic, and I welcome your interest, your participation, and your thoughts. Yet, despite this welcome I am often greeted by passive students who do not seem interested, do not readily participate, and have difficulty sharing their thoughts. Certainly there are those students who attend my course and who simply do not wish to participate. But more often than not, when I speak to students outside of my class they tell me that they want to participate, they want to engage the class, the texts, each other but they do not know how and it feels "strange." I am hesitant to simply attribute the problem to either a) my students general inability whether psychological or sociological or b) my own ignorance of how power works within dialogue. Moreover, I also recognize that despite my theoretical engagement with feminist theory which proposes to challenge gender norms, I often characterize my teaching as warm, approachable, and caring. Hence, my invitation becomes not feminist but rather conventionally feminine and does little to disrupt the structures of power which limit difference in the educational context. How then can my invitation to my courses become one that invites my students to participate despite the strangeness and difficulty of dialogue through difference but also without diminishing my own power as a subject?

As a possible answer to this query, Zelia Gregoriou writes of post-colonial teaching, "It [the receptacle] is a place we create when in hosting others we change, hybridize our discourses and identities, and let others teach us, from the beginning, how we are different and multiple within ourselves."[1] Gregouriou challenges feminist teachers who recognize gender, race, and class as structures within the classroom to become receptive hosts in our classrooms. And I would add, though she does not explicitly state this, that a teacher who is a receptive host does not simply host her students but is hosted by them.

This seems a counter response to the concept of hospitality that pervades modern philosophical and political thought whereby hospitality seemingly requires mastery of place to offer hospitality towards a guest or visitor. This counter response is a feminist response to a concept of hospitality that relies on mastery of place in order to invite. This mastery of place creates the conditions for an unchangeable, impermeable guest/host relationship. It is Immanuel Kant's essay, "Perpetual Peace" that establishes this concept of hospitality within the Western philosophical tradition. In the essay, he shows that peace is won through the establishment of certain conditions, one being the institution of hospitality. He writes, "The right of men as Citizens of the world in a cosmopolitical system shall be restricted to conditions of universal hospitality."[2]

A feminist reflection about hospitality cannot be content with this Kantian formulation of the concept, as it fosters an enacting of hospitality structured on hegemonic asymmetries. Feminist thinking in education needs an articulation of hospitality such as to allow for students and teachers to be reciprocally hospitable. Is there a text in Western philosophical thought which offers this kind of feminist response to the Kantian concept of hospitality?

I offer here a possible alternative to the Kantian text, a reading of the text of Plato's *Timaeus* as an entry point for a feminist reconsideration of hospitality. Not only does this text engage the concept of hospitality in a rich manner but it does so specifically by offering a picture of Socrates as a hospitable teacher offering a lens through which not only to engage a feminist understanding of hospitality but a feminist understanding of hospitality in the classroom. For this reason, a consideration of the complexities of this text from a feminist lens can provide interesting foundations to our daily practices of hospitality in the classroom.

In the Kantian context hospitality is extended towards the foreigner, not because he is "man" but because he is man within the cosmo-political state. He asserts further that, "A state of Peace among men who live side by side with each other, is not the natural state."[3] Moreover, hospitality is purposeful; it is an activity involving invitation into the abode of another nation. The right of hospitality is not extended as a matter of friendship but as something granted to the foreigner who wishes to dwell safely in another state. It simply ensures the "possibility of entering into social intercourse with the inhabitants of a country." Our conventional understanding of hospitality follows this. Through the name, "guest," the guest calls forth to be hosted by a host, as a matter of right. Elizabeth Telfer highlights this understanding with the following definition: "We can define 'hospitality' as the giving of food, drink and accommodation to guests—people who are not regular members of a household." And, thus, as host you are responsible for this guest.[4] We might think that this kind of hospitality is based on conditions. That is, the master or host ensures safety of the guest or visitor but only if the guest or visitor follows the rules and the conditions set up by the host and master.

When I tell my class "This is *my* class on such and such a topic" I offer only a Kantian vision of hospitality—the hospitality granted to a visitor who visits a foreign country. She can visit, she can view the art, she can eat the unfamiliar food. But she must not work, she must not break any laws, she must not get sick, she must not transgress upon this strange country. As her host, I must offer her this right to hospitality on the condition that she obey the laws. I cannot transgress upon her as the guest. We remain in a static relationship. Yet, without denying the right to both visit a foreign state and to be hosted properly by that state, we must question whether this sense of hospitality makes sense in the educational context. For the visitor must not leave her mark upon the country. Yet, this marking is exactly what we want from students! We do not simply wish our students to "visit" a field of study. We want students to locate themselves inside an unfamiliar field or discipline. We often want them to get lost in the questions of study and trace their way into answers that change the field in a new or positive way. We want them to critically read, comment, and reflect. We do not want visitors into our classrooms, mere tourists. We want students who make marks upon the field. We also want to change our students' lives; molding, impacting, enabling growth. Thus, our hospitality is misguided if we offer it only as masters of our classrooms, our work, and our disciplines encouraging passive and unreflective study instead of critical, active, and receptive scholarship in our students. And, I would argue by not allowing our students to host us, as teachers, we encourage our own sort of passivity that enforces hegemonic structures.

Feminist teaching calls for an engagement with hospitality that positions the student to be receptive and welcoming. As teachers we must engage students in a hospitality that situates them, as visitors who also receive us, and certainly the texts and ideas of our fields. This goes beyond the welcoming words of a host towards her guests. As feminist teachers we must engage in hospitality that goes beyond a general description of "nice" and "caring" towards hospitality that invites engagement and reception.

And though, in the educational field it is more often the *Meno* or the *Apology* where we turn to find Socrates the teacher, it is Plato's *Timaeus* (a strange and yet most welcoming dialogue) which offers us Socrates, the hospitable teacher. This ancient text offers us images of hospitality that challenge our modern, everyday, and ordinary use of the concept. Moreover, as Derrida and others have shown, this ancient text plays with the concept of hospitality by using the structure of gender. Plato's dialogue, *Timaeus*, is probably a dialogue from the late period of Plato's writing. In the dialogue, Critias, Hermocrates, and Timaeus attempt to tell Socrates the cosmology of the world. It is widely considered one of the most challenging of the Platonic dialogues.[5] There is great challenge in returning to ancient texts to uncover thinking about modern concepts. One reaction might be to ignore ancient texts for their age, their irrelevance to modernity. Another reaction might be to issue a complaint against interpretation or rather mis-interpretation because of the vast difference in language and culture. In feminist studies ancient texts are often cited for their misogynous language and ideals. However, it is through the recovery of these ancient texts and our modern interpretation of them that we issue new challenge to ourselves. We read and engage these texts, not in order to give credence to every idea or word held within them but to allow our own ideas and ideals to be challenged, refuted, reflected, and worked upon.

In the following discussion I will look at three episodes of hospitality in the *Timaeus* that give us hospitality considered beyond power, mastery, and place. I will move to a discussion of why this is a feminist vision of hospitality and close with a description of feminist hospitality in the classroom.

Locating Hospitality in Plato's *Timaeus*

In the following three episodes I will look at the three places in the *Timaeus* where Plato describes hospitality. In the first two there is a description that challenges the Kantian vision of hospitality. In the third episode Plato describes a conventional or Kantian vision of hospitality. I will note that both kinds of hospitality are necessary to the *Timaeus* but that the first two are emphasized. It is these first two episodes that offer a feminist understanding of hospitality.

As the purpose in this paper is not to add to scholarship on the *Timaeus* but to add the *Timaeus* as a text for those interested in looking at the concept of hospitality, the following account brackets many of the metaphysical questions raised by the *Timaeus* and concentrates on a textual interpretation of three main episodes in the dialogue that I believe highlight aspects of a feminist vision of hospitality.

Episode One: Socrates

The dialogue begins in the home of Critias, where Socrates is a visitor and guest. The conversation begins with Socrates asking Timaeus about a fourth man who appears to be missing. Socrates seems somewhat disappointed by the absence of this man, as if he expected to be the guest of not three men but of four! Moreover, he does not passively accept the man's absence, he entreats Timaeus to make up for the absence. To Timaeus' credit he stands up ready for this task that Socrates puts upon him.

> Socrates: One, two, three ... but now where's our fourth, my dear Timaeus, of yesterday's feasters and hosts of today? Timaeus: Some illness befell him, Socrates – he wouldn't have been left out of this meeting willingly. Socrates: Then does the task of filling the missing one's part belong to you and these fellows here? Timaeus: it certainly does, and we'll do everything in our power, at least, not to fall short in any way. Besides, it wouldn't be at all just for those of us who are left, after being entertained by you yesterday with gifts so befitting to guests, not to host you heartily in return.[6]

What we see in the beginning of this dialogue is a procedural conversation on the subject of how a guest and a host should act. The dialogue moves from procedure to content by each of the characters enacting either "guest" or "host" in an ambiguous way. Socrates, who is the "real" guest acts much like a host while his hosts act like guests. They challenge in their actions the norms of hospitality. Socrates takes charge of the procedural questions; he is the first to speak and he issues the challenge to the rest of the party. Moreover, Socrates does not speak first by thanking his hosts for having him over as a guest, but immediately challenges his hosts by noting that his expectations have not been met, as he had expected four men and there are only three. In this way he seems to act in the role of host—sending the invitation, ordering the sequence of the party. Likewise, Timaeus does not find this challenge antagonistic coming from the mouth of a guest and answers to Socrates that the hosts will try and make sure Socrates, the guest, has a good time. Timaeus, the one with the power of the host, becomes accommodating and accepting and takes on the characteristics of the conventional guest. Socrates, with a lack of power as a foreign guest, becomes directive and takes on the power of host.

Timaeus then, is the master of the coming conversation[7] but it is Socrates who *informs* the structure of the conversation. Socrates states, "then, after you had looked over it in common among yourselves, you agreed to pay me back today with my guest-gift of speeches; so here I am—arrayed for the occasion and readiest of all man to do my receiving."[8] Socrates, as guest, is the most prepared of all the men today and he is ready because he is not a passive guest. He has made himself present to the conversation by asking how it will proceed.

Yet, let it be clear that while Socrates and Timaeus challenge the roles of the host and guest they do not give up those named roles. Socrates is "the guest" and Timaeus et al. are the "hosts." Although Socrates is exacting and challenging he still considers himself hosted. Though he is ready to receive he does not do this as the master; note that he calls the speeches "guest-gifts." Thus, he does not take over the party; he simply rearranges the actions that are normally taken by guest and by host. He does not stop the conversation when he is told there are only 3 men and not 4 present, instead he seems to invite Timaeus to host him all the more better for the absence.

How do we know that he understands this receiving as a guest? Unlike a host, who may receive only that which is proper to his home, Socrates is prepared, in this dialogue, to accept almost anything from the three men. He accepts speeches, lectures, some poetry, and myth. These speeches will be received well by Socrates because they are invocations of the cosmic world, which includes all the ways that we describe the world. Moreover, Socrates will remain silent and receive each speech, not as mere stories but as the most truthful accounts possible. As he states, "you must speak; and I, in exchange for my speeches of yesterday, must keep my peace and listen in turn."[9]

Socrates is an out-of-place guest. He informs those who should master him. Socrates receives best of all the men because he is the guest. He is the one without a place from which to speak. He receives well because he will simply listen to the story being told. Socrates will remind his hosts that they too must receive the story well, as a song, as something beautiful. "Excellent, Timaeus! And it must be received entirely as you urge; so now that we've received your prelude so wonderfully, do for us what comes next in order and perform the song itself."[10] And he will thank them, he is a gracious guest.[11] Socrates and Timaeus in this section of the dialogue challenge the reader to reconsider the role of guest and host by showing how a guest—one without place or mastery—can invite and receive—be hospitable, and showing how a host—one with place and full mastery—can accept from a guest.

Episode 2: Khōra

We move here from the description of Socrates in the *Timaeus* to a similar description of reception without mastery or place—the *khōra*. Timaeus tells the story of the khōra after having told much of the story of the creation of the cosmos. Although we have been told that something called the demiurge has created the world Timaeus admits to leaving something out. It is important to recognize that the story of the *khōra* will be a difficult thing for Timaeus to tell. It is full of conflicting descriptions and illogical problems.[12] Timaeus tells us that he relates this story in a "bastard discourse."[13] The story is not easy to relate, and Timaeus must be sure to tell it well so that it is understood.

Here I will bracket much of the metaphysical arguments about place and space that the *Timaeus* brings up and concentrate simply on the description of the receptive *khōra*.[14]

Much like Socrates, *khōra* welcomes guests even as she itself has no place. Socrates received the dialogue from outside his place. The receiving imagined by *khōra* also is a receiving without place. Timaeus says:

> A third kind we didn't distinguish at that time, since we deemed that the two would be sufficient; but now the account seems to make it necessary that we try to bring to light in speeches a form difficult and obscure. What power, then, and what nature should one suppose it to have? This especially: that it's a receptacle for all becoming, a sort of wet-nurse.[15]

We find that this necessary cause, called receptacle, unlike the creator of the world, does not create the world but nurses the world, allows the world to become, is the "in-which" that things become within. While the creator created by seeing, the receptacle which will be renamed, *khōra*, at 52B, is reception enacted. In the passages which John Sallis calls the chorology[16] we receive the following names: "Molding stuff, (50C); Mother, Recipient, Container (50D3, 51A5); Recipient, (53A; 57C); The filled, (52E, 49A6, 51 A) Mother, Receptacle, (51A, 51A); Nurse, (49A); Place, Nurse (52D5, 88D); Nurse of Becoming, Khōra, Space (52B); Place, (52B)."[17]

Khōra is a receptacle, yet it is not a simply a container like something which holds things. Instead it is akin to a wet-nurse. The *khōra* is the ultimate receptacle. It only receives, but even in this it receives nothing that is not already received. It cannot be sensed or known. It receives beyond space and time. Khōra is that without a place, without a space. It is not being, it is not becoming. It is prior to all that which is. And it is simply "the in-which" that being resides. It has its own power. It does not take the shape of the things within it. The only material that Timaeus can compare it to is "gold" because he cannot think of a material that is worthy of comparative value. It receives all things.[18] It is wondrous. It is never without its own name. It is completely beautiful but is neither fire, nor water, nor air, nor earth.[19]

This ultimate receptacle then receives the elements within her, though she has no place of her own, no being of her own. Moreover, she does not simply allow them to abide there safely but nurtures them into some sort of order. They become within her. She does not array them by forcing them into shape but by shaking them as she herself sways irregularly.[20] It is as if her unintelligible, insensible backdrop allows for the becoming of sensible and intelligible beings. And this always moving necessary cause harbors and preserves. It grants stability to those things of the world which are in a state of flux, decay, and change.

If we think then of the *khōra* in terms of hospitality as understood through the terms of guest and host we see that *khōra* does not seem to act like a traditional host. She does not own a place. She is not a master of anything at all. And yet, despite this lack of mastery it is *khōra* that Timaeus tells us gives the world its shape and sense.

These two episodes then which describe Socrates' and *khōra*[21] in Plato's *Timaeus* begin to make us challenge the way we traditionally think of what it means to enact hospitable reception in the guest/host relationship. Socrates is a challenging guest that informs the party to which he has been invited. He does not give presents to his hosts, instead, his hosts give him gifts that he has helped prepare. It would be as if I had invited my guests to a party and they helped prepare some dough for bread, gave it to me, told me how to bake it, but then I gave it back to them as a gift.

In the episode of the *khōra* we find that *khōra*, which is as powerful and necessary to the world as the creator, does not make the world but allows the world to be informed upon her. She is all powerful and yet cannot even be described for what she is; she is the space upon which the whole of creation becomes. It would be as if we all went to a party and had a wonderful time in a house that we couldn't see or name! This is why the *Timaeus* as a text is so perplexing to theories of hospitality, for the work challenges our everyday notions of hospitality.

Yet, we cannot forget that our everyday notions of hospitality are not without ground. The world enacted reception in many ways before Timaeus told us his bastard discourse on the *khōra*. And Timaeus quickly returns us back to the Father, the cosmic body and soul. The following episode in the text of the *Timaeus* helps to underscore the differences between these modes of hospitality.

Episode 3: The Creator

The world Timaeus has portrayed is hospitable through and through. It is tempting to understand khōra as sole receptor for she is called receptacle, but we cannot allow the difficulty which Timaeus has in describing *khōra*[22] impede our understanding of the differences between *khōra* and the creator, or what Timaeus names, the demiurge.

The difference is not between two opposites but the difference is difference itself.[23] *Khōra* and demiurge are fundamental, *archic (first, before all,)* causes that must remain two. It is important that both *khōra* and the creator receive but that the receptions are irreducible to one another. When we move from *khōra* to demiurge we have moved kinds[24] of reception. For it is not true that the *khōra* receives and the cosmic body and soul do not! As Timaeus says: "For that one, having embraced all the intelligible Animals, holds them within itself, just as this cosmos holds and embraces us and all the other nurslings constructed as visible."[25]

Let us explore more fully the role of this father creator figure as it contrasts the *khōra*.

The demiurge/Father/creator receives as master. "And when the father who begat it noticed that it was moved and living—a sanctuary born for the everlasting gods—he rejoiced in it and, being well-pleased, thought of fashioning it to be more similar to its model."[26] So, the creator is the master who grants hospitality by making a peaceful place for the world to rest in. He does not receive being and the world in order to make being placed and to allow it to become as does *khōra*, instead, he grants sanctuary, a place of respite and peace The hospitality of the father is manifest in harmony, as whole. This is not a reception like *khōra*, instead this is an embrace or an enfolding. The constructor builds and that which he builds is nursed and grown within the hospitable cosmos.

This, that which is, hosts the cosmos as circle, it is turned in upon itself, there are no spaces, no gaps but instead a wholeness described here as one. This is a cosmos that is singular. It is complete within itself. It holds itself through its own strength. This cosmos has no need of others. It hosts them within its magnitude because it does not need or desire guests. This makes it happy. It flourishes in its excellence. It is a master of its own house; all in it are hosted as guest. Power is retained because it is held in place. It is able to be held within the intellect and intelligible.

> And so, as a circle turning within a circle he established a heaven that was one, alone, solitary—able by itself, because of its excellence, to be company to itself and to stand in need of no other at all, and sufficient unto itself as acquaintance and friend. For all these very reasons, he begat it a happy god.[27]

And the cosmos thus created does not simply stand alone. It is moved and living but yet excellent and eternal. It is a sanctuary: a place of worship, respite, gratitude. It invites guests but not as foreigners and not without its own place. It requires harmony as it is the master. Sanctuaries do not receive without place they simply protect, embrace within their own place. This is the hospitality that one finds in a fancy hotel spa. You are at peace, it is luxurious, and it is restful. But you do not become in such a place, you follow the rules and are ordered by the space itself.

The creator then is receptive, it is hospitable. But the activity of reception embodied by the demiurge is quite different from the reception embodied by Socrates and imagined by *khōra*. Importantly, *khōra* also receives the demiurge, she holds the creator! This underlines the importance of the kind of reception imagined by *khōra* in the *Timaeus*. Her reception is at least as important as the demiurge, for he is subject to the most necessary reception of *khōra*.

By considering these three episodes of reception in the text of the *Timaeus* I note two kinds of hospitality. One—that of the cosmic body and soul—is quite understandable and follows our conventional and Kantian understanding of hospitality. This is the hospitality offered by a master of a house who throws open the door, takes your coat, and gets you a glass of wine. He welcomes you into his home. You respectfully use the coasters and compliment him on his adorable dog. When the party is over he lets you know by escorting you quickly to the door and shutting it behind you.

Yet, the character of Socrates and *khōra* manifest themselves quite differently in regards to reception. They receive without mastery of place. Socrates is silent; *khōra* is described as the feminine absence of being. It is as if you were received into a party but there was no door, no host, no music, and no house. And you, yourself, only became welcomed after you began to dance to the music that wasn't even there!

Hospitality considered in this vein does not then rely on mastery of place but instead the action of invitation. If we return to the example of the classroom we might think then that a feminist invitation to the classroom would not begin with "Welcome to my classroom," but would begin with the question, "How should we act in this classroom?" The course would begin with a question that invited the action of reception from both the teacher and student, regardless of who was required or who had paid to attend the course rather than with a statement that immediately situated the teacher as a host and the student as a guest.

In the following section I will argue that the kind of hospitality enacted by Socrates and *khōra* are necessary for understanding a new way to look at hospitality that goes beyond mastery of place. Furthermore, this new understanding of hospitality is not simply new but is a feminist response to conventional understandings of hospitality.

A New Understanding Of Hospitality

The hospitality described in the text of the *Timaeus* then offers a feminist response to the idea of hospitality as mastery. In the described hospitality of Socrates and the *khōra* we find a reception that is hospitable not because it protects the foreigner (as the demiurgic creator does) but because it allows the foreigner to become and give place to itself. Its power does not create, does not give right, and does not own its "place" but it is archic—it is first, before all else. Its power comes because it is necessary to the world's sustainability. *Khōra* is hospitable without the need for location (place), mastery (power), or metaphysical presence; yet, this is not a passive reception—it is active and powerful. I will argue throughout the following section that this is a description of hospitality that aligns with critical feminist theory.

First I shall offer that it is in the text of the *Timaeus* that Plato has made space for a new understanding of hospitality which is feminist by calling *khōra* in the feminine form, not because, the *khōra* is feminine as female, but because Plato has marked the *khōra* as that which is different and yet as important as the creator. I think it most necessary to read Plato's use of the feminine gender to name *khōra* as a place in the text of the *Timaeus* that calls out for reading the

Platonic text against itself. I shall do so through a reading of Derrida's text, the *Khora*.

Derrida without considering himself a feminist theorist also challenges the concept of hospitality-as-right[28] from a reading of the *Timaeus*. Derrida finds the Platonic description of *khōra* (and hence Socrates, who seems *khōra* personified) as the description of hospitality which bests underscores the aporetic nature of authentic hospitality.

For Derrida, hospitality-as-right ensures the impossibility of the master receiving the guest into his home for in so doing the master gives up mastery of the domain. This is impossible for both the guest and the host must receive each other. In the moment of reception the guest becomes one with power, the host has disappeared and he can no longer retain mastery of the house. He labels this impossibility the *aporia (without place, full of paradox, puzzling)* of hospitality. Derrida attempts to recover the *aporia* of hospitality by understanding it as possibility within the horizon of the threshold or door. He considers the moment of hospitality then to be an impossible moment enacted within its own horizon of impossibility. Hospitality is its own horizon: a concept that defies objectivity. Derrida concentrates thus on the moment or activity of invitation.[29]

And, it is particularly the treatment of *khōra* as feminine that Derrida deconstructs at will in his chapter "Khōra." In his deconstruction of the *Timaeus* he finds that Plato too struggles with describing reception that allows being to become without mastery but yet is not passive. Derrida reads this in Plato as a necessary problem, for this indescribable reception is that which is necessary to keep the imagination of philosophy itself open.[30] This reading then makes it important for Derrida (and readers of Derrida like Gregoriou,[31] Aristarkhova, and Doufourmantell) to underscore that Plato in using the feminine, *khōra,* to name *Khōra* is not prescribing a feminine quality to hospitality, philosophy, or to the cosmos itself. Plato, according to Derrida's desconstruction, is playing with the feminine in order to challenge the metaphysical understanding of place in the role of philosophy.

According to Derrida then, we cannot essentialize *khōra* we cannot make her feminine, for this is Plato attempting to name something that is unnamable and beyond sex.[32] Thus, by keeping the concept of hospitality *aporetic*—without place—Derrida re-describes hospitality as only possible when power and place/ location are removed from the auspices of the action. As Anne Durfourmantell writes,

> To offer hospitality, he [Derrida] wonders, is it necessary to start from the certain existence of a dwelling, or is it rather only starting from the dislocation of the shelterless, the homeless, that the authenticity of hospitality can open up? Perhaps only the one who endures the experience of being deprived of a home can offer hospitality.[33]

I think we can agree with Derrida that simply reading *khōra* as "she" does not make this a feminist vision of hospitality. This is to equate feminism with feminine and does not challenge or disrupt gender norms in our society; rather this is to keep the woman in her place. But, by understanding that this is the feminine place in the *Timaeus* we allow the text to disrupt our everyday notions of hospitality and enable a reading of a most feminist understanding of hospitality, for in the *Timaeus* Socrates and *khōra* disrupt power and allow difference within the host/guest relationship and it is the feminine place that allows for this movement and mutual hospitality between the guest and host. The feminine gives possibility for the disruption of the ordinary understanding of the conditional host/guest relationship. It is "place" itself, that in the feminine uncovers for feminist theory a counter response to the idea of hospitality as mastery of place.

Later in the text, *khōra* is referred to again, not as *khōra* but as nurse of the becoming. Timaeus ensures that *khōra*, even as space, is a complicated, contradictory, and unintelligible space. Moreover, the action of *khōra* is to receive, which forces *khōra* back into its first naming, receptacle. I would argue that keeping *khōra* in the feminine space, keeping the definitions open between *khōra* as space and receptacle as nurse and nurturer[34] allows us to forgo closing down on a definition of *khōra*[35] and retain its key quality—that which is the "in which" of all becoming. It receives even though it does not have definition, space, mastery. It has power despite these qualities of lack![36] Here, Plato's insistence that this emptiness called *khōra* be gendered feminine allows us in modern feminist theory to take on this lack as the space to read new possibility in looking at ways to enact hospitality beyond right and power. We can now engage a hospitality that is not oppressive to either the host or the guest.

The dialogue's reliance on the description of the *khōra* "nurse as receptacle," especially the wet-nurse, is important to make any sense of this unintelligible, un-sensible form called *khōra*. The wet-nurse is feminine. The wet-nurse is not the natural mother. A woman who is a wet-nurse is lactating. She is rarely named, she can be any woman. The wet-nurse provides for the child after it has been born but also assists the child in growth, in becoming person. The wet-nurse then is not only a protector of the child but offers it her sustenance, milk. The lactating woman then provides milk from the breast which is not simply food but supplies the beginning nourishment. The wet-nurse becomes the basis from which the child grows. It is not the meat from outside provided by the community or the father but the milk of the woman created inside her from herself. It is this description that most powerfully underscores the need for this mode of reception to be considered in the feminine. She is the host as she receives but she does so in order to grow that which she hosts. And she does this by actively nurturing. She provides, as wet-nurse, not for her children but for that which is wholly different from herself.

Nancy Holland makes an argument that woman, as one who can give birth and host children within, foster this sense of hospitality that seems impossible. She posits that perhaps Derrida does not understand how the woman can actually understand this possible hosting of difference. For Holland, feminist hospitality is possible the way the woman experiences the world.

> [pregnancy] . . . yes, is a stranger, a guest, an alien but yet is also one of joy. . . .
> In the process you discover in yourself capacities you never knew you had.
> Capacities for love and nurture, but also the potential capacity to kill if the alien
> you harbor were threatened; the capacity to lie, freely and often, as needed; the

capacity to shift everything you believe about yourself and your world to accommodate the ever-changing needs of this stranger-becoming a person.[37]

I would argue that not only is this possible for woman, or pregnant women but is a way to understand feminist hospitality for all. It is not only the pregnant woman who can receive and be received in the world. It is possible that there are receptive acts that occur without mastery of place. When a small child in a preschool classroom who is mixing a bowl of sand and water to make the perfect building material asks her teacher to "feel this, it feels strange" her teacher can choose to receive the invitation and place his hands in the mixture and acknowledge with his student that yes, it feels strange. Likewise the teacher can ask another child nearby to follow suit and describe the sensation of sand in water. Together they may figure out that water and sand must lie in proportion in order to build sand castles.

Feminist hospitality reconsiders that the host and guest relationship cannot align along a model of power; instead, feminist hospitality aligns itself on a model of reception and invitation which does not oppress. Critical feminist theory further disrupts theories of hospitality by regarding reception as that which itself challenges the role of gender. In this reading, feminist hospitality enacts reception and invitation by enabling the feminine to be not merely a passive receiver but an active and challenging *reception*. This kind of hospitality is about openings and un-limit. It encourages possibility without bounds. It is beyond the polis and laws of the nation.

I do not accept a reading of this feminine reception and invitation as passive. Instead, I read Socrates and *khōra* as enacting powerful modes of feminist hospitality. Socrates receives as a guest. Socrates receives not those stories which he has accepted or is allowed by law. Instead, Socrates receives myths, allegories, and fantasy! This is quite a difference from the Socrates of *The Republic* who limits the kind of music, poetry, and myth in his utopian city. This reception makes a place for difference and other modes of knowing. Timaeus can tell the story of the cosmos without interruption, without fear that his story will not be well listened to. And yet, Timaeus still remains the host.

Likewise, the mysterious *khōra* makes a place for difference and possibility in the cosmos. She does not force a kind of creation but enables all that is to become all that it can become.

This kind of hospitality is one of reciprocal invitation. That is, the guest and host both invite each other to become as well as be welcome. The guest may challenge, the host may listen. The guest may listen and the host may tell a story. Yet, both retain full subjectivity and identity. Each welcomes the other in order to ensure the full freedom and possibility of each. Mustafa Dikeç writes of this kind of hospitality and calls it a mode of "mutual recognition":

> Although boundaries form an inherent part of the notion of hospitality, without which such a notion would perhaps be unnecessary, hospitality, I want to argue, is about opening, without abolishing, these boundaries and giving spaces to the stranger where recognition on both sides would be possible. In this sense, it implies the mutuality of recognition.[38]

It is possible to host and be hosted, mutually—the engendered episode of *khōra* and the challenging but yet silent figure of Socrates point us in these directions. This is a challenging notion of hospitality but it is one that I will argue contains the spirit of feminism.

Moreover it challenges the commonly held belief that education and learning are about mastery and offers to educational practice an example of feminist practice. By engaging in this new understanding of hospitality we can open up very real questions about our practices in education. How do we receive our students? How do we teach them to receive us? And perhaps most importantly for those of us engaged in the teaching of the liberal arts: how do we teach our students to receive texts, hospitably?

Possibilities for Education

In the educational context too often we believe that teachers have ultimate power and students retain a lack of power. But what is more usually the case is that the teacher has been forced to teach certain texts in a certain pedagogical style, and is merely a servant of a larger educational bureaucracy. And students, while demonized as greedy consumers who require amusing games to keep them occupied, instead often hold a false power over teachers as the stand-in consumers of their parents and the larger society. They do not have power but can call in power as needed or desired. If student and teacher then attempt to engage hospitality in the classroom that locates itself on mastery of place, or power of place, both engage in an inauthentic dynamic which simply enforces the static nature of an educational program based on the mastery of data and power. It is my belief that this is doomed to fail for two reasons. One, the teacher does not truly retain mastery of place so she or he cannot readily invite the student and the student understands this and thus is not comfortable being hosted by the teacher. And two, this kind of hospitality does not encourage the student to grow as a person who can use and create knowledge; this simply encourages students to take on static knowledge. We must then engage a new kind of hospitality in our classrooms, one that does more than simply flip the dynamic where the student becomes the host and the teacher becomes guest. This is to simply become the caring feminine teacher that does not engage questions of knowledge either. Instead, we must engage a feminist action of hospitality, one that encourages mutual reception between all within a place.

Education is about mastery: of facts, of certain kinds of data, of processes. We cannot deny that our first graders must learn their addition families and our ninth graders the history of the civil war. But as the text of the *Timaeus* shows us mastery cannot be the only form of reception in the world. The broader needs of education are not only about facts and sets of data but about the way that knowledge is appropriated, used, and incorporated into student's lives. Education and educational places must also be hospitable to these goals of education and they can only do so if they understand hospitality, not only as a right, but as mutual mode of being within the educational space. It is this reception which must move those of us in education. We must be shaken up and made ready to allow ourselves to be hosted by our students. This kind of hospitality in the classroom aligns with feminist pedagogy and theory not because it is feminine but because it challenges power, knowledge, language, and difference.[39]

In our classrooms we must encourage this kind of reception to the world by our students by first allowing them to host us. We must consider that we are not the masters in our classroom. Instead, all of us in the classroom must be "shaken and stirred" towards the world. It is in this space of no-place that we will all become. Luce Irigary reminds us:

> Welcoming does not take place simply in our dwelling, in ourselves, unless we arrange a space there which will never be ours, except as availability on our part. Welcoming will first take place outside of us, even if this outside has a corresponding part of ourselves.[40]

If we are to invite our students in, we must first make a place that allows for invitation outside of our mastered domains. Our students must be able to get lost in our fields and find their way back in new ways. They must host us in forging new understandings of our own disciplines. Our students can make us return to our foundational texts and read again.

Yet, we also must retain our own selves. We do not have to sit silently in our classrooms and simply allow a discussion to take place. We encourage critical discussions when we too engage in welcoming that is challenging, moving, suggestion. We can be active participants. I agree with Gregoriou that we cannot be feminized teachers but must be active feminist teachers:

> I suggest that we also reclaim receptivity from its pedagogically negative meaning as passive reception of fact (e.g., Freires' notion of a banking model of education). A practice of receptivity, though, must also be reclaimed from the feminized model of caring and receiving mother as an amorphous, immobile, and silent maternal substratum that envelopes and nurtures.[41]

When I welcome students into my class then I must be careful that I open up the space for a mutual recognition and mutual reception. I may say that this course is not my course nor is it yours. I may posit that the class is not even "ours" instead, it is mine and yours, it is a mutual classroom. I should lay out a foundation that makes space for multiple ways of knowing in my classroom, telling my class, as Timaeus told Socrates, that this may be a "bastard" discourse, and it may feel "strange" to be engaged, learning together. Yet, I do so, not to dismantle my own activity as a subject in the classroom but to empower all subjects in the classroom who come together to read and think in a discipline.

Thus, it is to philosophical reading and speaking to which I move for an example of what this kind of invitation should look like in my classroom. In a philosophical dialogue speech is received as a gift, created by two who move from their particular homes to forge thinking together. In the philosophical dialogue between reader and text or speaker and listener there must be a receiving without a home to grant reception. Philosophical dialogue centered not on argument but on reception means that both speaker and listener move into the text in order to make a place for different ways of valuing, believing, and understanding. When reading philosophically the text is encountered, not as an authority but as something to both enter into and take from. Similarly, a philosophical reader opens a text –not to devour it or to master it but to receive it, to be educated. She opens herself to the text—ready to argue, to concede, to learn, to question but importantly to receive something which is not herself. As she receives the text she allows the text to become something beyond the confines of the printed page. In philosophical reading and dialogue then we find that the readers and speakers make themselves ready to receive something different, may challenge, and cause growth.

When we enable our classes to become ready to receive, when we, as feminist teacher, make ourselves ready to receive in our classes, it is then when we are engaging a feminist vision of hospitality. As Timaeus says, we must listen and be *suitably* perplexed.[42]

Notes

1. Zelia Gregoriou, "Does Speaking of Others Involve Receiving the 'Other'?" In *Derrida & Education*, ed. Gert Biesta and Denise Egéa-Kuehne (London, Routledge, 2001), 146.

2. Immanuel Kant, *Kant's Principles of Politics including his essay on Perpetual Peace. A Contribution to Political Science*. Trans: W. Hastie. Edinburgh: Clark Printing, 1890. The Online Library of Liberty. http://oll.libertyfund.org/title/358/56090 (accessed May 2, 2008).

3. Kant, "Kant's Principles."

4. Elizabeth Telfer, "Hospitableness." *Philosophical Papers* XXIV no. 3 (1995): 183.

5. It both resists and calls out for interpretation. Scholars debate whether or not the dialogue takes place the day after the dialogue told in *The Republic*. The dialogue reads sometimes as myth, sometimes as allegory, and often as pure fantasy. Nevertheless, the metaphysics, physics, and ethics of the dialogue serve to highlight much of the questions that Western philosophy will undertake which makes the dialogue is an important piece in the Platonic opus.

6. Plato, *Timaeus*. Peter Kalkavage, Trans. (Newbury Port, Focus Publishing, 2001), 17A-B, 47.

7. A.E. Taylor, *A Commentary on Plato's Timaeus* (Oxford, Claredon Press, 1928), 45. "Line 17a: aunousia is the equivalent of the German *Stunde* and the French *conference*. The association is meant to colour the word here. Timaeus is about to deliver a lecture."

8. Plato, *Timaeus*, 20C, 50.

9. Plato, *Timaeus*, 29C, 59.

10. Plato, *Timaeus*, 29D, 60.

11. Plato, *Timaeus*, 20e, 51 "Critias: Hear, then, Socrates, an account most strange- and yet altogether true, as Solon, the wisest of the Seven, once claimed . . . a deed that would be fitting for us to remember now, so as to render our debt of thanks to you and at the same time to praise the goddess on her feast-day by singing as it were, in a manner both just and true."

12. Kenneth Sayre, "The Multilayered Incoherence of Timaeus' Receptacle" in *Plato's Timaeus as Cultural Icon*, ed. Gretchen J. Reydams-Schils (Notre Dame, University of Notre Dame Press, 2003).

13. Plato, *Timaeus*, 52B, 84.

14. One of the confusions is that Plato uses the name *khōra*, normally translated as "place" in Ancient Greek. In using *khōra* then Plato moves the concept from its geographical definitions in order to consider it for its philosophical significance. The analysis is much more sustained in Aristotle's *Physics* but Plato, here in the *Timaeus* begins to mark a difference between space and place. This entangles philosophers in considering the local vs. the universal, the particular vs. the general. Plato forces the Greeks (and us!) to think about what we mean when we say place instead of space. In the *Timaeus* specifically place is the concept that allows Plato to question how a culture both begins and ends, and how a culture can be limited and still grow. Gregoriou, that the *Timaeus* challenges us to ask questions about "movement and hybridization—displace [ing] the location of culture from polis to contact zones of transculturation." Gregoriou, "Does Speaking of Others," 142. She does so to understand ways that we can properly speak with others—those marginalized in our Western educational context. Although I appreciate Gregoriou's reading of the *Timaeus*, I think it might be important to look carefully at the way that *khōra* is described in the *Timaeus* in order to recover a mode of hospitality.

15. Plato, *Timaeus*, 49B, 81.

16. John Sallis, *Chorology* (Bloomington, Indiana University Press, 1999).

17. Plato, *Timaeus*, 48A-53B,80-6.

18. Plato, *Timaeus*, 50C, 83 "But one must put one's heart into speaking about this once more and with still more clarity. If someone having modeled all figures out of gold, should in no way stop remolding each figure into all the others then if someone pointed out one of them and asked . . . Rather one must be content whenever such a thing is willing to accept being called even 'of this sort' with any safety. It's the same account concerning the nature that receives all bodies. One must always call it by the same name, since it never at all abandons its own power. It both always receives all things, and nowhere in no way has it ever taken on any shape similar to the ones that come into is, for its laid down by nature as a modeling stuff for everything being moved and thoroughly configured by whatever things come into it and because of these, it appears different at different tiems, and the figures that come into it an go out of it are always imitations of the things that are, having been imprinted from them in some manner hared to tell of and wondrous, and which we'll pursue at a later point."

19. Plato, *Timaeus*, 51 B, 83.

20. Plato, *Timaeus* , 52E-53A, 85-86.

21. Jacques Derrida, *On the Name* (Stanford, Stanford University Press, 1995), 111 "Socrates is not khōra, but he would look a lot like it/her if it/she were someone or something. In any case, he puts himself in its/her place, which is not just a place among others, but perhaps, place itself, the irreplaceable place. Irreplaceable and unplaceable place from which he receives the word(s) of those before whom he effaces himself but who receive them from him, for it is he who makes them talk like this. And us too, implacably."

22. Plato, *Timaeus*, 48D, 80-81, "But now, let the following at least be held by us. We must not now declare the beginning concerning all things (or the beginnings, or whatever term seems to apply to them), fo no other reason than because it's difficult to make plain what seems to be the case according to the present mode of going through things. So, as for you, don't suppose that I must speak of it; and as for me, I in my turn wouldn't be able to persuade my own self that I'd be correct in trying to take upon myself so great a task; but by safeguarding what was declared at the very beginning –the power of likely accounts- I shall attempt to utter an account not less likely but more so, and to speak, as before from the beginning about things individually and together as a whole. So now too, at the beginning of our speeches, by invoking god the savior to grant us passage out of a strange and unusual narration to the decree based on likelihoods, let us once more begin to speak."

23. Claudia Baracchi, "Timaeus," New School University. Lecture Course, Spring 2008

24. Baracchi, "Timaeus," "If that is the right word."

25. Plato, *Timaeus* (30C, p.61).

26. Plato, *Timaeus* (37D, p.67).

27. Plato, *Timaeus* (34B, p.64).

28. Jacques Derrida, "Hostipitality," Angelaki: Journal of the theoretical humanities 5 no. 3 (December 2000), 5.

29. Jacques Derrida, "Hostipitality," 4 "At bottom, before even beginning, we could end our reflections here in the formalization of a law of hospitality which violently imposes a contradiction on the very concept of hospitality in fixing a limit to it, in determing it: hospitality is certainly, necessarily, a right, a duty, an obligation, the greeting of the foreigner other [l'aure etranger] as a friend but on the condition that the host, the Wirt, the one who receives, lodge or gives asylum remains the patron, the master of the household, on the condition that he maintains his own authority in his own home, that he looks after himself and sees to and considers all that concerns him [gu'il se garde et garde et regarde ce qui le regarde] and thereby affirms the law of hospitality as the law of the household, *oikonomia*, the law of his household, the law of a place, house, hotel, hospital, hospice, family, city , nation, language, etc.) the law of identity which de-limits the very place of proffered hospitality and maintains authority over it, maintains the truth of authority, remains the place of this maintaining, which is to say, of truth, thus limiting the gift proffered and making of this limitation, namely, the being-oneself in ones' own home, the condition of the gift and of hospitality."

30. Many readers of Derrida find this important. Perhaps Irina Aristarkov makes the clearest case in Aristarkhov, Irina, "Hospitality-Khōra-Matrix-Cyberspace" Filoofski Vestnik XXIII no.2 (2002), 27-43.

31. Gregouriou, "Does Speaking of Others," 146 "The receptacle is not to be found in a female nature or cultivated through attitudes of tolerance and self-reflective critique. It is apace we create when in hosting others we change, hybridize our discourses and identities, and let others teacher us, from the beginning, how we are different and multiple within ourselves."

32. Jacques Derrida, "Khora" in *On the Name*. Stanford, Stanford University Press, 1995. p. 98 "Khora must not receive for her own sake, so she must not receive, merely let herself be lent the properties (of that) which she receives. She must not receive; she must receive not that which she receives. To avoid all these confusions, it is convenient, paradoxically, to formulate our approach (to it/her) and always to use the same language about it/her."

33. Jacques Derrida and Anne Dufourmantell, *Of Hospitality*, (Stanford, Stanford University Press, 2000), 56

34. Emanuela Bianchi, "Receptacle/*Khora*: Figuring the Errant Feminine in Plato's *Timaeus*" *Hypatia* 21 no.4 (2006), 130 "Receptacle, *hupodochi* is derived from the verb *hupodechomai*, indicating the hospitality of entertaining or welcoming under one's roof, and, which, said of a woman, also means to conceive or become pregnant. *Khora*, by contrast, means space, place, position, but also a land, territory, or country, and especially the country opposed to the town. Receptacle and space are hardly cognates, so this reformulation deserves our close attention."

35. Derrida, *On the Name*, 103, "And yet, half-way through the cycle, won't the discourse on khōra have opened, between the sensible and the intelligible, belonging neither to one nor to the other, hence neither to the cosmos as sensible god nor to the intelligible god, an apparently empty space—even though it is no doubt not emptiness? Didn't it name a gaping opening, an abyss or a chasm? Isn't it starting out from this chasm, "in" it, that the cleavage between the sensible and the intelligible, indeed, between body and soul, can have place and take place? Let us not be too hasty about bringing this chasm named khōra close to that chaos which also opens the yawning gulf of the abyss."

36. Bianchi seems to argue this line finally: Bianchi, "Receptacle," 132 "What this choice does not acknowledge is the indeterminate directionality, the simultaneous giving and receiving implicated by hupodochi/*khōra*. For such giving and receiving to take place the distinctions required by the anthropomorphic schema between subjects and objects of giving are undermined."

37. Nancy J. Holland, "With Arms Wide Open of Hospitality and the Most Intimate Stranger" *Philosophy Today* 45 (2001), 134.

38. Mustafa Dikeç, "Pera Peras Poros Longings for Spaces of Hospitality," *Theory, Culture & Society*, 19 no.1-2, (2002), 229.

39. *Encyclopedia of Feminist Theory*, s.v "Feminist Pedagogy", ed. Lorraine Code, (London, Routledge, 2000), 381.

40. Luce Irigaray, *Sharing the World*, (London, Continuum, 2008) 18-9.

41. Gregoriou, "Does Speaking of Others," 139.

42. Plato. *Timaeus*, 55D, 89, "Now in reasoning about all these things, someone would do so musically if he raised the following point: perplexed as to whether he should say that there are indefinitely many cosmoses or that they're finite in number, he would consider the former decree to be that of someone genuinely inexperienced in matters in which he should be experienced. But as to whether it's appropriate to say that cosmoses are truly by nature one or five—if that's the stand he took, then he'd be more suitably perplexed. So then, in keeping with the likely account, our point of view discloses that the cosmos is by nature one goad, while someone else, having looked elsewhere to different considerations, will hold other opinions."

Selected Bibliography

Abdulrahim, Dima. "Defining Gender in a Second Exile: Palestinian Women in West Berlin." Pp. 55-82 in *Migrant Women: Crossing Boundaries and Changing Identities*, edited by Gina Buijs. Oxford: Berg., 1993.

Achugar, Hugo. "Postdictatorship, Democracy, and Culture in the Uruguay of the Eighties." Pp. 225-38 in *Repression, Exile, and Democracy: Uruguayan Culture*, edited by Saúl Sosnowski and Louis B. Popkin. Durham: Duke University Press, 1993.

Afkhami, Mahnaz. 1994. *Women in Exile*. Charlottesville: University Press of Virginia, 1994.

Algra, Keimpe. *Concepts of Space in Greek Thought*. New York: E.J. Brill, 1995.

Anidjar, Gil. "Secularism and the Theological-Political: An interview with Gil Anidjar," conducted by Nerman Shaik, *Asia Source*, (January 28, 2009). http://www.asiasource.org/news/special_reports/anidjar1.cfm (accessed March 16, 2010).

Aristarkhov, Irina. "Hospitality-Khōra-Matrix-Cyberspace." *Filozofski Vestnik* 23 no. 2 (2002): 27-43.

Auslander, Leora. "Bavarian Crucifixes and French Headscarves: Religious Signs and the Postmodern European State" *Cultural Dynamics* 12 no. 30 (2000): 283-309.

Balibar, Etienne. "Strangers as Enemies: Further Reflections on the Aporias of Transnational Citizenship," *Globalization and Autonomy Online Compendium* (May 9, 2006) http://www.globalautonomy.ca/global1/article.jsp?index=RA_Balibar_Strangers.xml (accessed March 16, 2010).

Baracchi, Claudia. "Timaeus." New School University. Lecture Course. Spring 2008.

Barnett, Clive. "Ways of Relating: Hospitality and the Acknowledgement of Otherness." *Progress in Human Geography* 29, no. 1 (2005): 5-21.

Bauman, Zygmunt. *Postmodernity and its Discontents*. Cambridge: Polity Press, 1997.

Benhabib, Seyla. "Democratic Iterations: The Local, the National, and the Global." Pp. 45-80, *Another Cosmopolitanism: The Berkeley Tanner Lectures*, ed. Robert Post, Oxford: Oxford Universty Press, 2006.

———. *The Rights of Others: Aliens, Residents and Citizens*, Cambridge: Cambridge University Press, 2004.

———. "In Search of Europe's Borders" *Dissent*, (Fall, 2002) http://www.dissentmagazine.org/article/?article=559 (accessed March 16, 2010).

Bennett, John B. "Hospitality and Collegial Community: An Essay." *Innovative Higher Education* 25 (2000): 85-96.

———. "The Academy and Hospitality." *Cross Currents: The Journal of the Associations for Religion and Intellectual Life* 50 no. 1-2 (2000): 23-35.

Bianchi, Emanuela. "Receptacle/Chopōra: Figuring the Errant Feminine in Plato's *Timaeus*." *Hypatia* 21 no. 4 (2006): 124-46.

Boersma, Hans. "Irenaeus, Derrida and Hospitality: On the Eschatological Overcoming of Violence." *Modern Theology* 19 no. 2 (2003): 163-80.

Booth, James William. "Foreigners: Insiders, Outsiders and the Ethics of Membership." *The Review of Politics* 59 (1997): 259-92.

Bowden, Peta. *Caring: Gender Sensitive Ethics*. London: Routledge, 1997.

Bretherton, Luke. "Tolerance, Education, and Hospitality: A Theological Proposal." *Studies in Christian Ethics* 17 no. 1 (2004): 80-103.

Bubeck, Diemut. *Care, Gender, and Justice*. Oxford University Press: Oxford, 1995.

Buijs, Gina. "Introduction." Pp. 1-20, *Migrant Women: Crossing Boundaries and Changing Identities*, ed. Gina Buijs. Oxford: Berg, 1993.
Carr, Marilyn, Martha Chen, and Renana Jhabvala, eds. *Speaking Out: Women's Economic Empowerment in South Asia*. UK: Intermediate Technology Publications Ltd., 1996.
Chávez, Denise. *A Taco Testimony*. Tucson: Rio Nuevo Publishers, 2006.
Cheal, David. *Towards an Anthropological Theory of Value: The False Coin of our Dreams*. Palgrave: New York, 2001.
Chopra, Radhika, Caroline Osella, and Filippo Osella, eds. *South Asian Masculinities: Context of Change, Sites of Continuity*. New Delhi: Kali for Women, 2004.
Cleaver, Frances. *Masculinities Matter! Men, Gender, and Development*. London: Zed Books, 2003.
Davies, Jacqueline. "Pornographic Harms." Pp. 127-45 in *Feminist Perspectives: Philosophical Essays on Method and Morals* edited by Lorraine Code, Sheila Mullett and Christine Overall. Toronto: University of Toronto Press, 1988.
―――――. "Premature M/Othering: Levinasian Ethics and the Politics of Fetal Ultrasound Imaging." Pp. 184-210 in *Embodiment and Agency: New Essays in Feminist Philosophy* edited by Sue Campbell, Letitia Meynell, and Susan Sherwin. University Park, PA: Penn State University Press, 2009.
De Certeau, Michel. *Culture in the Plural,* trans. Tom Conley, Minneapolis: University of Minnesota Press, 1997.
De Vries, Hent. "Hospitable Thought: Before and Beyond Cosmopolitanism." Pp. 296-431 in *Religion and Violence: Philosophical Perspectives from Kant to Derrida*. Baltimore and London: the Johns Hopkins University Press, 2001.
Derrida, Jacques. "The Principle of Hospitality." *Parallax* 2, no. 1, (January-March, 2005): 6-9.
―――――. *Rogues: Two Essays on Reason*. Translated by Pascale-Anne Blunt and Michael Naas. Stanford: Stanford University Press, 2005.
―――――. "A Discussion with Jacques Derrida" with Paul Patton. *Theory and Event*, 5 (2001):1-25.
―――――. "Hospitality." *Angelaki: Journal of the Theoretical Humanities* 5 no. 3 (December 2000): 3-18.
―――――. *On Cosmopolitanism and Forgiveness*. New York: Routledge, 1997.
―――――. *On the Name*. Stanford: Stanford University Press, 1995.
―――――. "A Word of Welcome." *Adieu to Emmanuel Levinas*. Palo Alto: Stanford University Press, 1999.
―――――. *Adieu to Emmanuel Levinas*. Translated by Pascale-Anne Blunt and Michael Naas, Stanford: Stanford University Press, 1999.
―――――. *Specters of Marx: The State of the Debt, The work of Mourning and the New International*. Translated by Peggy Kamuff, New York and London: Routledge, 1994.
―――――. *The Other Heading: Reflections on Today's Europe*. Translated by Pascale-Anne Brault and Michael B. Naas. Bloomington and Indianapolis: Indiana University Press, 1992.
―――――. "Violence and Metaphysics: An Essay on the Thought of Emmanuel Levinas." *Writing and Difference*. Translated by Alan Blass. Chicago: University of Chicago Press, 1980.
Derrida, Jacques and Anne Dufourmantelle. *Of Hospitality*. Stanford: Stanford University Press, 2000.
Deutscher, Penelope. "Derrida's Impossible Genealogies." *Theory & Event* 8 no. 1 (2005).

Dewey, John. *Democracy and Education*. Carbondale: Southern Illinois University Press, 1985.
Dikeç, Mustafa. "Pera Peras Poros Longings for Spaces of Hospitality," *Theory, Culture & Society*, 19 no. 1-2 (2002): 227-47.
Eastmond, Marita. "Reconstructing Life: Chilean Refugee Women and the Dilemmas of Exile." Pp. 35-54 in *Migrant Women: Crossing Boundaries and Changing Identities*, ed. Gina Buijs. Oxford: Berg, 1993.
El-Bizri, Nader. "Quit Etes-Vous, Kora?: Receiving Plato's Timaeus." *Existentia* 11 (2001): 473-90.
Engster Daniel. *The Heart of Justice: Care Ethics and Political Theory*. Oxford: Oxford University Press, 2007.
Everett, Wendy and Wagstaff, Peter. "Introduction." Pp. 1-19 in *Cultures of Exile: Images of Displacement*, eds. Wendy Everett and Peter Wagstaff. New York: Berghahn Books, 2004.
Feldman, Shelly. "NGOs and Civil Society: (Un)stated Contradictions." *Annals of the American Academy of Political Science* 554 (1997): 46-65.
"Feminist Pedagogy." Pp. 381-3 in *Encyclopedia of Feminist Theory* edited by Lorraine Code. London, Routledge, 2000.
Findly, Ellison Banks. "The Housemistress at the Door: Vedic and Buddhist perspectives on the Mendicant Encounter." Pp. 13-31 in Laurie L. Patton. *Jewels of Authority: Women in the Textual Tradition in Hindu India*. Oxford: Oxford University Press, 2002.
Fisher, Berenice and Joan C. Tronto. "Towards a Feminist Theory of Caring." Pp. 35-62 in *Circles of Care* edited by Emily K. Abel and Margaret K. Nelson. Albany: SUNY Press, 1990.
Ghorashi, Halleh. *Ways to Survive, Battles to Win: Iranian Women Exiles in the Netherlands and United States*. New York: Nova Science Publishers, Inc., 2002.
Gilligan, Carol. *In a Different Voice: Psychological Theory and Women's Development*. Cambridge: Harvard University Press, 1982.
Gilroy, Paul. *Postcolonial Melancholia*, New York: Columbia University Press, 2005.
Gole, Nilufer. *Modern Mahrem: Medeniyet ve Ortunme*, Istanbul: Metis, 1991.
Graeber, David. *Towards an Anthropological Theory of Value: The False Coin of Our Dreams*. New York: Palgrave, 2001.
Green, Judith. "Building A Cosmopolitan World Community Through Mutual Hospitality." Pp. 203-24 in *Pragmatism and the Problem of Race* edited by Bill E. Lawson and Donald F. Koch. Bloomington: Indiana University Press, 2004.
Gregoriou, Zelia, "Does Speaking of Others Involve Receiving the 'Other'?" Pp. 134-49 in *Derrida & Education* edited by Gert Biesta, and Denise Egéa-Kuehne. London: Routledge, 2001.
Guenther, Lisa. *The Gift of the Other: Lévinas and the Politics of Reproduction*. Albany, NY: State University of New York Press, 2006.
Gutiérrez y Muhs, Gabriella. *Communal Feminisms: Chicanas, Chilenas, and Cultural Exile*. Lanham: Lexington Books, 2007.
Hage, Ghassan. *White Nation: Fantasies of White Supremacy in Multicultural Society*. New York and London: Routledge, 2000.
Hamington, Maurice. *Embodied Care: Jane Addams, Maurice Merleau-Ponty and Feminist Ethics*. Urbana, Il: University of Illinois Press, 2004.
———. "Toward a Theory of Feminist Hospitality," *Feminist Formations* (formerly *National Women's Studies Association Journal*), 22:1 (April 2010): 21-38.
Heal, Felicity. "The Idea of Hospitality in Early Modern England." *Past and Present* no. 102 (1984): 66-93.

Held, Virginia. *The Ethics of Care: Personal, Political, Global.* Oxford: Oxford University Press, 2006.
Hershberger, Michele. *A Christian View of Hospitality: Expecting Surprises.* Scottdale, PA: Herald Press, 1999.
Herzog, Annabel. "Is Liberalism 'All We Need'?: Levinas's Politics of Surplus." *Political Theory* 30 (2002): 204-27.
Hirsi Ali, Ayaan. *Infidel.* New York: Free Press, 2007.
Hitchcox, Linda. "Vietnamese Refugees in Hong Kong: Behaviour and Control." Pp. 145-60 in *Migrant Women: Crossing Boundaries and Changing Identities*, ed. Gina Buijs. Oxford: Berg, 1993.
Hoffman, Eva. "Exile." Pp. 202-8 in *A Map of Hope*, ed. Marjorie Agosín, New Brunswick: Rutgers University Press, 1999.
Holland, Nancy J, "With Arms Wide Open of Hospitality and the Most Intimate Stranger." *Philosophy Today* 45 (2001): 133-37.
Honig, Bonnie. "Another Cosmopolitanism?: Law and Politics in the New Europe." Pp. 102-27 in *Another Cosmopolitanism*: The Berkeley Tanner Lectures, ed. Robert Post, Oxford: Oxford University Press, 2006.
———."Ruth, the Model Émigré: Mourning and Symbolic Politics and Immigration," Pp. 192-215 in *Cosmopolitics: Thinking and Feeling Beyond the Nation*, Phegh Cheah and Bruce Robbins, eds. Minnesota: University of Minnesota Press, 1998.
Huizinga, Johan. *The Waning of the Middle Ages.* New York: Doubleday, 1954.
Irigaray, Luce. *Sharing the World.* London: Continuum, 2008.
Jahan, Rounaq. *The Elusive Agenda: Mainstreaming Women in Development.* London: Zed Books, 1995.
Jahan, Rounaq, and Adrienne Germain. "Mobilizing Support to Sustain Political Will is the Key to Progress in Reproductive Health." *Lancet* 364 no. 8436 (2004): 742-44.
Kant, Immanuel. *Perpetual Peace and Other Essays*, translated by Ted Humphrey. Indianapolis: Hackett Publishing, 1983.
Kassam, Tazeen. "Response." *Journal of Feminist Studies in Religion.* 22 no. 1 (2006): 59-66.
Katz, Claire Elise. *Levinas, Judaism, and the Feminine: The Silent Footsteps of Rebecca.* Bloomington, Indiana: Indiana University Press, 2003.
Klepfisz, Irena. "Di yerushe! The Legacy: A Parable About History And Bobe-Mayses And Borsht And The Future Of The Jewish Past." In *From Memory to Transformation: Jewish Women's Voices.* Edited by Sarah Silberstein Swartz and Margie Wolfe. Toronto: Second Story Press, 1998.
Kotalova Jitta. *Belonging to Others: Cultural Construction of Womanhood among Muslims in a Village in Bangladesh.* Uppsala Studies in Cultural Anthropology 19. Uppsala, Sweden, 1990.
Kristeva, Julia. *Nations Without Nationalism.* Translated by Leon S. Roudiez. New York: Columbia University Press, 1993.
———. *Strangers to Ourselves.* Translated by Leon S. Roudiez, New York: Columbia University Press, 1991.
Kumar, Nita. *Friends, Brothers, and Informants: Fieldwork Memoirs of Banaras.* Berkeley: University of California Press, 1992.
Kuokkanen, Rauna. "Toward A New Relation of Hospitality in the Academy." *American Indian Quarterly* 27 no. 1 & 2 (Winter & Spring 2003): 267-95.
Lamb, Sarah. *White Saris and Sweet Mangoes: Aging, Gender, and Body in North India.* Berkeley: University of California Press, 2000.
Laws and Policies Affecting their Reproductive Lives—South Asia. Women of the World. Center for Reproductive Rights. Washington D.C., 2004.

Levinas, Emmanuel. *Otherwise than Being: Or Beyond Essence.* Translated by Alphonso Lingis. Pittsburgh: Duquesne University Press, 1998.
———. "Judaism and the Feminine." *Difficult Freedom: Essays on Judaism.* Translated by Seán Hand. London: The Athlone Press, 1990.
———. *Totality and Infinity: An Essay on Exteriority.* Translated by Alphonso Lingis. Pittsburgh: Duquesne University Press, 1969.
Lewis, Gail. "Imaginaries of Europe: Technologies of Gender, Economics of Power." *European Journal of Women's Studies*, 13:2 (2006): 87-102.
MacKinnon, Catherine. "Feminism, Marxism, Method and the State: An Agenda for Theory." *Signs: Journal of Women in Culture and Society.* 515 (1983): 7.
Manchanda, Rita. "Guns and *Burqa*: Women in the Kashmir Conflict." Pp. 42-101 in *Women, War, and Peace in South Asia*, ed. Rita Manchanda. New Delhi: Sage Publications, 2001.
Mandel, Ruth. *Cosmopolitan Anxieties: Turkish Challenges to Citizenship and Belonging in Germany.* Durham and London: Duke University Press, 2008.
Manderson, Desmond. *Proximity, Levinas, and the Soul of Law.* Montreal: McGill-Queen's University Press, 2007.
Marranci, Gabriel. "Multiculturalism, Islam and the Clash of Civilizations Theory: Rethinking Islamophobia." *Culture and Religion.* 5:1 (2004): 105-17.
Martínez, Rubén. *The New Americans.* New York: The New Press, 2004.
Mason, Andrew, "Plato and Necessity and Chaos." *Philosophical Studies* 127 (2006): 283-98.
Mohanty, Chandra Talpade. *Feminism Without Borders.* United States of America: Duke University Press, 2003.
Narayan, Uma. "Minds of Their Own: Choices, Autonomy, Cultural Practices, and Other Women." Pp. 418-32 in *A Mind of One's Own*, eds. Louise M. Antony and Charlotte E. Witt, 418-32. Boulder, CO: Westview, 2002.
Narayan, Uma, and Balakrishnan, Radhika. "Combining Justice with Development: Rethinking Rights and Responsibilities in the Context of World Hunger and Poverty." Pp. 230-47 in *World Hunger and Morality*, eds. William Aiken, and Hugh LaFollette. Upper Saddle River: Prentice Hall, 1996.
Murray, Harry. *Do Not Neglect Hospitality.* Philadelphia: Temple University Press, 1990.
Naas, Michael. "'One Nation… Indivisible': Jacques Derrida on the Autoimmunity of Democracy and the Sovereignty of God." *Research in Phenomenology* 36 (2006): 15-44.
———."'Alors, qui êtes-vous?' Jacques Derrida and the Question of Hospitality." *SubStance* 34 no. 106 (2005): 6-17.
———. *Taking on the Tradition: Jacques Derrida and the Legacies of Deconstruction.* Stanford: Stanford University Press, 2003.
Noddings, Nel. *Caring: A Feminist Approach to Ethics and Moral Education.* Berkeley: University of California Press, 1986.
———. *Starting at Home: Caring and Social Policy.* Berkeley: University of California Press, 2002.
Partnoy, Alicia. *You Can't Drown the Fire, Latin American Women Writing in Exile.* Pittsburgh: Cleis Press, 1998.
Pinchevski, Amit. *By Way of Interruption: Levinas and the Ethics of Communication.* Pittsburgh: Duquesne University Press, 2005.
Pitt, Mark, Shahidur Khandker, and Jennifer Cartwright. "Empowering Women with Micro finance: Evidence from Bangladesh." *Economic Development and Cultural Change* 54 no. 4 (2006): 791-831.
Plato. *Timaeus.* Translated by Peter Kalkavage. Newbury Port: Focus Publishing, 2001.

Popke, E. Jeffrey. "Poststructuralist Ethics: Subjectivity, Responsibility And The Space Of Community." *Progress in Human Geography* 27 no. 3 (2003): 298-316.
Raheja, Gloria Goodwin, and Ann Grodzins Gold. *Listen to the Heron's Words*. Berkeley: University of California Press, 1994.
Robbins, Jill, ed. *Is It Righteous to Be? Interviews with Emmanuel Levinas*. Palo Alto: Stanford University Press, 2001.
Rodríguez, María Cristina. *What Women Lose: Exile and the Construction of Imaginary Homelands in Novels by Caribbean Writers*. New York: Peter Lang, 2005.
Rosello, Mireille. *Postcolonial Hospitality: The Immigrant as Guest*. Stanford: Stanford University Press, 2001.
Rubin, Gayle. "The Traffic in Women: Notes on the 'Political Economy' of Sex." Pp. 157-210 in *Toward an Anthropology of Women* edited by Rayna Reiter. New York: Monthly Review Press, 1975.
Ruddick, Sara. "Care as Labor and Relationship." Pp. 3-26 in *Norms and Values: Essays on the Work of Virginia Held* edited by Mark S. Halfor and Joram C. Haber. Lanham Md: Rowman and Littlefield: 1998.
Russell, Letty M. "Postcolonial Challenges and the Practice of Hospitality." Pp. 109-33 in *A Just and True Love: Feminism at the Frontiers of Theological Ethics* edited by Maura A. Ryan and Brain F. Linnane. Notre Dame: University of Notre Dame, 2007.
Said, Edward. *Reflections on Exile and Other Essays*. Cambridge: Harvard University Press, 2000.
Sallis, John. *The Verge of Philosophy*. Chicago: Chicago University Press, 2008.
———. *Platonic Legacies*. Albany: State University of New York Press, 2004.
———. "Reception" in *Interrogating The Tradition: Hermeneutics And The History Of Philosophy* edited by Charles E. Scott and John Sallis. New York: SUNY Press, 2000.
Sayre, Kenneth. "The Multilayered Incoherence of Timaeus' Receptacle." Pp. 60-79 in *Plato's Timaeus as Cultural Icon* edited by Gretchen J. Reydams-Schils. Notre Dame: University of Notre Dame Press, 2003.
Sosnowski, Saúl. "As Seen from the Other Shore: Uruguayan Culture (Repression, Exile and Democracy)." Pp. 1-14 in *Repression, Exile, and Democracy: Uruguayan Culture*, eds. Saúl Sosnowski and Louis B. Popkin. Durham: Duke University Press, 1993.
Spivak, Chakravorty Gayatri. "Ghostwriting," *Diacritics*, 25:2 (Summer 1995): 65-84.
Still, Judith. "Language as Hospitality: Revisiting Intertextuality via Monolingualism of the Other." *Paragraph: A Journal of Modern Critical Theory* 1 (2004): 113-27.
Taylor, A.E. *A Commentary on Plato's Timaeus*. Oxford: Claredon Press, 1928.
Taylor, Chloe. "Lévinasian Ethics And Feminist Ethics Of Care." *Symposium: Canadian Journal of Continental Philosophy* 9 no. 2 (Fall 2005): 217-40.
Telfer, Elizabeth. "Hospitableness." *Philosophical Papers* 14 no. 3 (1995): 183-96.
Vaughn, Genevieve, ed. *Women and the Gift Economy: A Radically Different Worldview*. Toronto: Ianna Publications, 2007.
Vazquez Arroyo, Antonio Y. "Agamben, Derrida, and the Genres of Political Theory." *Theory and Event* 8 no. 1 (2005).
Wilder, Billy, director. *The Apartment*. DVD. Los Angeles: MGM, (1960) 2001.
Wilder, Billy and I.A.L. Diamond. *The Apartment*. The Internet Movie Script Database. http://www.imsdb.com/scripts/Apartment,-The.html (accessed June 24, 2009).
Wyschogrod, Edith. "Autochthony and Welcome: Discourses of Exile in Levinas and Derrida." *Journal of Philosophy and Scripture* 1 no. 1 (Fall 2003): 36-42.
Yeğenoğlu, Meyda. "Cosmopolitanism and Nationalism in a Globalized World," *Ethnic and Racial Studies* 28, no. 1. (January 2005): 103-31.

———. "Liberal Multiculturalism and the Ethics of Hospitality in the Age of Globalization." *Postmodern Culture* 13 no. 2 (2003).

Yoder, Paton. "Private Hospitality in the South, 1775-1850." *The Mississippi Valley Historical Review* 47 (1960): 419-33.

Index

30 Days (television show), 199–200
9/11, 106n44
A Christmas Carol, 6–7
aapayon, 117–22
Abdulrahim, Dima, 138–39
Addams, Jane, xiv, 37n35
Afkhami, Mahnaz, 132, 137, 153
Agosín, Marjorie, 136, 151, 153
anchor babies, 192, 201n2
Aquinas, Thomas, 95–96

Baier, Annette, 191
Bartky, Sandra Lee, 61–62, 64
Barvosa, Edwina, 194, 199
Bauman, Zygmunt, 166
de Beauvoir, Simone, 72, 76–79
bed & breakfast businesses, 207–20
Benhabib, Seyla, xiv, 172, 175–78, 187, 200
Bennington, Geoff, 39
Benveniste, Émile, 55
boarding houses, 238–53
body-dwelling, 65–67
Boisvert, Raymond, 23, 26
Bolchazy, Ladislaus J., xii–xiii, 74, 87n12
Bubeck, Diemut, 34n6
Buchanan, Pat, 188
Buddha, 14–15

care ethics, 20–23, 29–33, 111–12, 188–89, 196–99
Cantú, Norma, 130
care providers, 227–29
Carpendale, Jeremy, 44, 51n27
Catholic Worker Movement, xiv
de Certau, Michel, 165
Chacon, Justin Akers, 196
Chandler, Michael, 45
Cheal, David, 111
Chung, Sook Ja, 103
Clement, Grace, 191
Code, Lorraine, 46, 191
"comfort women," 27
Cook, Emily, 20
Crenshaw, Kimberle, xvii
Critchley, Simon, 25

Dallacroce, Michelle, 192

danadharma, 112–13
Day, Dorothy, xiv, 102
Derrida, Jacques, xiv–xv, 57–59, 67n13, 75–76, 83–86, 164, 167, 169, 173–74, 177–81, 190, 193–94, 197–98, 290–91; aporia of hospitality and, 57–8; neglect of gender and, 24–26, 58; *différance* and 39–40; "the gift" and, 40–41; openness and responsibility to the Other and, 42, 45–48
diakonia, 92–93
Dikeç, Mustafa, 292
Diprose, Rosalyn, 190
Dobbs, Lou, 187
Dubois, W.E.B., 148
Durfourmantell, Anne 290
Dyson, Michael Eric, 99

Engster, Daniel, 22, 32, 199

Fawlty Towers (television show), 210–11
Feder Kittay, Eva, 30–31, 34
female genital mutilation, 47
Fiorenza, Elisabeth Schussler, 92–94, 104n1
Foucault, Michele 63–64
Fraser, Nancy, 52n47
Frye, Marilyn, 197–98

Gadamer, Hans Georg, 49n10
Gail, Lewis, 181–82
Gaspard, Francoise, 172
Gauthier, David, 25–26
Ghorashi, Halleh, 127–29, 137, 156n4,
Gibbs, Robert, 46
Gilligan, Carol, 80–81
Gilroy, Paul, 181
Green, Judith, 20, 25, 37n35, 148–49
Green, Ronald M., xiii
Gregoriou, Zelia, 281, 294, 297n31
Gutierrez y Muhs, Gabriella, 129, 156n16, 156n17, 162n95

Hage, Ghassan, 164–65
Hamington, Maurice, 37n35
Harding, Sandra, xvii–xviii
headscarves, controversy over, 114, 141–42, 167–73, 175–80

Index

Hecht, Jennifer, 75–76
Heidegger, Martin, 50n20, 65, 76–78, 82, 273
Held, Virginia, xvi
Hoffman, Eva, 149–50
Holland, Nancy, 25–26, 291–92
Holtman, Sarah, 25–26
homophily, 103
Honig, Bonnie, 171–73, 177–78
hospitableness: agency and, 42, 46; conditions for, 4–5; as liberatory, 12–14, 16; as virtue, 5–7
hospitality: ancient forms of, xii, 73–75; Bible and, xiii, 73, 92–94, 102; Buddhism and, 9–11, 14–16; care ethics and, 20–23, 33; commercial forms of, 207–20, 238–53; conditional forms of, 175, 177–82. *See also* Derrida; Confucianism and, 37n33; education and, 293–95; domestic definition of, 77–78; feminism and, xvi–xix, 190–93; gender and, 24–29, 36n27, 56, 208, 210; immigration and, 35n8; marriage and, 36n24; medical care providers and, 227–31; medical patients and, 225–26, 229–31; oppression of women and, 11–13, 24–29, 76–78; as people's religion, 118–19; of privilege, 193; religion and, 112–13; shame and, 60–63, 65; as social change, 120–22; space and, 194, 209–11; unconditional forms of, 56–60, 173–82. *See also* Derrida
hostipitality, 194, 297n29
Hurricane Katrina, 91, 98–101

intersectionality, xvi–xvii
ipseity, 57
Iragaray, Luce, 73, 294

Jamison, Stephanie W., 193–94
Japanese "comfort women," 27, 31
Johnson, Allan, G., 195
Johnson, Mark, 202n32

Kant, Immanuel, xiv, 83, 177–78, 282
Kaufman, Gershen, 61
Kegan, Robert, 44–45
khōra (chora), 80, 286–93, 296n14, 297n32, 298n34
Khosrokhavar, Farhad, 172

Kierner, Cynthia, 193
Krell, David Farrell, 76
Kristeva, Julia, 80, 169–78, 198

LaCaze, Marguerite, 39
Lakoff, George, 202n2
Lazarus, Emma, 192
Levinas, Emmanual, xiv–xv, 56–58, the feminine other and, 79–82, 263–65, 267, 269–73, 275–77, 278n20; on reciprocity 24–25, 52n46
on feminine hospitality, 59–60
Lewis, Helen Block, 60–63
Livy, 73, 87n12
Lot, story of, 25–26, 31
Lugones, Maria, 194, 198

Manderson, Desmond, 277
Maurin, Peter, xiv
McIntosh, Peggy, 195
McNulty, Tracy, xii, xv, 57, 190
Merleau–Ponty, Maurice 65
Mexican immigrants, women, 189–90
moral luck, 195
Mothers Against Illegal Aliens, 192
Mullett, Sheila, 47

Narayan, Uma, 139–41, 143, 151
"The New Colossus," 192
Noddings, Nel, 22–23, 29–30, 197
Nussbaum, Martha, 200

Ortega, Marianna, 198
"other," xiv; intimate, 81; openness to, 39–43, 45–47, 50n15, 57. *See also* Derrida
"othering," 97
otherness, 81–82, 103, 270–72, 277n8, 278n14. *See also* Derrida

Partnoy, Alicia, 132, 137, 143, 152
Piaget, Jean, 43–46
Plato, 283–84, 289–91
Playful world traveling, 198
Poats, Lillian, 100

Raymond, Janice, 72
reciprocity, 29–33
Rich, Adrienne, 59–60
Robinson, Fiona, 197
Rosello, Mireille, xv, 48, 187, 194

Ross, Loretta, 100
Russell, Letty M., 96–99

Said, Edward, 127–28, 131–32, 137, 149, 158n43, 162n88
Saint Martha, 91–94, 103
Sallis, John, 286
Samaj, 114
Sanchez, Rob, 188
Scarry, Elaine, 68
Serres, Michel, 73
Settlement Movement, xiv
Shyrock, Andrew, 197
Socrates, 282, 284, 289
Spurlock, Morgan, 199–200
standpoint theory, xvii–xviii
Statue of Liberty, 192
Stevens, Allison, 191

Tancredo, Tom, 195
Telfer, Elizabeth, 21–23, 28, 282

Tessman, Lisa, 23–24
The Apartment, 263–77
The Kite Runner, 19, 27–28
Timaeus, 282–95
Tomasello, Michael, 43
Tronto, Joan, 22, 36n18, 223, 230, 232

Uberfremdung, 165
Uncle Octave, 25

Vaughn, Genevieve, 110–11
veil, controversy over. *See* headscarves, controversy over
de Vries, Hent, 174

Wilder, Ben, 263–66, 270–73, 276
Wilson, James Q., 100

Yamaguchi, Satako, 103
Young, Marion Iris, 46, 48, 64, 76–78, 86n1

Contributor Biographies

Fauzia Erfan Ahmed has worked for over two decades in development programs in various countries. Her current research focuses on Islam, masculinity, and feminist theory. She is writing a book entitled, *Redefining Manhood: Gender Empowerment, Poverty Alleviation and Masculinity*, based on her ethnographic research with Grameen Bank sharecropper families. Her writings have appeared in *National Women's Studies Association Journal*, *International Feminist Journal of Politics*, and *Encyclopedia for Women in Muslim Cultures*. She is currently Assistant Professor of Sociology and Women's Studies at Miami University in Ohio.

Patricia A. Boling teaches feminist theory, public policy, women and the law, and bioethics at Purdue University. She is the author of Privacy and the Politics of Intimate Life, editor of Expecting Trouble, articles on public-private distinctions, family policies, and feminist agenda-setting in Japan, and is currently working on a project comparing work-family reconciliation policies in four countries.

Stephanie Burdick-Shepherd is a doctoral student in Philosophy and Education at Teachers College, Columbia University. She currently teaches in the Educational Foundations Department at Montclair State University. She obtained her M.Ed. in Philosophy for Children from Montclair State University. She is a co-author on "Education, Values, and Valuing in Cosmopolitan Perspective" in *Curriculum Inquiry* (December, 2009).

Jacqueline Davies is an Associate Professor of Philosophy, cross appointed to the Department of Gender Studies, member of the Jewish Studies Faculty Advisory Committee, and associate of the Cultural Studies Graduate Program at Queen's University at Kingston, Canada. Her current teaching and research interests include intersectionality, and feminist thought, as well as Jewish philosophy, and twentieth century continental thought. Recent projects focus on the work of Emmanuel Levinas viewed through the lens of 20th century aesthetic and communications technologies (cinema, medical imaging, and the internet). Among these are "Others in the Ether: On Levinasian Internet Ethics by Design" in *Design Principles and Practices: An International Journal.* Vol. 3, 2009, and "Premature M/Othering: Levinasian ethics and the politics of fetal ultrasound imaging" in *Embodiment and Agency: New Essays in Feminist Philosophy,* Sue Campbell, Letitia Meynell, and Susan Sherwin eds. (Penn State University Press, 2009).

MariaLaura Di Domenico is Lecturer in Organizational Behaviour at the Open University Business School, UK. Her research emphasis spans critical theoretical and empirical approaches to work, organization and society, with a particular focus on issues of identity, enterprise and discourse. Key research interests include the interface between home and work in small firms and family businesses. Her research is published in leading international academic journals such as *Human Relations, Organization Studies, Regional Studies* and *Gender, Work and Organization*, as well as in books and monographs.

M. Christian Green is Alonzo L. McDonald Family Senior Lecturer and Senior Research Fellow at the Center for the Study of Law and Religion at Emory University School of Law. She holds a J.D./M.T.S. from the Law and Religion Program at Emory University School of Law, and a Ph.D. in ethics from the University of Chicago. She has taught ethics at De Paul University, Harvard Divinity School, and the Candler School of Theology at Emory University. Her research is in the areas of law and religion, feminist ethics, comparative religious ethics, and human rights.

Daniel Haggerty is Associate Professor of Philosophy at the University of Scranton. His research in moral psychology, ethics, and epistemology deals with such topics as emotions, affectivity, justification, and reasons for acting. His writings include studies of classical theorists as well as critiques of contemporary thinkers in both the analytic and continental traditions.

Maurice Hamington is Associate Professor of Women's Studies and Philosophy and Director of the Institute for Women's Studies and Services at Metropolitan State College of Denver. His publications include *Feminist Interpretations of Jane* Addams (Penn State Press, 2010) an edited volume; The *Social Philosophy of Jane* Addams (University of Illinois Press, 2009); Socializing *Care: Feminist Ethics and Public Issues* (Rowman & Littlefield, 2006) co-edited with Dorothy C. Miller; *Embodied Care: Jane Addams, Maurice Merleau-Ponty and Feminist Ethics* (University of Illinois Press, 2004); *Revealing Male Bodies* (Indiana University Press, 2002) co-edited with Nancy Tuana et al; and, *Hail Mary? The Struggle for Ultimate Womanhood in Catholicism* (Routledge, 1995).

Barbara J. Howe received her Ph.D. in American and English history from Temple University. At West Virginia University, she served as director of the Center for Women's Studies, taught courses in American women's history and West Virginia women's history, and focused much of her public service work on West Virginia women's history and current issues. Her publications include "Patient Laborers: Women at Work in the Formal Economy of West(ern) Virginia," in *Neither Lady, Nor Slave: Working Women of the Old South*, edited by Michele Gillespie and Susanna Delfino (Chapel Hill: The University of North Carolina Press, 2002); "Urban Wage-Earning Women in a Rural State," in *Beyond Hill and Hollow: Original Readings in Appalachian Women's Studies*, edited by Elizabeth Engelhardt (Athens: Ohio University Press, 2005; "Practicing Medicine in Mid-Nineteenth-Century Wheeling: The Story of Dr. Eliza Clark

Hughes," *Journal of Appalachian Studies* 12 (Fall 2006): 7-35; and "Pioneers on a Mission for God: The Order of the Visitation of the Blessed Virgin Mary in Wheeling, 1848-1860," forthcoming in *West Virginia History: A Journal of Regional Studies*, Spring 2010. Dr. Howe served as president of the National Women's Studies Association from 2006 to 2008.

Jo-Ann Pilardi, Professor Emerita of Philosophy and Women's Studies, Towson University (Maryland), says that her academic feminism was born of her activism in Baltimore's "women's liberation" movement. From this and from her philosophical specialty, twentieth century continental philosophy, she has published articles and a book on Simone de Beauvoir (*Simone de Beauvoir: Philosophy Becomes Autobiography*), and articles on social and political philosophy and feminist theory. At Towson, she taught both philosophy and women's studies (e.g., social and political philosophy, race/class/gender, feminist theory/ philosophy, postmodernism), and for many years chaired the Women's Studies Department. A native of Pittsburgh, her roots—and her love of hospitality—are in the Italian-American working class.

Maureen Sander-Staudt is an Assistant Professor at Arizona State University where she teaches Feminist Ethics, Bioethics, Environmental Ethics, and World Literature. She specializes in feminist ethics of care, and has published on the topics such as care ethics and virtue ethics, artificial womb technology, the moral status of embryos, and the political agency of care-givers. Her ongoing interests are in the areas of reproductive equality, care as political practice, and family ethics. She is currently working on projects that explore care as a corporate virtue and polygamous marriages in the U.S. She is the co-editor of two forthcoming anthologies on care ethics and business ethics, and motherhood and philosophy, and the author of the forthcoming book, *Care Ethics and Reciprocity*. She lives in El Mirage where she is creating an oasis in the desert with her three children, husband of fifteen years, and animal companions.

Helen Daley Schroepfer is assistant professor of philosophy at West Chester University of Pennsylvania. Her areas of specialization include philosophy of religion and religion in contemporary continental thought. One area of her research focuses on the intersection between religion and public life, and her most recent publication addressed the use of religious rhetoric in the Bush administration. Her other area of research revolves around how the notion of hospitality in contemporary continental thought provides a rich avenue for rethinking what is meant by religion, and what this hospitable openness might mean for human flourishing.

Nancy E. Snow is an associate professor of philosophy at Marquette University in Milwaukee, Wisconsin. Her primary research areas are virtue ethics and moral psychology. She is the author of a number of articles on virtues and virtue-ethical topics, as well as of a recently published book, Virtue as Social Intelligence: An Empirically Grounded Theory (Routledge). For the past several years, she has been interested in Asian philosophy.

Ileana F. Szymanski is Assistant Professor at the Philosophy Department in the University of Scranton. She completed her PhD at the University of Guelph, where she wrote a dissertation on Aristotle and sense-perception. Her current research is on Feminism, Philosophy of Gastronomy, and Self-Identity. She endeavors to inform her research in contemporary subjects with the history of Philosophy. Her most recent publication is "Philosophy of Food: How Our Choices with respect to Food Create Habits That Can Be Mirrored in the Choices We Make to Find Happiness in Every-day Life" in *Journal for the Society of Philosophy in the Contemporary World*, Fall 2009.

Meyda Yeğenoğlu is a professor of Sociology at the Middle East Technical University, Ankara, Turkey. She has held visiting appointments at Columbia University, Oberlin College, Rutgers University, New York University, University of Vienna and Oxford University. She has published in the fields of orientalism, globalization, postcolonial theory, cultural studies, and migrancy. She is currently working on a book entitled *Secular Apprehensions: Islam, Migrancy and Hospitality in Europe*. She is the author of internationally well-cited *Colonial Fantasies; Towards a Feminist Reading of Orientalism* (Cambridge University Press, 1998). She has published numerous essays in various journals and edited volumes such as *Feminist Postcolonial Theory, Postcolonialism, Feminism and Religious Discourse, Nineteenth Century Literature Criticism, Postmodern Culture, Race and Ethnic Relations, Culture and Religion, Radical Philosophy, Inscriptions, Toplum ve Bilim, Defter,* and *Doğu-Bat.* She has extensively contributed to the literature on post-colonial theory and orientalism. She teaches in the fields of cultural studies, postcolonial theory, contemporary critical theory, orientalism and feminist theory.